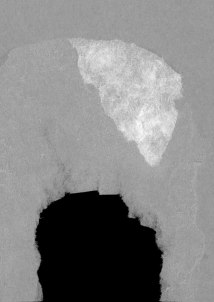

# AMERICAN
# ECONOMIC DEVELOPMENT
# SINCE 1860

# AMERICAN
# ECONOMIC DEVELOPMENT
# SINCE 1860

edited by
William Greenleaf

UNIVERSITY OF SOUTH CAROLINA PRESS
Columbia, S.C.

**To David**

# CONTENTS

# Introduction

## William Greenleaf

The economic development of the United States since the Civil War encompasses the most rapid and striking transformation of a major social order in the history of mankind. In little more than a century, a predominantly agrarian nation of small producers and entrepreneurs, generally hostile to consolidated business wealth, has undergone a transition to the managed capitalism of contemporary America, where the business corporation, as an economic and social institution, has found public acceptance on a scale unrivaled in the Western world. Today Americans are not so much concerned with the size of private enterprise as with its stability and productiveness, and one hears less of proposals to reform the structure of the American economy than of suggestions for a more equitable redistribution of the enormous wealth produced by it. Despite the wide gulf between actual performance and unfulfilled social needs and aspirations, a nation which with only 6 per cent of the world's population turns out more than 40 per cent of the world's goods, and whose gross national product increased from less than $7 billion in 1870 to approximately $800 billion in 1967, carries the credentials of an impressive material growth.

The wellspring of that growth has been an expanding industrial capitalism rooted in a set of peculiarly congenial conditions. Some of these conditions were active in the emergent phase of our industrial economy before 1860, but the Civil War, through an accident of history, brought into sharper focus pre-existing tendencies whose incremental thrust completed the basic process of industrialization within a half century after Appomattox and laid the foundation for subsequent phases of our economic development. Perhaps the most important condition was the social creed of untrammeled freedom for the producer, which was used to legitimize the physical exploitation of the continental domain after 1865. This precept grew in the soil of an economic experience richly seeded by the business individualism of Jacksonian democracy, antedating the postwar philosophical formulations of unrestrained free competition by the dis-

1

ciples of Herbert Spencer and the Social Darwinists. On the eve
of the Civil War, the energies of business individualism were pressing against the limits of the farm and village economy which President Lincoln described in his message to Congress in December,
1861. The small producer was the archetypical citizen of this society where relatively few owned capital and hired or bought others
to work for them. Said Lincoln: "Men with their families—wives,
sons, and daughters—work for themselves, on their farms, in their
houses, and in their shops, taking the whole product to themselves,
and asking no favors of capital on the one hand, nor of hired la-
borers or slaves on the other." There were, Lincoln noted, large
numbers of men who mingled "their own labor with capital," and
worked alongside hired hands, but this "mixed class," as he termed
the swelling ranks of small entrepreneurs, only underscored the fact
that the wage hand was not permanently fixed to his station and
could rise to a position of independence. "This is the just, and generous, and prosperous system, which opens the way to all," said
Lincoln; "gives hope to all, and consequent energy, and progress,
and improvement of condition to all."

Yet the balance of this agrarian society, with its network of commercial centers and interregional trade arteries, had been gradually
and perceptibly shifting for at least a decade. In the 1850's Lincoln
himself, as a lawyer who handled cases for the Illinois Central Railroad and the McCormick reaper interests, became involved in the
nexus of spreading industrialism. Lincoln's economic attitude might
be described as that of a Whig nationalist: friendly to the "mixed
enterprise" of locally subsidized internal improvements, hospitable
to invention and technological innovation, and, as shown in his
message to Congress in December, 1862, keenly aware of the economic illogic and impracticability of disunion, and alert to the
pivotal economic significance of the "great interior region," as he
called it, that was destined to become the booming internal market
of the postwar era. Lincoln's career as a corporation lawyer did not
lead to any close identification with industrial interests even after
the patchwork Republican platform of 1860 included concessions to
manufacturers. He continued to envision an economic order dominated by independent artisans, farmers, and small merchants. In
this he was not essentially different from the Radical Republicans,
as much as they took issue with him on high policy. The once
widely accepted view that the Radicals were the tool of Northern

financial and industrial interests has collapsed under its own monolithic weight. A good deal of historical writing on the Radicals has misrepresented their economic position, as W. R. Brock has pointed out in his incisive study, An American Crisis: Congress and Reconstruction, 1865–1867 (1963). Despite diverse economic interests and views, the Radicals as a group retained up to about 1870 much of the social idealism and egalitarianism which had attended the birth of the Republican party. They were hostile to monopoly; they favored free labor because it possessed rights denied to slave labor, not because it was "free" for exploitation; and they regarded themselves as spokesmen for "producers" as against "nonproducers," a distinction that traced back to the Jacksonian era which had schooled many a Radical in politics. "They did not think of themselves as the agents of the masters of capital," observes Brock, "but of the small businessman, the active farmer, and the enterprising working man."

To such men, it was fitting in 1860 that the federal government should continue to occupy in the economy the minimal role it had played since the early nineteenth century, when Hamilton's vision of a systematically developed nationalist economic program began to fade away. The adoption of Hamilton's neo-mercantilist strategy probably would have accelerated the rise of capitalist enterprise, especially in the industrial sector, and led sooner to the establishment of federal regulatory powers over business. As matters developed, it was the unforeseen demands of war, compelling the North to draw upon every available resource in the critical months after First Bull Run, that brought the national government into the economy in a way scarcely imagined by anyone when Lincoln was inaugurated. Through currency inflation and massive purchasing, the government became a stimulator of aggregate demand; through need of money to prosecute the war, it reorganized the banking system; through land grants to railroads, agriculture, and education, it became a prodigious dispenser of undeveloped public resources; and through increases in the protective tariff enacted originally to raise revenue for an empty Treasury, it built a wall against foreign industrial competition. In economic affairs, the Civil War signified the beginning of a historic reversal. Under the intense pressures of war and nationalism, the centrifugal tendencies of business enterprise, hitherto oriented toward the state and the locality, started flowing in the opposite direction as the North created new instrumentalities for organizing its economic energies. Yet all of these accomplishments in no way interrupted the continuity of a well-grounded *laissez-faire* tradition.

At the outbreak of the war, the country had no national currency and no national banking system. The sole currency was a bewildering profusion of 7,000 different varieties of bank notes issued by 1,600 state-chartered banks. In addition, there were about 5,500 kinds of spurious notes; in 1862, only 253 banks issued notes which had not been counterfeited or altered. True to the sacrosanct hard money standard, the federal government accepted only coin in payment of debts. Specie redemption was a principle of orthodox banking, but the bulk of daily business transactions was not in coin but in bank currency. In most Northern states the bank notes were not adequately secured, and were frequently subject to sharp discounting or "shaving." In late 1861 it became clear that the limited resources of the state banks, whose combined circulation amounted to only $132 million, would not be equal to financing the war for the Union. The hoarding of coin forced the suspension of specie payments at the end of 1861. The government had two emergency routes for escaping financial disaster. It could sell its bonds below par to bankers, who could then use them for expanding bank credit or for issuing bank notes at a profit; or it could, for the first time in the history of the republic, issue a genuine national currency controlled and regulated by public authority. There was no time to spare, for in early 1862 military contractors and other public creditors were clamoring for payment in a circulating medium receivable for private obligations and for claims and demands on the Treasury. At this time the Northern economy had been in a business recession since the autumn of 1860, when it had barely recovered from the severe financial panic of 1857, and it is conceivable that the persistence of an inadequate money supply might have paralyzed the economy of a nation fighting for its preservation. To meet the urgencies of the moment, a legal tender bill was introduced in January, 1862. The ensuing Congressional debate on the greenbacks saw the constitutional objections of hard money men who drew their teachings from past example pitted against the arguments of practical necessity and of popular refusal to countenance the selling of government securities below par to "note shaving" bankers (see Selection 1).

The greenbacks depreciated in value and helped to produce inflation. But the price advance that eroded purchasing power would have occurred even without the greenbacks, and the inflationary surge was hardly more severe than the inflation generated in the United States by World War I. The wild fluctuation in the wartime value of the legal tender notes was due chiefly to the hoarding of gold, which was sold at a premium with greenbacks by speculators on the New York money market, and to the changing military fortunes of the Union. Historians of another day, who wrote in the shadow of the sound money precepts of the late nineteenth century, tended to exaggerate the ruinous effects of the greenbacks. Altogether the legal tenders accounted for only about one-sixth of the national debt at the end of the war. Their positive effects were overlooked. In issuing fiat money backed solely by the public credit, the national government created its own purchasing power, as it has done in every major war since. The expansion of the money supply stimulated a business boom that was well under way by the summer of 1862, and the fresh capital reserves created by the greenbacks, mingled with large wartime profits, benefited industrial entrepreneurs and gave others—John D. Rockefeller is one example— the liquid capital they needed to invest in industry.

Adopted as an interim expedient to serve the financial needs of the government until a realistic tax program and a national banking system could be set afoot, the greenbacks proved to be the most controversial of all of the financial measures enacted by Congress during the Civil War. The stormy and protracted debate over contraction and resumption for more than a decade after the war really centered on the issue of "easy" versus "tight" money, and in time greenbackism became so intimately associated with farmer demands for monetary inflation that it was forgotten that its origins lay not in the depressed agrarian sector but in a depressed business community eager for an expanded money supply. In the swift and turning stream of history, interests are more enduring than the means used for promoting them. Thus we find that Representative George H. Pendleton of Ohio, a Democratic hard money man who in 1862 levelled an assault on the constitutionality of the greenbacks, sought political profit in 1867 when he sponsored before his agrarian constituency the so-called "Pendleton Plan" or "Ohio idea" for the redemption of certain types of government bonds in greenbacks, a proposal that necessarily involved monetary inflation. But it was not until the price of farm commodities dropped sharply after 1869 that agrarian debtors became receptive to inflation as a device for closing their cost-price gap.

The main object of a national banking system, as proposed by Secretary of the Treasury Salmon P. Chase in December, 1861, was to finance the war by providing a ready market for government bonds, and another of its purposes was the establishment of a uniform national currency. Although the National Banking Act of 1863, as revised in 1864, did not create a strong central bank on the Hamiltonian model, it eliminated the worst defects and excesses of the ramshackle state banking system inherited from the Jacksonians. Some Western states, such as Wisconsin, Michigan, and Missouri, tolerated the "wildcat" banks and excessive note issue that contributed to economic instability. The National Banking System incorporated the principle of free banking that had been successfully applied in several states with well-regulated banking institutions, notably New York, which required bond-secured note issues and the maintenance of specie reserves against deposits. National banks had to invest at least one-third of their capital (greenbacks being acceptable) in government securities and were authorized to issue a new kind of paper currency called national bank notes up to 90 per cent of the market or par value, whichever was lower, of the deposited bonds. The total issue of national bank note circulation was limited to $300 million. The notes were receivable for all government debts except import duties and were payable for all government obligations except interest on bonded indebtedness.

At first, the organization of national banks proceeded slowly. By the end of 1863 only 138 national banks had been chartered. But more favorable provisions in the revised act of 1864 promoted a rapid increase and, according to Hugh McCulloch—the hard money president of the well-managed State Bank of Indiana who became the first head of the National Banking System—accomplished a "great financial revolution" under wartime conditions without disturbing the business of the North (see Selection 2). By the end of 1865 there were 1,600 banks. While the National Banking System was developed too late to serve its intended purpose in financing the war, it asserted the capacity of the national government as controller and regulator of the money supply, and ended the divorce between the federal government and banking that dated from the Independent Treasury Act of 1846. In observing that the new system represented "a combination between the interests of private individuals and the government," Senator John Sherman of Ohio, one of the leading advocates of the banking measure, might well have been echoing Hamilton. For some, however, the legislation did not go far enough. The Radical leader, Representative Thaddeus Stevens of Pennsylvania, a soft money man who voted for the greenbacks and later opposed contraction, delayed the passage of the National Banking Bill in the House because he believed that a national currency issued by private banks was "unregulated enterprise" favoring a moneyed aristocracy. In 1866 Stevens said: "I think every dollar of paper circulation ought to be issued by the Government of the United States." The same view was voiced later in the century by the agrarian-debtor movement and in 1913 by the agrarian wing of the Democratic party when the National Banking System was being overhauled. Stevens' call for tighter federal control over monetary policy went unheeded. But his position hardly squares with the historical myth that a Radical juggernaut in Congress wrote the statutes that entrenched the power of a Northern big business oligarchy.

The National Banking System required banks to observe uniform standards stricter than those of the prewar era, afforded greater security for depositors and stockholders, and drove out the heterogeneous and disorderly array of state banknotes. Yet the system had obvious defects. There was a serious imbalance in the regional distribution of the national bank currency, a disproportionate amount being concentrated in the Northeast. The seasonal movement of country bank deposits to the central reserve banks in New York City, and the outflow of these funds in the autumn to service farm credit needs at harvest time, caused instability in the money markets and stock exchanges in the East. The banking system had no central mechanism for regulating and stabilizing the flow of money and credit, and practically no capability for mobilizing reserves. Since the note issues of the private banks were tied to the size of the national debt, and not to the volume of commercial debt, the national bank currency was inelastic—that is, it failed to expand and contract in timely response to changing levels of business activity. And, at a time when check money was being used in more business transactions, the lack of a national clearing house made interregional bank payments slow and cumbersome.

At first, beginning in the early 1870's, the National Banking System became the target of agrarian condemnation that employed the rhetoric of the Jeffersonian and Jacksonian traditions against "moneyed monopoly." The national banks were disliked not only by the farmers but also by the small businessmen in the hinterland who depended upon the farm trade, for most of these banks were situated in the cities or sizable towns, were not allowed to make loans against real estate, and did not provide long-term farm credits. Later, Greenbackers and Populists looked upon the national banks as conservative devices for limiting the supply of currency. By the end of the nineteenth century, however, the system's inflexibility, and its diminishing ability to service the commercial banking functions of an expanding industrial economy, were evoking criticism from the business community. From about 1880 on, investment bankers loomed as key figures in underwriting large-scale business enterprise, and their influence over the national economy aroused concern about the existence of a "money trust" in the early twentieth century. A movement to reform or reorganize the National Banking System was well developed even before a House subcommittee headed by Representative Arsène Pujo of Louisiana declared in 1912 that there was an "established and well-defined identity and community of interest between a few leaders of finance which had been created and is held together through stock holdings, interlocking directorates, and other forms of domination over banks, trust companies, railroads, public-service and industrial corporations, and which has resulted in a vast and growing concentration of money and credit in the hands of a comparatively few men."

By 1910 some members of the financial community, dissatisfied with the banking system for technical reasons, were advocating a plan for a central bank under private control. Progressives and neo-Populist agrarians, on the other hand, called for expanded government control over money and banking. A searching assessment of the National Banking System and a provisional plan for currency and banking reform was drawn up by a House committee in 1913 (see Selection 3), and was used by President Woodrow Wilson as a basis for his own legislative recommendations embodied in the Federal Reserve Act. At the insistence of Western and Southern spokesmen for the agrarian wing of the Democratic party, the governing board of the Federal Reserve System was made a wholly public body, and the new Federal Reserve notes, secured by commercial paper and gold, were made an obligation of the United States government.

In view of its present stature and functions, it is tempting but misleading to overestimate the powers of the Federal Reserve System in its first twenty years. The term "central bank" was anathema to the agrarian Democrats whose support was vital to the passage of the Federal Reserve Act. At the outset, the primary concern of the new system was the improvement of commercial banking. Like all major institutions, the Federal Reserve System underwent a process of evolution. It did not start life with any policy-making powers over the monetary system. Its authority was decentralized. Effective power resided in the twelve district banks, each of which set its own rediscount rates. During World War I the Federal Reserve was harnessed to the expansionary credit policies of the Treasury, and it failed to play a constructive role in the recession of 1920–1921, when the rediscount rate fixed by the New York district bank reached its historic high of 7 per cent. Only in the early 1920's did the Federal Reserve begin to understand the usefulness of open market operations for stimulating business activity or checking excessive speculation. General confidence in the agency was weakened by its performance before and after the Wall Street crash of 1929.

The Federal Reserve was not armed with adequate authority until the Banking Acts of 1933 and 1935 reorganized the governing board and gave it centralized powers over the rediscount rate, open market operations, and reserve requirements. These tools of monetary policy were set aside during World War II, when the Federal Reserve guaranteed the price of government bonds in order to assist the Treasury's easy money policies and to hold down the interest rate on the national debt. At the end of the war the Federal Reserve, in moving to recover its monetary powers as an anti-inflationary weapon, became involved in a policy clash with the Treasury, which contended that higher interest rates would slow down economic growth and increase the cost of servicing the debt. In 1951 an agreement with the Treasury enabled the Federal Reserve to follow an independent policy of monetary management. Since that time, the Federal Reserve has initiated "tight" or "easy" money policies, as the occasion seemed to require, in the face of a delicately balanced complex of changing conditions, including recessions, over-exuberant business booms, excessive stock market speculation, and record government spending. As supple as this policy has been, it had been demonstrated by 1967 that monetary management alone cannot carry the burden of preventing excessive inflation.

In every society, ancient or modern, a particular form of organized economic activity—the English wool trade of the fifteenth century, or the shipping and commerce of the Dutch in the seventeenth century—becomes a focus of the most advanced energies and techniques of material growth. In post-Civil War America, the greatest single force for economic development and change was the railroad. It provided faster and more reliable transportation than any earlier mode of movement by land or water; it speeded Western settlement; it made the United States a nation of cities, and integrated them into a national market; its stupendous financial requirements summoned into being the prototype of the modern securities market; and for many years, as the leading user of capital, goods, and labor, it exerted a "multiplier" effect upon public and private investment. There is a strong case for Walt W. Rostow's assertion in *The Stages of Economic Growth* (1960) that the introduction of the railroad was "the most powerful single initiator" of the take-off into self-sustaining growth. The railroad became the driving force behind the industrial economy of the late nineteenth century, when the United States achieved an exceptionally high rate of economic growth. In 1860 the nation had 30,626 miles of railroad. In 1916, when railroad mileage reached its all-time peak, the figure stood at 254,251, of which 162,720 miles were added between 1860 and 1900. In 1967 the United States had 216,000 miles of railroad.

Even though construction of new mileage was curtailed during the Civil War, old trackage was replaced and new facilities, such as shops and stations, were built. The railroad business prospered as never before in the first of the modern wars that saw the railroad become an essential part of military operations. The Civil War strengthened the financial position of many roads, enabling them to scale down indebtedness with inflated profits, and giving railroad securities the status of a preferred investment in the years just after the war. The construction of a national rail network had a direct impact on the rise of the steel industry, while the increasing scope and complexity of railway operations attested the emergence of the first corporate managerial structure that recognizably belongs to the new era of big business (see Selection 4).

The mixture of government paternalism and *laissez-faire* that marked public policy without offending the business individualism of the new enterprisers after 1860 was first typified by the building of the transcontinental railroads. The policy of federal aid to railway promoters was established in 1850, when the government, using states as intermediaries, granted tracts to a few rail enterprises, notably the Illinois Central Railroad. That road received a total of about three million acres in alternate sections of land on each side of the right of way, thus setting the basic pattern for similar land grant legislation that throughout the 1850's disposed of approximately eighteen million acres. In 1862 Congress, responding to the urgings of promoters, approved the construction of the Union Pacific and the Central Pacific as land grant roads. The federal government was the direct grantor of this largesse, which it approved as conducive to national unification and as useful to "the safe and speedy transportation of mails, troops, munitions of war, and public stores." The land grant policy was extended to other transcontinentals, such as the Northern Pacific, on even more generous terms. Altogether, in 1850–1871, the federal government granted about 175,350,000 acres to railroads. They actually received about 131,-350,000 acres, having forfeited some 34,000,000 acres because of unfulfilled construction agreements. The Union Pacific received twenty million acres, while the Northern Pacific was given forty-two million. It is suggestive of the part railroads played in Western settlement that four Western roads—the Union Pacific, the Northern Pacific, the Southern Pacific, and the Sante Fe—received 73 per cent of the total land grants.

Did the American social economy receive reasonably full value for the aggregate public and private investment in the railroad network? The answer is beyond precise determination. The record of railroad development after the Civil War is marred by fraud, corruption, graft, and financial manipulation by dishonest promoters and public officials interested solely in reaping quick profits from construction companies and "watered" securities. For decades after the network was laid down, many of the roads had a heavy burden of overcapitalization and a history of missed dividends and postponed interest payments. But there were railroad leaders like Cornelius Vanderbilt of the New York Central and Charles E. Perkins of the Chicago, Burlington & Quincy who developed good roads and services and the administrative organizations for running them.

Until about 1920, when the automobile and the motor truck began to tilt the balance, the railroads had a quasi-monopoly of dependable and relatively cheap long-distance and short-haul transportation. Still unregulated in 1865, they were free to charge excessive and discriminatory rates where competitive conditions permitted. In prosperous times, demand did not lag behind the available supply of transportation, and rates, although cut by two-thirds between 1865 and 1887, were generally stable in a good market. But when business slackened, the railroads in built-up areas with more than one line generally resorted to rate-cutting wars. The railroad managers generally disliked rebates, bowing to them as a necessary evil dictated by powerful industrial shippers with superior bargaining power. Pools and similar agreements to assure the participants a fair share of the carrying trade were not always effective because they usually broke down during recessions. The rate-setting practices of the roads were arbitrary and chaotic. Toward the end of the Civil War, farmers in Wisconsin and Minnesota were disturbed by rate increases, and before long farmers elsewhere, as well as merchants and other small shippers, were in the vanguard of regional and local movements for cheap transportation.

In the early 1870's, as a result of agitation by farmers and merchants, a number of Midwestern states, among them Wisconsin and Illinois, passed so-called Granger Laws regulating the rates of railroads and grain elevators. Meanwhile, a gathering tide of discontent with extortionate rates and other abuses found an outlet in Congress, where the Windom Report of 1874, a landmark in the history of national regulation, detailed many of the unfair and unethical practices that had been attacked by reformers (see Selection 5). In 1887, after the Supreme Court made it clear that only Congress could enact railroad legislation reaching across state lines, the Interstate Commerce Commission ushered in the federal regulation of business enterprise.

In the same year of 1887, the annual construction of new mileage reached its peak, raising the prospect that disastrous cut-throat competition might be precipitated by overbuilding. The railroad promoters and managers turned from unsatisfactory voluntary cooperation to the strategy of consolidation as a more effective way of preventing wasteful and unprofitable competition. By 1900, the greater part of American railroad mileage had been consolidated in six major systems (see Selection 6). Consolidation provided no conclusive answer. Some of the largest empires, such as the Morgan and Harriman systems, did not endure, and the industry as a whole became bogged down in bankruptcy and receivership. Although the Transportation Act of 1920 proclaimed the encouragement of consolidation as official policy, and the Interstate Commerce Commission in 1929 drew up a plan for grouping the railroads into twenty-one systems, nothing came of this. At present, mergers are the favored device where financial and technological considerations enhance the advantages of consolidation. The establishment in 1966 of a new federal Department of Transportation may in time produce a unified railroad policy the nation has lacked to this day.

Business as a system of power, with consolidating and centralizing tendencies that have profoundly affected social patterns and institutions, became discernible with the rise of the large industrial corporation between 1880 and 1914. The separation of ownership and management, and the concentration of policy-making powers in a board of directors and the chief executive officers, has made the big corporation, with its long-term capacity to allocate and develop resources, a vehicle of economic planning under private auspices that has altered classical models of business behavior. "It is plainly contrary to fact," wrote Adolf A. Berle, Jr., in 1954, "to represent that the great collective enterprise known as a corporation follows a course similar to the limited private enterprise of Ricardo's individual entrepreneur."

The formation of these huge aggregates owed much to mass technology in an urbanizing society, as shown by the commercial development of the telephone, which began in 1880, when the American Bell Telephone Company took over the Bell patents. The telephone was only one example of the many applications of electricity in an industrial economy. Although electrical energy as a usable power source had been foreseen well before the Civil War, it remained for Thomas Alva Edison, one of the most fertile minds in the history of invention, to develop its earliest practical possibilities for lighting and power. The response was immediate, and the demand for machinery to generate and transmit electricity from central or isolated plants soon created a new industry (see Selection 7) that was destined to grow as electricity became the basic power of industrial civilization. Edison's insistence on using an expensive and cumbersome direct current system hindered the transmission of high-tension electricity over long distances. The development by

George Westinghouse and his associates of a transformer for conducting high-voltage alternating current made the broad-scale use of electrical power technically and commercially feasible. After a patents cross-licensing agreement had been concluded by General Electric and the Westinghouse Electrical and Manufacturing Company in 1896, the industry became a leader in systematic research and development.

No industry was more basic to American industrial power than that of iron and steel. The huge iron ore resources of the Lake Superior district, discovered in 1844 and exploited after the Civil War, provided most of the iron for the steel industry until after World War I. The output of the Lake Superior iron ranges, together with the abundant coal deposits of western Pennsylvania and eastern Ohio, made the area bounded by Buffalo on the east, Pittsburgh and Wheeling on the south, and Chicago and Milwaukee on the west, the principal iron and steel producing area, as it remains to this day. The first commercial steel made in the United States by the Bessemer process was poured in September, 1864, at an iron works established at Wyandotte, Michigan, some ten miles from Detroit, by Captain Eber B. Ward and his associates. The Ward group purchased and consolidated the separate patents covering the methods independently developed by Sir Henry Bessemer and the Kentucky ironmaster, William Kelly. The Wyandotte Iron Works had the first laboratory of any American iron and steel mill for the scientific analysis of iron ore. Almost at the same time that the Wyandotte venture was being organized, a number of Easterners, including Erastus Corning of Albany, took out in 1863 a license to manufacture Bessemer steel. The plant for this operation, designed and built at Troy, New York, by Alexander L. Holley, produced its first Bessemer steel in February, 1865.

To Holley belongs the credit for having furnished the technological underpinning of the Bessemer steel industry in this country. Of the dozen Bessemer plants built here between 1867 and 1881, Holley designed and constructed eight, and strongly influenced the layout of another three. Among Holley's disciples who carried improved methods throughout the industry were Bill Jones, who became Andrew Carnegie's chief ironmaster, and the brothers John and George Fritz. An imaginative factory engineer, Holley saw that the Bessemer converter was less important in itself than as an element in an integrated sequence of production embracing blast furnaces, bloomeries, and rolling mills concentrating in one place all of the operations for changing iron ore into finished steel. Holley designed for Carnegie the J. Edgar Thomson Steel Works in the Pittsburgh district, the most modern steel mill at the time it began production in 1875. Holley's technological insights had organizational implications which were followed to their logical conclusion of vertical integration by Carnegie and his able lieutenants, who devised the far-flung and complex movement of materials that gathered at one point, as Carnegie put it, "four pounds of materials manufactured into one pound of steel, for which the consumer pays one cent." Carnegie's unrelenting insistence on cost-cutting through progressive technology reduced the price of a ton of steel from $65 a ton in 1872 to $20 a ton in 1897. Between 1889 and 1900, Carnegie boosted his annual steel output from 322,000 tons to 3 million tons. During that time his profits increased eight times over, reaching $40 million in 1900.

The key to expanded production, in an industry peculiarly vulnerable to recessionary movements, was diversified output for a broader market. During its developmental phase the growth of the industry was dependent upon the production of steel rails, first for steam railroads and later for electric urban and interurban street railways. The first American rails for commercial use were rolled in 1867. In 1870 practically all of the Bessemer steel produced was going into rails; and of the eleven Bessemer plants in the country in 1880, all but one concentrated on the production of rails. It was in the developmental years 1870–1895 that the industry achieved a position of strength which enabled the United States to overtake Great Britain as the world's leading steel producer (see Selection 8). The direction the industry would take had been foreseen by Alexander Holley in 1875, when he urged American Bessemer steelmen to diversify their production, as Europeans had already done, and develop a market for steel ships, bridges, and structural shapes. The drive toward diversification resulted in further integration and consolidation, bringing fears of destructive competition among a handful of giants. To forestall this, J. P. Morgan & Company in 1901 initiated the consolidation of the Carnegie and other properties into the United States Steel Corporation. At the time, U. S. Steel controlled over 50 per cent of the market. Today, although it is still the largest firm in this highly integrated industry, its share of the market has declined to 30 per cent.

Ranking with electricity and steel as forces that shaped modern industrial America is the internal combustion engine harnessed to the automobile. The nation's largest industry is the production of motor vehicles, and automobile sales are a primary indicator of the national economy. The gasoline motor car, powered by Gottfried Daimler's modification of the Otto four-cycle engine, was a European invention and was being manufactured commercially in France in 1892, shortly before J. Frank Duryea operated the first American-built gasoline car in 1893. By 1905 the United States was the leading maker of automobiles. In Europe, the automobile long remained a luxury item. Here, it became a necessity for the middle class, which comprised the first mass market for the motor car. Just after the turn of the century, that market was found largely in the small towns and in the hinterland, where the rising curve of farm commodity prices, especially in the Midwest and the Plains states, buttressed a seemingly limitless farm market for automobiles until 1920.

Between 1900 and 1920, the industry changed rapidly from custom-building to mass production, and from a multiplicity of small firms to a high degree of concentration. Huge integrated companies with superior financial, manufacturing, and distribution resources were already dominant in the 1920's, which witnessed the attrition of most of the remaining independent firms. Since the Great Depression, the "Big Three"—General Motors, Ford, and Chrysler—have among them accounted for an ever-growing share of the market as the few remaining independents have dropped out or merged.

The volume production of cars was pioneered by Ransom E. Olds, who in 1903 manufactured 4,000 curved-dash Oldsmobiles. It was Olds who first followed the formula of producing a relatively low-cost car for a mass market, foregoing high unit profits for volume sales at a lower margin of profit. The formula was perfected by Henry Ford, who with his associates established the Ford Motor Company in 1903 and in 1908 introduced the Model T. This became the most widely used single model in automotive history. Altogether, more than 15,000,000 were produced before the Model T was discontinued in 1927. More than any other single producer, Ford showed the industry the way toward mass production, pushed America into the motor and urban age, and made the car both a social and a technological innovation.

In the first decade of the twentieth century, when entry into the auto industry was comparatively easy because of modest capital requirements (the Ford Motor Company began with a paid-in capital of $28,000), the life expectancy of new firms was short and the annual turnover was high. Very early in the history of the industry, however, large-scale organization made its appearance with the establishment of a holding company, General Motors. Created in 1908 by William C. Durant, the career of General Motors, first in the Durant period of overambitious expansion, and then under the regime of Alfred P. Sloan, Jr., is a case history in the transformation of the automobile industry into big business (see Selection 9). The Sloan revolution in corporate management, one of the most brilliant achievements in the annals of business organization, produced the "standard volume" formula whereby long-range financial and market planning assure a high level of net return on invested capital. Price-making in the automotive industry is a conspicuous instance of the managed or "administered" price.

While indigenous technological contributions and a general lack of social resistance to technical change have helped to promote American industrial leadership, by and large our innovations have been interdependent with the achievements of other industrially advanced countries. From an early date, Americans were resourceful borrowers of technology. In Great Britain, home of the Industrial Revolution, rigid social institutions, worker opposition to technical innovation, the very slow evolution of new industrial organizations and a labor surplus acted as brakes on the fullest possible exploitation of new technology. In the United States, social fluidity, the rise of the large corporation, capital-intensive industry, and a scarcity of skilled labor nourished innovative technology in the setting of a mass market.

The eagerness with which American manufacturers adopted labor-saving machinery in an economy chronically short on skilled labor was demonstrated in the early nineteenth century by Eli Whitney when he innovated machine methods for the accurate production of interchangeable parts for army muskets. After the Civil War, however, a labor shortage was no longer the determining reason for the acceptance of machine technology. More important was the urgent necessity of factory cost economies in the face of heavy capital investment and a fluctuating business cycle. In good times, technological improvements were dictated by the burgeoning market demand for sewing machines, farm machinery, bicycles, and other articles assembled from machine-made interchangeable components. The quick march of technology spurred new advances in machine tools used for the precision shaping and cutting of metal. Progress in the steel industry made available alloy steels that enabled improvements in the speed, capacity, and versatility of lathes, borers, planes, drills, and other machine tools. The resulting gains in productivity contributed to the rise of the United States as a leading industrial power. In the last two decades of the nineteenth century the machine tool industry became a frontier of technological progress. Revolutionary advances were made in specialized automatic and semi-automatic machine tools and in the application of electricity and compressed air to drive them at high speed.

In the early twentieth century, the mounting pressures of the machine process tended toward a system of factory management incorporating the principle of continuous motion. The progressive utilization of machine tools in the mass production of the automobile raised new problems in the handling and assembling of machined parts. The traditional method of passing the work down a line of fixed stations was no longer compatible with the crowding stream of materials and components on the factory floor. Congestion and strains at weak points led to breakdowns that held up the flow of production. The past offered no guide. The principle of continuous flow production can be traced as far back as 1783, to the automatic water-driven flour mill designed by the Pennsylvania inventor, Oliver Evans, and built by him in 1784–1785, but this machine taught nothing about assembling a variety of fabricated parts into a unified whole. Suggestions of the assembly line principle have been found in the post-Civil War meatpacking plants of Cincinnati and Chicago, where hogs suspended from overhead conveyors were slaughtered, cut, and cleaned as they moved along from worker to worker. In the 1890's freight cars were assembled as they rolled along tracks between teams of workmen mounted on scaffolds.

The Highland Park plant of the Ford Motor Company, built specifically for the mass production of the Model T, was in 1910, the year it opened, one of the most advanced centers for the design or modification of special purpose tools used to replace hand labor or to perform high-speed multiple operations. By 1912 sequential production lines had been set up in the vast plant, but the thickening juxtaposition of men, machines, and components threatened to clog the smooth flow of the work in progress. Conveyors, gravity slides, and rollways were installed to improve the handling of materials, but these piled up sub-assemblies as the car neared the end of the assembly process. Finally, by persistent trial and experimentation, the continuously moving assembly line was evolved at Highland Park in 1913–1914 (see Selection 10). One of the culminating developments of modern technological history, this new mode of mass production was defined by Henry Ford in 1926 as "the focusing upon a factory project of the principles of power, accuracy, economy, system, continuity, speed, and repetition." This dynamic method of factory production was quickly adopted by other auto-makers and was later used in the production of a wide range of consumer appliances.

After 1914, the further refinement and extension of industrial mechanization and standardization held out the possibility that repetitive manual operations might be radically reduced or even eliminated. In the late 1920's the A. O. Smith Company of Milwaukee, which made most of the car frames used by the automobile industry, installed a completely automatic assembly line producing a completed unit every ten seconds. The next significant step in this direction was taken in 1947 by a Ford Motor Company executive, Delmar S. Harder, who suggested a company "Automation Department" for developing mechanical methods to replace manual operations. "Detroit automation," as it came to be known, involved the use of materials-handling transfer and conveyor equipment phased with multi-stage machine tools into systems that kept work moving along the factory floor with a minimum of human intervention. In 1949, Ford began building at Buffalo and Cleveland the first plants specifically designed for "Detroit automation." Less than a decade later, engine blocks which once required nine hours to be machined were being turned out in about fourteen and one-half minutes. Such processes, although revolutionary in their impact, were actually a logical sequel to the historical evolution of automatic factory machinery.

A genuinely new departure that opened up another era in technology was the utilization of electronic devices to instruct and control machines in performing factory and office operations. This innovation, commonly designated as "automation" in its current meaning, was made possible chiefly by the development and use of the electronic computer, which has vast capabilities for storing information, carrying out basic instructions at high speed, and directing and adjusting its programmed operations on the feedback principle. Developed during and just after World War II, the electronic computer was first used commercially in the early 1950's. Within a few years it was being applied to many industrial and business activities (see Selection 11). As yet, the prediction of a "factory without men" has not been borne out, but it has been approximated in continuous process industries such as petroleum refining, where the nature of the operation lends itself to centralized and integrated electronic control. The most advanced type of computer process control, known as the closed-loop system, eliminates the operator and sets the controls automatically. Such a system represents automation at its fullest. In 1965, however, less than a dozen closed-loop systems were operating or being tested in the United States.

The emergence of large-scale industry after 1865, accompanied by sweeping changes in business organization and market behavior, clashed with fundamental assumptions about the nature of private economic power inherited from the egalitarian and competitive credo of a pre-industrial society of small producers. Startling changes in scale, efficiency, output, and market power, epitomized by the rise of the Standard Oil trust, which in 1882 controlled about 95 per cent of the refining capacity in the United States, foreshadowed the coming era of consolidation and concentration. Antitrust sentiment took its first strong impetus from the Granger movement, which just after the Civil War channeled farmer opposition to monopolies into the movement for regulating the railroads. By 1880 anti-railroad feeling was inseparable from resentment against industrial monopolies. Henry Demarest Lloyd's article, "The Story of a Great Monopoly," which appeared in the *Atlantic Monthly* for March, 1881, and told of the rebating arrangements between Standard Oil and several railroads, was primarily concerned not with Standard Oil but with the railroads, "the greatest of monopolies." To a people still firmly wedded to the ideology of *laissez-faire* and the abstract mechanics of a self-adjusting economic order, Lloyd announced: "The time has come to face the fact that the forces of capital and industry have outgrown the forces of our government." The 1880's brought a crescendo of trust-building that intensified hostility to big business and provoked wide discussion. Samuel C. T. Dodd, the Standard Oil attorney who originated the trust device, openly admitted toward the end of the decade that there was "an earnest popular prejudice against trade combinations." The Greenback and Union Labor parties included antitrust planks in their platforms, and in 1888, in response to the national temper, both the Democratic and Republican national platforms condemned trusts and other "combinations of capital."

What was destined to be the first national antitrust legislation began with the introduction of a resolution by Senator John Sherman of Ohio in July, 1888. The character of Sherman's antitrust philosophy was expressed in the resolution's emphasis on the need of public policy "to preserve freedom of trade and production, the natural competition of increasing production, [and] the lowering of prices by such competition." These aims were embodied in a bill introduced by Sherman in August, 1888. After some two years of debate, revision, and parliamentary maneuvering and delay, a new measure was introduced by Sherman in March, 1890. By this time several Southern and Western states had enacted or proposed antitrust laws. The final version of the bill was drafted by the Senate Judiciary Committee, whose chairman, George Edmunds of Vermont, made most of the changes, assisted by George F. Hoar of Massachusetts and James George of Mississippi. The Sherman Antitrust Act was signed into law by President Benjamin Harrison on July 2, 1890. Subsequent experience demonstrated the wisdom of Sherman's observation: "All that we, as lawmakers, can do is to declare general principles." He and other supporters of the act conceded that it was an experimental and ambiguous statute whose scope and applicability would depend on judicial interpretation.

The federal government now had a new tool of business policy, presumably in alignment with the national credo of a competitive economy. Yet almost from the start the Sherman Act raised thorny questions for reformers and created uncertainty among businessmen. Was it the intent of the statute to draw a distinction between good and bad trusts, and between reasonable and unreasonable restraints on trade? Was the legislature abdicating its power to the courts? After 1900 various proposals were set forth for writing specific prohibitions into antitrust law and for establishing a government agency for the supervision and regulation of business. These aims were realized in 1914, with the passage of the Clayton Antitrust Act and the creation of the Federal Trade Commission, but the preliminary work of educating the public to the issues of business regulation was performed by President Theodore Roosevelt. Essentially a Social Darwinist who knew little about economics, and was interested in the trusts rather as a social and political issue, Roosevelt believed they were the natural, inevitable, and irreversible outcome of large-scale production and progressive technology. He never departed from the central aim he expressed before the New York State legislature in January, 1900: "We do not desire to destroy corporations; we do desire to put them fully at the service of the State and the people." While Roosevelt was the first President who vigorously enforced the Sherman Act, he regarded it as essentially impracticable because its negative policy on combinations did not recognize them as necessary and legitimate, and because its enforcement imposed an "impossible burden" on both the Department of Justice and the courts. As Roosevelt saw it, industrial combination was an accomplished fact, regardless of the Sherman Act, and after 1905 he called for a positive public policy of regulation and supervision administered by a federal agency. Following his retirement from the Presidency, Roosevelt took an even more advanced position, and the spirit of his New Nationalism anticipated the next broad advance in the federal regulation of business enterprise under the New Deal.

The Wall Street crash of 1929, by exposing structural weaknesses and unethical practices in investment banking and the securities market, turned public attention on the close link between commercial banks and their security affiliates. The economic breakdown and mass unemployment of 1930–1933 made the securities exchanges and the banks targets of reform. Direct federal control over security trading was established by the Securities Act of 1933 and the Securities Exchange Act of 1934, which established the Securities Exchange Commission and furnished long overdue protection for investors. The Banking Acts of 1933 and 1935 gave the Federal Reserve System centralized powers over margins for security trading and allowed the district reserve banks to restrict the security loans of member banks (see Selection 12).

When big business continued to grow after World War II, federal business policy sought to preserve a competitive model by strengthening some of its existing tools. One of these was a clarification of Section 7 of the Clayton Antitrust Act, a provision that was designed to prevent large companies in any industry from exercising a monopoly through the purchase of stock in competing firms. The failure of Section 7 to ban the acquisition of the physical assets of a competitor, however, proved to be a loophole, and beginning in 1926 the Federal Trade Commission asked Congress to remedy this weakness. At length, in 1950, Congress responded with the Celler-Kefauver Amendment to the Clayton Act. The growing complexity of case law and economic theory made it likely that a judicial finding on a proposed merger would require the court to engage in sophisticated economic analysis and to estimate the probable course of long-term trends in an industry. This was borne out in the first important judicial interpretation of the Celler-Kefauver Amendment (see Selection 13).

In spite of changing and even conflicting interpretations of antitrust, the courts have left no doubts about the illegality of collusive price-fixing agreements, partly because the power to set prices was always associated with monopoly and restraint of trade under the common law origins of the Sherman Act. Indeed, the first case brought under the Sherman Act, filed in a district court in Tennessee in 1890, involved an arrangement by mine operators and coal dealers for restricting output and fixing prices. It was declared illegal. In a similar case involving a group of California coal dealers, decided in 1898, a lower court rejected the argument of the defendants that the price-fixing arrangement constituted a "fair and reasonable restraint upon trade and commerce" because the participants sought beneficent ends. Intermittently, over a period of more than twenty years, the country had been through bouts of destructive competition. Even contemporary experts began to inveigh against undiluted *laissez-faire* as unsuited to a new stage of industrial development. Thus, in 1887 the distinguished economist, John Bates Clark, wrote that combinations "are the happy outcome of a competition so abnormal that the continuance of it would have meant widespread ruin." Might price-fixing, then, be considered "reasonable" under certain circumstances? In *U.S. v. Trans-Missouri Freight Association et al.*, 166 U.S. 290 (1897), the government proceeded against fifteen Western railroads which had combined to fix uniform freight rates. The district court judge, holding that the agreement was not prejudicial to the public interest, declared: "The public is not entitled to free and unrestricted competition, but what it is entitled to is fair and healthy competition; and I see nothing in the contract which necessarily tends to interfere with that right." This line of reasoning was accepted by the circuit court. The Supreme Court, however, reversed the judgment, ruling that the distinction between reasonable and unreasonable restraints was inapplicable to price-fixing. The doctrine that price-fixing is illegal per se was underscored in *U.S.* v. *Addyston Pipe and Steel Co. et al.*, 175 U.S. 211 (1899). In this action against a price-fixing combination of manufacturers of cast-iron pipe, the Supreme Court adopted the view of William Howard Taft, then a judge sitting on the Sixth Circuit Court of Appeals, who held that regardless of the excuse for the combination, "the illegality of the means stamps it as a conspiracy," thus bringing it within the scope of the Sherman Act. In the Standard Oil case of 1911 (*U.S.* v. *Standard Oil Company of New Jersey*, 221 U.S. 1), the high court laid down the "rule of reason." The Supreme Court, however, has never applied this rule to price-fixing agreements, even where collusion was directed primarily at controlling production, and where the defendants contended that the agreement prevented a weak market from collapsing into chaos.

The immediate origins of the movement for the public regulation of corporate business enterprise lay in consumer response to the exactions of the railroads and the trusts, but underlying the anti-big business hostility of the late nineteenth century was a fear that concentrated wealth might destroy the equilibrium of a pluralistic society based on the diffusion and limitation of power. It was not until the 1850's, as the capital requirements of industry grew larger, that the corporate form of business organization gained a foothold in industry. With the rise of large-scale industry between 1870 and 1890, an increase in the number of corporations was accompanied by the amassing of enormous personal fortunes by the captains of finance and industry. In the 1880's a growing list of millionaires for the first time provoked general discussion, and there was some concern that inherited wealth might become the base of a plutocracy. In the Gilded Age the social idealism which had marked the early Republican party vanished, and it became the political vehicle of big business. Like every nation that has been caught in the difficult transition from an agrarian society to an urban-industrial order, the United States began to show disquieting signs of social differences and inequities that were in glaring contrast to the society Lincoln had portrayed in 1861.

The post-Civil War business environment, with its sharp cyclical fluctuations and long-term price deflation, fostered economic concentration. Anxious to protect their share of the market and to shelter themselves against the gales of recession that swept over the economy, producers found it advantageous to expand their holdings, either by merger or by investment in new plant, and to use their strengthened resources to wage industrial warfare against weak competitors in an effort to drive them from the trade. Having won a position of market domination, the large concern could then fix output and prices. This was the technique of Rockefeller in oil, of Carnegie in steel, and of other industrial leaders. During the great era of trust-building in 1880–1900, the number of plants in many basic industries declined even as production increased. Behind this trend toward concentration was a quest for market stability and guaranteed profits, and the protection of heavy capital investments against destructive competition. A variety of devices—the pool, the trust, and the holding company—were used to promote these ends.

A great wave of mergers that began in 1898 and lasted until 1906, and was carried along by a boom market in securities, resulted in more and bigger trusts than had previously been established. The Sherman Act had proved no deterrent to size. In 1899 the Civic Federation of Chicago called a national conference on trusts attended by more than 700 delegates; throughout the year the issue was discussed at numerous other gatherings; and in December, 1899, President William McKinley drew Congressional attention to the widespread debate. Already, in 1898, Congress had established the United States Industrial Commission. This agency's preliminary report, based on extensive hearings, furnished an impressive survey of corporate concentration as it had crystallized by the beginning of the twentieth century (see Selection 14).

By the end of the 1920's, when a second great wave of mergers had run its course, it was apparent that corporate concentration had gone largely unchecked. Meanwhile, the pattern of market behavior changed. The earlier phase of open industrial warfare and cut-throat competition gave way to an era of "imperfect" or non-price competition. Markets came to be dominated by oligopoly—that is, by a few large sellers who recognized the advantages of tacitly following "price leadership" over the disadvantages of costly price rivalry and market instability. Economists differ on the role of oligopoly and on the significance of the still continuing trend toward concentration. The terms of the debate have changed (for the most part, they are far more technical), but not the basic issues.

Those who seventy years ago insisted that large combinations were the legitimate evolutionary result of technological progress, bringing social benefits through efficient organization and lower production costs, find an echo in John Kenneth Galbraith, who in 1966 told an audience: "Oligopoly is combined . . . with efficient production, expansive output and prices that are generally thought rather favorable to the public. The consequences of oligopoly are greatly condemned in principle and greatly approved in practice . . . to declare the big corporations illegal is, in effect, to declare the modern economy illegal." The most recent trend toward mergers, dating from the late 1940's, is closely allied to market and other strategies in an oligopolistic economy (see Selection 15).

Today, when the American economy is dominated by 500 large corporations, of which 150 are either worth a billion dollars or more, or annually transact at least a billion dollars' worth of business, Americans accord giant enterprise an acceptance that would have been inconceivable in the period 1870–1914 and would have seemed far-fetched even in the 1930's. The American people judge corporate capitalism by its economic performance and stability, and as long as it accomplishes this without eroding the opportunities of the millions of small "interstitial" enterprises in our economy, it is likely that big business will continue to enjoy a favorable public opinion. Nevertheless, American antitrust policy, reflecting official dedication to the preservation of a competitive model, stands virtually alone in its comprehensiveness and strict enforcement. Canada is the only other nation with a comparable body of statute law covering monopoly and restrictive business practices.

Probably no major American war has had so much or so little claimed for its economic impact as has the Civil War. Historians no longer accept the simplistic view that industrialism emerged practically full-blown from the crucible of that war, and most of them do not agree with a more recent hypothesis that the war actually retarded industrialization. No careful student will deny that an industrial order was in process of formation before 1860, and would have matured even if war had not intervened. But where the economic determinist insists that the Civil War was precipitated by the inevitable clash of two incompatible systems of production that could not continue to co-exist within the Union, a less doctrinaire analyst holds that the coming of the war coincided with but did not cause a transitional phase in American economic development. It would be naïve to suppose that the war was in the nature of a shock wave that produced something like a uniform effect in every part of the economic landscape. Its immediate impact was uneven, generating a boom in some sectors, and a decline in others. The Civil War accelerated tendencies that were already under way, and provided liquid capital for a host of enterprisers whose business plans and aspirations were enlarged by wartime feats of supplying the largest mass army that has ever fought on the North American continent. It is suggestive that from 1869 to 1883, the average annual rate of economic growth was about 9 per cent, a rate the American economy has never equaled since. A balanced estimate of the economic impact of the Civil War takes into account the long-term institutional effects created by war-induced policies and industrial activity (see Selection 16).

On the eve of its entry into World War I in April, 1917, the United States was little better prepared for industrial mobilization than the North had been in 1861. Yet the war in Europe had measurably affected the American economy since the spring of 1915, when Allied war orders stimulated business and agriculture, ending a recession that had been under way since 1913. In addition, the preparedness program of the Wilson administration had levied demands upon steel mills and shipyards. The volume of foreign trade increased five times over between 1914 and 1917. Industrial output grew by approximately 20 per cent between 1915 and 1916, while capital investment doubled and profits in mining and manufacturing reached new record levels. Even so, when the United States entered the war, it had no plan for the centralized mobilization of its resources. The Council of National Defense, established in 1916 to draw up a scheme of coordinated mobilization, was hampered by poor organization. The task of economic mobilization was taken over in July, 1917, by the War Industries Board, but its powers, which were partial at best, did not become really effective until after Bernard Baruch was appointed head of the WIB in March, 1918. Hastily dismantled after the armistice, the WIB marked the first time that the federal government had established an economic planning agency.

The financial requirements of fighting the war and aiding the Allies pushed government spending from about $2 billion in 1917 to $18.5 billion in 1919. In order to float its issues of war bonds, the government resorted to inflationary financing. Combined with inadequate controls over the economy, this contributed to price inflation. By late 1918 the general indexes of both wholesale prices and manufactured goods had climbed 98 per cent above the levels of 1913. The war brought a great increase in manufacturing facilities, with capital outlays for new buildings and equipment soaring from $600 million in 1915 to $2.5 billion in 1918. Most of this plant was later converted to peacetime production and became a permanent addition to manufacturing capacity. Demobilization and reconversion were carried out precipitously, but government deficit financing, maintained chiefly on bank credit, was the main impetus to expanded postwar purchasing power and to the flow of exports in 1919–1920 that helped to sustain the boom of 1919–1920 (see Selection 17).

As an expansionary economic force, World War II was without precedent in American history. When the European war began in September, 1939, the United States had just recovered from the severe recession of 1937–1938. It had nine million unemployed, considerable unused plant capacity, and a low level of business investment. Over the next two years, as the United States undertook to arm itself and to supply the European Allies, it utilized its idle plant resources and made large additions to its industrial resources. In 1940–1945, spending for new manufacturing facilities amounted to $25.5 billion, of which more than 75 per cent was provided by the government. During the same period the gross national product increased from $233.8 billion to $369.1 billion. When the production effort peaked out in 1944, war needs were taking about 80 per cent of durable goods output. Many of the plant additions, later sold to private firms as government surplus at a fraction of their original cost, substantially enlarged postwar industrial capabilities. While the industrial mobilization program was not free of confusion, shortcomings, and rivalries, the United States achieved in World War II the highest degree of centralized government planning and control of resources it has ever known.

World War II, by lifting the country from economic stagnation to full utilization of its resources, underscored the capacity of government to stimulate aggregate demand. Could it do the same in peacetime? The idea of deficit spending to take up business slack was not new. In the 1920's, the American economist William Trufant Foster had advocated increased public spending during depressions; and in January, 1933, a number of economists at the

University of Chicago, among them Paul H. Douglas, had called for a federal policy of deficit spending. When the New Deal came to power, it was pledged to fiscal orthodoxy. President Franklin D. Roosevelt resorted to deficit spending reluctantly, and only as a temporary expedient to be abandoned at the first opportunity of balancing the budget.

In 1936 the British economist John Maynard Keynes published his masterwork, *The General Theory of Employment, Interest, and Money,* in which he advocated a deliberate policy of compensatory spending as a contracyclical device for stimulating business investment and exerting a "multiplier" effect on the national income. Government deficits would be created in recessions, and surpluses in prosperous times. Keynesian policy stressed the short-term management of the business cycle rather than long-term economic growth. Moreover, as elaborated by one of the earliest of Keynes' American followers, Professor Alvin H. Hansen of Harvard, deficit spending or pump-priming differed from compensatory spending. Deficit spending gave the economy enough momentum to make maximum use of its resources without further government aid. Compensatory spending, on the other hand, involved the government continuously in the management of prosperity. The New Deal used pump-priming, but it never engaged in a culculated program of compensatory spending.

Even before Keynes won his first handful of American disciples in the late 1930's, there were administration advisers, most of whom had never read Keynes, who were urging on Roosevelt an overhaul of fiscal and monetary policy to expand purchasing power and business investment. One of these was Marriner S. Eccles, who envisioned the government as a regulator of cyclical fluctuations, compensating for inadequate activity in the private sector by running budgetary deficits during recessions, and restraining inflation by piling up surpluses in good times. When the exuberant business recovery of early 1937 encouraged Roosevelt to bring the budget into balance, he ordered sharp cutbacks in public spending. At the same time, growing tax collections for the new social security taxes reduced purchasing power. These factors, combined with underlying weaknesses in the economy, produced the fastest and sharpest business contraction on record, lasting from September, 1937, to June, 1938. After much vacillation, Roosevelt shifted back to deficit spending, but these renewed outlays never conformed to the economics of compensatory spending. As Keynes predicted in 1940, it required a vast defense mobilization to create full employment. In 1944, the unemployment rate was 1.2 per cent. The high economic levels of wartime America did not dispel anxieties that after victory the country would return to the stagnating "mature economy" of the 1930's, but as early as 1943 the performance of a mobilized economy led publicists, trade unionists, New Dealers, and a rising generation of American Keynesians to draw up proposals for giving fiscal and monetary policy a central role in sustaining high aggregate demand and full employment. Keynesian techniques attracted liberals and reformers committed to the goals of an expanding economy, higher living standards, and social security.

Liberal opinion on postwar economic policy crystallized in the Full Employment Bill of 1945, whose chief sponsors were Senator James E. Murray of Montana and Senator Robert F. Wagner of New York. Although the original version was considerably weakened by conservative and business opposition, the Employment Act of 1946 (which significantly omitted the word "full") nevertheless signified abandonment of the *laissez-faire* notion that government should not interfere with a self-regulating economy and represented a national commitment to the objectives of economic growth and stability (see Selection 18).

If the primary economic goal of the 1930's was recovery, and that of the immediate postwar era was stability and full employment, since the 1950's it has been growth. Until the recessions of 1953–1954 and 1957–1958, it was generally assumed that the economy, strengthened by the "built-in stabilizers" installed during the New Deal, had enough momentum to sustain growth. Meanwhile, the economic recovery of Western Europe after 1948, financed largely by the United States, stimulated high annual rates of growth in France, West Germany, and other nations, especially after 1955, in contrast to the average growth rate in the United States, which ranged between 2.5 and 3 per cent a year throughout the fifties. After 1956 economic growth figured more frequently in public discussion, and in the Presidential campaign of 1960, which was waged against the background of a business recession, the Democratic candidate, John F. Kennedy, made the growth rate one of his principal issues. A month after Kennedy took office, the unemployment rate stood at 8.1 per cent, although business improved after the spring of 1961.

Over the next two years a debate on economic policy was actively pursued in the White House circle, with Kennedy leaning toward those advisers who argued that tax reduction rather than increased public spending was the best means of creating a budget deficit conducive to economic growth. Foremost among the advocates of tax reduction was Walter W. Heller, Chairman of the Council of Economic Advisers. Heller stressed the "tax drag" theory, contending that high tax rates when production was rising siphoned off purchasing power and accumulated a budget surplus that retarded economic growth and full employment. For political reasons, Kennedy hesitated to commit himself, but he prepared the way, as in his address at Yale University on June 11, 1962, when he called on business and government to shed the "ideological preconceptions" of an earlier time and to approach in a spirit of pragmatic realism the common task of managing a modern industrial economy. By December, 1962, Kennedy had overcome his reluctance to use deficits as a stimulus to business investment and expansion, and, while still preferring tax reduction to public spending, became the first President to commit himself to a flexible policy of budgetary deficits as a tool of economic growth (see Selection 19). The longest boom in American history has been under way since late 1961, but what might have been almost ideal conditions for testing the ability of the "new economics" to manage high aggregate demand and full employment without substantial inflation was upset after the escalation in 1964–1965 of the Vietnam war. More fundamentally, in the economic environment of the Cold War that has prevailed for the last twenty years, the United States has not yet been able to demonstrate whether it can revise its priorities and organize comparable resources for expanded civilian production and social services.

After the Civil War, the development of an industrial society transformed agriculture without giving it a proportionate share of the benefits of technological progress and expanded production. The leading economic activity of the nation in 1860, farming had lost its primacy by 1890, when it was receiving a declining share of the national income. The root cause of its plight was the shift from subsistence farming to commercial agriculture in the North, and a vastly enlarged output that until close to the end of the century exceeded effective demand. Staple crop agriculture was accelerated by the Civil War, which introduced mechanization on a greater scale, and it made the farmer dependent on an impersonal and far-flung market system of railroads, banks, mortgage and insurance companies, middlemen, commodity exchanges, and foreign competitors. The wheat farmers who streamed into the trans-Mississippi West after 1865 competed not only with each other, but also with foreign growers who shipped wheat from newly opened lands in Canada, Argentina, Russia, and Australia.

Between 1870 and 1890—a period of declining world prices for wheat and other agricultural commodities—the number of farms in the United States rose from 2,660,000 to 5,737,000. Burdened by large capital outlays, heavy indebtedness, high and discriminatory transportation rates, excessive marketing costs, and an inequitable tax system, farmers on the Western prairies and plains responded to low prices by boosting production. The collective result was overproduction, market gluts, and still lower prices. Integrated into a money exchange economy, the farmer suffered from a disparity between the prices of farm produce and the prices of nonfarm goods and services he had to buy. In short, agriculture was out of balance with the rest of the economy. Organized farm protest was a post-Civil War phenomenon, and it did not grow rapidly until farm prices dipped sharply in 1872. The Granger movement mobilized agrarian sentiment against the concentration of private and corporate wealth, and paved the way for the anti-monopoly agitation of the 1880's. A deepening agricultural depression starting in 1887 intensified farm militancy in the Plains states, where the Northern Farmers' Alliance, predecessor of the Populist party, formulated a program of common action aimed at redressing the inequities which had diminished the status of agriculture in an industrial economy.

Populism, reaching its climax between 1890 and 1896, proved vulnerable to the silver inflation issue of the Bryan Democrats and crumbled after the return of farm prosperity in 1897. The period 1897–1914 has been termed the "golden age" of American agriculture because of the farmers' improved position in the economy. Farming expanded, but at a relatively modest pace; between 1900 and 1914, about 710,000 farms were added to the national total, compared to an increase of 1,172,000 for the single decade 1890–1900. This more leisurely growth was outpaced by the swelling demand of an urban industrial population augmented by a record stream of immigration. The result was an improved balance between domestic supply and demand, even though the proportion of wheat and other foodstuffs sent overseas actually decreased. The problem of huge surpluses vanished, and the price curve turned upward, stimulated partly by additions to the world gold supply after 1897. Between 1899 and 1909 the value of farm products climbed much faster than the general index of nonagricultural goods purchased by the farmer. While much of the increase in value was inflationary, between 1909 and 1914—the years later designated as "parity" base years—the prices of farm and nonfarm goods stood in virtually ideal relationship. No longer caught up in a race to avert foreclosure by producing more, many staple farmers began to diversify their production.

World War I unsettled the gradual stabilization and diversification of commercial agriculture. From 1914 to 1920, when foreign and domestic requirements promoted a massive shift to wheat and corn, there was no significant increase either in the number of farms or in gross agricultural output. The rise in farm income from $7.6 billion in 1914 to $16.9 billion in 1919 was almost entirely inflationary. American farmers came out of the war with a total debt of $8.5 billion, compared to $4.7 billion in 1914, and with a record number of farms, totalling 6,448,000 in 1920 compared to 6,406,000 in 1910. From late 1916 on, farm prices climbed faster than the general price level, and by June, 1920, crop prices were 252 per cent above the prewar level. In 1918–1920 the large-scale introduction of powered mechanization, in the form of the gasoline tractor, enhanced productivity. So did the first earnest acceptance of scientific agriculture by growers who had previously scorned "book farming," and were reached by the county agent system which came of age during the war. Beginning in the summer of 1920, a price decline in farm commodities ushered in the long agricultural depression that did not lift until World War II. By April, 1921, the price ratio of farm to nonfarm goods had dropped to 63 in terms of price equality in 1913 ( = 100). The staple farmer entered the 1920's facing the same problem of "disparity" that had beset him from 1870 to 1897 (see Selection 20).

Agricultural reform became one of the leading issues in the generally prosperous and otherwise politically tepid twenties. Leaders of the Congressional farm bloc, organized in 1921, supported the McNary-Haugen plan, a complicated scheme for bringing farm prices up to the level of a "fair exchange value" by skimming the agricultural surplus from the home market and selling it abroad through a government corporation. The McNary-Haugen plan was twice vetoed by President Calvin Coolidge. His successor, President Herbert Hoover, backed a proposal for stabilizing prices through the orderly cooperative marketing of surpluses. This was embodied in the Agricultural Marketing Act of 1929, which created a Federal Farm Board and authorized publicly financed commodity stabilization corporations to buy up surpluses in order to maintain a fair market price. The drop in farm prices after 1929 forced the government to purchase grain and cotton on the open market in the face of farmer refusal to restrict production voluntarily, and by 1931 the funds for price support operations were exhausted. Between 1929 and 1932 farm prices declined by more than 50 per cent, and the parity ratio fell from 89 to 55. The revival of agriculture and the restoration of its balance with the economy became high priorities of the early New Deal. Among the basic measures it adopted was the domestic allotment plan devised in 1932 by Milburn L. Wilson, a professor of agricultural economics at Montana State College. Crop restriction on the acreage allotment plan under the commodity programs of the New Deal was applied to basic commodities in the first Agricultural Adjustment Act of 1933. In later versions of farm legislation, where it was tied to "parity," it remained the central feature of agricultural policy (see Selection 21).

In World War II, agriculture regained its prosperity chiefly because, as in World War I, prices advanced faster than output. Between 1939 and 1944 production increased by some 23 per cent, despite a decrease in the farm labor force and only a small addition to the total cultivated acreage. The more intensive use of powered mechanization and chemical fertilizer raised man-hour output and per-acre yields. The technological revolution accelerated by the war reinforced the long-term trend toward larger farms, a growing concentration of output among large commercial growers, the dependence of many small farmers upon outside sources of income, the decline of the family farm, and the accumulation of surpluses despite government subsidy programs (see Selection 22). The number of farms dropped from 5.9 million in 1945 to 3.8 million in 1961 and 3.1 million in 1967, when the 11.5 million people on American farms accounted for less than 6 per cent of the population, compared to 17 per cent in 1945. The Vietnam war and the greater food needs of the developing nations have not disturbed the fundamental pattern of acreage restriction. In 1967 a Presidential body, the National Food and Fiber Commission, disagreed on the necessity for long-term federal assistance to agriculture, but it urged continuation of farm programs "until the problem of excess capacity in farming is alleviated and farmers are able to earn incomes from the market that are comparable to nonfarm incomes."

The rapid pace of American industrialization between 1870 and 1914 had a marked effect on the position of the United States in the international economy. A long-term shift toward more exports of manufactured and semi-finished goods—items which accounted for 48 per cent of total exports in 1914 as compared with 16 per cent in 1866—was largely instrumental in permanently establishing a favorable balance of trade in every year after 1873, with the exception of the years 1875, 1888, 1889, and 1893. Foreign trade grew from $800 million in 1870 to about $4.2 billion in 1914, expanding much faster than the economy as a whole. Most of this growth came between 1895 and 1914 and was partly related to overseas expansion, but during this entire period the bulk of American international trade was with Europe.

From 1865 to 1873 the United States had an annual surplus of imports over exports, as it did before the Civil War, and ran a deficit trade balance of about $100 million a year. The largest single deficit item in the balance of payments, it was supplemented by smaller debits on "invisible" items such as ocean freight and insurance charges, immigrant remittances, tourist expenditures, and interest payments. The total deficit in international accounts was made up by exports of gold and silver, and by foreign purchases of American securities, particularly railroad bonds. From 1874 to 1890 the trade balance shifted in favor of the United States, mainly as the result of record shipments of agricultural commodities to Europe, as well as the development of a large and tariff-protected internal market that held down the volume of imports. Even so, the trade surplus was smaller than the aggregate of "invisible" items, which rose owing to the decline of American merchant shipping after the Civil War, a stronger flow of remittances to Europe in the wake of growing immigration, and a greater volume of interest payments to foreign investors who during this period built up their holdings in railroads, cattle ranches, and land. At the same time, American capital was making its first sizable direct investments overseas, initiating a trend that has almost uninterruptedly been continued to this day.

After 1897 the volume of American exports increased disproportionately to imports, resulting in a trade balance that averaged a half billion dollars annually. These years, continuing into the early twentieth century, were the era of the "American commercial invasion" of Europe, when U.S. manufactured goods flooded the Continent and made the United States the successor to Great Britain as the world's supplier of cheap wares. After 1904, the trade balance of the United States approximated an equilibrium, being roughly equal to the deficit from "invisible" items. This reflected a major change in the international flow of capital; but a gap was created by foreign investments here, which rose from $3.3 billion in 1900 to about $6.5 billion by 1908. Between 1908 and 1914 foreign investment in this country increased to about $7.2 billion, while the United States held about $3.5 billion outside its borders. Thus, on the eve of World War I, the United States was a debtor nation.

World War I was a watershed in the development of the modern international economy. It disrupted the normal course of world economic relations, gravely weakened the economies of Germany and Central Europe, took Russia out of the world economy for about fifteen years, and raised the United States to a position of world financial supremacy. Between 1914 and 1919 the American export surplus exceeded $15 billion, a figure larger than that for the preceding four decades. This wartime export surplus was offset by Allied gold shipments of about $1 billion, the sale of American investments held by Allied nationals, American government and private loans to European countries, and remittances for European relief. By the end of 1919 the United States was a major creditor nation, with a net creditor position of $13.7 billion. Excluding the war debts, this gave America a net credit on private account of $3.7 billion.

It is probable that no nation has ever undergone a comparable transformation of its position in the world economy in such a short time. In the postwar period, economic logic recommended a smaller American export surplus, or even an unfavorable balance of trade, so that foreign debtors might develop needed dollar exchange for paying off their war debts and private obligations.

Throughout the 1920's, however, the United States continued to build up an excess of exports over imports, ranging from $375 million in 1923 to more than $1 billion in 1928. This expansion of the favorable trade balance was due to several factors, among them the long-term continuation of American industrial supremacy, which had been strengthened during the war at the expense of Great Britain and Germany, and the high protectionism written into the Fordney-McCumber Tariff of 1922. But probably most important of all were the large foreign loans floated in the United States, the liberal extension of private bankers' loans to Western and Central European nations, especially Germany, and American direct investment abroad. For practically every year between 1922 and 1929, there was a net capital flow out of the United States. America became the world's banker, and she financed her booming export trade by sending large supplies of dollar exchange overseas. But in 1928 the higher interest rates generated by the stock market boom lured American capital from Europe to the New York money market, and after the crash the withdrawal of capital continued. By late 1929, the United States had a net creditor position on long-term account of about $10 billion. With the coming of the Great Depression, restrictive nationalist policies, epitomized in the United States by the Smoot-Hawley Tariff of 1930, compounded the postwar economic dislocations and the war-induced changes in the international movement of capital (see Selection 23).

Between 1934 and 1939 a partial reversal of protectionism under the Reciprocal Trade Agreements Act of 1934 had no significant impact on American economic relations with Europe. The United States came out of World War II with the most powerful economy in the world. Of all the major combatants, it was the only one whose productive machinery escaped devastation. Early recognizing its stake in the restoration of world political and financial stability, the United States was the principal contributor to the United Nations Relief and Rehabilitation Administration, and later, through the Marshall Plan, underwrote the economic recovery of Western Europe in 1948–1951. With dollar shortages prevailing almost everywhere, the United States participated in creating mechanisms for promoting world trade, such as the International Bank for Reconstruction and Redevelopment, better known as the World Bank, and the International Monetary Fund. From 1949 on, however, the

American effort to contain communism became the chief factor in determining the composition of overseas spending, the bulk of which has gone for foreign military aid and the support of American military establishments and operations abroad. Though the United States continued to have an export surplus, it was more than offset by overseas military expenditures, foreign economic assistance programs, American direct investment, and tourist spending. As a result, the United States, beginning in 1958, has had an increasingly heavy balance of payments deficit which has made serious inroads into American gold reserves, impelling the United States to plug the gold drain by building up its trade surplus in the hope of bringing its international payments into approximate equilibrium (see Selection 24). Although controls over the outflow of private capital have been tightened, the balance of payments deficit has continued to grow, partly as the result of heavier American involvement in the Vietnam war.

The drive for expanding the volume of American exports was complicated by the economic resurgence of Western Europe and the establishment of the Common Market in 1958. Within this rich trading area the six nations comprising the Common Market have progressively reduced tariffs and stimulated the flow of goods. For years, however, the Common Market did not cut tariffs for nonmembers. To promote a freer flow of international trade, the United States led the way in proposing reduced tariffs under GATT (General Agreement on Tariffs and Trade), dating from 1947. The Trade Expansion Act of 1962 sanctioned the "Kennedy Round" of negotiations, which at their termination in 1967 projected a 35 per cent tariff reduction, phased out over five years, on $16 billion of American exports and imports. The greatest single effort in the liberalization of international trade, the agreement was signed by 46 nations in June, 1967. While the pact did not entirely dismantle protectionism, and was not wholly successful in relaxing restrictions imposed by the United States and the Common Market, the "Kennedy Round" reductions affected about three-quarters of the dutiable goods imported by the principal industrialized nations, excluding the Soviet Union. The planned tariff cuts must first run the gauntlet of industry and Congressional spokesmen for protectionism. By the fall of 1967 many proposals had been advanced for restrictive import quotas on a wide variety of products. If adopted, such non-tariff devices would invite retaliatory measures by foreign countries and seriously impair the trade policy envisioned at Geneva as well as the long-standing American commitment to the expansion of foreign trade.

At home and abroad the United States, as the world's most advanced industrial economy, faces awesome tasks and responsibilities. It is likely that future economic development at home will see an even closer mingling of public and private investment, and an ordering of long-range priorities determined not so much by economic goals as by pressing social problems. And, in a world where developing nations are now in the majority, the United States must reckon with the need for using its resources to close rather than widen the gap between itself and less affluent peoples.

# I. MONEY, BANKING, AND THE RISE OF FINANCE CAPITALISM

## 1. The Greenbacks

*The decision to issue irredeemable paper money, commonly known as "greenbacks," was a bold response to the exigencies of a civil war whose coming found the Union government in financial straits. In the summer of 1861 Congress failed to enact emergency tax legislation; when it met again in December, revenues were ebbing and the fiscal problems of the North were overwhelming. Government contractors and the army had to be paid. The Treasury could no longer turn to the large Eastern banks, which at the end of 1861 suspended specie payments. On January 22, 1862, Representative Elbridge G. Spaulding of the House Ways and Means Committee introduced a bill authorizing the emission of inconvertible, noninterest-bearing Treasury notes as legal tender in payment of public and private debts. The move touched off an uproar. Opponents of the measure condemned it as unconstitutional, immoral, and certain to produce a ruinous inflation. But some hard money men, notably Secretary of the Treasury Salmon P. Chase, swallowed their distaste and accepted the bill as an expedient dictated by grim necessity. In all, $350 million was due before mid-1862. "Immediate action is of great importance," wrote Chase as the bill lay before Congress. "The Treasury is nearly empty." Between February 1862 and January 1863, Congress authorized $450 million of greenback currency, of which $431.5 million was actually issued. A wartime improvisation, the greenbacks became a turning point in American monetary history.*

SOURCE: For I, *Congressional Globe*, 37th Cong., 2nd sess., remarks of Representative George H. Pendleton (Dem.-Ohio), January 29, 1862, pp. 549–51. For II, *ibid.*, remarks of Senator Henry Wilson (Rep.-Mass.), February 13, 1862, pp. 788–9.

## I

MR. [George H.] PENDLETON . . . I shall . . . confine myself this morning somewhat strictly to the special provisions of the bill before the committee. That bill provides for the issue of $100,000,000 of Treasury notes of the character and description therein mentioned. It provides that they shall not bear interest; that they shall be payable, at the pleasure of the Government, to bearer at the Treasury of the United States, or at the office of the Assistant Treasurer in the city of New York; they shall be receivable for all debts and demands due to the Government, and for all debts and demands due from the Government; and, in the language of the bill, "They shall be lawful money and a legal tender in payment of all debts, public and private, within the United States."

I have examined, Mr. Chairman, with some care, every law authorizing the issue of Treasury notes which has been passed from the foundation of the Government up to this hour, and I find that this bill differs from all of them in several essential particulars. Every other law authorizing the issue of Treasury notes provided that they should bear some rate of interest, whereas these are to bear none; that they should be payable at a fixed time prescribed in the note, whereas these are only to be payable at the pleasure of the United States; that the notes thereby authorized should be receivable in payment of public debts only by those who were willing to receive them at par, while these notes are to be received by every public creditor who is not willing to forfeit his right to payment at all. These notes are to be made lawful money, and a legal tender in discharge of all pecuniary obligations, either by the Government or by individuals, a characteristic which has never been given to any note of the United States or any note of the Bank of the United States by any law ever passed. Not only, sir, was such a law never passed, but such a law was never voted on, never proposed, never introduced, never recommended by any Department of the Government; the measure was never seriously entertained in debate in either branch of Congress. . . .

. . . The report of the Secretary of the Treasury, made at the opening of the session, contains no such recommendation. It is obvious, from the comparison which I have drawn between the bill before us and the laws heretofore passed, that if this bill shall pass, we are about to take a departure from the settled financial policy of the Government. We are about to launch ourselves, with sails all set, upon an ocean of experiment, upon which the wise men who administered the Government before we came into power, warned by the example of other nations, would not permit it even to enter. I believe that this Government has reached a crisis in its history. I believe that it is approaching a period in the history of its legislation which may determine the question of its continuance. By wisdom it may overcome the evils of secession; by its great powers and resources it may be able to defend itself against those in arms against it; but I firmly believe that it cannot maintain itself against the shock of the accumulated and manifold dangers which follow inevitably, closely in the wake of an illegal, unsound, and depreciated Government paper currency.

The feature of this bill which first strikes every thinking man even in these days of novelties, is the proposition that these notes shall be made a legal tender in discharge of all pecuniary obligations, as well those which have accrued in virtue of contracts already made as those which are yet to accrue in pursuance of contracts which shall hereafter be made. Do gentlemen appreciate the full import and meaning of that clause? Do they realize the full extent to which it will carry them? Every contract for the payment of money is in legal contemplation a contract for the payment of gold and silver coin. Every promissory note, every bill of exchange, every lease reserving rent, every loan of money reserving interest, every bond issued by this Government, is a contract to which the faith of the obligor is pledged that the amount, whether rent, interest, or principal, shall be paid in the gold and silver coin of the country. Every contract for the performance of some other thing than the payment of money carries with it, as the penalty of its infraction, that damages shall be assessed, and that these damages shall be paid, even if necessary at the end of an execution, in the gold and silver coin of the country. Every verdict which has been rendered, every judgment which has been entered up, every decree for the payment of money, has been made upon that hypothesis. That is the measure of the obligation of the one party, and of the right of the other.

The provisions of this bill contemplate impairing the obligation of every contract of that kind, and disturbing the basis upon which every judgment and decree and verdict has been entered. It proposes to say to a party who has entered into a contract, "You shall be discharged from the obligations of that contract by doing something else than that which you have agreed to do." It proposes to say to every party with whom a contract has been made, "Though you are entitled to demand one thing, you shall, perforce, remain satisfied with the doing of another." It proposes to say, "Although you have agreed to pay gold and silver, you shall be discharged upon the payment of these notes; although you are entitled to demand gold and silver, you shall rest content with the reception of this paper." It proposes, in one word, to release the one party from the obligation of his contract, and to divest the other party of the right which has been vested in him by that contract. Sir, I am sure I need only state the proposition to shock the mind of the legal profession of the country, so thoroughly has it been imbued with the idea of the sanctity of the obligation of contracts by those who have taught it the beneficent maxims of constitutional law.

As for the rest, this bill provides that it shall be illegal to make a contract for dealing in gold and silver coin; or, to state it more exactly, it provides that whatever executory contracts parties may make concerning the gold and silver coin of the country, they shall be discharged upon the performance of another and different duty —by the delivery of an equivalent number of dollars in these notes. Where, sir, does Congress get this power? Where is the grant to be found? One would suppose that a power like that—a power which involves the impairing of the obligations of such a vast class of contracts, which proposes to disturb vested rights to such an immense extent—would be worthy of a place in the express grants of the Constitution. . . .

The gentleman from New York [Elbridge G. Spaulding], in his argument yesterday, deduced this power from the general powers of the Government. He told us that Congress had power to lay and collect taxes; to raise and support armies; to provide and maintain a navy; and that all power necessary to effectuate these purposes was expressly given by the general grant of the Constitution. If I should admit his statement in the very language in which he has made it, am I not entitled to ask whether he has shown us any legitimate connection between making these notes a legal tender and the power to raise an army? Might I not ask whether the repudiation of the obligations of the Government to pay its interest is a legitimate means for providing and sustaining a navy? Whether impairing the obligations of contracts between private individuals throughout the country will, in any degree, assist the Government in its great duty of laying and collecting taxes? We had no demonstration of the necessity or propriety of these means to accomplish those ends.

The gentleman spoke quite at large in reference to the sovereign power of the Government. He told us that this power was not prohibited in the Constitution. He told us that in times of great emergency everything may be done except that which is prohibited; and he read an argument from the Attorney General, which concludes as it began, with the proposition that such a power is not prohibited to Congress. Sir, I repudiate this whole idea. I think it has no solid foundation in the Constitution. In all its external relations, standing among the nations of the earth, the Government of the United States is sovereign, and is invested with all the attributes of sovereignty; but in its relations to its own citizens, in its relations to the States, in its relations to its own constituents, it has no power except that which is granted. It has no original power; its powers are all delegated, and delegated by the terms of the Constitution itself. I repudiate the idea that all the sovereign power which rightfully resides in the nation must necessarily find expression in any department of the Government, whether it be national or State. I stand upon the provision of the Constitution, that all power which is not delegated to the Federal Government is reserved from it; and that all power which is not delegated to it, and thereby reserved from it, resides either in the States or the people. There are many powers which are denied by the Constitution to the States, and yet not delegated to the General Government. They find their proper repository in the people.

I would call the attention of the gentleman, in this connection, and in reference to the argument which he has made, to the fact that under the Articles of Confederation the Government of the United States had the power to raise armies, to provide a navy, to borrow money, and to emit bills of credit upon the faith of the United States. And yet the statesmen of that day never, even in all the distress and pressure of the financial difficulties of the Revolution, supposed that they possessed any such power as this. They desired that the bills emitted by the Government should be a legal tender, and they passed resolutions that they ought to be so considered, but they never deemed that they had the power to make them such, or sought to exercise it. . . .

When I come to examine the powers of Congress, according to the principles of interpretation to which I have said I adhere, I look to the grants of the Constitution. I find no grant of this power in direct terms, or, as I think, by fair implication. It is not an accidental omission; it is not an omission through inadvertency; it was intentionally left out of the Constitution, because it was designed that the power should not reside in the Federal Government. . . .

Sir, it seems to me that if the language of the Constitution, and the weight of authority can settle any proposition, it is that Congress has not the power to do that which it is proposed shall be done by the provisions of this bill. . . .

. . . I do not deny the power of Congress to borrow money and to issue notes in evidence of the indebtedness; I limit my objection strictly to the notes described in this bill.

But, even if I believed this bill to be constitutional in both aspects, I yet see enough in it to merit, as I think, the hearty condemnation of the House. It provides that these notes shall be redeemable only at the pleasure of the United States. The gentleman from New York [Mr. Spaulding] called them "demand notes." They have been so called throughout the country. They do not bear a single characteristic of a demand note. There is no time, from the hour when they shall pass into the hands of the holder, when he can by their terms demand that they shall be redeemed. There is no time when the faith of the Government is pledged to their payment. The holder may present them, and he is told that the time has not arrived at which, by the face of the bill, they are to be paid. They will inevitably depreciate. The wit of man has never discovered a means by which paper currency can be kept at par value, except by its speedy, cheap, certain convertibility into gold and silver. I need not cite gentlemen to history or to authorities —writers on political economy—to prove it. Unless convertible they have always depreciated; they always will depreciate; they ought to depreciate, because they are only valuable as the representatives of gold and silver; and if they are not convertible into that of which they are the representative, they must necessarily lose their value. You send these notes out into the world stamped with irredeemability. You put on them the mark of Cain, and, like

Cain, they will go forth to be vagabonds and fugitives on the earth. What then will be the consequence? It requires no prophet to tell what will be their history. The currency will be expanded; prices will be inflated; fixed values will depreciate; incomes will be diminished; the savings of the poor will vanish; the hoardings of the widow will melt away; bonds, mortgages, and notes, everything of fixed value, will lose their value; everything of changeable value will be appreciated; the necessaries of life will rise in value; the Government will pay twofold—certainly largely more than it ought —for everything that it goes into the market to buy; gold and silver will be driven out of the country. What then? The day of reckoning must come. Contraction will follow. Private ruin and public bankruptcy, either with or without REPUDIATION, will inevitably follow. . . .

Can we not learn something from the early experience of our own country? Can we not learn something from the overthrow of the revolutionary Government of France by this very over-issue of depreciated paper? Can we not learn something from those throes which the society of England endured during the long suspension of, and at its return to, specie currency in 1822? Can we not now rise to a wisdom of statesmanship which shall control the financial necessities of the country without plunging it into that gulf from which there is, with honor and safety, no recovery?

Sir, I beg gentlemen to permit me to read, in closing what I have to say, one more lesson of wisdom from that statesman of New England [Daniel Webster] to whom I have had occasion so often already to refer. I read it with the hope that it will be engraven on the memory of every man here, and that it will enable us to avoid the evils of which he has spoken by adhering to the course which he has wisely marked out:

> No nation had a better currency than the United States. There was no nation which had guarded its currency with more care, for the framers of the Constitution and those who had enacted the early statutes on the subject were *hard money men*. They had felt and duly appreciated the evils of a paper medium; they therefore sedulously guarded the currency of the United States from debasement. The legal currency of the United States was gold and silver coin. This was a subject in regard to which Congress had run into no folly. Gold and silver currency was the law of the land at home, the law of the world abroad; there could, in the present condition of the world, be no other currency.

Let gentlemen heed this lesson of wisdom. Let them, if need be, tax the energies and wealth of the country sufficiently to restore the credit of the Government. Let them borrow whatever money in addition may be necessary—borrow it to the full extent that may be necessary—and let us adhere rigidly, firmly, consistently, persistently, and to the end, to the principle of refusing to surrender that currency which the Constitution has given us, and in the maintenance of which this Government has never, as yet, for one moment wavered.

## II

Mr. [Henry] Wilson, of Massachusetts . . . Passing by the question of constitutional power, and coming to it simply as a practical question, it is a contest between brokers and jobbers and money-changers on the one side, and the people of the United States on the other. I venture to express the opinion that ninety-nine of every hundred of the loyal people of the United States are for this legal tender clause. I do not believe that there are one thousand persons in the State I represent who are not in favor [of] it. The entire business community, with hardly a solitary exception, men who have trusted out in the country in commercial transactions their tens and hundreds of millions, are for the bill with this legal tender clause. Yes, sir; the people in sentiment approach unanimity upon this question. What is true of Massachusetts is in my judgment true to a considerable extent of New England, and true to some considerable extent of the central States and the West. I believe that no measure that can be passed by the Congress of the United States, unless it be a bill to raise revenue to support the credit of the Government, will be received with so much joy as the passage of this bill with the legal tender clause. On that question I entertain no shadow of doubt. If you pass this bill with the legal tender, the legal tender cannot injuriously affect the credit of this currency you propose to circulate. No harm can certainly come of it. It seems to me, sir, the argument made by the Senator from Vermont and the Senator from Maine is an argument against issuing these notes as a currency at all. The legitimate inferences from their arguments are against this proposition for $150,000,000 of demand Treasury notes.

Now, sir, I believe that if this bill is to pass at all, if we are to issue these demand notes at all, we should do all in our power to preserve their credit and to protect the persons to whom we pay out this $150,000,000. In my judgment, if the legal tender clause is stricken out of the bill, you will have every curbstone . . . broker in the country, the bulls and the bears of the stock exchange, and the class of men who fatten upon public calamity and the wants and necessities of the people, using all their influence to depreciate the credit of this Government and break down the value of these demand notes. Under such circumstances and such influences these demand notes will be depreciated, and the persons to whom we pay them out, our soldiers in the field, the sailors upon the decks of our vessels, the persons who have furnished millions and tens of millions unpaid goods for the use of our Army and Navy, will be compelled to go into the market and submit to be shaved by the brokers and money-changers of the country. If we are to issue these demand notes at all, let us stamp upon them this legal tender; let us support their credit by taxation and by reducing the expenditures of the Government in every form down to the lowest possible rates. Let us sustain them by proclaiming that we are ever ready to put burdens upon the wealth of the country; that we mean to uphold and sustain the credit of the Government, and thus carry the country financially triumphantly through the contest in which we are engaged. . . .

We are told that it will not do to interfere in these private transactions. Sir, my opinion is to-day that no class in this country have more interest in this legal tender clause than the creditor class of the community. You will find that your manufacturers, your merchants, your men who have their hundreds of millions trusted out in all parts of the country, are for this measure, for it is their protection and their interest. You will find that the families of your soldiers, who are to receive a small pittance from the men who are fighting the battles of your country in the field, are in favor of stamping upon these notes the words "legal tender"; so that when that little pittance comes from the field to them, to support them at home, they can use it to pay their necessary debts, and support themselves without having to go through the process of broker shavings.

I look upon this contest as a contest between the curbstone brokers . . . the money-changers, and the men who speculate in stocks, and the productive, toiling men of the country. I believe the sentiment of the nation approaches unanimity in favor of this legal tender clause. I have received several letters from my own State on the subject; one a day or two ago, signed by several large commercial houses, representing millions of capital, and from others, and they say to me that they do not know a merchant in the city of Boston engaged in active business who is not for this legal tender. The intelligence I obtain from all portions of the country is to the same effect. I shall, therefore, vote against striking out that clause. If it is retained, I shall vote for the bill. If it is stricken out, I shall give my vote against putting on the people, upon the soldiers of the country, $150,000,000 of demand notes, and doing nothing to protect those upon whom we impose this Government paper.

# 2. The National Banking System Springs to Life

The National Bank Act of February 25, 1863, barely squeezed through an unenthusiastic Congress. Unquestionably, it would never have passed at the time save as an emergency measure to meet the urgent necessities of financing the war for the Union. Secretary of the Treasury Salmon P. Chase had supported the proposal since December 1861, partly because it promised to create a market for United States bonds. The measure had formidable foes, among them the state banks which had flourished since the 1830's and were determined to preserve their privilege of note issue against federal constraint, and their Democratic allies in Congress who remained loyal to the Jacksonian traditions of the "bank war." In the first year under the act, relatively few banks took out a national charter. An extensive list of amendments in an act of June 3, 1864, helped to speed up conversions. This second act served as the foundation of the National Banking System until passage of the Federal Reserve Act in 1913. A feature of the 1864 legislation was a 2 per cent tax on state banknote circulation. Under an act of March 1865, this tax was raised to a prohibitive 10 per cent.

SOURCE: Hugh McCulloch, "Report of the Comptroller of the Currency," *Report of the Secretary of the Treasury, 1864*, 38th Cong., 2nd sess., House of Representatives, Executive Document No. 3 (Washington, D.C.: Government Printing Office, 1864), pp. 46–52, 54.

November 25, 1864.

. . . Since my last annual report two hundred and eighty-two new banks have been organized, and one hundred and sixty-eight State banks have been changed into national ones. Of the one hundred banks last organized, sixty-seven have been conversions of State banks, and nearly all the papers now being filed are for the change of State banks into national associations.

There are now in existence, under the national currency act, five hundred and eighty-four associations, which are located in the following States:

| | |
|---|---:|
| In Maine | 18 |
| In New Hampshire | 9 |
| In Vermont | 10 |
| In Massachusetts | 67 |
| In Rhode Island | 2 |
| In Connecticut | 20 |
| In New York | 100 |
| In New Jersey | 16 |
| In Pennsylvania | 109 |
| In Delaware | 1 |
| In Maryland | 3 |
| In District of Columbia | 2 |
| In Virginia | 1 |
| In West Virginia | 2 |
| In Ohio | 84 |
| In Michigan | 15 |
| In Indiana | 34 |
| In Illinois | 38 |
| In Wisconsin | 15 |
| In Minnesota | 4 |
| In Iowa | 20 |
| In Missouri | 7 |
| In Kansas | 1 |
| In Nebraska Territory | 1 |
| In Kentucky | 1 |
| In Tennessee | 3 |
| In Louisiana | 1 |

The paid-in capital of the banks in the respective States and Territories, the currency delivered to them (a considerable portion of which has not been put into circulation), and the bonds deposited with the Treasurer to secure their notes, are as follows:

. . . A large proportion of the circulating notes which have been furnished by the Comptroller was intended to take the place and is taking the place of the circulation of such State banks as have been converted into national ones, or of those whose notes have

| State | Capital stock paid in | Circulation | Bonds |
|---|---|---|---|
| Maine | $ 2,749,800.00 | $ 1,887,880 | $ 2,244,500 |
| New Hampshire | 1,120,000.00 | 552,700 | 944,000 |
| Vermont | 1,490,000.00 | 1,311,800 | 1,636,000 |
| Rhode Island | 700,000.00 | 414,000 | 560,000 |
| Massachusetts | 25,909,040.00 | 12,536,850 | 16,888,650 |
| Connecticut | 5,176,638.00 | 4,084,050 | 4,525,500 |
| New York | 20,599,175.03 | 12,584,950 | 14,064,600 |
| Pennsylvania | 21,120,148.88 | 10,193,830 | 14,964,100 |
| New Jersey | 2,141,249.00 | 1,756,170 | 2,011,000 |
| Delaware | 300,000.00 | 200,000 | 250,000 |
| Maryland | 1,560,000.00 | 1,245,000 | 1,400,000 |
| District of Columbia | 600,000.00 | 477,000 | 534,000 |
| Virginia | 95,025.00 | 95,000 | 112,000 |
| West Virginia | 206,950.00 | 140,000 | 230,000 |
| Ohio | 10,035,165.86 | 7,505,880 | 8,749,850 |
| Kentucky | 200,000.00 | 162,000 | 184,000 |
| Indiana | 4,201,671.26 | 3,148,400 | 3,924,100 |
| Illinois | 4,147,837.25 | 3,396,560 | 3,794,600 |
| Michigan | 1,165,090.00 | 797,800 | 943,500 |
| Wisconsin | 1,040,277.00 | 774,500 | 903,050 |
| Minnesota | 590,000.00 | 442,000 | 603,000 |
| Iowa | 1,215,000.00 | 945,900 | 1,092,000 |
| Nebraska Territory | 40,000.00 | 27,000 | 30,000 |
| Kansas | 100,000.00 | 49,000 | 55,000 |
| Missouri | 1,621,530.00 | 722,000 | 865,000 |
| Tennessee | 340,000.00 | 234,380 | 263,000 |
| Louisiana | 500,000.00 | 180,000 | 200,000 |
| Total | 108,964,597.28 | 65,864,650 | 81,961,450 |

been voluntarily retired, or have been returned from those parts of the country in which the notes of the United States and of the national banks are alone current; so that the currency delivered to the national banks is not and will not be altogether an addition to the paper money of the country, but rather, to a considerable extent, the substitution of it for that of the State banks.

It is perhaps to be regretted that so many new banks have been organized in States where, before the passage of the act, there was no deficiency of banking capital. There would have been less cause for apprehension that banking capital in any of the States was being too rapidly increased, if, by suitable legislation of the States, State banks had been sooner authorized to avail themselves of the benefits of the national currency act, and the managers of banks, where the necessary legislation had been obtained, had more promptly discerned the inevitable tendency of the public sentiment, and co-operated with the government in its efforts to nationalize the bank note circulation of the country. It was not the intention of the originators and friends of the system, nor has it been the policy of the Comptroller, to swell, through the instrumentality of the national banks, the volume of paper money. On the contrary, the system was designed to check overissues by requiring ample security for every dollar which should be put into circulation, and it has been the aim of the Comptroller so to administer the law as to prevent, instead of encouraging, an unhealthy and dangerous expansion of credits.

I am happy in being able to say that my apprehensions of a too rapid increase of national banks have been much lessened by the recent action of many State banks. The legislature of Pennsylvania, following the example of the legislatures of Massachusetts, Connecticut, &c., has recently authorized the banks of that State to reorganize under the national system, and the stockholders of so many of them are availing themselves of this authority, as to render it quite certain that at an early day there will be in this great central State, without a dangerous increase of its banking capital, but one system of banking. In fact, the indications are now unmistakable that the time is not far distant when the people of the United States will be everywhere relieved of a bank note circulation of limited credit and uncertain value, and supplied with one of uniform credit and as solvent as the nation. It has been the earnest wish of the Comptroller that this desirable result should be brought about through the agency of existing banks, rather than by the organization of new ones, so that the national circulation might be introduced with as little increase of banking capital as possible. A national bank note currency will be one of the compensations for the heavy debt which has been incurred in the terrible contest in which the nation has been involved. If it can be everywhere introduced, as now seems probable, without creating a dangerous bank note inflation, it will prove to be a compensation which more than anything else will reconcile the people to the burdens which the war must necessarily impose upon them. It will be so by its tendency to regulate domestic exchanges, by the stability it will give to trade, in preventing unsecured issues and bank note panics, by saving the people from losses in the use of paper money, and by its influence in securing and perpetuating that national unity which is the ark of our safety.

It is an interesting fact, that this great change is taking place—this great financial revolution, if I may so call it, is being accomplished, without disturbing the business of the country. State banks, whose conversions are facilitated by enabling acts, are being daily reorganized without a curtailment of discounts, or even a temporary derangement of their affairs. Nearly all the banking capital of Philadephia has been recently nationalized, with scarcely an interruption of the business of the banks for a single day. In States where no enabling legislation has been obtained, the change from the State to the national system is attended with more difficulty. But even in these States, by the organization of national banks by the stockholders of State banks, and the transfer of the assets of the latter to the former, the change has been already, in many instances, effected without loss to the owners, and with very little practical inconvenience to the managers.

It is also an interesting fact, that the stock of State banks which have been changed into national associations has not been depreciated by the change; on the contrary, the shares of most of them have been appreciated, and I know of no instance in which their real or market value has been injuriously affected by it. This fact sufficiently refutes the charge, sometimes urged against the system, that it was being forced upon the country to the prejudice of the stockholders of State institutions.

It may be proper for me to state another fact in this connexion of interest to the public, which is, that the national banks are, without any known exceptions, in safe, although some of them are in inexperienced hands, and that the fears that the national banking system would be the means of filling the country with banks of fictitious capitals, and be a reproduction, on a large scale, of the stock banking systems of States in which they had proved to be a failure, if not a fraud, are, from present indications, without a real foundation.

The fact that such apprehensions were entertained or were professed to be entertained by the bankers of a State, in which a system similar in some of its main features was in practical operation, intimidated, for a while, the capitalists of other States, and retarded the reorganization of State banks, but worked no permanent injury to the national system. On the contrary, the expression of these fears has led to a thorough examination of the act, and a careful observation of its administration, and the result has been favorable to both. It has been discovered that in many important particulars the national system differs from, and is an improvement upon, the State system, which it the most closely resembles; that it restricts circulation to ninety per cent of the bonds on deposit with the Treasurer, and prohibits the banks from issuing notes to an amount exceeding their bona fide paid up capitals, sworn to by their officers; that every interior national bank, in addition to redeeming its notes at its own counter, is compelled to redeem at par, at some commercial centre, thereby tending to prevent high rates of exchange between the different sections of the country, and that, in case of the failure of a bank to redeem its notes according to the provisions of the act, these notes, instead of being depreciated, would be at once redeemable in lawful money, at the treasury of the United States. It has been also ascertained that the Comptroller is requiring the most satisfactory references or credentials in regard to the standing and responsibility of the persons proposing to organize national banks, and is instituting a system of examinations which will do much to expose and check improper practices on the part of the bankers, and violations of the wholesome provisions of the law.

This examination of the act, and the observation of the manner in which it is being administered, have resulted in the entering up of a popular judgment in favor of the national banking system; a judgment, not that the system is a perfect one, nor free from danger of abuse, but that it is a safer system, better adapted to the nature of our political institutions, and to our commerical necessities, giving more strength to the government, with less risk of its being used by the government against the just rights of the States, or the rights of the people, than any system which has yet been devised, and that by such amendments of the act as experience may show to be needful, it may be made as little objectionable, and as beneficial to the government and the people, as any paper money banking system that wisdom and experience are likely to invent. It promises to give to the people that long existing "desideratum," a national currency without a national bank, a bank note circulation of uniform value without the creation of a moneyed power in a few hands over the politics and business of the country.

Of course this system depends for its success upon the maintenance of the faith and credit of the nation, which, in their turn, depend upon the preservation of the national integrity. If these fail, the national banking system will fail; but it will go down with all other important interests, and will be but a part of the general wreck. That such a calamity is not in store for us is the confident hope and belief of all true men of the loyal States. The anxieties and apprehensions which have existed heretofore on this point are rapidly disappearing as the loyal mind of the United States has hardened to the inexorable resolution that the Union shall be preserved, and the public credit shall be maintained, no matter what sacrifices and burdens the execution of this resolution may involve.

It is a common objection to the national banking system, on the part of some who favor a national currency, that it will deprive the government of the privilege it might safely use, and the field it might profitably occupy, by the continued circulation of its own notes. Why, it is asked, should not the government drive out of circulation all bank notes, and continue to issue, as it has done since the commencement of the war, its own notes, and thus save the interest which otherwise will go to the banks? In answer, I would remark:

The banking interest in the United States is an important one; it has grown with the business of the country, and has been largely instrumental in developing the national resources and in increasing the national wealth. Banks of issue, badly and dishonestly as many of them have been managed, and disastrous as have been the failures which bad management and dishonesty have produced, have still been of unquestionable advantage to the people. The capital of the country has been largely, and in good faith, invested in them, and thousands of stockholders depend upon the dividends upon their bank stock for support. It is an interest which has stood by the government in its struggles with a gigantic rebellion; and now, when it is indispensable that the government should control the issues of paper money, there has been created a national banking system, not to destroy the State banks but to absorb them, and that, too, without prejudice to their stockholders.

Governments should not be bankers. None has existed which could be safely trusted with the privilege of permanently issuing its own notes as money. Circulating notes have been issued under peculiar circumstances by other governments, as it is now being done by that of the United States, but the judgment of the world is against it as a permanent policy, and nothing but an overpowering public exigency will at any time justify it. Under popular institutions like ours no more dangerous, no more corrupting power could be lodged in the hands of the party in possession of the government; none more perilous to official probity, and free elections. Give to a party dominant in the legislative and executive branches of the government the authority of issuing paper money for the purpose of furnishing the country with its currency, subject as it would be to no restraint but its own pleasure, and what guaranty would there be that this authority would be honestly and judiciously used? If there were no risk in the preparation of the notes, and checks were provided to make fraudulent issues an impossibility, the power of issuing government promises as a circulating medium is too dangerous a one to be conferred upon any party, except under extraordinary circumstances.

The present issue of United States notes as lawful money, and the decisions of the courts sustaining the constitutionality of the issue, have been justified by the consideration that under a great public necessity, when the nation's life is in peril, policies must be framed and laws must be interpreted with a view to the preservation of the government. This is the paramount consideration to which all others must bend. Whatever opinions may have been, in times past, entertained in regard to the propriety of the issue of United States notes, and the expediency as well as the constitutionality of the law making them a legal tender, there are now, I apprehend, very few intelligent persons who are not persuaded that without these notes, and the character of lawful money given to them by Congress and confirmed by the courts, the credit of the nation would have given way at the very outbreak of the rebellion. When the war has been concluded, and the exigency which made the issue of government notes a necessity has ceased to exist, there will be very few to advocate the continued use of them on the ground of economy.

If, however, there were no objections of the kind alluded to, there are other objections to the permanent issue of circulating notes by the government, which must be apparent to all who have considered the object and uses of a paper currency.

Paper money has been found to be useful, or rather an absolute necessity in all commercial countries for the convenient transaction of business, and as a circulating representative of values too large to be represented by coin. Although the fruitful cause of great evils, by reason of its unregulated use, and of its uncertain and frequently deceptive character, the general utility of it can hardly be questioned. Now, what is needed in a paper circulating medium, is, that it should be convertible into coin; that it should be sufficient in amount to answer the purposes of legitimate business; that it should not, on the one hand, by being overissued, encourage extravagance and speculation and give an artificial and unreliable value to property; nor, on the other hand, by being reduced below the proper standard, interrupt business and unsettle values. It should be supplied to just the extent of the demands of a healthy trade. It should be increased as the regular business of the country may require its increase, and be diminished as the proper demand for it is diminished.

It is not pretended that banks of issue have furnished this kind of circulation. Bank notes, with few exceptions, have been convertible into coin when there was no demand for coin, and inconvertible when there was. They have, too generally, been issued for the exclusive benefit of the bankers, and not for the convenience of the public, and they have encouraged speculation, when their true mission was to facilitate trade. It has been the bane of a bank note circulation, that it has been expanded by the avarice of the bankers, and contracted by the distrust that overissues have created.

Now, this objection to a bank note circulation applies with much greater force to government issues. There is always inducement enough for banks to keep up a full circulation, and against excessive issues there are the restrictions of law and the liability to redeem. Government notes, in the issue thereof, would be regulated only by the necessities of the government or the interests of the party in power. At one time they might be increased altogether beyond the needs of commerce and trade, thereby enhancing prices and inducing speculation; at another, they might be so reduced as to embarrass business and precipitate financial disasters. They would be incomparably worse in this respect than a bank note currency, because the power that should control circulation would be the power that furnishes it. Supplied by an authority not in sympathy with trade, they would not be accommodated to the requirements of trade. They might be the fullest in volume when there was the least demand for a full circulation, and the most contracted when there was a healthy demand for an increase. They would eventually become an undesirable circulation, because there would be no way in which the redemption of them could be enforced: they would be a dangerous circulation, because they would be under the control of political parties; an unreliable circulation, because, having no connexion with trade and commerce, they would not be regulated by their necessities.

There are objections to all kinds of paper money; but, in some form, it is a commercial necessity, and no form has yet been contrived so little objectionable as that which is authorized by the national currency act. Under this act the government performs its proper functions by exercising one of its constitutional powers for the regulation of commerce, by fixing the maximum of bank note circulation, securing its solvency, and giving to it nationality of character and uniformity of value. It takes the promises, which are to go among the people through the national banks, puts its seal upon them, and guarantees *their* redemption, as it takes the precious ore from the mines—the property of individuals—coins it into money of the United States and fixes the value thereof. It thus performs the proper offices of government. In doing so it interferes with no State rights, meddles with no man's lawful pursuits. It stands between the bankers and the people, and while it protects the latter from imposition in the use of a bank note currency, it trespasses upon no privileges of the former. Without becoming a banker, and without, as in the case of the charter of the United States Bank, conferring peculiar if not dangerous privileges upon a single corporation, it provides a national circulation, indispensable for its own use and safety in the collection of its internal revenues, and suited to the circumstances of the country.

But while the national currency act is restrictive in its general provisions, and is expected, when generally adopted, to prevent expansions, there is still danger that too much capital will be invested under it during the suspension of specie payments, and in the existing unsettled condition of our political and financial affairs. When money is plenty, and fortunes are being rapidly acquired, the country is always in a feverish and unhealthy state. This is especially true at the present time. The enormous expenditures of the government, and the great advances in prices since the commencement of the war, have made many persons suddenly rich, and, upon fortunes suddenly acquired, have followed reckless expenditures, extravagance, waste. Speculation is taking the place of sober and persevering industry, and thousands are deluded with the notion that the wealth of the nation is being increased by the increase of its indebtedness. The inauguration of a new system of banking, under such circumstances, is peculiarly hazardous, and I have been, from the time of my appointment, more apprehensive that too many banks would be organized, than that the system would not be sufficiently attractive to induce capitalists to become connected with it. The government is the great borrower. Its obligations compose a large portion of the discount line of the banks, which are making large profits on government securities at little apparent risk, and the danger is, that the national banking system, with all its restrictions, may, during the suspension of specie payments, and the continuance of the war, add to the plethora of paper money; and that, when the war is over, the banks, deprived of the existing means of investment in government obligations, and finding no legitimate use for their capitals, may be tempted to use them in encouraging operations that will eventually prove to be as unprofitable to themselves, as they will be injurious to the country. For the double purpose, therefore, of keeping down the national circulation as far as it has seemed possible to do it, consistently with the establishment of the system throughout the country, and preventing an increase of banking capital, that might hereafter be instrumental in keeping up the inflation, and retarding the resumption of specie payments, or prove unprofitable to its owners, I have felt it to be my duty to discourage, in many instances, the organization of new banks and in more instances to refuse my sanction to the increase of the capital of those already organized. In doing so, I may seem to have exercised a power not warranted by the act; but if not sustained by its letter, I have been by its spirit, and I am willing to let the future decide as to the correctnesss or incorrectness of my course. . . .

As long as there was any uncertainty in regard to the success of the national banking system, or the popular verdict upon its merits and security, I did not feel at liberty to recommend discriminating legislation against the State banks. It is for Congress to determine if there is any longer a reasonable uncertainty on these points, and if the time has not arrived when all these institutions should be compelled to retire their circulation. It is indispensable for the financial success of the treasury that the currency of the country should be under the control of the government. This cannot be the case as long as State institutions have the right to flood the country with their issues. As a system has been devised under which State banks, or at least as many of them as are needed, can be reorganized, so that the government can assume a rightful control over bank note circulation, it could hardly be considered oppressive if Congress should prohibit the further issue of bank notes not authorized by itself, and compel, by taxation (which should be sufficient to effect the object without being oppressive), the withdrawal of those which have been already issued. My own opinion is, that this should be done, and that the sooner it is done the better it will be for the banks themselves and for the public. As long as the two systems are contending for the field (although the result of the contest can be no longer doubtful) the government cannot restrain the issue of paper money; and as the preference which is everywhere given to a national currency over the notes of the State banks indicates what is the popular judgment in regard to the merits of the two systems, there seems to be no good reason why Congress should hesitate to relieve the treasury of a serious embarrassment, and the people of an unsatisfactory circulation.

# 3. Banking and Monetary Reform

The "money panic" of 1907 underscored the already felt need for fundamental banking and monetary reform adequate to the needs of a growing national economy. Wider interest was spurred by the detailed studies and the report of the National Monetary Commission (1908–1912). The commission drew attention to the glaring weaknesses of the National Banking System, but neither its report nor the so-called Aldrich bill advocated the establishment of a true central bank capable of mobilizing reserves. The substance of such a mechanism, although veiled in carefully guarded language to avoid offending Democrats hostile to a central bank, was a key feature of the report of the House Banking and Currency Committee drafted by Dr. Henry Parker Willis, an authority on banking who in 1912–1913 served as expert to the committee. *Willis was chosen by Representative Carter Glass of Virginia, who in June 1913 became committee chairman. Both Glass and Willis played important roles in shaping the basic technical structure of the Federal Reserve Act as finally adopted in 1913. Commenting on the origins of the act, Willis wrote in his authoritative study, The Federal Reserve System (1923): "It was not an 'original proposal' in the sense that it embodied anything new in regard to banking principle, but, on the contrary, it was the digested product of elaborate and careful study of European banking experience as adapted to American necessities and requirements."*

SOURCE: *Changes in the Banking and Currency System of the United States,* 63rd Cong., 1st sess., House Report No. 69 (Washington, D.C.: Government Printing Office, 1913), pp. 3–7, 11–12, 16–17, 19–20.

## DEMAND FOR ACTION

There has for a great while been strong public demand for remedial legislation on banking and currency. This demand was partly obscured during the controversy regarding the adoption of a monetary standard. Yet even before the adoption of the act of March 14, 1900, there had been a vigorous popular movement directed to the amendment of the national banking act. This took form in various voluntary organizations and in actions by bankers' associations as well as by organizations of business and commercial interests. It was practically universally admitted from 1898 onward that one of the basic commercial evils of the day was the lack of a suitable banking system.

This view has been frequently reiterated and restated ever since the earlier days of the banking discussion to which reference has been made. Of late it has taken form in renewed agitation following the panic of 1907 and promises of action have been made in nearly every political platform, by whatever party adopted, within recent years. The call is loud and comes from many sources of widely divergent character.

It is probable that not a single scientific student of currency and banking could be found who would approve the conditions which now exist in the United States or the banking system under which they have sprung up. Nowhere in the world to-day can there be found a banking system similar or analogous to that of the United States, or a situation as to credit which could be compared to that prevailing in this country at the present moment.

## REASONS FOR ACTION

The considerations which thus dictate action upon the banking and currency question at the present time have often been stated and from many different points of view. In the opinion of the committee there can be no doubt whatever with regard to the essential elements of the case. The general background of the situation which calls for banking reform is this: Half a century ago Congress, in the midst of a civil war, established a new system subsequently developed into the national banking system. The essential elements in this system were three in number: (1) The maintenance of the principle of free banking through the unrestricted organization of banking institutions; (2) the refusal to allow the extension of systems of banking throughout the country by the organization of branch banks; and (3) the adoption of a peculiar system of note issue whereby the banks were required to buy a minimum of national bonds when chartered and subsequently to deposit with the Treasury bonds to protect all currency received by them for circulation. The different elements in this system will be fully considered at other points in the present report. It is enough now to suggest the general bearings of the case. This system has continued substantially unamended to the present time, and to-day includes some 7,473 banking institutions within its range. These banking institutions vary in size from $25,000 capital to $25,000,000. They are entirely local. The only bond between them is found either in mutual stock ownership or in the redepositing of reserves as they are permitted to do under the national-bank act. In view of the lack of any factor of unity the national banks have failed to furnish to the nation as a whole a single and powerful system of credit. The strength of the credit situation in each community has depended upon the strength of the banks there situated, and, except in times of stress, has even in these communities been measured by the strength not of the strongest, but of the weakest institution there located. In times of stress the banks of such independent communities have at times in self-defense united to place their combined resources temporarily at the service of the public and of one another, but they have taken such action only under stern pressure. As a rule, they have been individualistic in the highest degree, and the country has lacked the capacity either to prevent credit disorders from breaking out locally and spreading to the centers, or to defend its own resources against the monetary demands of foreign nations or against the infection due to bad financial conditions in countries with which we stood in close relations.

The evidence that this system has not done its duty is not found in dishonesty or failure. While at times failures have been numerous among the national banks, as must necessarily be the case in any system of numerous and highly individualized banks, the average record of failure or irregularity has been small. No noteholder has ever lost a dollar, and the losses of depositors constitute in the aggregate a very small percentage of the total deposits held by the banks. The country has been enabled to do an expanding business, to its own great profit. But the evil of the situation has been perceived upon all those occasions when unusual pressure was brought to bear upon the banks of the country. In 1873, 1884, 1890, 1893, 1896, and 1907, to mention the most familiar occasions, it has been necessary for large groups of banks practically to suspend specie payments. They have done so as the result of concerted action, and one feature of the situation upon each of these occasions has been a genuine effort to relieve conditions by resorting to an issue of obligations for which the banks became jointly liable, and which in some measure helped to overcome shortage of currency and the stringency that was associated with it. In spite of all that could be done, however, the public has been put to great inconvenience and loss upon such occasions, the relations of the United States with foreign countries have been embarrassed, if not brought into jeopardy, the failure of firms, corporations, and individuals has been necessitated, and the loss of wealth has been tremendous. We think it is axiomatic that these conditions should not be allowed to repeat themselves, but that they should in some manner be relieved or prevented, if possible.

On the other hand, the national banking system, with its many merits, has not proved responsive to the seasonal needs of the community. At periods of exceptional demand for credit the movement of currency between various points, with attendant expense and delay, has been enormous, while the expansion of this currency has been slow and halting, local necessities being met by withdrawing circulating media from other regions. In consequence, the marketing of the country's annual crops has been slow, difficult, and expensive, and it has frequently happened that various sections of the nation have been obliged to depend too largely upon the limited extension of credit to them by banks located elsewhere.

Conversely, it has been found that whenever the seasonal needs of credit in agricultural regions throughout the United States had been met and when the crops there produced had been fully disposed of there was an accumulation of currency, partly borrowed from other portions of the country, partly of local origin, which could not be used to advantage upon safe or sound security throughout the less active portions of the business year, and which was therefore shipped to banks in distant cities, that it might be there put to some employment that would yield its owners an income. It has not always turned out that the employment thus found for it was desirable or, on the whole, conducive to the good of the country.

## NATURE OF EXISTING CONDITIONS

Turning from the general considerations which tend to prevent the acceptance of existing banking conditions as satisfactory, there is need of a recognition of the immediate status of the financial and business world at the present day. There can be no doubt that for some time past the national banks of the United States have been in a difficult situation. The committee has been amply warned and advised of this state of things, and a general knowledge of it is common to the country at large, certainly to all close or careful observers of existing conditions. In the reserve centers to-day banks are unable to extend the credit that they would under normal circumstances be disposed to grant, while merchants are frequently unable to get the accommodation to which they are entitled. A general tendency toward stringency evidently exists, and while this is not peculiar to-day to the United States it should not be felt here in anything like its present severity, inasmuch as this country has not had to bear the burden of warfare and destruction of capital that has been thrown upon the European countries. All over the western world there is now a distinct shortage of capital, both fixed and floating, while our banking and reserve situation is anything but reassuring. Under such circumstances it is highly desirable that the utmost efficiency should be given to the reserve resources in the hands of the banks and that they should be enabled to do all that circumstances will permit in extending to the business world the volume of loans that it needs, so long as they maintain themselves in position to protect the accommodation thus granted. Legislation which will relieve this pending condition of pressure and possible panic, which will place the banks in position to employ their resources to the best advantage, which will obviate the necessity of expensive transfers of funds between different parts of the country, and which will furnish loans upon an inexpensive but absolutely safe basis was never more urgently demanded than it is to-day. It is this condition of affairs that has most strongly moved the Committee on Banking and Currency in its effort to press a measure of relief upon the attention of the House.

## LACK OF PROTECTION AGAINST PANICS

Reference has just been made to the fact that the national banking system, among other defects, fails to afford any safeguard against panics and commercial stringencies or any means of alleviating them. This fact has received more attention than has thus far been given to any other in the whole range of the banking and currency discussion, and there has been more effort to apply some legislative remedy to this than to any other condition.

In practice, when commercial credit had hopelessly broken down and the banks of the country found themselves seriously threatened by danger of failure, they have united for mutual protection, and clearing-house associations in the chief cities of the country have joined in the issue of certificates good in liquidating obligations between banks. Sporadic and temporary as this remedy has been, it nevertheless has proven effective while in use, and after the panic of 1907 an attempt was made to provide for a permanent resort to this so-called clearing-house currency by passing the act of May 30, 1908, ordinarily known as the Aldrich-Vreeland law. This law will expire automatically on June 30, 1914, inasmuch as the act itself carries a provision limiting its own life to six years. The fact that this legislation will thus expire is regarded by many persons as an additional argument for action at the present time, inasmuch as the measure in question constitutes the only emergency protection against conditions of sudden difficulty in the money market that the country now has. The Aldrich-Vreeland law provides for the establishment of organizations of banks, to be known as National

Currency Associations, which are to be allowed to take out notes under certain conditions.

It is worth observing that up to date the Aldrich-Vreeland associations have been an entire dead letter. The situation regarding them was clearly sketched by the Comptroller of the Currency in his last annual report, in which he said:

> Under authority of the act of May 30, 1908, providing for the issue of "additional currency" secured otherwise than by United States bonds, 18 national currency associations have been formed, all of which, with the exception of the Los Angeles association, were formed prior to the current year. Each association has an aggregate capital and surplus of at least $5,000,000, and is composed of at least 10 national banks having an unimpaired capital and an unimpaired surplus of not less than 20 per cent of the capital, and having United States bonds on deposit to secure circulation to the extent of at least 40 per cent of its capital. There are 286 national banks forming these 18 national currency associations, their capital aggregating $321,105,710 and surplus $281,544,722. The capital represented is slightly in excess of 30 per cent of the paid-in capital stock of all national banks, as shown by the reports for September 4 last.
>
> The title, membership, capital, and surplus of each of the associations are shown in the following table:

National Currency Associations

| Associations | Number of banks | Capital | Surplus |
|---|---|---|---|
| National Currency Association of Washington, D.C. | 10 | $ 5,702,000 | $ 4,792,512 |
| National Currency Association of the city of New York, N.Y. | 33 | 117,052,000 | 127,175,000 |
| National Currency Association of Philadelphia, Pa. | 27 | 20,975,000 | 36,665,000 |
| National Currency Association of the State of Louisiana | 10 | 6,100,000 | 4,030,000 |
| National Currency Association of Boston, Mass. | 14 | 26,700,000 | 18,950,000 |
| National Currency Association of Georgia | 28 | 8,206,000 | 6,434,000 |
| National Currency Association of Chicago | 10 | 42,750,000 | 25,950,000 |
| National Currency Association of St. Louis, Mo. | 10 | 19,510,000 | 9,095,000 |

National Currency Associations—Cont.

| Associations | Number of banks | Capital | Surplus |
|---|---|---|---|
| National Currency Association of St. Paul and Minneapolis | 14 | 10,750,000 | 9,545,000 |
| National Currency Association of Detroit | 15 | 6,325,000 | 3,101,200 |
| National Currency Association of Albany, etc. | 11 | 3,560,000 | 3,385,000 |
| National Currency Association of Kansas City, etc. | 10 | 6,659,000 | 3,800,000 |
| National Currency Association of Baltimore | 18 | 12,340,710 | 7,752,010 |
| National Currency Association of Cincinnati | 10 | 14,300,000 | 6,450,000 |
| National Currency Association of Dallas | 14 | 3,760,000 | 3,100,000 |
| National Currency Association of Alabama | 25 | 5,700,000 | 3,497,500 |
| National Currency Association of Denver, etc. | 15 | 4,700,000 | 4,991,500 |
| National Currency Association of Los Angeles | 12 | 6,025,000 | 2,831,000 |
| Total | 286 | 321,105,710 | 281,544,722 |

In accordance with the terms of the Aldrich-Vreeland Act, $500,000,000 in currency has been printed and is now ready, in blank, for issue in case of a call from any of the banks or currency associations authorized to issue notes by the terms of the law. Individual banks may issue such notes by depositing at the Treasury State or municipal bonds of approved kinds, receiving in exchange 90 per cent of the par value of such bonds, provided they are worth at least par. The currency associations may obtain notes equal to 75 per cent of the face value of commercial paper left with them by the constituent banks of the association.

One reason why the Aldrich-Vreeland law has never been availed of is that the issue of the currency was made very expensive, owing to the imposition of a heavy tax on such notes as might be taken out, while the banks were for a long time reluctant to go into the currency associations because of the onerous conditions under which they were at first required to be authorized by the terms of the regulations laid down by the Secretary of the Treasury. The law is thus not likely to be resorted to except in cases of very severe necessity for notes; but, even if such were not the case, it would remain a temporary expedient and a mere extension of its life would be only the renewal of such an expedient.

No statement could make clearer the inadequate character of the Aldrich-Vreeland Act or its purely temporary character. It is a weak makeshift, soon to expire.

## RECOGNITION OF SITUATION

That under the conditions just sketched there is a responsibility resting upon those in charge of the Government of the United States no one can deny. No more serious obligation to-day exists in the whole range of national problems. This duty has been amply recognized by the Democratic Party. In platform after platform it has stood firmly for the adoption of sound and courageous legislation, and at Baltimore in 1912 it adopted without dissent the following plank:

We oppose the so-called Aldrich bill for the establishment of a central bank; and we believe our country will be largely freed from panics, and consequent unemployment and business depression, by such a systematic revision of our banking laws as will render temporary relief in localities where such relief is needed, with protection from control or domination by what is known as the Money Trust. . . .

## VALUE OF COMMISSION'S WORK

The work done at such great cost should not, indeed cannot, be ignored, but, having examined the extensive literature published by the commission, the Banking and Currency Committee finds little bearing upon the present state of things in the credit market of the United States. Most of the matter published by the commission is a revision or recasting of books and documents having only historical value or brought down to modern times by their authors or others. There is practically nothing of original value or of direct aid bearing upon the details of remedial legislation.

The bill favored by the commission and popularly known as the Aldrich bill, from the name of the chairman of the monetary commission, ex-Senator Nelson W. Aldrich, of Rhode Island, remains as the chief distinct trace of the commission's existence. It has not commended itself to the Banking and Currency Committee. The Aldrich bill is a lengthy and elaborate statute and no sufficient account of its contents or of the reasons for refusing to accept it can be given in brief space. Something, however, may be said of it. This bill has often been spoken of as a poisonous theoretical novelty and at other times as an ingenious scheme to create a central bank which would absorb all banking functions to itself. In fact it was neither of these things. Little of novel character is found in the ideas underlying the Aldrich bill. To mention only two of the many proposals embodying the same general ideas as those held by the framers of the Aldrich bill, the plans for banking and currency legislation suggested by Hon. Charles N. Fowler in his "A financial and banking system for the United States" (H. R. 23707, 60th Cong., 1st Sess.), and by Hon. Maurice L. Muhleman, in his "Plan for a Central Bank," reprinted from the *Banking Law Journal*, have the same purpose in view. They differ in several important details, none of which, however, is absolutely fundamental to the scheme presented.

The objects technically aimed at in all these measures were desirable and the criticism to be made of the Aldrich bill does not, in the opinion of the committee, reside in its confessed purposes, but in the methods by which it undertook to carry them out and the disregard of public welfare by which it was characterized.

The Aldrich bill was not a plan for a central bank as that term is properly used. It called for the creation of a national reserve association which was to do business only with banks, while the Government had but little power over the institution and the public neither business nor other relations with it. Without going further into the detailed analysis of the Aldrich bill it may be stated that the committee objects to the plan fundamentally on the following points:

1. Its entire lack of adequate governmental or public control of the banking mechanism it sets up.

2. Its tendency to throw voting control into the hands of the larger banks of the system.

3. The lack of adequate provision for protecting the interests of small banks and the tendency to make the proposed institution subserve the purposes of large interests only.

4. The intricate system by which the reserve institution it created was prevented from doing any business that might compete with that of existing banks.

5. The extreme danger of inflation of currency inherent in the scheme.

6. The clumsiness of the whole mechanism provided by the measure.

7. The insincerity of the bond-refunding plan provided for by it, there being a barefaced pretense that this system was to cost the Government nothing.

8. The dangerous monopolistic aspects of the bill.

## ESSENTIAL FEATURES OF REFORM

The other plans before the committee or examined by it have likewise been found unsatisfactory—some for reasons analogous to those which made the Aldrich bill unacceptable, others because of defective detail, erroneous principle, or faulty construction. An effort was, however, made to ascertain the constituent elements of these measures and of the Aldrich bill, common to all, which should be recognized and provided for in any new plan because representing the fundamentals of legislation. It is believed that these are as follows:

1. Establishment of a more nearly uniform rate of discount throughout the United States, and thereby the furnishing of a certain kind of preventive against overexpansion of credit which should be similar in all parts of the country.

2. General economy of reserves in order that such reserves might be held ready for use in protecting the banks of any section of the country and for enabling them to go on meeting their obligations instead of suspending payments, as so often in the past.

3. Furnishing of an elastic currency by the abolition of the existing bond-secured note issue in whole or in part, and the substitution of a freely issued and adequately protected system of bank notes which should be available to all institutions which had the proper class of paper for presentation.

4. Management and commercial use of the funds of the Government which are now isolated in the Treasury and subtreasuries in large amounts.

5. General supervision of the banking business and furnishing of stringent and careful oversight.

6. Creation of market for commercial paper.

Other objects are sought, incidentally, in these plans, but they are not as basic as the chief purposes thus enumerated.

The first problem in developing a measure was, of course, the consideration of various alternative courses which might be pursued.

## CENTRAL BANK QUESTION

At the outset of the committee's work it was met by a well-defined sentiment in favor of a central bank. This idea appeared to have become rooted with a large section of the banking community, and was the manifest outgrowth of the work that had been done by the National Monetary Commission, and those who believed that the recommendations of that body were well founded. While the institution which would have been created by the National Monetary Commission bill was not a central bank in the technical sense of the term, inasmuch as it did not do a general banking business, it was a central bank in many of the aspects that are usually regarded as characteristic of that term. The idea of the monetary commission bill had been accepted with great fervor by those who believed that the use of a centralization principle was necessary, as well as by others who deemed that their own objects would be served by the particular form that had been given to the proposal of the monetary commission in its bill.

Without allowing itself to entertain any prepossessions either for or against the central bank idea, the committee carefully examined this notion both at hearings and through private study. It reached in general the following conclusions:

1. The idea of centralization or cooperation, or combined use of banking resources, is the basic idea at the root of central banking argument.

2. It is not necessary in order to obtain the benefits of the application of this idea that there should be one single central bank whose activities should be coterminous with the limits of a nation's territory.

3. Equally good results can be obtained by the federating of existing banks and banking institutions in groups sufficiently large to afford the strength or cooperating power which is the chief advantage of the centralization.

4. In the United States, with its immense area, numerous natural divisions, still more numerous competing divisions, and abundant

outlets to foreign countries, there is no argument either of banking theory or of expediency which dictates the creation of a single central banking institution, no matter how skillfully managed, how carefully controlled, or how patriotically conducted.

5. It is therefore necessary to abandon the idea of a single central banking mechanism for the United States unless it shall be found that there are considerations of expediency which would dictate a resort to this policy. . . .

It was therefore decided that throughout its efforts to formulate a banking measure there should be no necessary attempt to base the result of the bill upon the central banking idea. Only in so far as that idea indicated an easy and natural adjustment to existing institutions and conditions was it to be given a place in the ultimate findings. . . .

## FUNDAMENTAL FEATURES OF REFORM

After looking over the whole ground, and after examining the various suggestions for legislation, some of which have just been outlined, the Committee on Banking and Currency is firmly of the opinion that any effective legislation on banking must include the following fundamental elements, which it considers indispensable in any measure likely to prove satisfactory to the country:

1. Creation of a joint mechanism for the extension of credit to banks which possess sound assets and which desire to liquidate them for the purpose of meeting legitimate commercial, agricultural, and industrial demands on the part of their clientele.

2. Ultimate retirement of the present bond-secured currency, with suitable provision for the fulfillment of Government obligations to bondholders, coupled with the creation of a satisfactory flexible currency to take its place.

3. Provision for better extension of American banking facilities in foreign countries to the end that our trade abroad may be enlarged and that American business men in foreign countries may obtain the accommodations they require in the conduct of their operations.

Beyond these cardinal and simple propositions the committee has not deemed it wise at this time to make any recommendations, save that in a few particulars it has suggested the amendment of existing provisions in the national-bank act, with a view to strengthening that measure at points where experience has shown the necessity of alteration.

## PROPOSED PLAN

In order to meet the requirements thus sketched, the committee proposes a plan for the organization of reserve or rediscount institutions to which it assigns the name "Federal reserve banks." It recommends that these be established in suitable places throughout the country to the number of 12 as a beginning, and that they be assigned the function of bankers' banks. Under the committee's plan these banks would be organized by existing banks, both National and State, as stockholders. It believes that banking institutions which desire to be known by the name "national" should be required, and can well afford, to take upon themselves the responsibilities involved in joint or federated organization. It recommends that these bankers' banks shall be given a definite capital, to be subscribed and paid by their constituent member banks which hold their shares, and that they shall do business only with the banks aforesaid, and with the Government. Public funds, it recommends, shall be deposited in these new banks which shall thus acquire an essentially public character, and shall be subject to the control and oversight which is a necessary concomitant of such a character. In order that these banks may be effectively inspected, and in order that they may pursue a banking policy which shall be uniform and harmonious for the country as a whole, the committee proposes a general board of management intrusted with the power to overlook and direct the general functions of the banks referred to. To this it assigns the title of "The Federal reserve board." It further recommends that the the present national banks shall have their bonds now held as security for circulation paid at the end of 20 years, and that in the meantime they may turn in these bonds by a gradual process, receiving in exchange 3 per cent bonds without the circulation privilege.

In lieu of the notes, now secured by national bonds and issued by the national banks, and, so far as necessary in addition to them, the committee recommends that there shall be an issue of "Federal reserve Treasury notes," to be the obligation of the United States, but to be paid out solely through Federal reserve banks upon the application of the latter, protected by commercial paper, and with redemption assured through the holding of a reserve of gold amounting to 33⅓ per cent of the notes outstanding at any one time. In order to meet the requirements of foreign trade, the committee recommends that the power to establish foreign branch banks shall be bestowed upon existing national banks under carefully prescribed conditions and that Federal reserve banks shall also be authorized to establish offices abroad for the conduct of their own business and for the purpose of facilitating the fiscal operations of the United States Government. Finally and lastly, the committee suggests the amendment of the national-bank act in respect to two or three essential particulars, the chief of which are bank examinations, the present conditions under which loans are made to farming interests, and the liability of stockholders of failed banks. It believes that these recommendations, if carried out, will afford the basis for the complete reconstruction and the very great strengthening and improvement of the present banking and credit system of the United States. The chief evils of which complaint has been made will be rectified, while others will at least be palliated and put in the way of later elimination.

## FEDERAL RESERVE BANKS

The Federal reserve banks suggested by the committee as just indicated would be in effect cooperative institutions, carried on for the benefit of the community and of the banks themselves by the banks acting as stockholders therein. It is proposed that they shall have an active capital equal to 10 per cent of the capital of existing banks which may take stock in the new enterprise. This would result in a capital of something over $100,000,000 for the reserve banks taken together if practically all existing national banks should enter the system. . . . How many State banks would apply for and be granted admission to the new system as stockholders in the reserve banks can not be confidently predicted. It may, however, be fair to assume at this point that the total capital of the reserve banks will be in the neighborhood of $100,000,000. The bill recommended by the committee provides for the transfer of the present funds of the Government included in what is known as the general fund to the new Federal reserve banks, which are thereafter to act as fiscal agents of the Government. . . .

. . . The committee's proposals provide for the transfer of bank reserves from existing banks which hold them for others to the proposed reserve banks. At present the national banking act recognizes three systems of reserves:

1. Those in central reserve cities, where banks are required to hold 25 per cent of their deposit liabilities in actual cash in the vaults, while banks situated outside of such cities are allowed to make certain deposits with them which shall count as a part of the reserves of such outside banks.

2. Those in reserve cities, 47 in number, which are required to keep a nominal reserve of 25 per cent, 12½ per cent of this being in cash in their own vaults, while 12½ per cent may consist of deposits with banks in central reserve cities.

3. Those in the "country," by which is meant all places outside of central reserve and reserve cities, it being required that such banks shall nominally keep 15 per cent of their deposit liabilities, of which 6 per cent is held in cash in their vaults and 9 per cent may be held in the form of balances with other banks in reserve and central reserve cities.

The original reason for creating this so-called "pyramidal" system of reserves was that inasmuch as central banking institutions were absent, and inasmuch as banks outside of centers were obliged to keep exchange funds on deposit with other banks in such centers, it was fair to allow exchange balances with such centrally located banks to count as reserves inasmuch as they were presumably at all times available in cash. This is an absolutely anomalous and unique system, found nowhere outside of the United States, and dangerous in proportion as the number of the reserve centers thus recognized increases beyond a prudent number. The law has almost necessarily been liberal in recognizing the power to increase the number of such centers, with the result that whereas but few existed just after the organization of the national bank act, there being then 3 central reserve and 13 reserve cities, there are to-day 3 central reserve and 47 reserve cities. Even had this extension of the number of centers not occurred, the system established under the national banking act would still have been unsatisfactory. As matters have developed, it has been vicious in the extreme. Coupled with the inelasticity of the bank currency, the system has tended to create periodical stringencies and periodical plethoras of funds. Banks in the country districts unable to withdraw notes and contract credit when they have seen fit to do so, because of the rigidity of the bond-secured currency, have redeposited such funds with other banks in reserve and central reserve cities and have thus built up the balances which they were entitled to keep there as a part of their reserves. Moreover, the practice of thus redepositing funds having been once established, it has been carried to exteme lengths, and at times has been decidedly injurious in its influence. The payment of interest on deposits by banks in the centers has been used for the purpose of attracting to such banks funds which otherwise would have gone to other centers or to other banks in the same centers or which would have been retained at home. The funds thus redeposited, even when not attracted by any artificial means, have of course constituted a demand liability, and have been so regarded by the banks to which they were intrusted.

In consequence, such banks have sought to find the most profitable means of employment for their resources and at the same time to have them in such condition as would permit their prompt realization when demanded by the depositing banks which put them there. The result has been an effort on the part of the national banks, particularly in central reserve cities, to dispose of a substantial portion of their funds in call loans protected by stock-exchange collateral as a rule. This was on the theory that, inasmuch as listed stock-exchange securities could be readily sold, call loans of this type were for practical purposes equivalent to cash in hand. The theory is of course close enough to the facts when an effort to realize is made by only one or few banks, but is entirely erroneous whenever the attempt to withdraw deposits is made by a number of banks simultaneously. At such times, the banks in central reserve and reserve cities are wholly unable to meet the demands that are brought to bear on them by country banks; and the latter, realizing the difficulties of the case, seek to protect themselves by an unnecessary accumulation of cash which they draw from their correspondents, thereby weakening the latter and frequently strengthening themselves to an undue degree. Under such circumstances the reserves of the country, which ought to constitute a readily available homogeneous fund, ready for use in any direction where sudden necessities may develop, are in fact scattered and entirely lose their efficiency and strength owing to their being diffused through a great number of institutions in relatively small amounts and thereby rendered nearly unavailable. This evil has been met in times past by the suspension of specie payments by banks and by the substitution of unauthorized and extra-legal substitutes for currency in the form of cashiers' checks, clearing-house certificates and other methods of furnishing a medium of exchange. Needless to say such a method of meeting the evil is the worst kind of makeshift and is only somewhat better than actual disaster.

The committee believes that the only way to correct this condition of affairs is to provide for the holding of reserves by duly qualified institutions which shall act primarily in the public interest and whose motives and conduct shall be so absolutely well known and above suspicion as to inspire unquestioning confidence on the part of the community. It believes that the reserve banks which it proposes to provide for will afford such a type of institutions and that they may be made the effective means for the holding of the liquid reserve funds of the country to the extent that the latter are not needed in the vaults of the banks themselves. . . .

# II. THE AGE OF THE RAILROADS

## 4. The Railroads: Energizers of Economic Development

Although the railroad revolution was in the making for twenty years before 1860—by that year only two states, Oregon and Minnesota, had no railroads—it was not until the Civil War that many of the lines in the North for the first time reaped large profits and declared generous dividends. In the main, however, opportunities for the reinvestment of earnings were ignored, and for thirty years after Appomattox railroad mismanagement continued to be a serious problem. After the war the trans-Mississippi West, which in 1860 had been hardly penetrated, became the most important single region of railroad expansion. When the book from which this excerpt is taken was published, the United States was enjoying the greatest railroad boom in its history. The 12,878 miles of track built in 1887 set a record that was never surpassed; nor did any other decade rival the 73,441 miles of new construction added in the 1880's. The extension of the rail network from 30,626 miles in 1860 to an all-time high of 254,037 miles in 1916 was matched by an increase in total capitalization from $1,149,000,000 to $21,049,000,000. In the following selection Ringwalt, who was editor of The Railway World, illuminates the impact of the railroad revolution on the post-Civil War industrial economy and its influence on new patterns of business management. This early appraisal confirms the recent observation of Peter F. Drucker, an expert on corporate management: "The first modern business, the first truly organized enterprise, was the large railroad. . . ."

SOURCE: J. L. Ringwalt, Development of Transportation Systems in the United States. . . . (Philadelphia, 1888), pp. 181–3, 198–201, 362–3.

THE seventh decade [1860–1870] was probably the most prosperous period ever known, in the matter of enabling a number of northern and western railways to earn and declare large dividends.

79

At the same time, it was one of the most unfortunate of eras in the way of stimulating competitive construction, and in infusing a reckless speculative spirit, which has rarely, if ever, been paralleled, into various railway operations. The enormous expenditures of the Government during the war, immense issues of greenbacks, contraction of a gigantic debt by the United States, and of large debts by many cities and counties, protracted suspension of specie payments, heavy premium on gold, which at one time rose to 185, and remained above 100 for a considerable period, large number of fortunes made by contractors and speculators in staple products, cotton goods, gold, petroleum, coal, bubble companies, and railway stocks, and other analogous influences, helped to bring about a state of affairs which apparently placed railways on a new basis. By many they were no longer regarded as struggling enterprises, which could scarcely hope for success unless they were carefully managed, and remarkably fortunate in their location and surroundings, but rather as bonanzas, which could scarcely fail to enrich all who were prominently connected with them, either in construction or operation. Roads that had previously been prosperous increased their dividends, and roads that had been on the verge of bankruptcy suddenly became profitable. It was not merely by a marked increase in the business of many lines, arising from the movement of troops, war material, and diversified products, that railways were benefited, but by the changes in the laws and usages relating to the currency, which enabled them to pay with greenback dollars debts, or the interest on debts, contracted on a gold basis, and thus conferred a liberal share of the sort of prosperity that helped to enrich all the debtor classes of that period who were engaged in active business. Many railway stocks advanced greatly in nominal value, not only on account of the large dividends earned, and inflation of the currency, but because an unusually large number of persons had suddenly acquired fortunes which they wished to invest, and as the standard rate of the dividends of a number of companies was about 10 per cent, and frequently more, they furnished one of the best of available investments.

## PROFITS OF CONSTRUCTION

In addition to the substantial returns of the older companies, it was generally believed, and in some cases there were apparently good grounds for such belief, that a number of large fortunes had been made out of the mere construction of railways, not only or mainly by the intricate process of superintending, as contractors, the operations of large numbers of men engaged in the actual work of tunneling or graduation, but by participation in the profits of construction companies, which made favorable bargains with co-adjutors acting as directors. In connection with the Pacific roads subsidized by United States bonds, and various land-grant roads, devices for speedily securing profits out of construction were specially numerous, but even with other classes of roads, during eras when unbounded confidence in the success of railways prevailed, and when bonds could be readily sold, means were devised for rendering construction a profitable operation.

## CHANGES IN BUSINESS SYSTEMS

Aside from all temporary and speculative influences a radical and permanent change in many vital matters affecting the business of the country was progressing. The local and state spirit which had previously prevailed was, to a great extent, supplanted by broad nationalism. It was largely on account of this change that consolidations, the establishing of fast frieght lines, or other methods for facilitating intercourse between distant points became popular. The entire Republic was opened up to all its citizens and the disposition to conduct commercial transactions with distant communities was greatly increased. Manufactures of many kinds began to flourish to an extent never known before, and as a substitute for a great temporary diminution in the exports of cotton, exports of petroleum, breadstuffs, and provisions began to assume tremendous proportions. After the close of the war, and the withdrawal of an immense number of men from military service, many of them sought new employment in comparatively new fields of agricultural development, such as portions of Texas and various western, north-western, or south-western states and territories, and also petroleum regions, and gold, silver, copper, lead, iron, and coal-mining districts. These outbursts of national activity each helped, in one way or another, to promote railway construction, by greatly expanding the area in which there was a demand for a marked increase of facilities for transportation.

## DIVIDENDS OF THE SEVENTH DECADE

The profitable nature of many of the railway operations of portions of the decade is partly illustrated by the following statement of some of the dividends paid:—

Of the New England roads, the Boston and Albany, formed by a consolidation of the Boston and Worcester and the Western, which had paid dividends of 8 per cent from 1859–60 to 1861–62, and a dividend of 9 per cent in 1862–63, paid dividends of 10 per cent per annum in each year from 1863 to 1869, and increased its capital stock from $9,650,000 in 1864 to $16,411,600 in 1869. The Boston and Maine paid dividends of 8 per cent from 1862–63 to 1864–65 and of 10 per cent from 1865 to 1869. The New York and New Haven, after large payments on account of the Schuyler fraud, to which it had been subjected, began to declare 10 per cent dividends. A number of the short New England roads raised their annual rate of dividends to 10 per cent before the close of the decade. The Boston and Providence paid dividends of 8 per cent during five years of the decade, 9 per cent in one year, and 10 per cent in four years. The Boston and Lowell paid dividends of 8 per cent from 1865 to 1869. A number of New England roads seem to have been less affected by the war than the lines of any other section. They were prosperous before and continued to be so. A table of the net earnings of seven railroads leading into Boston in 1860 and 1863 gives their net earnings in each of these years as follows:—

|                          | 1860      | 1863      |
|--------------------------|-----------|-----------|
| Boston and Lowell        | $197,909  | $167,051  |
| Boston and Maine         | 475,720   | 482,657   |
| Boston and Providence    | 349,486   | 397,729   |
| Boston and Worcester     | 439,285   | 488,358   |
| Eastern                  | 367,653   | 394,594   |
| Fitchburg                | 302,400   | 328,042   |
| Old Colony and Fall River| 329,208   | 411,544   |

Of the Western, which, in combination with the Boston and Worcester, subsequently became the Boston and Albany, it was reported that its net earnings had increased from $888,254 in 1860 to $1,228,706 in 1863. Vigorous efforts to promote such a consolidation were progressing in 1864.

The Hudson River Railroad and the New York and Harlem, of both of which roads Cornelius Vanderbilt was president, each declared dividends of 8 per cent or more during portions of the decade, prior to the consolidation of the New York Central with the Hudson River, which went into effect October 1st, 1869, after which time Cornelius Vanderbilt became president of the consolidated company. The Rome, Watertown and Ogdensburg declared dividends of 10 per cent from 1863 to 1869. The New York Central paid a dividend of 7 per cent in 1862–63, 9 per cent in 1863–64, 6 per cent from 1864 to 1868, and 8 per cent in 1868–69. The Erie paid two dividends of 8 per cent and one of 3½ per cent on its common stock, and five dividends of 7 per cent and one of 8½ on its preferred stock during the decade.

A committee of the New York Central reported in 1864 that the net earnings of that company had been sufficient to pay all interest on indebtedness, a 7 per cent dividend, and to yield "a surplus of a million and a quarter of dollars, applicable to permanent increase and improvement of the company's property and reduction of debt." The committee suggested that at a future period the question should be duly considered "whether such large additions to the permanent value of the company's property ought not to be represented by a corresponding increase in value in the amount of its capital stock."

The United Companies of New Jersey paid a cash dividend of 10 per cent during 1869, and permanently maintained that rate throughout the decade.

The class of companies which apparently profited most extensively by the events of the period were the anthracite railways. The Delaware and Hudson Canal Company paid a dividend of 8½ per cent in 1862–63; of 20 per cent in each of the two following years; of 16 per cent in each of the two succeeding years; of 14 per cent in 1867–68, and 10 per cent in 1868–69. The Delaware, Lackawanna and Western declared a dividend of 9 per cent in 1863; dividends of 20 per cent in two of the years of the decade; a dividend of 15 per cent in another year, and dividends of 10 per cent in other years of the decade. The Lehigh Valley declared a dividend of 20 per cent in 1865–66, and of 10 per cent in six other years of the decade. The Philadelphia and Reading declared cash, stock, or optional dividends ranging from 5 to 15 per cent in each year of the decade.

The Pennsylvania Railroad declared cash dividends ranging from 6 to 10 per cent during each year of the decade and the following stock dividends: May, 1864, 30 per cent; May, 1867, 5 per cent; May, 1868, 5 per cent. Pennsylvania Railroad shares, par $50, were selling at from $75½ to $77½ shortly after a 30 per cent stock dividend had been declared in the early part of 1864, so that the original holder of 100 shares which had cost $5,000 could have sold his dividend of 30 shares for from $2,265 to $2,325. The stock dividend represented surplus profits, applied to permanent improvements or investments, which had not been divided among the stockholders.

The net revenue of the Baltimore and Ohio was enormously increased while the war was progressing, and it declared substantial dividends, but applied a considerable portion of its net earnings to a reduction of its funded debt and sundry investments or improvements. A similar policy was pursued by the Philadelphia, Wilmington and Baltimore, which also had its net revenue largely increased above the usual standard during the war.

The prosperity of the Pittsburgh, Fort Wayne and Chicago is indicated by the fact that it was leased to the Pennsylvania in 1869, on terms which guaranteed a dividend of 7 per cent on the capital stock, after the amount of the latter had been increased from $11,500,000 to $19,583,947.71. A prospectus issued in 1864 by promoters of a new company stated that in 1863 the Cleveland, Columbus and Cincinnati divided 15 per cent; the Cincinnati, Hamilton and Dayton divided 10 per cent; the Little Miami 30 per cent; the Michigan Central 18 per cent; and the Lake Shore, Cleveland, Painesville and Ashtabula, 23 per cent.

The Illinois Central paid dividends of 8 per cent in 1863 and 1864, and of 10 per cent from 1865 to 1869, inclusive. The Chicago and Rock Island paid dividends of 6 per cent in 1860–61, 1861–62, and 1862–63; a dividend of 8 per cent in 1864–65, and dividends of 10 per cent in each of the four following years. The Michigan Central declared dividends of 8 per cent in 1862–63; 12 per cent in 1863–64; 18 per cent in 1864–65; 9 per cent in 1865–66, and 10 per cent in each of the three following years of the decade. The Chicago, Burlington and Quincy declared large dividends, and also distributed a considerable amount of stock. The Chicago and North-western in 1867–68 declared a dividend of 10 per cent, payable in stock, and in 1868–69 a dividend of 10 per cent, payable in cash. The Milwaukee and St. Paul, the forerunner of the Chicago, Milwaukee and St. Paul, declared a dividend, for the earnings of 1869, on preferred stock of 7 per cent, and 3 per cent on common stock, and on common stock of 3 per cent in cash, and 7 per cent in common stock.

Various other dividends of the period are of a character similar to those already mentioned. So far as any general deduction can be drawn from them, it is probably to the effect that the prevailing standard of the period for prosperous railways more nearly approximated 10 per cent per annum than any other figure, and that sanguine investors were more apt to suppose that this rate would be maintained, and occasionally increased by stock dividends or cash returns exceeding 10 per cent per annum, than that dividends would fall below that rate. . . .

## BREAKERS AHEAD

While the increase of the dividends, and the usual rate of the dividends, of a number of northern and western railways helped to greatly increase public confidence in railway enterprises and to stimulate the organization of new projects, success was by no means universal. The Atlantic and Great Western, built while the war was progressing, which commenced operations with great expectations, was in the hands of receivers before the decade closed. For the year ending June 30th, 1869, its net earnings were reported to be $1,638,078.34, and at that time its capital stock was $30,000,000, and its various classes of indebtedness amounted to $63,897,472.50. Aside from this disastrous showing of one of the most important of the new companies a number of the old lines extensively engaged in competitive movements found, before the decade had closed, that the rate of profit on a given amount of business had woefully decreased, and declines in gross earnings were common. This was one of the most noticeable developments of the period. The Baltimore and Ohio, for instance, reported on gross earnings of $10,138,876 in 1864, a net revenue of $5,692,680, while in 1868 it reported gross earnings of $8,472,218 and $2,692,106 of net revenue. The Philadelphia, Wilmington and Baltimore reported $3,828,464.06 of gross earnings and $1,574,554.39 of net revenue in 1864–65, while in 1868–69 its gross earnings were $2,565,302.31, and its net revenue $874,094.48—the net revenue being in the latter year 34.15 per cent of the receipts, and in the former 54.29 per cent. The Erie reported in 1863–64 that its gross earnings were $12,551,480, and its net earnings $3,493,726, while in 1868–69 its gross earnings were $16,721,500, and its net earnings were $2,179,395. Some important roads were able to ward off similar changes, by improving their facilities, diminishing the cost of freight movements, and obtaining advantageous new connections or classes of traffic; but in the absence of exceptionally favorable influences, there was a strong tendency towards a marked reduction of railway profits, and some of the companies which did not promptly counteract this tendency either by reducing expenses per ton per mile, or other expedients, were drifting towards a disastrous condition. The roads that had been most materially benefited by new influences, and had failed to provide new sources of profit or to greatly reduce expenses, were the heaviest sufferers, but many lines were adversely affected by the new order of things. . . .

.   .   .

The seventh decade was prolific in railway improvements of various kinds, but there was none which left a more permanent and important impression than the commencement of efforts to substitute steel for iron rails. No other single influence has been equally effective in reducing the cost of transportation and improving the general condition of leading lines. The movement gained a great impetus from a variety of causes, one of which was the relative scarcity, at some periods, of the supply of iron rails, and another the inferiority of many of the iron rails then in use, and consequent necessity of frequent renewal of tracks.

The condition of the iron rail industries of the country during the early portion of the decade is indicated by the following statements:—

## CAPACITY OF IRON RAIL MILLS IN 1865

A letter sent to the Commissioner of Internal Revenue, in 1865, by Samuel J. Reeves, Esq., the chairman of the executive committee of the American Iron and Steel Association, embodied, in a lengthy discussion of proposed changes in the duty on rails, the following statements:—

1st. That the quantity of railroad iron now being produced in the loyal states is over 275,000 tons per annum, with an ultimate capacity, in the present mills, of double that quantity.

2d. That they are able to keep all the present roads in repair, and furnish a surplus equal to the requirements of nearly 2,000 miles of new track per annum.

3d. That from June 30th, 1861, to June 30th, 1864, all the rails required by the railroad companies, as well as the demand of the United States government for military purposes (with the exception of 206,000 tons imported during the three fiscal years), were supplied by the American mills.

About the same time a table was published giving the names, address, capacity, and production for the year ending November 16th, 1864, of the railroad iron mills of the United States. The total number was 38, capacity 684,000 tons, production 283,560 tons. The capacity of the mills located in Pennsylvania was 291,000 tons, and their production 138,000 tons. The mills that had severally produced 20,000 tons or more, during the year named, were the following: Cambria Iron Company, Johnstown, 40,000 tons; Lackawanna Iron Company, Scranton, 22,000; Pennsylvania Iron Company, Danville, 20,000.

It was announced as a notable event that in the six working days ended March 19th, 1864, the Cambria Iron Company rolled 993 tons of rails, equal to an average of 165½ tons per day. . . .

## AMERICAN RECOGNITION OF THE UTILITY OF STEEL RAILS

. . .

The Pennsylvania Railroad annual report, dated February 15th, 1864, says:—

"The rapid destruction of iron under the high speeds and heavy locomotives now used upon railways has become a subject of serious consideration, not only to the managers of these improvements in this country, but also in Europe. When the Pennsylvania Railroad was planned a locomotive weighing from 45,000 to 50,000 pounds was considered as the extreme limit of these machines, justified by prudence. But the demands of the public for high speeds has compelled the introduction upon all thoroughfares of more powerful engines. These could only be obtained by adding to their dimensions and weight, which has produced its natural result—great wear and tear of iron rails, and the superstructure of the road. This evil has been still further increased by the inferiority of the rails now manufactured, compared with those placed upon railways when the edge-rail was first introduced. It was then deemed essential that rails should be made from the best refined iron produced from selected ores. The great increase in the demand for iron under the rapid development of the railway system in England and this country soon caused the substitution of an inferior article, which seemed for a time to answer the purpose, but which experience has proven to be insufficient to resist the causes referred to as continually operating for its destruction. A return to the quality of the iron originally used on railways would be the natural remedy for this difficulty, but this would require time, as none of the rail mills have the required furnaces to refine their metal. In Europe this subject has been longer considered, and the determination appears to be general to gradually substitute a still more expensive material, either a rail made wholly of steel, with a steel head only, or the wearing surface converted into steel after the iron rail is made. The present high cost of rails made entirely of steel will probably prevent their general adoption, although the rapid destruction at the termini and stations, where the iron rail in some positions does not last six months, will fully justify their introduction. For the purpose of testing the relative value of steel and iron rails in such positions, we have procured 150 tons of rails made wholly of cast steel. A trial is also being made of a rail with a steeled wearing surface passed through the rolls, when drawn from the converting furnace, which promises well. It is understood that favorable results have been obtained from rails, the top plate in the pile from which they were made being puddled steel. If the two metals can thus be firmly welded together, this improvement in railway bars will be generally adopted. This is a subject of such great importance to the company that it will continue to meet the earnest attention of your directors, and, if necessary to effect the reformation desired in the quality of rails, it should become important to erect works to effect that object, such a policy will be adopted. The frequent renewal of rails is not only expensive, but it adds to the interruption of the traffic of the line."

The Pennsylvania Railroad report for 1864, dated February 18th, 1865, says: "Notwithstanding our unremitting efforts to secure the best rails that are made, each succeeding year adds its testimony to those preceding it of the want of a better material than that now used. In addition to their rapid destruction from ordinary wear, is added the risk to the trains from their frequent breakage. To obviate this our new rails have been increased in depth to an extent (4½ inches) that will give them 30 per cent additional vertical strength, which it is believed will, with increased care in the selection of ores and the manufacture of the rails, prevent further damage from this source. The steel rails introduced upon the road show no evidence of wear, but their great cost at present precludes their general introduction. The manufacture of rails with a steeled-wearing surface, referred to in our last annual report, has not proved successful upon a scale that would render it of practical value."

## RESULTS OF EXPERIMENTS ON THE PENNSYLVANIA RAILROAD

Two years later, describing operations of the Pennsylvania Railroad Company, for the year 1866, President [J. Edgar] Thomson in his report dated February 19th, 1867, says: "Every effort to materially improve the quality of the iron to meet the wants of the augmenting traffic of the trunk lines, having heretofore failed, attention was directed to the introduction of steel rails, and, with a view to test their efficiency, the president, while in England, in 1862, ordered a few hundred tons for trial. These proved so satisfactory that larger importations of Bessemer steel have been made, which entirely confirmed our expectations of their success. The cost of steel rails is at present about twice that of the best iron rails, while their durability is fully eight times greater. It is confidently believed, however, that with enlarged works, increased knowledge of the ores required to produce the best quality of this metal, and great experience in its production, they will be successfully manufactured at home, and the price very largely reduced. At present the demand is equal to the supply, and prices are maintained. To avoid the heavy annual outlays, that a change from a cheap to a dearer material would necessarily entail upon the revenues, it is proposed to continue for the present to reroll the worn-out rails, and replace the annual wear and tear with steel rails. The general introduction of steel rails is now wholly a commercial question, in which the cost of the increased capital required for their purchase becomes the chief impediment to their general adoption. While the business of a line is small, it will still be economy to use the iron rails, at an ordinary rate of interest upon capital until the cost of producing steel is reduced to its minimum. When that result is accomplished the general public will be materially benefited by the reduced cost of transportation which the introduction of steel rails will enable railway companies to afford."

## IRON AND STEEL RAILS ON THE ERIE RAILWAY

In a letter written by H. Riddle, general superintendent of the Erie Railway, to John S. Eldridge, president of that road, dated March 3d, 1868, he states that during the preceding three winter months "the iron rails have been broken, laminated, and worn out beyond all precedent, until there is scarce a mile of your road, except that laid with steel rails, between Jersey City and Salamanca or Buffalo, where it is safe to run a train at the ordinary passenger-train speed, and many portions of the road can only be traversed safely by reducing the speed of all trains to twelve or fifteen miles per hour, solely on account of the worn-out and rotten condition of the rails. Broken wheels, axles, engines, and trains off the track have been of daily, almost hourly, occurrence for the last two months, caused mostly by defective rails. Fully one thousand *broken rails* were taken from the track in the month of January, while the number removed on account of lamination, crushing, or wearing out was much greater. February will show a worse record than January. . . . With the ten miles laid with the John Brown Bessemer steel no fault need be found. Only one rail has broken during the winter, and no lamination and very little wear is perceptible. Twenty steel rails were laid in Jersey City yard last March. The iron rails adjoining, subject to the same wear, have been renewed four times since the steel was put down, and I have no doubt the steel rails will outlast three times as many more iron rails. This winter's experience has satisfied me that the quality and weight of the iron rails in use cannot be depended upon to sustain the weight of the Erie Railway. Forty-two-ton locomotives, hauling trains of fifty and sixty loaded cars, and passenger engines weighing thirty-seven tons, running at a speed of thirty to forty miles per hour, literally crush and grind out the iron rails beneath them. Instances have been reported to me of rails removed from track, too much worn for safety, where the first imperfection was visible but the day before." . . .

It is claimed that the first steel rail rolled in America was made at the Chicago Rolling Mill, under the direction of W. F. Durfee, engineer, on May 25th, 1865. The ingots used had previously been manufactured at the Wyandotte Rolling Mill, located at Wyandotte, Michigan, in accordance with the Kelly process, an American patented invention, which conflicted with the claims based on the Bessemer patent to an extent that presumably led to a postponement of the active operations subsequently undertaken until these antagonisms were reconciled. . . .

## ORGANIZATION OF THE EARLY AMERICAN STEEL-RAIL INDUSTRIES

In 1882, in a letter addressed to Judge Kelly, Mr. James M. Swank gave the following account of the organization of the early steel-rail works of this country:—

"Each of the two experimental Bessemer steel works which were established in this country in 1864 and 1865, one at Wyandotte, Michigan, and the other at Troy, New York, lost money. The Wyandotte works were abandoned in 1869, and were almost a total loss. The Troy experimental works were succeeded in 1867 by permanent works, and these were burned in 1868. New works were completed in 1870, and it was not until after this event that any money was made in the manufacture of Bessemer steel at Troy.

"The first works established in Pennsylvania expressly to manufacture Bessemer steel were those of the Pennsylvania Steel Company, near Harrisburg, which were commenced in 1865. In 1867 steel was first manufactured at these works, since which time they have been steadily in operation. But it was not until 1873, eight years after the erection of the works had been undertaken, that a cash dividend was declared, and then it amounted to only two per cent upon the capital stock. At this time the stock exceeded one and three-quarter million dollars. A short time prior to this dividend one of the stockholders sold his stock for one-half its original value.

"The second Bessemer steel works in Pennsylvania were those of the Freedom Iron and Steel Company, near Lewistown. They were undertaken in 1866. In 1868 they commenced to make steel, and in 1869 the company failed, and the works were subsequently dismantled. Over one and a half million dollars, in capital and bonded and unbonded debts, was sunk in this abortive enterprise.

"The Cambria Iron Company, at Johnstown, Pennsylvania, has manufactured Bessemer steel since 1871, but it was originally organized in 1853 to manufacture iron rails. Its capital stock was one million dollars. In 1854 the company failed, and in 1855, fresh capital having been added, it failed again. The works were then leased. In 1861 the company was reorganized, and placed upon a firm financial basis, the original stockholders, who had paid a million dollars, surrendering their stock, and receiving in exchange one hundred thousand dollars of new stock, or one hundred dollars for every thousand dollars they had invested. Thus the original promoters of this enterprise absolutely lost nine hundred thousand dollars.

"The Bethlehem Iron Company, at Bethlehem, Pennsylvania, was organized in 1863 to manufacture iron rails, and in 1873 it commenced also to manufacture Bessemer steel. It has continued the manufacture of Bessemer steel until the present time. From 1869 to 1873 only stock dividends were made, and from 1873 to 1879 neither stock nor cash dividends were declared. In these latter years the company's operations were conducted at an actual loss. In 1874 a bonded debt of a million dollars was created, and in 1877 additional bonds were issued to the amount of $278,000.

"The effort to establish the Bessemer steel industry in the west has been attended with many discouraging vicissitudes. The works of the Joliet Iron and Steel Company, at Joliet, Illinois, were commenced in 1870, and in 1873 they first manufactured Bessemer steel. In 1874 the company failed, and the works were stopped. The company made another effort to achieve success, but after a long struggle again failed, but not until fresh debts had been created, the whole investment aggregating three million seven hundred thousand dollars. After passing through bankruptcy, the works were sold in 1879 for a sum not sufficient to pay all the bondholders, and the original capital was lost. The works of the Vulcan Steel Company, at St. Louis, Missouri, were built in 1872 to roll iron rails, but in 1875 the company commenced the erection of Bessemer steel works. In 1876 these works were completed, and steel was made by them in that year. Soon afterwards the company failed to meet its obligations, and the works were stopped, but, after many serious losses, it has been reorganized, and the works are now in operation. Probably two million dollars has been expended in building up this enterprise, which has until very recently been exceedingly unprofitable."

## PROGRESS IN AMERICAN STEEL-RAIL-MAKING

The following table shows the annual production in gross tons of Bessemer steel rails in the United States since the beginning of their manufacture in 1867, together with the average annual price at which they have been sold at works in Pennsylvania and the rates of duty imposed on foreign rails:—

| Years | Production in gross tons | Price in currency | Duty |
|---|---|---|---|
| 1867 | 2,277 | $166.00 | 45 per cent ad valorem |
| 1868 | 6,451 | 158.50 | |
| 1869 | 8,616 | 132.25 | |
| 1870 | 30,357 | 106.75 | |
| 1871 | 34,152 | 102.50 | $28 per ton to Aug. 1st, 1872; $25.20 to Mar. 3d, 1875; $28 from that date to July 1st, 1883 |
| 1872 | 83,991 | 112.00 | |
| 1873 | 115,192 | 120.50 | |
| 1874 | 129,414 | 94.25 | |
| 1875 | 259,699 | 68.75 | |
| 1876 | 368,269 | 59.25 | |
| 1877 | 385,865 | 45.50 | |
| 1878 | 491,427 | 42.25 | |
| 1879 | 610,682 | 48.25 | |
| 1880 | 852,196 | 67.50 | |
| 1881 | 1,187,770 | 61.13 | |
| 1882 | 1,284,067 | 48.50 | |
| 1883 | 1,148,709 | 37.75 | |
| 1884 | 996,983 | 30.75 | $17 per ton from July 1st, 1883 |
| 1885 | 959,471 | 28.50 | |
| 1886 | 1,574,703 | 34.50 | |
| 1887 (March) | | 39.50 | |

The lowest average annual price at which Bessemer steel rails have been sold in this country was reached in 1885, namely, $28.50, but sales were made at still lower figures in both 1884 and 1885.

The outlays for steel rails, which commenced in the seventh decade, continued to represent a large expenditure on account of increase in the quantity used, which was generally accompanied by a large annual decrease in price per ton, except during years when unusually large amounts of new railway construction were progressing. It was estimated in 1885 that up to that year 10,000,000 tons of steel rails had been produced in this country, of which less than 50,000 tons had been made before July, 1870, and the price had fallen from $106.75 per ton in 1870 to such an extent that sales were reported in 1885 at less than $30 per ton, or $28.50 at the mills.

The limited product of rails in American Bessemer mills before 1871 indicates that the works of this country before that time had only been making preparatory efforts for the gigantic labors they subsequently performed.

. . .

## SYSTEMS OF RAILWAY ORGANIZATION

. . .

As in the past, so in the present, there are some small roads which might have furnished the groundwork of the description of a humorous writer who credits a president with saying that he is the principal owner; and also "the board of directors, treasurer, secretary, general manager, superintendent, paymaster, track master, general passenger agent, general freight agent, master mechanic, ticket agent, conductor, brakeman, and boss. The engineer does his own firing, and runs the repair shop and round-house, all by himself."

One writer of high railway standing, H. S. Haines, in referring to this subject, says: "There are those among us whose memory goes back to the patriarchal stage of management, when most corporations owned not more than fifty or a hundred miles of track; when the treasurer sold tickets at the principal passenger station on the road, and the freight agent at the same station was virtually the head of the transportation department; when no bill was paid except upon the order of the president, and periodical reports and statistical statements were unknown." In referring to a similar stage of development, Charles Francis Adams says he can easily remember when the first railroads were organized in Massachusetts. "An apothecary was president of the Old Colony Railroad, which

## Table Showing the Production, Importation, Consumption, and Price of Rails in the United States from 1860 to 1880, with the Mileage of Railroad Built

| Year | Production | | | Imports[1] | | Apparent consumption[2] | Miles of railroad built | Average price of iron rails | Average price of steel rails |
|---|---|---|---|---|---|---|---|---|---|
| | *Iron* | *Steel* | *Total* | *Iron* | *Steel* | | | | |
| 1860 | 205,038 | ...... | 205,038 | 139,835 | | 341,873 | 1,846 | 48 | .... |
| 1861 | 189,818 | ...... | 189,818 | 83,429 | | 273,247 | 651 | 42⅜ | .... |
| 1862 | 213,912 | ...... | 213,912 | 9,644 | | 223,556 | 834 | 41¾ | .... |
| 1863 | 275,768 | ...... | 275,768 | 19,138 | | 294,906 | 1,050 | 76⅞ | .... |
| 1864 | 335,369 | ...... | 335,369 | 132,959 | | 468,328 | 738 | 126 | .... |
| 1865 | 356,292 | ...... | 356,292 | 86,820 | | 443,112 | 1,177 | 98⅝ | .... |
| 1866 | 430,778 | ...... | 430,778 | 87,368 | | 518,146 | 1,742 | 86¾ | .... |
| 1867 | 459,558 | 2,550 | 462,108 | 163,049 | | 625,157 | 2,449 | 83⅛ | .... |
| 1868 | 499,489 | 7,225 | 506,714 | 250,081 | | 756,795 | 2,979 | 78⅞ | 158½ |
| 1869 | 583,936 | 9,650 | 593,586 | 313,163 | | 906,749 | 4,953 | 77¼ | 132¼ |
| 1870 | 586,000 | 34,000 | 620,000 | 399,153 | | 1,019,153 | 5,690 | 72¼ | 106¾ |
| 1871 | 737,483 | 38,250 | 775,733 | 566,202 | | 1,311,935 | 7,670 | 70⅜ | 102½ |
| 1872 | 905,930 | 94,070 | 1,000,000 | 381,064 | 149,786 | 1,530,850 | 6,167 | 85⅛ | 112 |
| 1873 | 761,062 | 129,015 | 890,077 | 99,201 | 159,571 | 1,148,849 | 4,105 | 76⅔ | 120½ |
| 1874 | 584,469 | 144,944 | 729,413 | 7,796 | 100,515 | 837,724 | 1,901 | 58¾ | 94¼ |
| 1875 | 501,649 | 290,863 | 792,512 | 1,174 | 18,274 | 811,960 | 1,917 | 47¾ | 68¾ |
| 1876 | 467,168 | 412,461 | 879,629 | 287 | ...... | 879,916 | 2,856 | 41¼ | 59¼ |
| 1877 | 332,540 | 432,169 | 764,709 | ...... | 35 | 764,744 | 2,281 | 35¼ | 45½ |
| 1878 | 322,890 | 559,795 | 882,685 | ...... | 10 | 882,695 | 2,687 | 33¾ | 42½ |
| 1879 | 420,160 | 693,113 | 1,113,273 | 19,090 | 25,057 | 1,157,420 | 4,721 | 41¼ | 48¼ |
| 1880 | 493,762 | 968,075 | 1,461,837 | 132,459 | 158,230 | 1,752,526 | 7,174 | 49¾ | 67½ |

[1] Fiscal year to 1867.

[2] Including imports per fiscal year to 1867.

carried 250 passengers a week, considered something wonderful forty years ago."

Enlarged systems of organization were necessitated by additions to mileage and the growth of business. Thirty years ago the model management of a first-class road of that era was divided first into two grand departments. One related to financial affairs and all accounts, and was managed by the president, secretary, treasurer, attorney, and directors. The other was the operating department, with a commercial branch and a mechanical branch. They were, in turn, subdivided under the direction of a general superintendent. His principal officers were first, a superintendent of road, whose chief assistants were road masters, the employes under their direction being section men; second, a superintendent of machinery, whose chief aids were a foreman of a machine shop in which machinists worked, a foreman of a blacksmith shop and blacksmiths, a foreman of a car shop and carpenters, a foreman of a paint shop and painters, engineers (not on trains) and firemen, and car masters who directed operations of oil men and cleaners; a general passenger agent whose leading assistants were conductors and mail agents who directed the labors of brakemen, engineers (on passenger trains), and ticket agents, station agents, express agents, and police; a general freight agent whose principal assistants were conductors who directed labors of brakemen and engineers on freight trains, freight station agents, weighers, gaugers, and yard masters; a supply agent and a fuel agent, who each had appropriate assistants.

## GENERAL PRINCIPLES OF ORGANIZATION

A report made to the stockholders of the New York and Erie Railroad in 1856, by D. C. McCallum, stated that the following general principles should be observed in arranging the organization of railway forces:—

"First. A proper division of responsibilities.

"Second. Sufficient power conferred to enable the same to be fully carried out, that such responsibilities may be real in their character.

"Third. The means of knowing whether such responsibilities are faithfully executed.

"Fourth. Great promptness in the report of all derelictions of duty, that evils may be at once corrected.

"Fifth. Such information to be obtained through a system of

daily reports and checks that will not embarrass principal officers nor lessen their influence with their subordinates.

"Sixth. The adoption of a system, as a whole, which will not only enable the general superintendent to detect errors immediately, but also point out the delinquent.

"A system of operations to be efficient and successful should be such as to give to the principal and responsibile head of the running department a complete daily history of details in all their minutiæ."

Such principles have been respected, to a considerable extent, for the protection and benefit of companies, but as the magnitude of operations increased various modifications or additions were found desirable or necessary.

Of the present large railway organizations Charles Francis Adams, in addressing students of Harvard University, in March, 1886, said:—

"In the modern railroad there are five departments. First is the financial department, which is the sinew of the whole body, its ways and means; second, the construction department, of which the head is the chief engineer, who lays out the road; thirdly comes the operating department, with the superintendent at the head; fourth comes the commercial department, looked after by the general traffic manager; and, then, fifth, comes the legal department. The counsel for the company looks after all legal papers, suits, &c., and has a vast amount of business to attend to. The duties of these departments are as varied as those of the United States government, and the heads constitute a sort of cabinet, and the pivot wheel around which the whole machinery moves is the president. In the beginning of the building of railways $1,000,000 was deemed a large capital for a railroad. The capital of the Union Pacific is represented by $270,000,000 of securities of the forty or fifty roads which are combined in this general system. Its income is $25,000,000 a year, and in profitable times reaches $100,000 a day. It employs 12,000 men, and has a monthly pay-roll of $800,000; 12,000 cars are run by 550 locomotives; 25,000 tons of steel rails are used in replacing worn-out rails, and 2,000,000 ties are used in keeping the road-bed in condition. If you compare this with the United States government, the affairs of the latter during the first fifty years of its existence were trifling. Yet this is only one system, and there are five more by the side of which—for example, the

Pennsylvania—the Union Pacific is insignificant. If this is the growth of forty years, what will be that of sixty or eighty years. I confess that I am unable to forecast it. This great principle of consolidation and aggregation, like the principles of gravitation, has as yet but begun to develop its results."

# 5. Railroad Abuses and the Call for Regulation

The campaign against railroad abuses began at the state level in the Midwest shortly after the Civil War and drew much of its strength from farmers, but the movement for regulation was also initiated by Eastern merchants and manufacturers in states like New York and Massachusetts, where small shippers denounced rebating and pushed for the public control of rates. As early as 1869 the outcry against extortionate and discriminatory charges led Granger spokesmen in Congress to ask for laws to help Western growers by regulating rates on shipments of farm commodities. The campaign for national regulation was given its first significant impetus in 1874 by the report of a Senate committee headed by William Windom of Minnesota. Many of the evils listed in this pioneer Congressional investigation of railroad abuses could be found some ten years later in the report, submitted by the Senate committee headed by Shelby M. Cullom of Illinois, which recommended the establishment of an independent commission authorized to regulate railroads engaged in interstate commerce. The Windom Committee shied clear of such a proposal, but it concluded that the best hope of reducing transportation costs lay in building more inland waterways and in constructing one or more government-operated railroads to serve as competitive yardsticks for the private roads.

SOURCE: U. S. Senate, Report of the Select Committee on Transportation Routes to the Seaboard, 43rd Cong., 1st sess., Senate Report No. 307, Part 1 (Washington, D.C.: Government Printing Office, 1874), pp. 71–2, 115–19, 121–2.

## DEFECTS AND ABUSES OF EXISTING SYSTEMS OF TRANSPORTATION

Concisely stated, the defects and abuses alleged against the existing systems of transportation are insufficient facilities, unfair discriminations, and extortionate charges.

With reference to the matter of facilities, it is believed that the improvements of natural water-ways and the construction of additional channels of water communication have been wholly inadequate to the growing demands of trade; and by reason of this neglect on the part of the Government, the commerce of the country has been compelled to accept the more expensive methods afforded by railroads . . . railway companies, having thus secured a substantial monopoly of the business of transportation, have failed to recognize their responsibilities to the public, or to meet the just demands of the rapidly-increasing commerce between the interior and the seaboard.

Discriminating and extortionate charges, however, constitute the chief grounds of complaint. The principal causes which are supposed to produce such charges, and which have aggravated and intensified the public discontent, may be summarized as follows:

1. "*Stock-watering*," a well-known process by which the capital stock of a company is largely increased, for purely speculative purposes, without any corresponding expenditure on the part of its recipients.

2. *Capitalization of surplus earnings.* By this process the net profits, over and above the amount paid on interest and dividends are supposed to be expended in permanent improvements, and charged up to capital account, for which additional stock is issued, and increased charges rendered necessary to meet the increased dividends required. It is insisted that this is a double form of taxation: first, in the exorbitant charges from which such surplus profits are derived; and, second, in the conversion of such surplus into capital-stock, thereby compelling the business of the country to pay increased charges on all future transactions, in order to provide dividends on capital thus unjustly obtained. It is argued, with great force, that as all the legitimate claims of railroad companies are met by the public, when it has paid a fair and reasonable return for the capital invested and services rendered, any surplus earnings expended in improvements should inure to its benefit, instead of being made the basis for future exactions. In brief, the people believe that by this process they are first robbed, and then compelled to pay interest on their own money.

3. The introduction of intermediate agencies, such as car-companies, fast-freight lines, &c.

4. "Construction rings" and other means by which the managers

are supposed to make large profits in the building of railways, which are charged up to the cost of the road.

5. Unfair adjustments of through and local rates, and unjust discriminations against certain localities, whereby one community is compelled to pay unreasonable charges in order that another more favored may pay less than the services are worth. This will be fully considered hereafter, in the discussion of "equal mileage rates."

6. General extravagance and corruption in railway management, whereby favorites are enriched and the public impoverished.

7. Combinations and consolidations of railway companies, by which free competition is destroyed, and the producing and commercial interests of the country handed over to the control of monopolies, who are thereby enabled to enforce upon the public the exorbitant rates rendered necessary by the causes above named.

8. The system of operating fast and slow trains on the same road, whereby the cost of freight movement is believed to be largely increased. This is perhaps the misfortune rather than the fault of railway companies. It is doubtless a necessity, growing out of the conditions under which our railway system has been developed.

Of the defects and abuses above enumerated, perhaps none have contributed so much to the general discontent and indignation as the increase of railway capital by "stock-watering," and capitalization of surplus earnings. . . .

## COMPETITION IN THE UNITED STATES

Let us now inquire to what extent railway competition exists in our own country, and how far its permanence may be relied upon to regulate and cheapen transportation.

The theory here has always been, as in England, that the transportation business, like other commercial affairs, would regulate itself on the principle of competition. On this theory our railroad system has attained its present gigantic proportions. Believing that additional lines would create and stimulate competition, and thereby reduce rates, towns, cities, counties, and States have made haste to burthen themselves with debt in order to secure the coveted boon. The General Government having never interfered, and, until recently, the States having made but little effort to control or direct it, the system has developed itself under the influence of the natural laws which govern that kind of business. Hence the tendencies and results evolved by the operation of those laws, if carefully studied by the light of the experience of other countries, will enable us to form an opinion as to what may be anticipated from railway competition in the future if left to regulate itself by the ordinary laws of trade. That there is effective competition in the matter of charges at many points cannot be doubted, but that the same natural laws which have destroyed it in other countries are vigorously at work here, and will ultimately produce the same results is also obvious. The history of railway combinations in Europe, and especially in Great Britain, discloses the fact that during the period of development, and while each corporation was struggling to appropriate to its exclusive control as large a district of country as possible, competition was very sharp. When, by the consolidation of separate links, through trunk-lines were formed between the principal centers of population and trade, competition at once sprung up between those points. But self-interest very soon suggested to the competing companies that as the traffic must be divided, it was desirable to divide its profits between themselves rather than with the public. The result was an agreement as to rates and an end of competition. Having become strong and rich, the trunk-lines began the work of extending their power by the construction of branches and the absorption of weaker lines extending into the adjacent districts. Then followed a great struggle for territorial dominion, during which sharp and active competition re-appeared at numerous points in the contested districts. Its duration and vigor were measured chiefly by the relative strength of the giants contending for the prize, but the ultimate result was seldom long delayed and never doubtful. By purchase, lease, arrangement of rates, or some other of the numerous forms of combination and consolidation, one point after another disappeared from the competing list, and finally the disputed territory passed under the exclusive control of one of the contestants.

The same motives and influences which operated in Great Britain are rapidly producing similar results in this country. The existing competition, whatever may be its extent and value, is gradually disappearing from the trunk-lines, and is found mainly at points in the outlying districts from which these roads draw their support. The contest between the great companies for territorial dominion is still progressing in our country, and the struggle for control of the trade at some of the common termini and points of intersection of branch lines and feeders owned and operated by them, is apparent in the reduced charges which prevail at those places. The number of such competing points is, however, constantly diminishing, as each of the great corporations absorbs, one after another, the inferior lines which have served as allies to its rival. Thus every additional absorption defines with constantly increasing precision, the boundaries of the territory which is certainly and rapidly passing under its exclusive domination. The wide extent of our country, and the colossal proportions of our railway system (equaling one-half of the railway mileage of the globe), requires a longer time for complete development than in some of the states of Europe, and hence the influences which induce competition will extend through a longer period, but the ultimate result will probably be the same. And when the natural tendencies of corporate power working through railway organization shall have wrought out their inevitable conclusions, the magnitude of our combinations will probably be in proportion to the extent of the field in which they operate.

In illustration of the statement that competition has already substantially disappeared from the main trunk-lines, take those which center in Chicago from the east—the Pennsylvania line, running to New York and Philadelphia; the Lake Shore and Michigan Southern, running in connection with the Erie and New York Central; and the Michigan Central Railway, in connection with the last two, and also the Grand Trunk. These lines all have agents at Chicago who meet together and agree on prices for east-bound freight; and the prices established by such agreement bind the eastern roads. Mr. Homer E. Sargent, general superintendent of the Michigan Central Line, when asked upon what principle their rates are fixed, answered, "The rates from there east-bound are fixed somewhat according to the demand for transportation. The Western men generally meet together and agree upon prices. The managers of the Eastern roads meet together at New York and arrange matters."

Mr. C. M. Gray, assistant general freight agent of the Lake Shore and Michigan Southern Line, said, "We meet together, and if we deem it proper to advance, we do so, and the same is usual in the way of reduction. We are governed by the quantity moving and the price of freight on the lake. The lake craft take the lead in reducing rates, and they also have a very decided influence in the advance of rates when it comes toward winter. If they are carrying very high, so that it comes near to the railway, we immediately advance a little, and keep a little above them all the time."

Mr. E. D. Worcester, secretary of New York Central Railroad, testified that in fixing rates, "*the only question is what will the property bear,* keeping always in view the future development of the business, and the elements of public prosperity involved in such development."

Mr. Joseph D. Potts, president of the Empire Transportation Company, says, "The method of fixing the rates is about this: The various freight representatives of the different roads going eastward from Chicago usually fix unitedly upon the rates which are to govern all shipments out of Chicago by each of the lines, their own roads and the lines running over them."

Mr. Hayes, general manager of Blue Line, testified, "That the rates eastward are made by the general freight agents of western roads centering in Chicago. *They get together and find what the water communications are doing, their rates, &c., and base their rates upon that as a competing rate.*"

The tariffs on all freights moving eastward over these lines are thus fixed by agreement between the western agents; and the charges on westward-bound freight by agents with like powers at the eastern termini. It is obvious from these statements, that there is no competition between these lines in the matter of charges, and that the principle upon which they are adjusted is not what are the services worth, but *how much will the article bear, and what is the extent of water competition?* This combination for the establishment of charges does not formally include the Baltimore and Ohio line. Mr. Homer E. Sargent testified that he did not know whether the agents of that line were always present at the meetings, "but they adopt the same prices that the other roads make"; and that any road that should reduce fares without consulting with the other agents would be regarded as 'cutting.' "

"Cutting" is considered dishonorable among railway men, and at once gives rise to what are well known as "railway fights," which temporarily reduce charges below a paying rate at points of competition, accompanied generally by an increase at the non-competing points, and when the "war" is over, by enhanced rates on the entire line in order to make good the losses.

The two great companies which largely control the traffic of Wisconsin and Minnesota—the Chicago and Northwestern, and the Milwaukee and Saint Paul—afford another illustration of the value and extent of railway competition when regulated by its own laws. Towns and cities favored with a line belonging to, or controlled by, one of these companies eagerly contributed to aid in the construction of a second, which should be in the interest of the other company. For several years, while those great corporations have been extending their branches and absorbing weaker lines, competition has at times been active at certain places, but the territory which each can hope to control being now pretty well defined, an agreement as to rates has been made, and the people are alarmed by rumors, but too well founded, of a contemplated arrangement for pooling receipts. Thus the people of the great wheat-growing region of the continent, after having hoped and struggled for years for reduced rates through competition, and after having in many cases imposed upon themselves grievous burdens of taxation for that purpose, now find that instead of bringing into the field a competitor, they have not only doubled the power with which they have to contend, but that they have quartered upon themselves a new and expensive organization which must be supported from the products of their toil.

Very suggestive illustrations of the progress of combination and centralization of power are readily found in the history of the great trunk lines having their base at Boston, New York, Philadelphia, and Baltimore. But a quarter of a century ago there was no connection by rail between the great lakes and any of the eastern cities, or between Boston and New York. When subsequently the connection was formed between Albany and Buffalo it was composed of ten distinct links, each owned by a separate company. In 1850 the Pennsylvania Company was endeavoring to find its way over the mountains, which, by means of an inclined plane and stationary engine, it accomplished in 1851. In 1853 the Baltimore and Ohio united the Chesapeake Bay with the Ohio River. In 1850 there were but ten miles of road westward from Chicago, and three years thereafter that city was first connected by rail with the Atlantic Ocean. At that time not more than one company in the United States owned over two hundred continuous miles of road, and but few had half that number. Consolidations proceeded slowly, until about ten years ago, when a spirit of railway aggrandizement took possession of the stronger companies, since which the work of centralization and absorption has progressed without a parallel in the railway history of the world.

But it is not our purpose to multiply illustrations of this subject. The same forces which have produced the colossal combinations now in existence are still at work everywhere, and in our opinion will not cease to operate, if uncontrolled by legislative power, until railway competition shall have substantially disappeared from the country.

Combination assumes various forms, which, commencing with the simplest and most common, may be described as follows, viz.:

1. An agreement as to rates and fares between competing points.

2. An arrangement to forward traffic over one another's lines, each company receiving all the profits earned on its own line.

3. An arrangement which permits each company to run its cars over the line of the other, the profits being divided in certain fixed proportions.

4. An agreement to "pool earnings," or, as it is called in England, a "joint-purse," by which it is agreed that by whichever route the traffic goes, the line that carries it shall retain a certain proportion of the gross receipts, and pay over the balance to the other.

5. Lease of one road by another, under which a certain fixed sum is annually paid by the lessee, or an annual interest on the stock of the leased road.

6. A form of combination very similar to the last is where one company agrees to operate and maintain the line of another, paying over a certain proportion of the earnings.

7. Consolidation, as where one company purchases the stock of another, or where each road is valued and stock issued, and divided in proportion to the respective values of each. . . .

Additional railway lines have been suggested as the means of increasing competition and reducing the cost of transportation. Is it probable that relief will be found in that direction if such lines are to be under corporate control? What reason have we to suppose that the same principles of combination which govern existing lines will not control the new ones? If, as already shown, competition with the water-routes, and "the highest charge the commodity will bear" now rule the rates, have we any guarantee that they will not do so on the additional lines? In fact every new line from the Mississippi to the Atlantic Ocean will add from seventy-five to one hundred millions of dollars to the capital on which the transportation business of the country must pay at least $5,000,000 to $7,000,000 annual interest, in addition to the cost of maintaining the new organization. Will not this afford an irresistible inducement to combine with existing companies, in order to make the largest possible profits out of the business to be performed? Is there anything in experience, or in the known principles of railway management, which teach us to hope that the new competing line would not at once participate in the councils of its rivals and be governed by their policy?

# 6. The Consolidators

As noted by the Windom Committee Report, a trend toward railroad consolidation appeared after the Civil War. This tendency accelerated in the 1880's, when it also swept through industry, and reached new heights after the panic of 1893. In the first two years of the ensuing depression, about 25 per cent of the nation's aggregate railway capitalization went through bankruptcy proceedings. Among the bankrupt major lines were the Union Pacific, the Northern Pacific, the Santa Fe, and the Baltimore and Ohio. The large-scale reorganization of the roads, a process dominated by J. Pierpont Morgan, made investment bankers a decisive force in the railroad economy and enabled the stronger roads to absorb the weaker ones. By 1900, as this selection indicates, most of the railroad mileage in the United States was controlled by a handful of groups. While "Morganization" undoubtedly produced some salutary results, it had the long-term effect of increasing bonded indebtedness, thus adding to the financial problems of the railroads in the decade before the outbreak of World War I. Although the Transportation Act of 1920 and subsequent rail legislation reflected a change in public policy toward consolidation, viewing it as a means of promoting efficient and economical regional systems, these laws failed to stimulate important consolidations undertaken in the public interest.

SOURCE: M. G. Cunniff, "Increasing Railroad Consolidation," World's Work, III (February, 1902), pp. 1775–80.

. . . The very history of American railroads is a tale of consolidation. Cheap roads were built in the thirties from town to town, much as our trolley lines are built. By 1850 the Eastern

States were full of little lines, ten thousand miles of them, that bumped along from one town to another and then changed passengers and freight for the next town, where another transfer was made. Later, they were consolidated. The consolidations were fought in the State Legislatures just as vehemently as the Northwestern Governors have fought the Northern Securities Company, but they went on notwithstanding. We should have a curious system or railroads now if they had not—if passengers from New York had to change eight times to reach Albany and ten times between Albany and Buffalo, or even if eighteen arrangements had to be made for any through passage. In the consolidations, as railroads increased, the well-managed, conservative roads absorbed the badly managed ones. Over-capitalization, excessive bonding, rash expansion, brought hundreds of roads into the hands of receivers, and in the reorganization periods the firmly established roads acquired adjoining lines at little expense. . . . A railroad crash in 1893 [sent] one fifth of the entire mileage of the country . . . into the hands of receivers. By the wiping out of excessive indebtedness that came with reorganization, by the merging of competing lines under unified control, and by the employment of economical methods of operation, the railroads have been placed since 1896 in the best condition they have ever known, with the cheapest freight rates, the best equipment, the fastest service, and the largest dividends in the world. In this period of prosperity the great systems grew to their present transitional form.

The Vanderbilts have merely expanded a system that Commodore Vanderbilt began; the Goulds have increased and strengthened Jay Gould's system; Mr. E. H. Harriman and the interests he represents are now in possession of the Huntington roads; Mr. Cassatt and his associates have marvelously improved the Pennsylvania that Col. Thomas A. Scott and others had made a great railroad; Mr. Hill, the only railroad builder among the financial giants now owning the greater part of the transportation lines of the country, has added to the Great Northern, which he built, the Northern Pacific and the Burlington, built up by Henry Villard, John M. Forbes and other men; and Mr. J. P. Morgan typifies in his great organizing powers, even better than Mr. Harriman, the force that has taken a multitude of railroads from the hands of builders and placed them in the hands of financiers. The contemporary phase of railroad history is this last.

## Mileage Controlled by Syndicates

108

| VANDERBILT SYSTEM | | PENNSYLVANIA SYSTEM | | GOULD-ROCKEFELLER SYSTEM | | MORGAN-HILL SYSTEM | |
|---|---|---|---|---|---|---|---|
| ROAD | MILEAGE | ROAD | MILEAGE | ROAD | MILEAGE | ROAD | MILEAGE |
| New York Central System (Including the main line, the Beech Creek, the Fall Brook, the Mohawk and Malone, the New York and Harlem, the Rome, Watertown and Ogdensburg, the West Shore, and many others.) | 3,107 | Pennsylvania R. R. (east of Pittsburgh & Erie) (Including the New Jersey lines, the Allegheny Valley R. R., the Philadelphia and Erie, the Northern Central, and many others.) | 5,530 | Controlled by the Gould-Sage interests | | Controlled jointly | |
| Lake Shore & Michigan Southern | 2,084 | | | Missouri, Pacific and Iron Mountain | 5,372 | Northern Pacific (Which owns twenty-three million acres of land.) | 5,487 |
| Michigan Central (Including the Canadian Southern.) | 1,635 | Pennsylvania R. R., (west of Pittsburgh & Erie) (Including the Pennsylvania Company, the Peoria and Western, the St. Louis, Vandalia & Terre Haute, the Pittsburgh, Chicago, Cincinnati and St. Louis, the Cleveland, Akron and Columbus, the Grand Rapids and Indiana, and others.) | 4,405 | International and Great Northern | 891 | Great Northern | 5,417 |
| New York, Chicago & St. Louis. (Nickel Plate) (Including the Pittsburgh and Lake Erie.) | 523 | | | Wabash (Including the Wheeling & Lake Erie, and the Omaha and St. Louis.) | 2,968 | Chicago, Burlington and Quincy | 8,171 |
| Chicago & Northwestern (Including the Chicago, St. Paul, Minneapolis & Omaha and the Fremont, Elkhorn and Missouri Valley.) | 8,769 | | | St. Louis and Southwestern | 1,293 | Erie | 2,605 |
| Cleveland, Cincinnati, Chicago & St. Louis. (Big Four) | 2,287 | | | Texas and Pacific | 1,619 | Lehigh Valley | 2,178 |
| Boston and Albany | 394 | Long Island | 391 | Rockefeller and Gould interests | | Controlled by Mr. Morgan | |
| Lake Erie & Western | 725 | Baltimore and Ohio (Including the Cleveland, Lorain and Wheeling, the B. & O. Southwestern, and others.) | 4,025 | Missouri, Kansas and Texas | 2,480 | Philadelphia and Reading (Including the Central of New Jersey.) | 1,677 |
| | | | | Denver & Rio Grande (Including the Rio Grande Western.) | 2,301 | Hocking Valley (Including the Toledo and Ohio Central, and the Kanawha and Michigan.) | 882 |
| | | | | | | Chicago, Indianapolis and Louisville | 546 |
| | | | | | | Southern Railway (Including the Central of Georgia, the Alabama, Great Southern, the Cincinnati, New Orleans and Texas Pacific, and the Mobile and Ohio.) | 10,627 |
| Total Mileage | 19,524 | Total Mileage | 14,351 | Total Mileage | 16,924 | Total Mileage | 37,590 |

## CONTROLLED JOINTLY BY THE PENNSYLVANIA AND THE NEW YORK CENTRAL

| ROAD | MILE-AGE |
|---|---|
| Chesapeake and Ohio | 1,616 |
| Norfork & Western | 1,685 |
| Total Mileage | 3,301 |

## BELMONT SYSTEM

| ROAD | MILE-AGE |
|---|---|
| Louisville and Nashville | 5,188 |
| Nashville, Chattanooga and St. Louis | 935 |
| Total Mileage | 6,123 |

## HARRIMAN-KUHN-LOEB SYSTEM

| ROAD | MILE-AGE |
|---|---|
| Union Pacific (Including the Southern Pacific, the Oregon R. R. and Navigation Co., and the Oregon Short Line.) | 15,163 |
| Chicago and Alton | 918 |
| Illinois Central | 5,000 |
| Kansas City Southern | 873 |
| Total Mileage | 21,954 |

## IMPORTANT INDEPENDENT SYSTEMS

| ROAD | MILE-AGE |
|---|---|
| Atchison, Topeka and Santa Fe | 7,481 |
| Chicago, Rock Island and Pacific | 3,818 |
| St. Louis and San Francisco | 2,887 |
| Colorado and Southern | 1,142 |
| Chicago, Milwaukee and St. Paul | 6,461 |
| Pere Marquette | 1,747 |
| Atlantic Coast Line | 2,177 |
| Seaboard Air Line | 2,600 |
| Plant System | 2,207 |
| New York, New Haven and Hartford | 2,038 |
| Boston and Maine | 3,338 |
| Total Mileage | 35,896 |

An approximately accurate list of the systems grown great by consolidation accounts for over 150,000 miles of the 200,000 miles in the country as shown in [ the table on pages 108–109.]

Clear-headed financiers set about devising some means of stopping the rate-cutting that under the anti-pooling and anti-trust laws was driving the roads into bankruptcy. Whether Mr. Huntington or Mr. Morgan first evolved the community-of-interest idea, it was already in the air. The result was consolidation from 1896 to the present at an unprecedented speed. The Santa Fé was expanded by the merging of lines from a road of 471 miles in 1896 to one that now measures nearly 7,500 miles and reaches the Pacific Coast. By lease the New York Central acquired the Boston and Albany and thus reached Boston, a port whose business is rapidly increasing; and by purchase of a majority of the stock the Union Pacific gained control of the Southern Pacific. Syndicates represented by houses like J. P. Morgan & Company secured reorganized roads by such processes as getting themselves appointed voting trusts with power to manage the road for the stockholders. All these were common enough forms of consolidation. The community-of-interest idea exemplified by the New York Central and the Pennsylvania in the Trunk Line district and the Chicago & Northwestern and the St. Paul in the Old Northwest is a newer policy. In this community-of-interest arrangement the controllers of Railroad A own some stock in Railroad B, possibly have directors on the board, and the result is an understanding between the roads, without an actual community of ownership and without any pool within the meaning of the law. In the form of control illustrated by the Northern Securities Company a company is formed for the sole purpose of holding the securities of a number of roads—community-of-interest carried to the point of legal recognition and chartered responsibility. With full understanding, like that in the Harriman-Kühn-Loeb syndicate, such control is the closest form of community-of-interest holding. All these forms of combination have been recently exploited so fast as actually to double the mileage of roads like the Union Pacific and the Pennsylvania in the course of a year or two.

Clearly to understand the railroad situation in the United States, the country may be roughly divided by a line drawn from San Francisco through St. Louis to Newport News, and another down the Mississippi Valley from Chicago to Galveston, making four railroad districts. Through the Northwestern section run two vast railroads that strike westward from St. Paul to connect with steamships for the Orient at Seattle. Over them went the settlers that many "feeders" distributed in the prairie and mountain States, and east and west in long lines of heavy freight cars go the wheat and all the rich products of the great farms of the world, that these colonists win from the land. One of the roads, the Northern Pacific, still owns twenty-three million acres that will one day be settled. Connecting at Chicago for the East over the Erie, the Great Northern and the Northern Pacific furnish a line controlled by two men, Mr. Morgan and Mr. Hill, which not only runs from coast to coast, but connects at each terminal with steamship lines controlled by the same men, thus reaching more than half way round the world. In the Southern section Mr. Morgan has so firm a grasp . . . that it looks as if he would in time dominate the region. As the Southern Railway, moreover, connects with other Morgan roads running as far north as Buffalo, the Hill-Morgan interests are impregnably fortified in two of the four great railroad divisions, with outlets at all main ports.

In the Southwest the Harriman system grows stronger as the new line from Salt Lake creeps through the sage-brush toward Los Angeles. Up and down the Mississippi runs the Illinois Central, west of the Morgan sphere of control, and east of the Gould sphere. The possession of the shortest line from Chicago to the Pacific Coast via the Union Pacific and the Central Pacific throws a monopoly of transportation west of Ogden into the hands of the Harriman interests, possession of the shortest line from Denver to the Northwest gives domination along that avenue, and the Southern Pacific and its connections follow a nearly straight line from New Orleans to San Diego, and thence to Portland, Oregon. The Gould system, strong in the eastern part of the Southwest, is reaching out to the coasts by the Denver & Rio Grande in one direction, and by the Wabash in the other.

In what is known as the Trunk Line district the Vanderbilt and Pennsylvania systems dominate, with an outlet for the Vanderbilt lines to Boston, and feeders in the Hill-Morgan territory in the Old Northwest as far as St. Paul.

The very unsatisfactory and incomplete state of this whole arrangement is convincing enough evidence of its instability, even if there were not vigorous warfare going on or alliances in process of making to strengthen the position that each system holds.

In the Trunk Line district, President Cassatt of the Pennsylvania Railroad, and the Vanderbilts of the New York Central, have so carefully fostered pleasant relations by acquiring in common the Chesapeake & Ohio and Norfolk & Western to exploit the coal regions without friction, that the New York Central has been left to its far-reaching improvements, and the Pennsylvania to its vast expansion and its great undertakings, with no fear of war. But as the Hocking Valley, the Erie and the Lehigh, Morgan roads, compete with these larger systems; as the Lackawanna, a Rockefeller road, though acting in harmony with the New York Central is really an independent factor; and as the Gould roads, already assured of entrance into Pittsburgh over the Pittsburgh, Carnegie & Western, are said to be seeking, thence, a line to New York, there is still room for the extension of the community-of-interest principle.

In the South four independent roads, the Louisville & Nashville, the Atlantic Coast Line, the Seaboard Air Line and the Plant System, and the Illinois Central as well, dispute the control of Mr. Morgan's Southern Railway. . . .

In the West there has been open warfare. There is still rate-cutting in the region, and there has been also battling for control. The spectacular feature of the contest has been the rise of Mr. E. H. Harriman as a railroad man.

When Mr. C. P. Huntington was building the Southern Pacific and Mr. J. J. Hill the Great Northern, Mr. J. P. Morgan was a New York banker with a reputation as a financial organizer, and Mr. E. H. Harriman was another New York banker known among railroad men as the Vice-president of the Illinois Central. In the reorganization of the Northern Pacific by J. P. Morgan & Company, Mr. Hill and his friends bought more than a quarter of a million dollars' worth of stock in the reorganized road, which, after a brief competition with the Great Northern, practically joined forces with it. In the reorganization of the Union Pacific Mr. Harriman came into prominence by acquiring with Kühn, Loeb & Company the control of the line.

After Mr. Huntington died the Harriman interests by a brilliant financial coup obtained a majority of the Southern Pacific stock for the Union Pacific, and took over the system that Mr. Huntington had hoped would perpetuate his name. The inside history of the scattering of the Huntington control is a tale of a great opportunity lost by one syndicate and snapped up by another in a moment. By acquiring the Oregon Short Line and the Oregon Railroad & Navigation Company, the Harriman-Kühn-Loeb syndicate became master of all Pacific Coast traffic south of Portland, with the exception of that pursuing the Santa Fé route, completed not long before. Last May came the tug-of-war. Mr. Hill invaded Union Pacific territory by buying the Burlington. Mr. Harriman retaliated by buying control of Mr. Hill's Northern Pacific, though the stock was "skied" to a thousand dollars a share in the operation. To adjust the trouble Mr. Morgan organized the Northern Securities Company, with a capitalization of $400,000,000, to hold the securities of the Northern Pacific, the Great Northern and the Burlington; and Mr. Harriman, Mr. Stillman and Mr. Schiff, of the Union Pacific, were made directors. Though this would seem to have ended the war, the retirement of the Northern Pacific preferred stock, now accomplished—the stock that gave the Union Pacific its control in Northern Pacific— may affect in no small measure the position of the Union Pacific in the Securities Company. It looks at the time of writing, then, as if the Hill-Morgan combination had secured a line competing with the Union Pacific by extending to them a community of interest which they did not desire to possess.

The key to the Western situation is the independent Santa Fé. Whichever interest secures it will dominate the Western trade. The Gould system, moreover, may build from its Western terminals to the Pacific Coast, just as it is said to be aiming at an Atlantic outlet by purchase. Western railroad affairs, accordingly, are highly unsettled. There is much competition. The decrease in business due to the partial failure of the corn crop has led to rate-cutting. Some community-of-interest *modus vivendi* can hardly be long delayed.

Here, then, is a vast continent belted and banded and criss-crossed with 200,000 miles of railroads. Many of the roads are great independent lines, and some are systems controlled by groups of men outside the five large syndicates. But practically half the stupendous network, affecting in one way or another every inhabitant in the country, is in possession of five little bodies of men with headquarters in New York. A strip of land hundreds of miles wide, beginning at the Washington ports in the Northwest and sweeping east to the lakes, is practically an industrial fief of Mr.

Hill and Mr. Morgan. In Mr. Harriman's hands in some measure is the prosperity of California and the Southwestern States, as well as of a broad strip up the Mississippi Valley, a fertile band through the prairie States, and all the habitable land reaching west from the Rockies to the coast. The Central Atlantic States live to the rhythm of the New York Central and the Pennsylvania Railroad. It is true that one can go from Boston to San Francisco, from the Gulf to St. Paul, and travel not a mile on the roads of the railroad giants, but only through a very narrow pathway and for the most part within view of competing syndicate lines on either side. . . . When it is remembered, furthermore, that Morgan men are directors in Vanderbilt roads, Hill men in Pennsylvania roads, Gould men in Harriman roads, and that every other possible inter-weaving of common control exists throughout the great groups, the lines of demarcation melt away and we see dimly outlined a condition of affairs which may possibly take the hue of monopoly.

Thus far the unification of control has been a blessing. Where many sets of railroad officials formerly managed many roads from many centres, one set now manages a single system from a single headquarters. That means economy. The other day, for example, the Burlington, directed before the merger from three widely separated offices, concentrated its management in Chicago. Nor does such concentration spell the elimination of employees; the expansion of the railroad army at the rate of 240 men a day shows the opposite tendency. Vast capital has permitted of improved rails, bridges, locomotives and cars, the building of efficient ter-minals and the straightening of lines. Efficient management has produced such economical methods that foreign railroad men come here as to a school of railroading. And since unification of control is by no means synonymous with unification of ownership, the insurance companies, the savings banks, the trust companies and private individuals reap in the increased value of the stocks and bonds they own the benefits of the improvements. Skilful opera-tion has resulted in lower freight and passenger rates, so that shippers and travelers have prospered with the prosperity of the rail-roads.

Twenty years ago shippers and even whole districts suffered from unfair discriminations in competitive regions, and from almost prohibitive rates in regions where single roads possessed a monop-oly. The railroads of the country were carrying about thirty-five million tons of freight at a cent and a quarter a ton for each mile. Now the average rate is a little over seven mills and the tonnage is more than one hundred and forty millions. The tonnage has gradually increased; the rate has gradually gone down. The passenger rate has likewise gone down, and the passenger traffic is growing fifty million a year. Immigrants have been carried at a rate on which there is practically no profit, to develop the country fed by Mr. Hill's lines, just as Mr. Huntington carried them into California. Branch lines open up districts everywhere. Not all of the growth that this economy has produced came about through consolidation, for there are many independent roads that are run efficiently, cheaply and profitably, but it is beyond question that consolidation has been the main impetus to it all.

The railroad problem consists of working out the best method of conserving the advantages gained and securing more without allowing any institution to arise that shall injure the Republic. The Northwestern Governors believe that the way to do it is to go back to competition. Railroad men and the Interstate Commerce Commission favor pooling. A return to competition is a return to a wasteful economic condition. It will never pay either stockholders or shippers to have freight hauled over a mountain road, simply to preserve the competitive principle, if there is a valley road alongside. Pooling might preserve the status quo for a time, but it may be questioned how long it would last. Suppose the case of a pooling arrangement between the Southern Pacific and the Union Pacific two years ago. Would that have prevented the Harriman interests from securing the road when the time was ripe? A pooling arrangement, moreover, is wasteful in cases where a direct line divides freight with a roundabout line that cannot haul it so cheaply. The shipper, in the long run, pays for the waste. We may have a pooling law or not: the economic saving produced by monopoly is a strong enough incentive to bring about monopoly, law or no law. Whether it will be a private monopoly or a Government monopoly remains to be seen.

# III. THE EMERGENCE OF MODERN INDUSTRY

## 7. The Threshold of the Electrical Age

Thomas Alva Edison's invention of the electric incandescent lamp, patented in 1879, and the central generating station he opened in New York City in 1882, required a complex system of technology that swiftly called into being a new industry. When Edison's financial backers, among them J. P. Morgan, refused to furnish additional money for both his central station project and the manufacturing plants to supply the needed equipment, the inventor organized his own companies. Among these enterprises was the Edison Machine Works in Manhattan. The advent of electric street traction and a practical system of alternating current in 1885–1887 created a vast and immediate need for electrical power that heralded the end of the Age of Steam. The sudden boom in business so quickly overtaxed the facilities of the Edison manufacturing works that late in 1886 Samuel Insull, Edison's business aide, purchased a former locomotive shop in Schenectady, New York, and moved the Edison Machine Works and other units to it. The Schenectady plant, managed by Insull, opened with a force of two hundred workers. By 1892, when it was absorbed by the newly organized General Electric Company, it had six thousand employees. Few industries in late nineteenth-century America grew as fast as electrical manufacturing.

SOURCE: "A Day With Edison at Schenectady," *Electrical World*, XII (August 25, 1888), Supplement, 1–3, 5, 10–12.

PASSING swiftly through the suburbs of the sedate old city of Schenectady, on the New York Central Railroad . . . one's attention is arrested by a huge range of factory buildings and by the numerous signs of pressing activity in and around them. Massive and handsome, lifting themselves boldly up from the level meadows

of the Mohawk Valley, their appearance, as one after another of
the roofs swings into the line of vision, arouses curiosity, for it is
easily to be seen that the place is the home of an industrial enterprise of no mean order. . . . Beyond the factory, as it lies solidly
athwart the view, with its long facade to the railroad and its remote rear bordered by the Erie Canal, winds and doubles the
placid Mohawk River, hemmed in by green banks and girdled by
uprolling mountains well away to the northward. There, in the
legendary background, the atmosphere hangs drowsily, as well it
might, over the quaint homesteads built by the ancestors and off-
spring of sundry Rip Van Winkles; but here the air is astir with
the sharp outburst of steam and smoke and athrob with the pulsa-
tion of machinery. There, along the circuitous highways, the heavy
wagons, with heavier teams, are hauling slowly to market the
growth of farm and make of dairy; but here in the forefront, and
fixing the eye as insistent energy and bustle always do, especially
when on the grand scale, are trains of freight cars alive with men
unloading raw material at the factory yard, while others at half a
dozen different points are carrying away the finished product of
the works.

. . . We are looking at one of the greatest exemplifications of
the power of American inventive genius, and at an establishment
where, from beginning to end, a new art is illustrated by new
processes. One would hardly seek for the latest developments of
scientific discovery and engineering skill in this peaceful rural
region; but they are here, and amid people and scenes that even
in Europe would wear an ancient air, we can watch the manufacture of the novel appliances of modern electricity. It is, indeed,
not a little singular that the quiet city of Schenectady, seated by
the still waters of the Mohawk . . . and the center of a rich dairy
district, should have become closely identified with the most striking advances in American commerce and manufacture. Not only
were its fortunes at one time fostered by the opening of the Erie
Canal, whose importance even at the present time is so great, but
it built some of the earliest locomotives, and nearly sixty years
ago it was running passenger trains to and from Albany. To-day
it has as its most prominent and prosperous industry the manufacture of dynamo-electric machines, electric motors and kindred
apparatus in an establishment over which floats the name of
Edison.

There are few chapters in American national life so interesting as those which concern the careers of the inventors—the men who have revolutionized the world by their genius and their skill. If ours be an industrial civilization, wherein each discovery that makes for the welfare, comfort and broader information of the people is a victory over the brute forces of nature, then the scientists and inventors fighting for every new foothold of truth and struggling to master some new fact, must be accounted the worthiest heroes and the essential rulers. . . .

No one, we believe, will deny to Mr. Edison his well-earned position among these men who shape the times; and it certainly cannot be gainsaid that in the popular mind and estimation his name has been peculiarly and distinctively associated with the great electrical arts and applications that belong to the last twenty-five years. . . . If reckoning be made of all the various factories in America, Europe and Asia, where Edison inventions are manufactured, it will be found that a total of several thousand artisans is easily reached. Of these establishments, one of the most extensive and noteworthy is . . . the Edison Machine Works at Schenectady.

If the reader will take the trouble to run through the pages of Dr. Benson Lossing's admirable *History of American Industries and Arts*, issued at the time of the Centennial Exposition, he will discover that complete as the work is it makes no mention of dynamo building. The fact is significant as to the youth of the new industry and as to its growth. The case in point illustrates some stages of the evolution. The Edison Machine Works represent the amalgamation of three businesses, all based on the dynamo. One was the old Edison Machine Works at Goerck street, New York, founded and owned by Mr. Edison, and started in March, 1881. The second was the Electric Tube Company, of which Mr. John Kruesi was manager, with factories first in New York and then in Brooklyn; and the third was the Edison Shafting Company, which was carried on as a department of Goerck street. The company representing these combined interests removed to Schenectady in December, 1886, prosecuting its work with such vigor that inside of the first year the plants and tools were reinstalled, the shops were reorganized, and treble the business was done.

. . . The property [of the Works] is triangular in shape and covers thirteen acres, of which about five acres are under cover, there being, all told, twenty-six separate buildings in use. The chief boundaries are the New York Central Railroad, the Delaware & Hudson Canal Company Railroad, with both of which there are siding connections, and the Erie Canal, on which the Works have a fine dock frontage. It will be seen, therefore, that the situation is eminently favorable for the handling of freight, and the advantages have been enhanced by the laying of rails all through the yards and shops. There is a total of nearly two miles of track, and the finished product can be loaded into the cars at five different shipping points.

As regards prime power, the Works are well equipped. There are two Brown engines of 100 h.p. each, one of which, it is interesting to note, by the way, was brought from Mr. Edison's well-known old laboratory and workshops at Menlo Park. These are in the principal machine shops. There is also a Straight Line engine of 100 h.p., which operates the foundry and supplies light, running twenty-two hours a day. Another Straight Line engine of 50 h.p. is in use in the dynamo testing department, and the shops Nos. 3 and 6 are driven by large Edison dynamos employed as motors. Steam is furnished by two extensive boiler rooms, the main one being attached to shop No. 1, while the other adjoins the foundry. The piping is so arranged as to take steam from any boiler to any engine. The boilers not only feed the engines but warm the buildings in winter, overhead heating being successfully employed. The exhaust is used, supplemented whenever necessary by live steam. Light is given by about 900 Edison lamps scattered throughout the factory, while gas is put to its appropriate duty by being used as fuel. The Works make their own fuel gas, and it is in great demand for heating and manufacturing purposes. The supply of coal is conveniently and cheaply maintained. Water is drawn from a series of no fewer than twenty driven wells all over the works, and a partial supply comes also from the city water-works. Provision against fire is made with the large tank . . . having a capacity of 20,000 gallons.

The Works employ from 750 to 850 hands, according to the season of the year, and at the time of the writer's visit, about 775 were on the rolls. Work is chiefly done on the contract basis. There are occupied on the business of the Works, outside, from 50 to 100 employes. Large as this force may seem, there is every promise of an increase, and the Works are now in course of extension. Although the products of the Works are in a sense restricted, as no lamps or fixtures are made here, the business has several very distinct departments, any one of which would suffice to tax the highest executive ability. These departments include the building of Edison dynamos; the construction of Sprague electric motors for stationary and street railway work; the manufacture of Edison electric tubes for underground work; every branch of the insulated wire business for all classes of service; Sims-Edison torpedo work; the Edison processes for dealing with refractory ores; and a general business in shafting, pulleys and hangers, and in millwright and foundry work. It is always gratifying to see a self-centered and sel-contained establishment such as is here found. The company purchase[s] only pig-iron, bare copper wire, copper ingot and rough forgings, and these passing through the various stages and complemented by the different parts that go to form the whole, come out in shapes of beauty and utility.

. . . [The No. 2 Machine Shop] is not less than 122 feet wide and 306 feet long. . . . Its central aisle is 40 feet wide, and there is a cathedral-like airiness and distance in its long perspectives. Five hundred men can easily find elbow room here for their work, with all the machinery. . . . Here are 6,000 feet of shafting and some 50,000 feet of belting, driving nearly 400 separate mechanisms, in the production of apparatus whose birth was yesterday. Right and left are gigantic machine tools of every kind and style; here a planer 60 by 60 inches and 32 feet long; there a special boring mill, built to order at a cost of $6,000. The value of the tools, in fact, runs up into hundreds of thousands of dollars, and their multiplicity is understood on looking at the variety and extent of the work in hand. At one end of the shop immense pulleys and lines of shafting are passing through the necessary processes, and a quantity of gearing for electric street cars is being cut. As a rule there are from 200 to 250 dynamos in course of assembling in the central aisle. The Works not only build dynamos of the standard Edison type, but often are called upon to meet special wants. Such are ship lighters, run at slow speed and connecting directly to the engine, and those for the United States cruiser *Yorktown* were seen in course of construction. Others, of quite another type, are those generating current for telegraph circuits. . . . Altogether, at the time of the writer's visit, 262 dynamos were under way, varying in capacity from 5 ampères to 1,000; about 200 stationary motors, from ½ to 20 h.p., and more than that number of street car motors of 7½ h.p. each. The largest Edison dynamo then building was a giant of 1,000 ampères and 140 volts, known as No. 56. Its weight, roughly, is 27,500 pounds. . . . Eight of these machines were being pushed through for the new Edison central station at Philadelphia. The machines to be used in the New York stations are . . . known as No. 32's; the weight is 16,200 pounds and the output is 575 ampères at 140 volts. . . .

One might linger in this shop a week, so endless are the points of interest that it presents. A casual question as to some strange tool elicits the information that the company construct all their own tools here, except those ordinarily to be had in the market. All the machinery for the foundry department is made here, and a month or two ago upon the receipt of an order for 25,000 feet of a specially insulated cable, the machinery was at once designed and built on the spot. Resources of this nature give an establishment courage and daring for the most onerous enterprises. It should be added that in this shop also the commutators for the dynamos and motors are made—mica being used between the bars —and the general work of assembling is done. By means of the overhead power traveler, handling ten tons, the big machine, whose bed-plate, fields, pole pieces, keeper and bearings were widely scattered a few hours since, is hoisted into line as a solid entity, and if need be, before the night whistle blows, it will be fitted with its armature and be far on its way to the place where work awaits it. . . .

[In 1882 the Edison Electric Illuminating Company of New York opened the Pearl Street central station in downtown Manhattan. It was the first city generating station in America for the sale and distribution of electric light and power.]

. . . To-day the station started . . . in 1882 is still in operation, and as we look around the big machine shop where the dynamos are constructed, we are reminded at every turn of the extension that the business has enjoyed. The Pearl street station was a notable installation in its day, and has its place in the history of the art, but one needs only to visit it to become informed as to the advancement that has been made, and that is illustrated also by these machines around us for the new stations in New York, Chicago and Philadelphia. With the equipping of Pearl street station began that part of the operations of the Machine Works. In 1883 the dynamos were supplied for the central station at

Roselle, N. J., on the two-wire system, and then a little later that year were built those for the first station on the three-wire system at Sunbury, Pa. Now the list of stations began to lengthen, with Brockton and Fall River in Massachusetts, Piqua, Circleville, Tiffin and Middletown in Ohio, and Mt. Carmel, Ashland and Shamokin in Pennsylvania. Up to the present time, the Works have built machines for no fewer than 140 stations in this country, as stated before. These stations are to be found in all parts of the Union, utilizing every kind of prime power, from crude petroleum and natural gas to waterfalls and artesian wells, in addition to steam engines of all the well-known and approved makes. The Works have latterly been required also to furnish dynamos of the municipal type, giving an electromotive force of 1,200 volts, for street lighting plants, such as those at Rochester, N.Y.; Denver, Col.; Lockport, N.Y.; Reading, Pa.; Somerville, Mass. The Lockport plant was started as long ago as 1885 by the local gas company, which says: "We find that whether for streets or for interiors the sale of electric light is more profitable to us than gas."

It is in connection with this central station business that a remarkable development affecting the Works is going on. Slowly but surely the stations are getting upon their proper basis of supplying current, not simply for lighting, but for all the other demands that may arise for it. A station is no longer a place where intense activity for five or six hours is succeeded by leisure and dullness the rest of the twenty-four. The telegraph office, requiring current for its circuits; the telephone exchange, with its magnetos to be run; the medical establishment, with patients to be cured by electricity; the printing offices, the ice cream saloons, the buildings with elevators, the wood-working factories, the chemical works with bad ventilation, the jeweler's workshop, the clothier's store— each of these and hundreds of other places need current all day long for direct use or to drive motors, and they are all becoming customers of the central stations. The Edison Machine Works have within the last year, besides building a large number of special generators, sent out thousands of horsepower of Sprague motors to these stations, and the tasks to which the motors are put multiply daily. To Laramie motors have gone to operate a large flouring mill and a rolling mill. At Hutchinson and Abilene, in Kansas, as well as at Detroit, the motors are printing daily papers, and they are also running newspaper presses at Elgin, Ill.; New Brunswick,

N.J.; Cincinnati, O., and other places. At Des Moines, Ia., the motor, with its current from the central station, brushes down the horses, while at Pawtucket, R.I., it follows the dusty trade of stone-cutting. It is now not at all an unusual thing to go into an office which ought to be hot and there be saluted with a refreshing breeze which comes from one of these motors stowed away with a fan up in some corner. In these and similar ways, the use of motors is so rapidly on the increase that, to go no further, there is already promise that before 1890 all the Edison stations will have been supplied from the Machine Works with motors for day service, up to the limit of their generating capacity, while in several stations an increase in plant will have been rendered necessary by the demand for electric motive power. The significance of this development is quite beyond estimation.

So much for the great central stations of the day, as here illustrated by the work doing on their account. The record is impressive, but it has a counterpart in the output of machines for isolated lighting. At this moment there are not far short of 1,500 isolated Edison plants running in the United States alone. The first commercial plant of this kind is said to have been that installed on board the steamer *Columbia* for the Oregon Railway and Navigation Company in 1879. Now over 90 steamships, yachts, ferryboats, men-of-war and other craft in our waters enjoy the light —such craft as Jay Gould's *Atalanta*, James Gordon Bennett's *Namouna*, and William Astor's *Nourmahal*, being on the list, in company with the noble Sound steamer *Pilgrim* and the gorgeous *Monmouth*; the war ships *Trenton* and *Dolphin*. The Works have also built dynamos for a number of foreign vessels in the different navies, as well as in the mercantile marine. Several of the dynamos now in hand are for mills and factories, and some conception of the vogue enjoyed by the light among manufacturers and others may be formed when we state that the Works have furnished machines for more than 160 cotton, woolen and textile fabric mills; nearly 70 flour mills and grain elevators; just upon 100 iron works, car shops and machine shops; over 60 furniture and other woodworking establishments; about 100 miscellaneous factories, etc.; more than 50 newspaper and publishing offices; some 70 asylums and public institutions; a round 50 theatres and places of amusement; nearly 250 banks, clubs, apartment houses, office buildings and fine residences; and paper mills, oil refineries, pumping stations, special works and the like to the number of 300 or 400 more. Such figures explain of themselves the activity which we have already noted as so characteristic of the Works. Some of these plants are, in fact, larger than an average central station and often include half a dozen dynamos. Thus the plant of the "Dakota" apartment house and the streets adjoining, in this city, is of 5,000 lights capacity. That of the beautiful Hotel Ponce de Leon and Alcazar, at St. Augustine, runs up to 4,100 lights. The isolated plant of the Astor building in Wall street, this city, is used for nearly 1,400 lights; the Custom-house at New Orleans has 1,200; the new "Rookery," at Chicago, represents 4,000. A recent order received at the Works is for dynamos to operate what will be when finished by far the largest isolated plant in existence, that of the new Auditorium in Chicago. Among the mills, there are a great many big plants, to which from time to time a new machine is added. The success of the electric light in the mills has been perhaps as pronounced as anywhere else, and a trip by night through New England reveals building after building brilliant with the electrics flashing into sight, until it looks as though no other illuminant were known or tolerated by the busy manufacturers in that section of the country. It may be mentioned that the business of supplying isolated plants was undertaken at first by the Edison Company for Isolated Lighting, in 1881, but since 1886 it has been carried on by the Edison United Manufacturing Company.

Beyond this demand for machines from central stations and isolated plants, there comes a steady flow of orders from abroad. This is one of the facts that speaks volumes for the progress made by America in electrical arts. There is no denying the popularity abroad of American electric lighting apparatus. According to the popular idea, our ingenuity is most typically represented in the export trade by sewing-machines, street cars, axes and Yankee clocks. Well, each of these is a good exemplar in its way of the manner in which, through the ability of its inventors and mechanics, America bids fair to monopolize in time some leading branches of industry, but recognition is certainly due of the preference manifested in Europe and other quarters of the globe for American electrical apparatus. From these Works, for example, machines have been dispatched to regions as remote as Finland, China, Brazil and South Africa. The demand for electric lighting in South America may be said to be wholly met from this country, and the machines undergo all the trials of a long sea voyage as well as the handling of inexpert natives. A large contract filled not long since at Schenectady was for a plant for Tokyo, Japan, where light is now being supplied to the Mikado and to a large portion of the city. Even the "hermit kingdom" of Korea has sent orders to the Works. . . .

As likely as not the visitor who reached the Works early in the day to find everything at the highest pitch of activity, leaves them at night still in the full tide of productiveness, for the inrush of new business allows of little lull or rest. After all, the work to do has been but barely touched, the experimental stages have scarcely been past, and the pioneers are still among us. Millions of incandescent lamps are burning, and thousands of dynamos are throwing their currents into the mazes and miles of circuits of our great cities, but that is only the beginning. Electric motors are now in use everywhere, but their number for power purposes is to increase in a geometrical ratio for years to come, and their superiority for urban passenger traffic is only just across the threshold of its triumphant demonstration.

# 8. Iron and Steel

This rise of the United States in 1870–1900 to the position of the world's leading industrial power was largely the result of its primacy in iron and steel production. During this period the improved Bessemer process was the most common method of making steel, and when the United States, in 1886, overtook Great Britain in steel output, new mills using Bessemer converters were under construction in the major producing areas of the Middle Atlantic states and the Great Lakes region. The Siemens-Martin open-hearth furnace did not become important here until Andrew Carnegie installed his first one at the Homestead Works in 1888. The production of open-hearth steel increased in the 1890's, and by 1910 had taken a commanding lead over Bessemer output. American supremacy in steel-making owed much to improved technology, especially larger and more efficient furnaces generating more heat with less fuel and using coke instead of coal. Until the late 1880's the demand for steel rails for new construction, double trackage, and replacement continued to be the largest single market for steel in the

United States. Specialized production, coinciding with a declining demand for rails, was a response to diversified need, and as 1900 approached the large consolidated enterprises were turning out steel tubes, tin plate, ordnance and armor plate, structural shapes, wire, alloy steel, and bridge iron.

SOURCE: All the selections are from the Commercial and Financial Chronicle: for I, Vol. XLII (February 13, 1886), 199–200; for II and III, Vol. XLIV (February 5, 12, 1887), 163–5, 198–9; for IV, Vol. LX (March 2, 1895), 373.

I

. . . It is true that up to the present time iron has been regarded as the so-called barometer of our industries, but with the increasing uses to which steel is being put and the cheapening of its manufacture, the time may not be far distant when iron will be supplanted by steel, and the latter be accepted as the guide—as far as any one trade can be a guide—to our industrial condition.

But be that as it may, it is a fact that while in the case of iron the production for 1885 was considerably below the best previous total, in the case of steel the production of ingots in that year was the largest on record. Nor is this all. New steel plants are being put up all sections of the country. In the Bulletin of the Steel Association for February 10, 1886, we find no less than 13 works for the manufacture of Bessemer steel that have either recently been completed or are in process of construction and expect to be in operation some time in the present year. These new works are going up in a great many different States—Pennsylvania, New York, New Jersey, Ohio, Illinois, West Virginia—and it is true, as the Bulletin says, that the Bessemer steel industry is no longer confined to a few establishments located in three or four States.

With this great increase in the producing capacity, speculation might be indulged in as to whether there was not danger of an oversupply, except that it is so evident that the demand has also in very decided measure increased. It must be remembered too that these new plants do not cover any particular kind of product, but embrace various and different kinds. Quite a number are to be used in the manufacture of ingots for rolling into nail plate, but others cover steel for structural purposes, for wire rods, for boiler plates, for sheets, bars, &c. Indeed, the distinctive feature not only of the new works, but of the old works and their production in recent years, is the increasing proportion of the steel devoted to miscellaneous uses. The Bessemer steel process, as is known, has been free to the use of all for some years—the patents having run out—and this process has, of course, greatly cheapened the manufacture of steel, and, besides, with each year steel is being adapted to new and wider uses. Then the diminished demand for rails, to which the old plants were originally almost exclusively devoted, has induced many of the producers to seek and find other outlets for the capacity of their works. Contemporaneously, and because of the fall in price and the cheapening of the manufacture, steel has been extensively substituted for iron, being more durable and for many purposes much more desirable.

In the matter of rails, it has almost altogether supplanted iron, as we show below, but of course the demand for rails had been so unduly stimulated and inflated during the years 1881–82, by our excessive railroad construction, that even with the replacement for iron the present production of steel rails falls far below the total then reached. This, however, makes the fact that the production of all kinds of steel (including the decreasing total of rails), is larger than ever before, all the more noteworthy, and emphasizes the growth that has taken place in the use of the same for miscellaneous purposes. Here is a table showing the production of Bessemer steel ingots in the United States in each year since 1874, in net tons of 2,000 pounds, and also the principal States among which it was distributed. It should be stated that very little is produced by the open hearth or any other process than the Bessemer.

| Production of Bessemer steel ingots | Net Tons of 2,000 Pounds | | | |
|---|---|---|---|---|
| | Pennsylvania | Illinois | Other states | Total |
| 1874 | 85,625 | 62,492 | 43,816 | 191,933 |
| 1875 | 148,374 | 136,356 | 90,787 | 375,517 |
| 1876 | 258,452 | 171,963 | 95,581 | 525,993 |
| 1877 | 328,599 | 111,299 | 120,689 | 560,587 |
| 1878 | 426,481 | 179,500 | 126,245 | 732,226 |
| 1879 | 514,165 | 250,980 | 163,827 | 928,972 |
| 1880 | 643,894 | 304,614 | 254,665 | 1,203,173 |
| 1881 | 844,501 | 375,763 | 318,893 | 1,539,157 |
| 1882 | 933,631 | 397,436 | 365,383 | 1,696,450 |
| 1883 | 1,044,396 | 273,325 | 336,906 | 1,654,627 |
| 1884 | 1,031,484 | 339,068 | 170,043 | 1,540,595 |
| 1885 | 1,109,034 | 366,659 | 226,064 | 1,701,757 |

It will be seen that the production has steadily increased year by year, 1883 and 1884 being the only exceptions, and that now the yearly total reaches 1,701,757 tons, against only 191,933 tons but eleven years ago, in 1874. The increase over 1884 alone was 161,000 tons. In this steady extension of the production have we not a modifying cause for any set-back that pig iron production may have received? To prove that this growth in steel, in the more recent years at least, has not been in the item of rails, we now give the following statement of the yearly production of steel rails in the same years. The statement embraces also rails produced by the open hearth process, and likewise iron rails. In a word, it shows the total production of rails in each year since 1874.

| | | Net Tons of 2,000 Pounds | | | |
|---|---|---|---|---|---|
| Production of rails | Bessemer steel | Open-hearth steel | Total steel | Iron rails, all kinds | Total iron and steel |
| 1874 | 144,944 | ..... | 144,944 | 584,469 | 729,413 |
| 1875 | 290,863 | ..... | 290,863 | 501,649 | 792,512 |
| 1876 | 412,461 | ..... | 412,461 | 467,168 | 879,629 |
| 1877 | 432,169 | ..... | 432,169 | 332,540 | 764,709 |
| 1878 | 550,398 | 9,397 | 559,795 | 322,890 | 882,685 |
| 1879 | 683,964 | 9,149 | 693,113 | 420,160 | 1,113,273 |
| 1880 | 954,460 | 13,615 | 968,075 | 493,762 | 1,461,837 |
| 1881 | 1,330,302 | 25,217 | 1,355,519 | 488,581 | 1,844,100 |
| 1882 | 1,438,155 | 22,765 | 1,460,920 | 227,874 | 1,688,794 |
| 1883 | 1,286,554 | 9,186 | 1,295,740 | 64,954 | 1,360,694 |
| 1884 | 1,116,621 | 2,670 | 1,119,291 | 25,560 | 1,144,851 |
| 1885 | 1,074,607 | 1,400 | 1,076,007 | 14,692 | 1,090,699 |

Thus while the out-turn of steel ingots in 1885 was 161,000 tons larger than in 1884 and 5,000 tons larger than in 1882, the quantity of these ingots converted into rails was 42,000 tons less than in the previous year, and 364,000 tons less than in 1882—that is to say, the increase in the use of steel for other purposes has apparently increased that much in the three years. To state it in another way, of the 1,696,450 tons steel ingots produced in 1882 only 258,295 tons could have been for anything else than rails; in 1885, out of 1,701,757 tons, over 600,000 tons were for miscellaneous uses. As regards rails made from iron, these seem to have become almost a thing of the past. In 1885 but 14,692 tons all told of that kind of rail were produced; in 1880 the amount had been 493,762 tons, and in 1881 488,581 tons. Taking all kinds of rails together, the production for 1885 is the smallest since 1878, and the total is only 1,090,699 tons, against 1,844,100 tons in 1881, the decline having been continuous since the latter year.

## II

In no department of trade is the industrial growth of the United States so strikingly seen as in the case of coal and iron. . . .

As in the case of coal, the United States is the second largest producer of iron in the world. Great Britain leads, but the United States is rapidly gaining on it—so rapidly, indeed, that it would seem it must in a few years surpass Great Britain. In the United States the increase [in 1886], compared with the previous year, reached 1,836,819 tons of 2,000 lbs., or full 40 per cent. Nor does this measure the extent of the revival that has taken place, for with this enlarged production stocks in makers' hands were diminished from 416,512 tons to 249,504 tons; furthermore, our imports of iron of various kinds reached 1,230,390 tons, against only 647,895 tons the previous twelve months. In values the year was one of steady improvement from beginning to end, the revival of railroad building of course contributing greatly to this result.

In Great Britain, on the other hand, there was hardly a sign of promise during the first six months, and in fact this continued till towards the close of the year, when the great activity and increased demand in the United States stimulated the trade in the United Kingdom and gave hope of a better state of affairs in the current year. . . . The improved tone . . . would appear to be very largely based upon the revival in the United States, for while the exports of iron and steel from the United Kingdom in 1886 did expand, and reached 3,795,901 tons (of 2,000 lbs.), against 3,503,809 tons in 1885, the United States contributed 910,049 tons of the amount in 1886, against only 453,959 tons in 1885—that is to say, the demand from the United States was doubled, and formed nearly one quarter of the entire exports, while the movement to the rest of the world fell off. Moreover, notwithstanding the increase in total exports and the diminution in the make of iron stocks in Great Britain at the end of the year were stated to have increased, the London *Economist*, in an article in its issue of January 15, estimating the total in public stores and in makers' hands at the large figure of 2,500,000 @ 2,600,000 gross tons, equivalent of 2,800,000 @ 2,912,000 net tons of 2,000 lbs.

We make these remarks to show that in contrasting our production for 1886 with that of Great Britain for the same year, allowance must be made for the fact that in the one case the conditions governing the output were favorable in the extreme, and in the other they were just the reverse. We now annex a table giving our own make of pig and that of the United Kingdom for each of the last 17 years, the figures being all expressed in tons of 2,000 lbs., and the production of the United States being stated in detail according to the kinds of fuel used.

Yearly Production of Pig Iron in United States According to Fuel Used, and Total Production in United Kingdom

| Tons of 2,000 lbs. | United States | | | | Production in Great Britain |
|---|---|---|---|---|---|
| | Anthra-cite[1] | Char-coal | Bitumi-nous | Total | |
| 1870 | 930,000 | 365,000 | 570,000 | 1,865,000 | 6,679,137 |
| 1871 | 956,608 | 385,000 | 570,000 | 1,911,608 | 7,422,440 |
| 1872 | 1,369,812 | 500,587 | 984,159 | 2,854,558 | 7,550,960 |
| 1873 | 1,312,754 | 577,620 | 977,904 | 2,868,278 | 7,354,425 |
| 1874 | 1,202,144 | 576,557 | 910,712 | 2,689,413 | 6,710,377 |
| 1875 | 908,046 | 410,990 | 947,545 | 2,266,581 | 7,129,317 |
| 1876 | 794,578 | 308,649 | 990,009 | 2,093,236 | 7,342,716 |
| 1877 | 934,797 | 317,843 | 1,061,945 | 2,314,585 | 7,401,304 |
| 1878 | 1,092,870 | 293,399 | 1,191,092 | 2,577,361 | 7,146,777 |
| 1879 | 1,273,024 | 358,873 | 1,438,978 | 3,070,875 | 6,714,777 |
| 1880 | 1,807,651 | 537,558 | 1,950,205 | 4,295,414 | 8,679,141 |
| 1881 | 1,734,462 | 638,838 | 2,268,264 | 4,641,564 | 9,121,783 |
| 1882 | 2,042,138 | 697,906 | 2,438,078 | 5,178,122 | 9,617,081 |
| 1883 | 1,885,596 | 571,726 | 2,689,650 | 5,146,972 | 9,552,816 |
| 1884 | 1,586,453 | 458,418 | 2,544,742 | 4,589,613 | 8,749,134 |
| 1885 | 1,454,390 | 399,844 | 2,675,635 | 4,529,869 | 8,305,325 |
| 1886 | 2,099,597 | 460,917 | 3,806,174 | 6,366,688 | 7,800,000[2] |

[1] Includes iron made with mixed anthracite and coke, as well as that made with anthracite alone.
[2] Estimated on basis of reports published in English trade papers.

This shows interesting changes. The production in the United States has been steadily extending, till in the late year the make amounted to 6,366,688 tons, against only 1,865,000 tons in 1870, and against but 3,070,875 tons as recently as 1879. There have been set-backs of course, involving periods of declining totals, but after each decline a higher level has been reached, and with the extraordinary development in the late year, the 1886 aggregate is decidedly the heaviest on record. The increase since 1879 is over 100 per cent, and since 1870 nearly 250 per cent. Great Britain also has enlarged its production, as compared with both 1870 and 1879, but in a more moderate way, and during the last four years has been experiencing a steady decline. About this decline, however, there is nothing so very striking, since our production had also been declining between 1882 and 1885, and only in the late year did the recovery which subsequently became so marked begin. . . . It is significant of the controlling influence that the United States has had in this respect in the past, that in the previous era of falling totals, the United Kingdom made its lowest total in 1879, and then steadily and largely increased till it reached its highest aggregate in the same year that we did ours, namely, in 1882—the increase in those three years being from 6,714,777 tons in 1879 to 9,617,081 tons in 1882, from which there has since been a decline to 7,800,000 tons.

Bearing in mind that in using the results for 1886, we are taking Great Britain at her worst, the comparison of the figures of the two countries affords a good measure of the great progress that the United States has made in this industry. In 1870 the make of iron in the United States, as already said, was only 1,865,000 tons, but in Great Britain the make was 6,679,137 tons; that is, the product of the British Isles was nearly 3½ times that of the United States. In 1879 the United Kingdom still had more than twice as much as the United States, the totals being respectively 6,714,777 tons and 3,070,875 tons. In 1886, however, we find this country up to 6,366,688 tons, and Great Britain at 7,800,000 tons, a difference in favor of the latter of only about 1,400,000 tons or less than 25 per cent.

In the one particular of home consumption the United States would appear already to be decidedly in advance of Great Britain. A considerable proportion of the United Kingdom's make of iron is exported in one form or another. On the other hand the exports from the United States are so small as to count practically for nothing. As stated further above, in 1886 the shipments of iron and steel from Great Britain to foreign countries amounted to 3,795,901 tons, not including hardware or cutlery. If against this we allow for 132,630 tons of unwrought steel and of iron imported in the shape of bar, angle, bolt and rod, we have a net export of

3,663,271 tons. Deducting this from the 7,800,000 tons produced in the year, there remains say about 4,100,000 tons for domestic consumption, leaving out of consideration altogether the increase of stocks during the year. In the same period the United States has apparently used up its production of 6,366,688 tons imported besides 1,230,390 tons, and reduced stocks in makers' hands 167,008 tons, affording a grand total of over 7¾ million tons consumed at home. Hence consumption in the United States would seem to be 90 per cent greater than in the United Kingdom. . . .

With reference to the production of the Southern States, the increase during 1886 has not been very marked. In view of the great prominence these States have latterly assumed in the public mind, this may seem surprising, but as has been truthfully declared 1886 was a year of preparation in the South rather than of realization. To indicate what a small proportion of the whole the Southern States yet hold in the iron production, we have prepared the following table showing first the output in those States individually and collectively, and then the output of all other large producing States.

We see here that notwithstanding the extension of iron manufacture into so many new fields, Pennsylvania still retains its preeminence. Not only has it gained absolutely but also relatively. In 1880, with a total production of 4,295,414 tons, Pennsylvania had not quite one half, or 2,083,121 tons. In 1886, with a total production of 6,366,688 tons, it had more than one half, or 3,293,289 tons. It will also be noticed that Western States, like Ohio and Illinois, have greatly added to their production and that these rather than Southern States are to be mentioned for their gains. Indeed, the nine Southern States together produced only 876,539 tons, while Ohio alone had 908,094 tons, and even Illinois had 501,795 tons. If we compare with the 3,293,289 tons of Pennsylvania, the 876,000 total of the Southern States appears still more diminutive. But the growth of the South has at least been steady and continuous, only one year since 1880 having failed to record an improvement on its predecessor, and the 1886 total being more than twice as great as that of 1880, which was only 397,301 tons. Moreover, it must always be borne in mind, that owing to the large number of new furnaces recently erected or now in process of erection, the past offers absolutely no guide to the future. . . .

It may be thought that under the large production and active demand, manufacturers on the whole had a very profitable year.

Production of Pig Iron by States

| Tons of 2,000 lbs. | 1880 | 1881 | 1882 | 1883 | 1884 | 1885 | 1886 |
|---|---|---|---|---|---|---|---|
| | Tons | Tons | Tons | Tons | Tons | Tons | Tons |
| South'n States | | | | | | | |
| Alabama | 77,190 | 98,081 | 112,765 | 172,465 | 189,664 | 227,438 | 283,859 |
| Virginia | 29,934 | 83,711 | 87,731 | 152,907 | 157,483 | 163,782 | 156,250 |
| Tennessee | 70,873 | 87,406 | 137,602 | 133,963 | 134,597 | 161,199 | 200,526 |
| West Virginia | 70,338 | 66,409 | 73,220 | 88,398 | 55,231 | 69,007 | 98,618 |
| Kentucky | 57,708 | 45,973 | 66,522 | 54,629 | 45,052 | 37,553 | 54,844 |
| Georgia | 27,321 | 37,404 | 42,440 | 45,364 | 42,655 | 32,924 | 46,490 |
| Maryland | 61,437 | 48,756 | 54,524 | 49,153 | 27,342 | 17,299 | 30,502 |
| Texas | 2,500 | 3,000 | 1,321 | 2,381 | 5,140 | 1,843 | 3,250 |
| North Carolina | ...... | 800 | 1,150 | ...... | 435 | 1,790 | 2,200 |
| Total | 397,301 | 471,540 | 577,275 | 699,260 | 657,599 | 712,835 | 876,539 |
| Pennsylvania | 2,083,121 | 2,199,786 | 2,449,256 | 2,638,891 | 2,385,402 | 2,445,496 | 3,293,289 |
| Ohio | 674,207 | 710,546 | 698,900 | 679,643 | 567,113 | 553,963 | 908,094 |
| New York | 395,361 | 359,519 | 416,156 | 331,964 | 239,486 | 160,157 | 233,618 |
| New Jersey | 170,049 | 171,672 | 176,805 | 138,773 | 82,935 | 73,667 | 157,886 |
| Illinois | 150,556 | 251,781 | 360,407 | 237,657 | 327,568 | 327,977 | 501,795 |
| Michigan | 154,424 | 187,043 | 210,195 | 173,185 | 172,834 | 143,121 | 190,734 |
| Wisconsin | 96,842 | 102,029 | 85,859 | 51,893 | 52,815 | 24,632 | 65,933 |
| Missouri | 105,555 | 109,799 | 113,644 | 103,296 | 60,043 | 51,408 | 74,523 |
| All others | 67,998 | 86,849 | 89,625 | 92,410 | 43,818 | 36,613 | 64,277 |
| Grand Total | 4,295,414 | 4,641,564 | 5,178,122 | 5,146,972 | 4,589,613 | 4,529,869 | 6,366,688 |

133

But this conclusion hardly seems warranted. In the first place, though prices were better than in the previous year, no decided improvement occurred till towards the close, so that the average for the year will not range much above that for the previous year, which with one exception (1878) recorded the lowest average in the history of the trade. Taking the commonly accepted standard, No. 1 anthracite pig at Philadelphia, we find that it was not till October that the price got above $18.50, but after that the rise was rapid, the quotation touching $20.50 in the last week of December. The rise, however, came so late as to have but little effect on the average value, which would seem to have been not much above $18⅝, against $18 for the year 1885. Moreover, much iron produced in 1886 must have been to fill orders taken at the very low prices of 1885. The following table shows the opening, highest, lowest, closing and average prices for each year since 1870.

Range of Average Monthly Prices for Pig Iron (No. 1 Anthracite at Philadelphia) for Seventeen Years

| *Tons of 2,240 lbs.* | *Opening* | *Highest* | *Lowest* | *Closing* | *Average* |
|---|---|---|---|---|---|
| 1870 | $36¼ | $36¼ Jan. | $31¼ Dec. | $31¼ | $33¼ |
| 1871 | 30½ | 37¼ Nov. | 30½ Jan. | 37¼ | 35⅛ |
| 1872 | 37 | 53⅞ Sept. | 37 Jan. | 47⅝ | 48⅞ |
| 1873 | 45⅙ | 48⅜ Mch. | 32½ Dec. | 32½ | 42¾ |
| 1874 | 32 | 32 Jan. | 24 Dec. | 24 | 30¼ |
| 1875 | 25⅔ | 27 Mch. | 23½ Dec. | 23½ | 25½ |
| 1876 | 23¼ | 23¼ Jan. | 21¼ Dec. | 21¼ | 22¼ |
| 1877 | 20¾ | 20¾ Jan. | 18 Aug. | 18 | 18⅞ |
| 1878 | 18½ | 18½ Jan. | 16½ Nov. | 17 | 17⅝ |
| 1879 | 17¼ | 30½ Dec. | 17¼ Jan. | 30½ | 21½ |
| 1880 | 40 | 41 Feb. | 23 June | 25 | 28⅛ |
| 1881 | 25 | 26 Mch. | 24 June | 26 | 25⅛ |
| 1882 | 26 | 26¼ Oct. | 25½ April | 25¾ | 25¾ |
| 1883 | 25 | 25 Jan. | 21 June | 21 | 22⅜ |
| 1884 | 20½ | 20½ Jan. | 18½ Dec. | 18½ | 19⅞ |
| 1885 | 18 | 18¼ Oct. | 17¾ June | 18¼ | 18 |
| 1886 | 18½ | 20½ Dec. | 18¼ June | 20½ | 18⅝ |

## III

. . . [The foregoing excerpt] showed how greatly the make of pig iron in this country had increased; we now have the figures for measuring the extent to which that increase is due to the enlarged use of iron for the manufacture of steel. There have been a great many new works for steel production erected in different parts of the country, while railroad construction has been prosecuted with great vigor; the result is that our largely increased consumption of rails has continued to be almost wholly of our own manufacture.

In brief, we may say that the statistics show even more strikingly than those of iron production the extraordinary strides forward the United States has made in recent years, and especially last year. The make of iron in 1886, compared with 1885, increased 40 per cent, but the production of Bessemer steel ingots increased 49 per cent and the production of steel rails 63 per cent. In amount the make of iron increased 1,836,819 tons, that of Bessemer steel ingots 839,731 tons, and of Bessemer steel rails 675,292 tons, from which some idea can be formed of the extent to which each is responsible for the expansion of the others, as the increased production of rails of course contributed to the increased use of ingots, and the increased use of ingots in turn added to the demand for iron. What makes the increase in the case of steel (ingots) particularly noteworthy, however, is that the total of the previous year had been the heaviest in our history, notwithstanding that the production of Bessemer rails had then been steadily declining for three years. A further increase now therefore of almost 50 per cent, marks a wonderful degree of growth. Moreover, the Iron and Steel Association states that only about 100,000 tons of the 839,731 tons increase, is the result of the starting up of new plants, the remainder being the result of the increased production of the older plants. We have referred in our figures to the Bessemer product alone, because very little steel is made by any other process. In the following table, however, we also state the production of the other kinds, to make the exhibit complete. . . .

In 1870 our Bessemer production was only 42,000 tons, and our total steel production only 78,500 tons. In 1880 the Bessemer was 1,203,173 tons and total steel 1,397,015 tons. Now for 1886 we have 2,541,493 tons of Bessemer and say 2,800,000 tons of total steel. In the last six years we have added 1,400,000 tons to the output—that is, we have more than doubled it in this period—and of this increase about 850,000 tons were the growth of the late year. Pennsylvania still retains its lead as preeminently the largest steel-producting State in the country, though its percentage of the total

Production of Steel in United States

| Tons of 2,000 lbs. | Bessemer steel ingots | | | | Open hearth steel | Crucible steel | All other steel | Total steel production |
|---|---|---|---|---|---|---|---|---|
| | Pennsylvania | Illinois | Other states | Total | | | | |
| | Tons | Tons | Tons | Tons | Tons | Tons | Tons | Tons |
| 1870 | ...... | ...... | ...... | 42,000 | 1,500 | 35,000 | | 78,500 |
| 1871 | ...... | ...... | ...... | 45,000 | 2,000 | 37,000 | | 84,000 |
| 1872 | ...... | ...... | ...... | 120,108 | 3,000 | 29,260 | 7,740 | 160,108 |
| 1873 | ...... | ...... | ...... | 170,652 | 3,500 | 34,786 | 13,714 | 222,652 |
| 1874 | 85,625 | 62,492 | 43,816 | 191,933 | 7,000 | 36,328 | 6,353 | 241,614 |
| 1875 | 148,374 | 136,356 | 90,787 | 375,517 | 9,050 | 39,401 | 12,607 | 436,575 |
| 1876 | 258,452 | 171,963 | 95,581 | 525,996 | 21,490 | 39,382 | 10,306 | 597,174 |
| 1877 | 328,599 | 111,299 | 120,689 | 560,587 | 25,031 | 40,430 | 11,924 | 637,972 |
| 1878 | 426,481 | 179,500 | 126,245 | 732,226 | 36,126 | 42,906 | 8,556 | 819,814 |
| 1879 | 514,165 | 250,980 | 163,827 | 928,972 | 56,290 | 56,780 | 5,464 | 1,047,506 |
| 1880 | 643,894 | 304,614 | 254,665 | 1,203,173 | 112,953 | 72,424 | 8,465 | 1,397,015 |
| 1881 | 844,501 | 375,763 | 318,893 | 1,539,157 | 146,946 | 89,762 | 3,047 | 1,778,912 |
| 1882 | 933,631 | 397,436 | 365,383 | 1,696,450 | 160,542 | 85,089 | 3,014 | 1,945,095 |
| 1883 | 1,044,396 | 273,325 | 336,906 | 1,654,627 | 133,679 | 80,455 | 5,598 | 1,874,359 |
| 1884 | 1,031,484 | 339,068 | 170,043 | 1,540,595 | 131,617 | 59,662 | 5,111 | 1,736,985 |
| 1885 | 1,109,039 | 366,659 | 226,064 | 1,701,762 | 149,381 | 64,511 | 1,696 | 1,917,350 |
| 1886 | 1,507,577 | 535,602 | 498,314 | 2,541,493 | | | | 2,541,493 |

NOTE. For 1886 the figures of open hearth steel, crucible steel and "all other steel" . . . [had not] yet been furnished.

Bessemer product is not as great as in the previous year. However, it had a million and a half tons out of a total of 2½ millions. Illinois comes next, but a great way behind, its output standing at 535,602 tons. Outside of these two States only 498,314 tons was produced, which, however, is more than double the amount of the previous year; in fact the ratio of gain is decidedly heavier than in the case of the two principal States.

One effect of the large extension of production in the late year, is, that it raises the United States to the position of the largest steel producer in the world. We called attention last week to the fact that in the case of pig iron we were making steady and rapid progress toward that point, but in the case of steel we have already reached it. We have for some years produced more Bessemer steel than the United Kingdom, but the latter produces a large amount of steel by the open hearth process, so that our *total* production did not equal that of Great Britain. Now, however, not only our Bessemer product but our total product is the larger. The figures for the United Kingdom are always more or less incomplete, the statistics covering merely the production by the two processes mentioned, and these have not yet been published for 1886. Taking however the totals for the first half of the year, and making a liberal allowance for gains in the second half, we get approximate results, as below, which we use in comparison with the actual figures for previous years back to 1877. For the period preceding 1877 no reliable data are obtainable. We have added a column to show the Bessemer rails produced in the same years. We can find no figures whatever bearing upon the production of other kinds of rails. In 1880 it was reported that about one-third the open hearth steel ingots (then 281,000 tons) had been converted into rails; in 1886, however, out of a total production of open hearth steel of 379,943 tons in the first six months, the British Iron Trade Association had details as to the uses to which 238,423 tons had been put, and of this 238,423 tons only 7,373 tons represented rails. With this explanation, the table following will not be open to any misconstruction. We should say that in Great Britain it is customary to take 2,240 lbs. as the standard of a ton, but we have stated the figures all in tons of 2,000 lbs.—the commonly accepted standard now in this country.

Thus, of Bessemer steel ingots, the United Kingdom in 1886 produced only about 1,630,000 tons, against our production of

## Production of Steel and Steel Rails in Great Britain

| Tons of 2,000 lbs. | Bessemer steel ingots | Open hearth steel ingots | Total, two kinds | Bessemer steel rails |
|---|---|---|---|---|
| | Tons | Tons | Tons | Tons |
| 1877 | 840,000 | 153,440 | 993,440 | 569,408 |
| 1878 | 904,430 | 196,560 | 1,100,990 | 709,781 |
| 1879 | 934,652 | 196,000 | 1,130,652 | 582,084 |
| 1880 | 1,169,708 | 281,120 | 1,450,828 | 828,699 |
| 1881 | 1,614,725 | 378,560 | 1,993,285 | 1,146,589 |
| 1882 | 1,874,486 | 488,320 | 2,362,806 | 1,384,079 |
| 1883 | 1,739,786 | 510,160 | 2,249,946 | 1,228,835 |
| 1884 | 1,455,637 | 532,280 | 1,987,917 | 879,164 |
| 1885 | 1,460,622 | 653,988 | 2,114,610 | 791,373 |
| 1886 | 1,630,000[1] | 765,000[1] | 2,400,000[1] | 870,000[1] |

[1] Estimated.

2,541,493 tons. Of Bessemer and open hearth steel together it produced about 2,400,000 tons. Good authorities have in recent years added 100,000 tons more annually to represent the miscellaneous production of steel. Adding that to the 1886 figures would make the total product for that year 2½ million tons. Even then, however, the United States production is greater, for our total is 2,757,081 tons—and that on the basis of no change from 1885 in the production of open hearth, crucible and miscellaneous forms of steel; only a slight increase in any of these would raise our aggregate to 2,800,000 tons.

As to steel rails, there is reason why the United States production should grow rapidly. Our railroad mileage is very large, and consequently we need a large amount for repairs and renewals; then we are all the time constructing new roads, and last year added no less than 8,000 miles. To be sure, Great Britain makes a good many rails for export, and some years has sent a considerable amount to the United States; but the recent years of depression have checked that trade, so that even with the help of that item the United Kingdom is not placed on a parity with the United States. These facts afford the explanation why we should have produced 1,749,899 tons of Bessemer rails last year, while Great Britain's aggregate reaches approximately only 870,000 tons. How many rails of other descriptions, in addition to Bessemer, Great Britain produced, we do not know, but the amount could not have been sufficient to diminish materially the above difference. In the

United States the production of open hearth steel rails in 1885 was only 4,793 tons, and the production of iron rails 14,815 tons, or 19,608 tons together; in default of any later returns we use the same figures for 1886 in the comparison below. The following table gives the production of all kinds of rails in the United States in each year since 1870. To show how completely steel rails have displaced iron rails, it is only necessary to say that while in 1872 the production of iron rails was over 900,000 tons, in the late year it was practically nil. In the same interval the production of Bessemer steel rails has risen from 94,070 tons to 1,749,899 tons. It will be noticed that after reaching a total of 1,438,155 tons in 1882, there was a steady decline in the Bessemer rail production year by year till in 1885 the quantity manufactured was only 1,074,607 tons, from which at one bound the total was raised to 1,749,899 tons.

It will be seen from this table that though the production of Bessemer steel rails for 1886 is decidedly the largest ever made, the *total* production of rails, owing to the diminished amount of iron rails manufactured, is about 75,000 tons below that of 1881. If we have regard for the imports in addition, the difference is very much greater. In 1886 we imported only 46,577 tons of rails, which added to the 1,769,507 production, makes a total for the year of 1,816,084 tons. In 1881, however, the imports were 386,321 tons, making the total of imports and production 2,230,421 tons. Hence, since rails are not carried in stock like pig iron, the consumption of rails in the late year was about 400,000 tons less than in 1881, when, however, the new mileage constructed was 9,779 miles, and was followed by 11,599 miles in 1882. Though the 1886 total of 1,800,000 tons is not the heaviest on record, it would, at 100 tons to the mile, suffice to lay 18,000 miles of road, which gives an idea of the quantity of rails used in new construction, in laying second track, sidings, &c., and for renewals. When in August, 1885, the manufacturers agreed to restrict the output of rails, they fixed 775,000 gross tons as the limit of production for 1886, and even in December, 1885, when the demand had become so heavy as to make an extension of the limit necessary, the amount was placed no higher than a million tons. The actual production, we have seen, was 1,750,000 net tons, and this shows better than any figures of consumption what an extraordinarily favorable year 1886 was.

## Rail Production of the United States

| Tons of 2,000 lbs. | Bessemer steel rails | | | | Open hearth steel | Iron rails, all kinds | Total, iron and steel |
| --- | --- | --- | --- | --- | --- | --- | --- |
| | Pennsylvania | Illinois | Other states | Total | | | |
| | Tons | Tons | Tons | Tons | Tons | Tons | Tons |
| 1870 | .... | .... | .... | 34,000 | .... | 586,000 | 620,000 |
| 1871 | .... | .... | .... | 38,250 | .... | 737,483 | 775,733 |
| 1872 | .... | .... | .... | 94,070 | .... | 905,930 | 1,000,000 |
| 1873 | .... | .... | .... | 129,015 | .... | 761,062 | 890,077 |
| 1874 | 66,902 | 48,280 | 29,762 | 144,944 | .... | 584,469 | 729,413 |
| 1875 | 112,843 | 111,189 | 66,831 | 290,863 | .... | 501,649 | 792,512 |
| 1876 | 203,750 | 133,713 | 74,998 | 412,461 | .... | 467,168 | 879,629 |
| 1877 | 250,531 | 89,519 | 92,119 | 432,169 | .... | 332,540 | 764,709 |
| 1878 | 308,093 | 143,785 | 98,520 | 550,398 | .... | 322,890 | 882,685 |
| 1879 | 368,187 | 197,881 | 117,896 | 683,964 | 9,397 | 420,160 | 1,113,273 |
| 1880 | 495,716 | 257,583 | 201,161 | 954,460 | 9,149 | 493,762 | 1,461,837 |
| 1881 | 688,276 | 346,272 | 295,754 | 1,330,392 | 13,615 | 488,581 | 1,844,100 |
| 1882 | 759,524 | 336,122 | 342,509 | 1,438,155 | 25,217 | 227,874 | 1,688,794 |
| 1883 | 819,544 | 231,355 | 235,655 | 1,286,554 | 22,765 | 64,954 | 1,360,694 |
| 1884 | 763,223 | 290,185 | 63,213 | 1,116,621 | 9,186 | 25,560 | 1,144,851 |
| 1885 | 736,522 | 308,242 | 29,843 | 1,074,607 | 2,670 | 14,815 | 1,094,215 |
| 1886 | 1,097,943 | 430,975 | 220,981 | 1,749,899 | 4,793 | .....1 | 1,749,899 |

¹ No statistics for 1886 available to compiler of this table. [Ed.]

## IV

We have noted on previous occasions that however unsatisfactory the general condition of the iron and steel trades might be, there was at least one very encouraging feature in the situation, namely the increasing consumption of steel. This feature is very strikingly shown in the statement of steel production for the calendar year 1894, which has now been published by the American Iron & Steel Association at Philadelphia.

It will be remembered that the statistics of the production of pig iron . . . showed an output for 1894 smaller than for either 1893 or 1892, the figures being 6,657,388 tons for 1894, 7,124,502 tons for 1893 and 9,157,000 tons for 1892. In the case of the Bessemer steel production, the output for 1894, though half a million tons less than the output for 1892 (which was decidedly the largest ever reached in any year in the country's history), is 363,000 tons in excess of the output for 1893—that is, in the make of steel a very decided recovery has already occurred after the drop in 1893. Here is the record back to 1888 in half-yearly periods. It will be observed that for the last six months of 1894 the c itput was not far from two million tons (1,911,647 tons), and that it has happened only three times that the half-yearly product has reached or exceeded two million tons.

Production of Bessemer Steel Ingots in Gross Tons

| 1894 | 1893 | 1892 | 1891 | 1890 | 1889 | 1888 |
|---|---|---|---|---|---|---|
| Tons | Tons | Tons | Tons | Tons | Tons | Tons |
| | | | First Half | | | |
| 1,667,454 | 2,092,057 | 2,058,928 | 1,427,764 | 1,822,535 | 1,268,495 | 1,235,971 |
| | | | Second Half | | | |
| 1,911,647 | 1,123,629 | 2,109,507 | 1,819,653 | 1,866,336 | 1,661,709 | 1,275,189 |
| | | | Total | | | |
| 3,579,101 | 3,215,686 | 4,168,435 | 3,247,417 | 3,688,871 | 2,930,204 | 2,511,160 |

The full significance of this favorable comparison does not appear unless we consider it in conjunction with the small steel-rail production. In 1894 only 899,120 tons of Bessemer steel rails were manufactured, against 1,036,353 tons in 1893, 1,458,732 tons in 1892, 1,797,489 tons in 1899 and 2,044,818 tons in 1887. We would have to go back to 1885 to find a product as small as that for 1894. It is proper to state too that the total for 1894 would be even smaller except for an increasing consumption of rails for street railways. Of the total of 899,120 tons for 1894, 155,196 tons were street rail; in 1893 the amount was but 133,423 tons, in 1892 111,580 tons, in 1891 81,302 tons and in 1890 98,529 tons. If we deduct the street rails, there remains for 1894 a total of not quite three-quarters of a million tons. In the following we show the Bessemer rail output in half yearly periods.

Production of Bessemer Steel Rails in Gross Tons

| 1894 | 1893 | 1892 | 1891 | 1890 | 1889 | 1888 |
|------|------|------|------|------|------|------|
| Tons | Tons | Tons | Tons | Tons | Tons | Tons |
| | | | First Half | | | |
| 399,404 | 704,240 | 772,436 | 517,794 | 922,016 | 642,475 | 692,197 |
| | | | Second Half | | | |
| 499,716 | 332,113 | 686,296 | 702,080 | 875,473 | 827,792 | 673,724 |
| | | | Total | | | |
| 899,120 | 1,036,353 | 1,458,732 | 1,219,874 | 1,797,489 | 1,470,267 | 1,365,921 |

It deserves to be pointed out that the foregoing does not include a small quantity of rails manufactured from purchased blooms, nor a small amount of other kinds of rails turned out. It is estimated that the aggregate rail output for 1894 was 1,014,034 tons, which compares with 1,136,458 tons in 1893, 1,551,844 tons in 1892, 1,885,307 tons in 1890 and 2,139,640 tons in 1887. As in the other case, the product is the smallest of any year since 1885. Deducting the street rails in this case, the quantity remaining in 1894 is 858,838 tons. We know that new railroad construction in 1894 was exceedingly light, but nevertheless about 1,900 miles of new track were laid. The 858,838 tons can hardly be considered sufficient to meet the ordinary requirements of the roads for renewals, not to speak at all of the rails for new lines, from which it is evident how great has been the economy that the railroads have been forced to practice.

It is this falling off in the use of steel for the manufacture of rails that invests the large output of Bessemer steel ingots with so much importance and significance. Only a few years ago the greater part of the whole steel output was for this one purpose—the manufacture of rails. But now the situation in that particular has changed, and the steel producers are no longer dependent almost exclusively for their activity upon the demand for rails. . . .

# 9. The Giant Corporation

The General Motors Corporation, the largest manufacturing company in the world, won its present eminence after its administrative structure was revamped under the direction of Alfred P. Sloan, Jr., who at the behest of the du Ponts became its president in 1923. Assisted by gifted associates like Donaldson Brown and John Lee Pratt, Sloan evolved a doctrine of business organization based on centralized policy-making and long-range planning by the general managers at headquarters, and decentralized decision-making by the operating executives within the autonomous divisions. The basic reforms, carried out between 1921 and 1925, strengthened General Motors, whose future had been uncertain after the recession of 1920–1921, and enabled it to challenge successfully Ford's leadership in the automotive industry. Between 1924 and 1927 General Motors' share of the car market more than doubled, and the corporation seized the ranking position it has since held in the industry. In subsequent years the management pattern of General Motors became a model for the diversified multidivisional corporation. In U.S. v. E. I. du Pont de Nemours et al., 353 U. S. 586 (1957), the Supreme Court ordered the Du Pont Company to divest itself of its holdings in General Motors. In the following selection, the variant spelling "Du Pont" has been left unaltered.

SOURCE: U. S. Congress, Senate Judiciary Committee, Bigness and Concentration of Economic Power—A Case Study of General Motors Corporation, Staff Report of the Subcommittee on Antitrust and Monopoly, 84th Cong., 2nd sess., Senate Report No. 1879 (Washington, D.C.: Government Printing Office, 1956), pp. 2–3, 7, 24–35.

General Motors and its wholly owned subsidiary, General Motors Acceptance Corp., are respectively the largest manufacturing and sales finance companies in the world. In its manufacturing operations General Motors operates 119 plants in 64 cities in the United States as well as plants in 18 foreign countries. It employs more than one-half million persons in its worldwide activities. General Motors Corp. and its sales finance subsidiary utilize banks in 289 cities, including all cities with populations of over 350,000 persons and some below that level. It owns and operates insurance companies and a capital financing unit for dealerships. It is the leading producer of passenger cars, trucks, automotive parts, buses, and locomotives in the world and an important producer of off-the-highway earth-moving machinery. It is the single largest prime contractor for defense equipment in the country. Also, contrary to the popular belief that soaps, cigarettes, and breakfast-foods manufacturers are the leading advertisers, General Motors has the country's largest advertising budget, about $100,000,000.

General Motors produces 5 passenger car lines in the United States and 3 abroad. Since 1931 it has been the leading producer in this field, and in each of the past 2 years it has sold more cars in the United States than all other producers combined; General Motors has also been the leading producer of trucks since 1936. Its position in the bus field has advanced continuously while there has been a gradual exit of competing firms. In 1955 General Motors produced in excess of 80 per cent of intercity and city buses.

In the production of locomotives General Motors' market share is of comparable importance to its position in the bus field. Its percentage share of units delivered to railroads in the first 8 months of 1955 was 76 per cent, including all the passenger locomotives, and 83 per cent of the freight diesel locomotives according to its own statistics. Only in the diesel switcher did other firms have significant market shares.

General Motors holds significant shares of the markets for many household appliances, including refrigerators, ranges, washers, food freezers, and many other products. As late as 1936 the refrigerator was the only major appliance sold by General Motors, and many of its products in this field have been introduced since the war. It has recently designed entire kitchens, internally wired and plumbed, for installation as complete units by builders. Its position in the housing industry is assured. In addition to kitchen appliances, it also manufactures air-conditioning, heating, and water systems.

General Motors' 17 parts and accessories divisions produce and distribute a broad array of parts and accessories used in the automotive, aviation, and marine industries. It is claimed by General Motors that its share of the automotive replacement parts and accessories industry is 23 per cent. There is reason to believe that this share has been rising. The remainder of the market is supplied by upwards of 2,000 producers, and General Motors is without doubt the largest producer in the industry.

A firm whose gross sales total $12 billion, whose assets exceed $5 billion, and whose profits after taxes exceed a billion dollars, cannot help but have considerable effect upon our economy. Any investment program it undertakes or any significant change in its sales or labor force is bound to have important repercussions. It cannot act without some realization of its effects. In short, in whatever industry it operates, regardless of market proportions, General Motors presents the problem of size.

After the Subcommittee's early announcement that it would seek to determine what the national antitrust policy should be with respect to bigness, the staff initiated preliminary inquiries seeking to obtain information from various sources, both governmental and private, concerning the larger corporations. While abundant information was publicly available on many such companies, it was discovered that none of the Government agencies have made any comprehensive economic study of the General Motors Corp. in recent years.

Industries dominated by one or a few large companies pose many difficult competitive problems. The officials in charge of the 2 Government agencies which enforce the antitrust laws expressed their concern over the structure of the automobile industry, in which 3 companies produce about 95 per cent of the total output. They felt that this high degree of concentration was the basic problem confronting the industry. General Motors posed especially difficult problems, not only because of its relative market position, but also because of its absolute size. . . .

This study of many aspects of General Motors leads to the conclusion that the structure and financial strength of the corporation increased the certainty of success in any new field the corporation entered. Its financial resources are such that the capital barrier to entry faced by most business today is nonexistent for General Motors. Because of the integrated character of the corporation, and because of the dealer franchise system, much of the corporation's activities are sheltered from meeting the test of the market.

A defense of the giant corporation has been that broad stock ownership assures a community of interest between the corporation and the country. General Motors has in excess of one-half million stockholders. However, General Motors' ownership is highly concentrated. The 15 major stockholders own one-third of the entire outstanding common stock of the corporation.

One of the most striking characteristics of the General Motors operation is the extremely high profits earned by the company. In 1955, profits before taxes represented a return of 65 per cent on capital invested or net worth. After allowances for taxes, profits in that period were 48 per cent more than in 1954 and equal to a return of about 31 per cent on investment. Earnings of the other two major automobile producers have also been favorable but not as high as those of General Motors. By comparison the rate of return after taxes for American manufacturing firms as a whole last year was approximately 12 per cent, while for those firms with assets of $100 million or more, the average rate of return was less than 15 per cent. . . .

Sales by General Motors exceed the combined sales of all other passenger-car producers. In an attempt to minimize the significance of this fact it has been suggested that General Motors' share of the automobile industry is no larger than the share held by the Ford Motor Co. in years past. But there is a marked difference in the importance of market shares between the periods 1921 and 1954. In 1921, when Henry Ford had over 60 per cent of the automobile market, total passenger cars in use were approximately 1 per 13 persons. In 1954, when General Motors produced more than half the passenger cars in the United States, there were over 48 million passenger cars registered, or approximately 1 for every 3 persons. In this intervening period, the automobile has changed the lives of all people in our country. Thousands of towns today are entirely dependent upon automotive transportation. The entire movement of population from the center of cities to the suburbs is dependent upon the automobile. No part of our economic and social life is independent of the passenger car and truck today.

In 1955, General Motors' sales were $12.4 billion, and profits, after taxes, were $1.2 billion, 48 per cent more than in 1954. Income taxes in 1955 are in excess of $1 billion. Its assets exceed $6 billion, and its capital represents in excess of $4 billion. In 1954, General Motors sold almost 3 million passenger cars manufactured in the United States. In 1955, General Motors' sales of such passenger cars increased about 40 per cent over 1954. But cars and trucks are not its only products. It makes tanks, locomotives, tractors, engines for airplanes and ships, and brakes for bicycles. It makes guns, rockets, ammunition, radios, clocks, oil well drills, ice-cream cabinets, ice-cube makers, mirrors, and keys. It finances the dealer selling these products, finances the consumer's purchase, and, in some cases, insures the product against fire and theft. General Motors has plants in 18 foreign countries where it produces passenger cars, trucks, automotive parts and consumer appliances. It produces Vauxhall cars and Bedford trucks in England, Opel cars and trucks in Germany, and Holden cars and utility vehicles in Australia.

There is probably no company in the United States that affects the lives of the citizens of the country as much as General Motors. Of the total value of goods and services produced in the United States in 1954, it is estimated that General Motors sales accounted for 3 per cent. Its sales in 1954 were almost equal to the combined gross national products of Norway and Sweden.

General Motors was organized in 1908 by William C. Durant. Prior to that time leadership in the automobile industry was vested in those firms which subsequently formed the nucleus of General Motors, i.e., Buick, Olds, and Cadillac. From 1900–1904 the Olds Motor Works produced between 25 and 33 per cent of industry output. Cadillac, an important producer, accounted for 12 per cent of industry output in 1904 and 16 per cent in 1905. Buick, organized in 1903, was taken over by Durant in 1904, and by 1908, the year General Motors was organized, was the leading firm in the industry. The formation of General Motors by William C. Durant concentrated one-fourth of industry output in the hands of the largest firm in the industry. Shortly thereafter, Ford output exceeded General Motors, but from 1910 to 1932, except for 2 years, these 2 firms were the industry leaders.

Early in 1908 Durant and Benjamin Briscoe had proposed a consolidation of Ford, Maxwell-Briscoe, Reo, and Buick. Ford demanded $3 million in cash, and Olds then demanded similar treatment. Negotiations fell through. Durant and Briscoe thereupon attempted a merger of their companies and sought the backing of J. P. Morgan for new capital. Disagreement between Durant and the Morgan attorneys caused the abandonment of this project. Durant thereupon proceeded to organize General Motors in September 1908. His original plan to consolidate other firms with his organization was not abandoned, however. In the latter part of 1909 Durant secured an option to purchase the Ford Motor Co. for $8 million. His acquisitions during this period had reduced available funds and Durant was unable to raise the necessary money to buy out Ford.

Briscoe, after withdrawing from negotiations with Durant, proceeded to organize the United States Motor Co. in 1910. Within 2 years this firm was in receivership and reorganized as the Maxwell Motor Company. Ultimately, from this discouraging start, emerged the present Chrysler Corporation.

Durant organized the General Motors Co. as a holding company to acquire the stock of the Buick Motor Co. In the year it was organized, General Motors acquired the Olds Motor Works and the following year, the Cadillac Motor Car Co. By 1910, General Motors marketed 10 brands of automobiles, representing 21 per cent of the entire industry output. Within the first 2 years of the organization of the firm, Durant consolidated over 20 different companies into his organization. The overextension of the firm due to these acquisitions made it necessary, however, to raise capital, which could only be accomplished under onerous conditions, including the relinquishment of control of the organization by Durant. A condition of the banking group which supplied the necessary capital was that a voting trust be established, with the understanding that it would have control of the board of directors. Durant remained as a vice president and director, but ceased active participation in the firm for the period of the voting trust.

The recent Government antitrust case against Du Pont, General Motors and United States Rubber disclosed a great deal of information about the early history of General Motors. The inclusion of material from this trial is not for the purpose of reviewing the legal issues involved but to present primary source material bearing upon the growth of this large corporation. Mr. Ewart Harris, one of the attorneys for the Department of Justice in the case, appeared as a witness before the Subcommittee, and much of the following history of General Motors and its relationship to Du Pont is based upon his testimony and exhibits presented at these hearings. . . .

During the period of the voting trust Durant was not inactive. In 1911 he organized the Chevrolet Motor Co., which grew considerably in the next few years. Durant used the profits of Chevrolet to purchase General Motors stock and so reacquire control of the company. At the expiration of the voting trust in 1915, Durant had sufficient stock to challenge the bankers who controlled the voting trust. It was in this early period that the Du Ponts' influence in the corporation was first manifested. The Du Ponts began investing individually in General Motors in 1914. At the time of the struggle for control of General Motors, Pierre du Pont owned 2,200 shares of General Motors and John J. Raskob about 1,200 shares. The reorganization of the board of directors provided an equal number of appointees by the banking syndicate and by Durant. Pierre du Pont became chairman of the board of General Motors and was empowered to name three members of the board as neutral directors. The members appointed by Pierre du Pont were all representatives of the Du Pont interests.

Following termination of the voting trust and the reaccession to control by William C. Durant, General Motors' earnings rose rapidly and the firm embarked upon another period of expansion. The Du Ponts, realizing that Durant had control of the corporation, accepted his offer to exchange their stock for Chevrolet stock. Out of this association grew the plan for greater participation by the Du Ponts in General Motors.

The Du Ponts at that time had considerable funds for investment. Net profits during World War I were $232 million and Du Pont, while the war was still in progress, sought postwar uses for its facilities. Paint and varnishes which the automobile industry used in large quantities appeared attractive, and in 1917 Du Pont acquired Harrison Bros. & Co., one of the larger paint, varnish, and chemical manufacturers. Cawley Clark & Co., pigment manufacturers, and the Bridgeport Wood Finishing Co., varnish manufacturers, were purchased before the end of 1917. Prior to the war, Du Pont had entered the artifical leather and, in 1916, the rubber-coated fabric fields. Both products were major materials used in the automobile industry. In 1915 the Du Ponts also entered the celluloid field, also an important material used by the automobile industry. Nitrocellulose, the principal raw material used in the manufacture of smokeless powder by the Du Ponts, was also the material from which artificial leather and celluloid were produced.

Thus the development of the interests of the Du Ponts from manufacturers of gunpowder to major stockholders in General Motors was a logical progression. The close association between Du Pont and the automobile industry, its largest customer, convinced Du Pont of the industry's great potential. Obviously, an important consideration was the desire to maintain an interest in the company which promised to become in the future its greatest single customer.

In December 1917 Durant invited the Du Ponts to invest $25 million in General Motors. At that time, John J. Raskob, director and member of the finance committee of the Du Pont Co., prepared a report to the Du Pont finance committee recommending the investment. The report stated that with Durant, Du Pont would control General Motors with considerably more than a majority of the outstanding stock. Of a total of 1,080,000 shares, Durant would hold 280,000 shares, and the Du Pont Co. would acquire 273,000 shares as a result of their investment. Holdings of Du Pont friends would approximate 100,000 shares. Raskob stated:

> It is the writer's belief that ultimately the Du Pont Co. will absolutely control and dominate the whole General Motors situation with the entire approval of Mr. Durant who, I think, will eventually place his holdings with us, taking his payment therefor in some securities mutually satisfactory.

Raskob's summary of the management structure was that Durant would continue as president, Pierre S. du Pont would continue as chairman of the board, and Du Pont representatives would dominate the finance committee. In urging the investment, Raskob stated that Du Pont had $50 million to invest and—

> Our interest in the General Motors Co. will undoubtedly secure for us the entire Fabrikoid, Pyralin, paint, and varnish business of those companies, which is a substantial factor.

By this investment the Du Ponts secured a 23.83 per cent interest in the common stock of the enlarged General Motors Co. In the latter part of 1918, General Motors purchased the McLaughlin Buick properties in Canada, issuing common stock in payment thereof. Before the end of the month in which this transaction occurred, the Du Ponts had purchased from the McLaughlins the bulk of the General Motors stock they had acquired. At the end of 1919 Du Pont owned 28.74 per cent of the outstanding General Motors stock.

In 1920 the General Motors Corp. was in need of capital. A report by Raskob to the finance committee of the Du Pont Co., dated March 19, 1920, stated:

The General Motors Corp., in order to carry out a development program which has been reduced to the greatest degree possible without sacrificing its position in the industry, will need $60 million of new capital.

Mr. Raskob continued his report stating that the investment conlitions in the world, particularly in the United States, were such hat it was impossible to raise the new capital through the sale of ,tock, and since the capital would be required permanently in the )usiness, he felt it should be secured from the common-stock 10lders or new partners. New partners were acquired in the Nobel nterests, who had been associated with the Du Ponts in Canadian Explosives, Ltd., and in J. P. Morgan & Co. Subscription rights of )oth Durant and the Du Ponts to the new stock were to be illocated to Nobel.

The relationship of J. P. Morgan to the automobile industry lates back many years. As indicated previously, J. P. Morgan was interested in financing an early merger sponsored by W. C. Durant. Morgan's direct participation in General Motors, however, apparently dates from the interest of the Du Ponts in the corporation. Durant had been aided by other banking interests in his formation of Chevrolet. In the 1920 General Motors financing operations, the firm of J. P. Morgan was used. It acquired a considerable stock interest in General Motors at that time and representation on the board of directors. It is understood that Morgan was brought into General Motors financial affairs at the instance of the Du Ponts.

J. P. Morgan & Co. was to underwrite the stock issue of 1920 and head a syndicate to stabilize the market during the issuance of public shares. Durant charged that the syndicate did not carry out its functions. He attempted stabilization operations with disastrous results to himself. The syndicate utilized only $2 million of the $10 million authorized, and Durant was faced with a continuously falling market. . . .

On November 22 the Du Ponts purchased almost the total Durant holdings at $9.50 a share. Simultaneously, a bloc of stock was purchased from the syndicate at over $17 a share. It would appear that Durant was squeezed out of the corporation. In the Du Pont annual report for the following year, it was stated that Durant requested that Du Pont take over the management and control of the corporation. Durant demurred to this, saying:

On the evening of November 15, a personal friend of mine, representing the Du Pont interests, called at my apartment and informed me that my resignation as president of the General Motors Corp. was desired and would be accepted.

As a result of these acquisitions, Du Pont ownership of General Motors stock in early 1921 reached 35.8 per cent of the total outstanding common stock.

The events surrounding the ouster of Durant are not too clear. Alfred P. Sloan, Jr., who had been associated with Mr. Durant since 1916, was a director of General Motors. While he was on the executive committee with Durant and occupied an office next to him, he testified before the Subcommittee that he was not in consultation with Durant on the problems of the car manufacturing units. Mr. Sloan, however, also reported that one of his criticisms of Durant was that Durant's relation with the car manufacturing units was a personal one. Officials reported directly to him. Sloan was also a participant in the stock syndicate of 1920. In the reorganization of General Motors upon Durant's resignation, Donaldson Brown, treasurer and member of Du Pont's executive committee, assumed Mr. Durant's position on the General Motors finance committee. Pierre du Pont became president. J. Amory Haskell, director and vice president of Du Pont, who had joined the General Motors board in 1915, became vice president in charge of operations. Raskob continued to head the finance committee, and Mr. Sloan was placed in charge of the general advisory staff. In 1923 Mr. Sloan became president of General Motors, and immediately thereafter a director of the Du Pont Co.

Certain significant changes occurred in General Motors from the period of the voting trust to the time of acquisition by the Du Pont interests. During the voting trust from 1910 to 1915, various passenger car lines were discontinued. Buick, Cadillac, Olds, Oakland were continued and three other makes were consolidated in the General Motors Truck Co. The market share of the company declined considerably during this period. The end of the voting trust witnessed a new expansion in General Motors.

In 1916 United Motors Corp. was organized to acquire various companies formerly producing parts for sale to General Motors and to other corporations. The promoters of this consolidation were Durant, Raskob, and Louis G. Kaufman, a New York banker who had backed Durant in Chevrolet. The companies involved in this consolidation were Dayton Engineering Laboratories Co., Remy Electric Co., Hyatt Roller Bearing Co., New Departure Manufacturing Co., the Perlman Rim Corp., and shortly thereafter, Harrison Radiator Corp., and the Klaxon Co. Mr. Sloan, president of Hyatt, was made president of United Motors Corp. In 1918 General Motors took over the United Motors Corp. by the payment of cash and the exchange of stock.

In this same year, General Motors expanded in other lines. It purchased the Chevrolet Motor Company of Canada and the McLaughlin Carriage Co. (the Canadian Buick producing company). It purchased the outstanding stock of the Scripps Booth Corp., a company in which it already held a minority interest. It also entered the tractor industry, purchasing the Samson Sieve-Grip Tractor Co., and the Janesville Machine Co.

The year 1919 saw a major expansion of General Motors. It built the largest office building in the world at that time, organized General Motors Acceptance Corp. (GMAC), acquired the Guardian Refrigerator Co. and various parts producing firms. It also purchased an interest in the Fisher Body Corp.

The Fisher Body Co. had been organized in 1908 to make bodies for automobile producers. Its expansion was meteoric and as the largest builder of bodies in the industry, it was soon considering entry into the automobile industry. Three automobile firms were interested in associating themselves with Fisher. General Motors offered the most advantageous proposition. In 1919 General Motors acquired a 60 per cent stock interest in the firm for almost $28 million. Control of Fisher was vested in a voting trust, the Fisher brothers sharing control with General Motors. General Motors contracted to purchase substantially all its bodies from Fisher on a cost-plus basis for a period of 10 years.

Fisher Body thereafter expanded further. In 1920 it acquired the controlling interest of the National Plate Glass Co., a recently merged organization of three major glass producers, and in the same year acquired the Ternstedt Manufacturing Co., producer of automobile body hardware.

The General Motors-Fisher arrangement was extremely profitable to the Fishers, and General Motors sought an end to the cost-plus arrangement. In 1926, with 3 years of the cost-plus contract remaining, General Motors succeeded in purchasing the outstanding 40 per cent Fisher Body Corp. stock, offering General Motors stock in payment. The shares issued in payment equaled 11 per cent of the entire common stock outstanding. By acquiring the Fisher Body Corp., General Motors obtained a firm which was not only the largest body producer but also operated hardwood mills and plants producing glass and automobile hardware.

In 1931 both Pittsburgh Plate Glass Co. and the Libbey-Owens-Ford Glass Co. negotiated with General Motors for the purchase of the National Plate Glass Co. General Motors was willing to sell this firm if an agreement could be negotiated which would assure a supply of glass at a favorable price. In July 1931 such an agreement was consummated with Libbey-Owens-Ford. In addition to a payment of $9.5 million, Libbey-Owens-Ford agreed to supply General Motors with the greater portion of its glass requirements. The initial agreement, which was to run for 7 years, called for a price of 27½ cents per square foot for the first 20 million square feet and 26½ cents per square foot for purchases in excess of this amount. In subsequent years prices were to be adjusted proportionately to changes in the prices of materials, fuel, power, and labor. Similar contracts to supply General Motors' glass requirements were concluded in 1936 and 1945, and now the arrangement between Libbey-Owens-Ford and General Motors is to run until August 31, 1958.

In 1925 General Motors transferred the assets of its truck division to a new firm, the Yellow Truck & Coach Manufacturing Co., of which General Motors held 57 per cent of the stock. . . .

In 1925 General Motors attempted to purchase the properties of Dodge Bros. put on the market by the Dodge heirs. Dodge was the third largest producer in the industry from 1919 to 1922, but began to decline upon the death of the founders. Dillon, Read & Co., of New York, by offering the greater amount of cash, acquired the Dodge properties. Ultimately, the firm was sold to the Chrysler Corp.

Large corporations in the United States generally pride themselves on their broad distribution of stockownership. This is also true of General Motors. The number of General Motors shareholders at the end of 1955 totaled more than 540,000, compared with 487,639 at the end of the previous year. It is obvious from these statistics that there are a great many shareholders of General Motors common stock. But little more than this can be stated. Historically, the ownership and control of General Motors has been highly concentrated. In only one period of the company's history—the period of the voting trust, 1910 to 1915—can it be said that voting control of the corporation has been other than in the hands of William C. Durant or those invited by him into the corporation. When the Du Ponts first came into the organization, they, together with Durant, controlled in excess of 50 per cent of the voting stock of the corporation. At the end of the year 1920, stockholdings of the Du Pont Co. represented 23.96 per cent of the outstanding stock of General Motors Corp. This was only the ownership of the Du Pont Co., and not the personal holdings of any of the Du Pont family or those persons who customarily participated with the Du Ponts in their enterprises. In 1921, after purchasing Durant's stockholdings in the corporation, the proportion of ownership of General Motors stock held by the Du Pont Co. rose to 35.8 per cent of the outstanding stock. Stock ownership by J. P. Morgan & Co., the bonus fund controlled by the Du Ponts, and the holdings of the Nobel interests, also associated with the Du Ponts, together with the Du Pont direct holdings, exceeded 50 per cent of outstanding stock in 1921.

In 1923 a bonus plan was prepared in order to secure the loyalty of the former Durant associates. Various key men in the organization, selected by the finance committee of General Motors, were sold stock in a holding company whose assets were General Motors stock. Du Pont supplied General Motors stock to a new corporation, Managers Securities Co., which in turn issued its stock, one-third to General Motors' executives, two-thirds to Du Pont, so that voting control of the General Motors stock remained unaffected. This distribution of stock under the Managers Securities plan was the forerunner of the General Motors' bonus plan for executives.

Today ownership of the General Motors Corp. is still concentrated. The 15 largest stockholders in General Motors own 33 per cent of the outstanding common stock. The 50 largest stockholders own 39 per cent of the outstanding common stock. Of this total, the Du Pont Co. holds 23 per cent. This again does not include ownership of General Motors stock by individual members of the Du Pont family as private investment. The importance of Du Pont stock at General Motors' stockholders' meetings can be seen from the total shares of common stock represented by persons or proxy at such meetings from 1928 to 1938. The number of shares of common stock entitled to be voted by the Du Pont Corp. represented 52 per cent in 1928 and 40 per cent in 1938. If we consider large individual stockholdings by persons in the corporation who were either associated with the Du Ponts or who held substantial stockholdings by virtue of the stock distribution offered under the General Motors bonus plan, it is clearly seen that there is little possibility of a significant stockholders' group in opposition to the Du Pont interests.

The General Motors bonus plan now in effect works to allocate to General Motors executives a considerable number of General Motors shares each year. The amount of funds available for bonuses is 12 per cent of the net earnings after deducting 5 per cent return on capital, but not in excess of the amount paid out as dividends on the common stock of the corporation during the year. According to Harlow H. Curtice, General Motors president, the common stock so disbursed is purchased by the corporation in the open market, and in the last few years has represented average daily purchases of 2,000 shares. In the last 4 years over 2 million shares of General Motors common have been purchased by the corporation for bonus purposes. In this same period, total transactions of General Motors stock on all public exchanges were 13 million shares. Since it is likely that the shares traded on the exchange were traded more than once per share, and the shares awarded as bonus to General Motors executives were more than likely retained for investment purposes, it appears that the bonus plan has operated to remove a substantial number of shares of General Motors stock from the public market. If continued at the current rate, it will tend further to concentrate ownership of the corporation.

The financial affairs of General Motors are controlled by the financial policy committee, a committee of the board of directors under the direction of Albert Bradley, executive vice president. This committee is also responsible for the legal affairs of the corporation. Testimony before the Subcommittee of top company officials concerning this committee and the existing financial controls was illuminating.

The operation of the financial policy committee historically has always been an extremely important function of the General Motors management. The committee determines financial policies and accounting procedures. The various financial officers such as the vice president in charge of finance, the treasurer, comptroller, divisional comptrollers, and other financial officers, all report to the chairman of the financial policy committee. The committee approves all appropriations, but delegates to the operations policy committee all appropriations not over a million dollars. The financial and insurance subsidiaries also report to the financial policy committee. Mr. Bradley, as chairman of the financial policy committee, and Mr. Frederick G. Donner, vice president in charge of the financial staff, are on the board of directors of the General Motors Acceptance Corp.

When the Du Ponts agreed with Durant to share in the management of the corporation, it was in the finance committee that direct participation occurred. By August 1917, Pierre du Pont and John Raskob were members of this committee. With formal participation in General Motors the financial management of the company fell largely to Du Pont interests. The finance committee, as reported in the 1917 annual report, consisted of John J. Raskob, chairman, who simultaneously was a director of both the Du Pont Corp. and Christiana Securities, and a member of the finance committee of Du Pont, together with the following: H. F. du Pont, Irénée du Pont, Pierre S. du Pont, W. C. Durant, J. A. Haskell, and J. H. McClement. Mr. Haskell was a director and vice president of Du Pont at that time. By the end of 1918 McClement was dropped and the finance committee consisted of four Du Ponts, Raskob, Haskell, and Durant.

Mr. Raskob was chairman of the finance committee from 1917 until 1929, at which time he was succeeded by Donaldson Brown, also a director and member of the finance committee of Du Pont. In 1937 the finance committee and the executive committee were combined into a single committee, the policy committee, under the chairmanship of Alfred P. Sloan, Jr. In 1946, the finance committee was reestablished and Albert Bradley became chairman.

Today the financial policy committee in addition to Mr. Bradley includes: Henry C. Alexander, Donaldson Brown, Walter S. Carpenter, Lucius D. Clay, Lammot duP. Copeland, Harlow H. Curtice, Frederick G. Donner, Alfred P. Sloan, Jr., and George Whitney. Mr. Alexander and Mr. Whitney are respectively president and chairman of J. P. Morgan, long associated with the Du Ponts in General Motors. Of the remainder, all but Lucius D. Clay are either members of the Du Pont family or employees of General Motors—the firm in which the Du Ponts long held the controlling interest.

General Motors has been an extremely profitable corporation consistently enjoying a higher return on investment than leading firms in other major American industries. It was, therefore, one of the purposes of the Subcommittee to study General Motors' pricing practices and financial policies.

In the early twenties, Mr. Bradley, together with Mr. Donaldson Brown, then vice president of the finance staff, prepared a system of pricing procedures which has been used by the corporation since that time.

The essential feature of the General Motors financial policy is the desire to maintain a planned rate of return on capital.

> An acceptable theory of pricing must be to gain, over a protracted period of time, a margin of profit which represents the highest attainable return commensurate with capital turnover and the enjoyment of wholesome expansion, with adequate regard to the economic consequences of fluctuations in volume. Thus, the profit margin translated into its salient characteristic rate of return on capital employed is the logical yardstick with which to gage the price of a commodity with regard to collateral circumstances affecting supply and demand.

Mr. Curtice, when asked if the test of efficiency would be the ability of management to learn and perform the skills necessary to operate large-scale industry in order to make a satisfactory return on investment, answered:

> That is certainly it, but we have to do better than that because each year we must have something, either greater value or lower price, for the customer.

When asked what attainable return has been used in pricing policy, Mr. Bradley indicated that there was a standard which has not been changed in a period of over 20 years, a yield between 15 and 20 per cent on the net capital employed over the years. A yield of 20 per cent was also expected by Mr. Curtice on new investment.

In planning this return, the corporation has a long-term view. The capital on which this return is expected always is assumed to be in excess of immediate requirements. It is expected that facilities will be utilized to the extent of 80 per cent of capacity, so that the return on investment is translated into a markup on costs computed at 80 per cent of capacity operations. This planned level of operations for cost accounting purposes is called standard volume. This planned level, or standard volume, has been constant over the years.

Since 1948, actual return after taxes and after provision for employee bonuses has been in excess of the standard described by Mr. Bradley.

Return on Net Worth after Taxes

| | Per cent | | Per cent |
|---|---|---|---|
| 1948 | 24.5 | 1952 | 20.5 |
| 1949 | 31.4 | 1953 | 20.1 |
| 1950 | 34.9 | 1954 | 24.4 |
| 1951 | 20.9 | 1955 | 31.3 |

In the past 8 years, General Motors return has exceeded the standard it has established for itself. The question was therefore raised why are not the prices of its products lowered. Mr. Curtice indicated this would not benefit dealers, and argued that General Motors' pricing was fair. He stated that the lowering of prices now would not be beneficial in the long run, since the company would have to raise prices if volume declined in order to maintain its planned return.

Returns in excess of the standard would normally occur when production exceeds standard volume, either because of underestimation of the demand for products and subsequent underinvestment, or because of a change in the planned attainable return used in pricing. This study of General Motors' standards of return on investment shows that General Motors both possesses and exercises market power. In this light, the return earned by General Motors can be likened to a public-utility return. A utility's prices are determined so that an agreed-upon rate of return on capital is secured. Public authority determines the standard used and usually the price charged.

The pricing procedure outlined previously could be called a formula pricing method for the establishment of a base price. Actual prices probably differ from formula prices for individual products, the necessity of meeting competition being the major cause of such differences.

The mechanics of pricing in the corporation provide for individual divisions to recommend prices for their products to a price review committee. The committee reviews the suggested price and makes its recommendations to the operations policy committee. If approved by the latter committee, the price is final. The price suggested by the producing division must be in conformity with the basic pricing policy outlined previously, since a person in charge of a division is judged by the top management by his ability to earn the rate of return on capital held attainable by the corporation. His ability to accomplish this includes proper forecasting of demand at the suggested price, his ability to keep costs at projected levels or below such levels, and accurate forecasting of capital requirements. Thus, while the individual division manager may have independence of action, such action is limited by the knowledge that his tenure requires achievement of company earning goals.

The price review committee consists of the president of the corporation, Mr. Bradley and Lewis C. Goad, executive vice presidents, and Mr. Donner, vice president in charge of the financial staff. The operations policy committee in addition to these 4 also includes the vice presidents in charge of the major operating groups and the 2 largest car divisions. It seems unlikely that a recommendation of the price review committee would not be approved by the operations policy committee. The price review committee appears to be strategically located to coordinate operating division policies and financial policy controls of the company.

# IV. THE TECHNOLOGICAL REVOLUTION

## 10. The Moving Assembly Line

*The concept of the moving assembly line in the mass production of a complicated mechanism fabricated from machined parts was the direct outgrowth of Henry Ford's commitment to the manufacture of a low-priced, standardized car turned out in enormous numbers. In order to replace the ordinary methods of skilled labor with speedier and simplified processes, Ford production managers and engineers devised new techniques for keeping the final assembly of the Model T synchronized with antecedent operations in the sequence of production. An intensive subdivision and repetitiveness of the labor function was combined with the principle of bringing the continuously moving work to the man at a level entailing the fewest waste motions. The separate elements of moving mass assembly may be traced as far back as Oliver Evans and Eli Whitney, and to pioneers of time and motion studies such as Frederick Winslow Taylor and Frank Gilbreth. In evolving a new and unique combination of these elements, the Ford production men worked independently and empirically, in direct response to immediate need. The major contribution to the moving assembly line at the Ford Highland Park plant in Detroit, as described below, was made by Charles E. Sorensen, who anticipated this technological breakthrough in an experiment conducted in 1908. For Sorensen's account of the evolution of moving assembly, see his reminiscences, My Forty Years With Ford (New York, 1956).*

SOURCE: Horace Lucien Arnold and Fay Leone Faurote, *Ford Methods and the Ford Shops* (New York: The Engineering Magazine Company, 1915), pp. 102–5, 109, 111–12, 114–16, 135–40, 142. Reprinted by permission of *Factory* magazine, copyright 1915, 1943, McGraw-Hill, Inc., New York.

. . . The Ford motor and chassis assembling methods are believed to show the very first example of minutely dividing the assembling operations of so large and heavy a unit assembly as an

161

automobile. These Ford motor and chassis assembling lines are believed also to show the very first examples of chain-driving an assembly in progress of assembling. . . .

The Ford shops assembling practice is to place the most suitable component on elevated ways or rails, and to carry it past successive stationary sources of component supply, and past successive groups of workmen who fix the various components to the principal component, until the assembly is completed and ready to leave the assembling line.

In some cases, where the shape of the component is unsuited to travel on rails, the principal component is pushed along on a finished iron table from one man or group of men to another man or group of men, past sources of component supply, each workman or group of workmen completing the placing, or the placing and fixing, of one component before moving the assembly in progress to its next station.

In case the assembly in progress moves on elevated rails or ways, it is common Ford practice to drive the assembly in progress by means of a slow-moving chain, and if the components are perfectly to gauge, so that all operations can be performed in predetermined times, it is better to drive the assembly in progress at a fixed suitable speed by chain, at a uniform rate, than to move it on the ways by pushing.

This Ford method of moving the assembly in progress has effected remarkable labor-saving gains over stationary assembling with all components brought to the one point for each assembly, the labor-saving gains being in all cases accompanied by great reductions in floor space required for the assembling operations.

Thus, up to September, 1913, the Ford car chassis assembling occupied 600 feet length of floor space, and required 14 hours of one man's time to assemble one chassis, standing still in one place while being assembled.

April 29, 1914, with the chassis chain-driven while assembling, 1,212 Ford chassis were assembled on three parallel elevated-rail assembling lines, by 2,080 hours of labor, giving one chassis assembled for each 93 minutes of labor, as compared with 840 minutes of labor in September, 1913.

The stationary chassis assembling in 1913 took 600 feet in length of floor space, while on April 29, 1914, the assembling lines were only 300 feet long.

As for Ford motor assembling, in October, 1913, 9,900 labor hours were required to assemble 1,000 motors in one day, which gives 9 hours 54 minutes = 594 minutes for each motor assembled; May 4, 1914, 1,003 motors, chain-driven on rails, were assembled with 3,976 labor hours, or 238,560 minutes = 237 minutes and 52 seconds time for each motor-assembly completed, a saving of 356 minutes 8 seconds = 5 hours and 56 minutes, per motor. In other words, more than 2½ motors were assembled on May 4, 1914, in the time it took to assemble 1 motor in the month of October, 1913, when the motor assembly was made by first-class American mechanics, working in what was believed by the Ford engineers in the month of October, 1913, to be the very best manner possible.

Besides these almost unbelievable reductions in assembling time, the Ford shops are now making equally surprising gains by the installation of component-carrying slides, or ways, on which components in process of finishing slide by gravity from the hand of one operation-performing workman to the hand of the next operator, this use of work slides being in some instances combined with operation divisions.

All of this Ford practice is of great importance to manufacturers at large, because the Ford engineers assert that these improved methods of handling work by slides, of moving assemblies in progress, and in minutely dividing assembling operations, can be applied to any and all small-machine manufacturing, with very large reductions of labor-cost. . . .

. . . The Ford engineers are now moving over 500 machine tools in the Highland Park shops, and are having a large number of new machine tools constructed, many of them showing striking novelties of design, in order to take full advantage of the new things they themselves have learned in the last ten or twelve months. . . .

## THE FORD PISTON AND CONNECTING-ROD ASSEMBLING

To show what may be done by simply dividing an operation seemingly already reduced to its lowest terms, and placing a short work-slide lengthwise of the assembling bench[,] the first example of the improved Ford practice . . . is the piston and connecting-rod assembling, changed within the last two months, so that now

14 men assemble 4,000 pistons and connecting-rods in one 8-hour day, instead of the 28 men employed to do exactly the same work less than two months ago, and with no change whatever in the tools used, nor in the ultimate operations performed. . . .

The best time record for 7 men, 6 assemblers and 1 inspector, is 2,600 piston and rod assemblies turned out in 8 hours, equal to one assembly in $77\frac{1}{13}$ seconds of one man's time. Average time, 2,400 assemblies in 8 hours, with 7 men, gives one assembly in 84 seconds of one man's time, or better than double the work of one man doing the entire job with no inspector, and with a saving of 101 seconds of time of assembling. . . .

This piston-assembling job teaches two lessons of first importance. The first is that there are great savings in labor to be made by splitting operations to such an extent that the workman does not need to change the position of his feet, and the second lesson is that a work-slide so located that the workman can drop his completed operation out of his hand in a certain place, without any search for a place of deposit, and also can reach to a certain place and there find his next job under his hand, is also a very important time-saver. . . .

## HEIGHT OF MOVING ASSEMBLY LINES

It was in this same assembling department that the first moving assembly line, that for assembling the Ford fly-wheel magneto, was installed. Of course, every one had everything to learn, and this first Ford assembling rail-line was built 8 inches lower than it should have been. The correct height for the magneto assembling . . . is 35 inches above the floor for this job. There were the same uncertainties as to the best height in the case of the chassis-assembing ways. In all instances it is of first importance that the workman should stand upright. A stooping posture very soon tires the workman, and greatly reduces his efficiency. When the chassis ran on its own wheels on the floor it brought things about "work-high"; some of the operations were too high for convenience, and platforms were placed on the floor where needful. When the first high line was placed for chassis assembling, with the chassis sliding on its axles on top of the rails, it was made $26\frac{3}{4}$ inches high; two other chassis lines were installed each $24\frac{1}{2}$ inches high, one on each side of the middle $26\frac{3}{4}$-inch rail-line. These two heights, $26\frac{3}{4}$ and

24½ inches, are retained with much satisfaction, the tall men being worked on the high line and the shorter men placed on the two low lines. The Ford engineers attach so much importance to this "work-high" condition that they are now placing a great number of gray-iron raising bases under various machine tools, particularly under presses, to bring the work at such a height that the workman can either stand or sit erect, any stoop being now well known to cause a marked reduction in the worker's ouptut.

The first fly-wheel magneto moving assembling line was installed, ready for work, about May 1, 1913, but the desirability of general application of the moving assembly line to the Ford motor assembling and the chassis assembling was not at once fully conceded by all the Ford engineers.

## FLY-WHEEL MAGNETO MOVING ASSEMBLY

This moving-assembly line is of historical importance as being the first moving assembly placed in work anywhere, so far as revealed by information to date. It is, of course, possible, or perhaps probable is the better word, that the moving-assembly line has been used somewhere in the world, but it is new to the Ford engineers and entirely novel to me. If the moving-assembly line has been used elsewhere, probably this publication will bring the previous use to public knowledge.

The fly-wheel-magneto-assembling story will not be told in full at this time. The Ford motor is the only one used for automobile driving which fires the charge by current generated by a magneto built directly on the fly-wheel, and hence sure to run as long as the fly-wheel revolves—which, of course, gives a more direct and certain magneto drive than can be had with a separate magneto, gear-driven from the motor crank-shaft, after the usual practice. . . .

Previous to the installation of this moving magneto-assembling line, the Ford fly-wheel magneto had been a one-man assembly, each workman on this job doing all the assembling of one fly-wheel magneto and turning out from 35 to 40 completed assemblies per 9-hour day. The work was done by experienced men, but was not so uniformly satisfactory as was desired, and was costly as a matter of course, as all one-man assembling must of necessity be forever.

Forty assemblies per 9-hour day, best time for one-man work, gives nearly 20 minutes time to each one.

When the moving-assembly line was placed in work with 29 men, splitting the one-man operations into 29 operations, the 29 men began turning out 132 magneto assemblies per hour, or 1,188 per 9-hour day, one man's time producing one fly-wheel magneto assembly in 13 minutes 10 seconds, a saving of nearly 7 minutes time on each assembly, or more than one-third of the best one-man time.

A new high line with chain-drive was installed for magneto assembling about March 1, 1914, when the Ford work day had been shortened to 8 hours. At that time the magneto-assembling force had been improved by substitutions and experience, and 18 men were assembling 1,175 magnetos in 8 hours, or a little more than 7 minutes of one man's time to assembling one magneto.

The chain-drive speed was a matter of trial; it was first made 5 feet per minute, which was much too fast; then 18 inches per minute was tried, and found much too slow; the third trial was 44 inches per minute (3 feet 8 inches), and is yet in use, though the foreman believes it could now be increased to advantage. The chain drive proved to be a very great improvement, hurrying the slow men, holding the fast men back from pushing work on to those in advance, and acting as an all-round adjuster and equalizer.

As soon as the men became accustomed to the automatically moving assembly 4 men were taken out of the line and the production was 160 in excess of previous performance; 14 men working 8 hours assembled 1,335 magnetos, making 5 minutes of one man's time assemble a magneto, as against 20 minutes when one man assembled the entire job.

The next attempt at moving the assembly in progress was made with the job of placing the crank-shafts in the en-bloc cylinders. An accident occurred which resulted in personal injury and put a stop to new installations of the moving assembly for a time, but in June, 1913, the foreman of the assembling room took courage and split the transmission-cover assembling into 23 operations, not on rails but on flat-top metal tables, the shape of the transmission cover making rail-sliding impracticable.

One man assembling the entire transmission cover produced from 20 to 30 assemblies per 9-hour day, 18 minutes for each one.

At the present time 23 men, each working one of the 23 operations for 8 hours, complete 1,200 transmission assemblies, which gives 9 minutes 12 seconds for each assembly, or a little more than one-half the best time with one man doing the whole job.

These great labor savings led to the first trial of full-length assembling ways for motor assembling, in November, 1913. Motor assembling on separate benches gave, in October, 1913, 1,100 men working 9 hours to assemble 1,000 motors.

By installing full-length motor-assembling lines and building some new tools to go into the motor-assembling line, along which the motors in process of assembling are moved by hand, now, May 8, 1914, 472 men working 8 hours assemble 1,000 motors.

In November, 1913, it took nearly 594 minutes of one man's time to assemble one motor.

Now, one motor is assembled in 226 minutes of one man's time, as against that 594 minutes in November, 1913.

This very great saving is due to the continuous line assembling, to the installation of work-carrying chutes, and to holding the motor as nearly as may be at one level during the entire course of motor assembling. . . .

## FORD CHASSIS ASSEMBLING

The Ford chassis assembling in moving lines affords a highly impressive spectacle to beholders of every class, technical or non-technical. Long lines of slowly moving assemblies in progress, busy groups of successive operators, the rapid growth of the chassis as component after component is added from the overhead sources of supply, and, finally the instant start into self-moving power—these excite the liveliest interest and admiration in all who witness for the first time this operation of bringing together the varied elements of the new and seemingly vivified creation, on the three Ford chassis assembling lines where over 1,200 have been put together and driven out of doors into John R[1] Street in one single 8-hour day.

## CHASSIS ASSEMBLING IN CHAIN-DRIVEN LINES

Up to August, 1913, the Ford chassis was assembled in one location. First the front and rear axles were laid on the floor, then the

[1] One of the main Detroit thoroughfares adjoining the Ford Highland Park plant. [Ed.]

chassis frame with springs in place was assembled with the axles, next the wheels were placed on the axles, and the remaining components were successively added to complete the chassis. All components needed to make up one chassis had to be brought by hand to each chassis-assembling location. This routine of stationary chassis assembling was, in September, 1913, worked with two lines of assembling-floor space, 600 feet long, 12 feet chassis-to-chassis centers, 50 assembling locations in each 600-foot line, 100 cars in process of assembling in the two lines. Working in this routine 600 men were employed, 500 being assemblers who were supplied with components by 100 men acting as component carriers.

About April 1, 1913, the first sliding asembling line, used for assembling the Ford fly-wheel magneto, was placed in work and immediately showed a large reduction in assembling labor-cost. Consequently, the possibility of lowering chassis-assembling costs by introducing the moving assembling line for chassis assembling became a matter of discussion among the Ford engineers.

In the month of August, 1913 (the dull season) 250 assemblers, with a stationary assembling location for each chassis, the assemblers being served by 80 component carriers, worked 9 hours per day for 26 days to turn out 6,182 chassis assemblies. Total labor hours $330 \times 9 \times 26 = 77,220$ hours, giving 12 hours and 28 minutes for labor time on each chassis, about as good as was ever done with stationary chassis assembling.

The assembling line was long—600 feet—but even at that did not give room enough, and 12½ hours of labor time seemed altogether too much for one chassis. It was in the dull season, and an experiment was made with rope and windlass traction on a moving assembly line 250 feet long. Six assemblers traveled with the chassis as it was slowly pulled along the floor by the rope and windlass past stationary means of component supply, and the chassis-assembling time was reduced to 5 hours and 50 minutes of one man's time, over 50 per cent saving.

October 7, 1913, on a moving-assembly line 150 feet long, with no helpers, components being piled at suitable locations, 140 assemblers in the line completed 435 chassis assemblies in one 9-hour day, 2 hours and 57 minutes of one man's time for each chassis assembling.

The assembling line was lengthened by degrees to 300 feet, giving the men more room, and on December 1, 1913, 177 assemblers working 9 hours turned out 606 completed chassis assemblies, about 2 hours 38 minutes of one man's time to each chassis.

December 30, 1913, working two assembling lines, 191 men completed 642 chassis assemblies in one 9-hour day, a little less than 2 hours 40 minutes of one man's time for each chassis, the cars being pushed along by hand.

January 14, 1914, one assembling line was endless-chain driven, with favorable results.

January 19, four chassis-assembling lines were worked, only one line being chain-driven. The wheels were put on as soon as the axles and the chassis frames were assembled, and the assemblies in progress ran with their front wheels on the floor and their hind wheels carried in 3-wheeled cradles, used to give easy placing of the rear wheels on the motor-starting drive at the end of the line.

February 27, 1914, the first high line of rails with chain drive was used. The chassis slid on its axles as pulled by the chain, and the wheels were applied only a short distance before the motor-starting was reached. This first high line was made with rails 26¾ inches above the shop floor, and at once showed great advantages, the best time for one chassis assembling being only 84 minutes, while the worst time was 2 hours. Two other high lines were soon installed, 24½ inches high, with chain drives; tall men worked on the line 26¾ inches high, and short men on the other two lines, 24½ inches high.

The Ford engineers make a point of "man-high" work placing, having learned that any stooping position greatly reduces the workman's efficiency. The differing heights of the chassis-assembling high lines are believed to be decidedly advantageous.

On these three high lines, on April 30, 1914, 1,212 chassis assemblies were completed in one 8-hour day, each chassis being assembled in 1 hour 33 minutes of one man's time, as against 12 hours 28 minutes, the best time with stationary chassis assembling, September, 1913—93 minutes as against 728 minutes—and it must be borne in mind that the September, 1913, Ford practice in chassis assembling was fully abreast of the best known in the trade. Very naturally this unbelievable reduction in chassis-assembling labor costs gave pause to the Ford engineering staff, and led to serious search for other labor-reduction opportunities in the Ford shops, regardless of precedents and traditions of the trade at large.

The chassis was not completed when it ran out into John R

Street, and the first practice was to let the driver run the chassis up and down until he thought best to abandon it to the motor inspector and the rear-axle inspector, and to return to the end of the assembling lines for another chassis to drive out into John R Street. The bodies were allowed to slide down an incline from the second floor, and were then dragged along the pavement by one man and stood on end in a bunch south of the chute.

When the assembly was completed on the John R pavement, and had been inspected by the motor inspector and the rear-axle inspector, it was again boarded by a driver and taken to the bunch of bodies, where four men lifted a body into place on the chassis, and the completed automobile assembly was then driven to the shipping-clerk's office, between the railway tracks, ready for shipment.

This procedure afforded plenty of gaps and vacancies for discretionary proceedings on the part of all the men working outside under the head assembler. The next radical improvement was made by laying down the angle-iron John R street track, running southward from the exit door, under the body-chute and something more than a chassis length to the south of the chute; and the chute itself was presently equipped with a car-body handling rig, not regarded as the final thing, but serving to place a body on the chassis with one handling only. The ground plan of the three chassis-assembling lines inside the shop, and of the John R street track, is given to scale on this page. . . .

## CHASSIS-ASSEMBLING OPERATIONS

It must be clearly understood that the moving-assembly speed is varied to suit exactly each individual assembling job. As each operation is performed while the work passes slowly across the station occupied by each assembler or assembling gang, the time of transit past this station must be sufficient for good work and no more.

The first assembling line established in the Ford shops (for the magneto) was originally speeded at 60 inches per minute, which proved much too fast. The next speed tried, 18 inches per minute, was found to be as much too slow. The third guess, 44 inches per minute, answered so well that it is yet retained.

The dash-assembly line travels 72 inches per minute; the front-

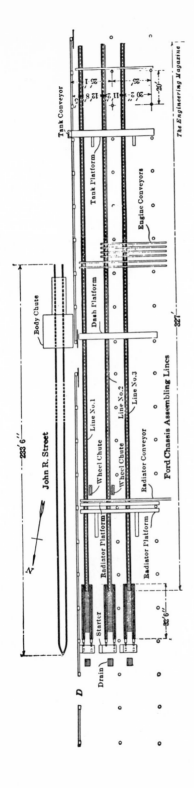

## Plan of Chassis-Assembling Lines

The chassis assemblies begin at the south (right-hand) end, and move to the north (left-hand) end, under the overhead gasoline-tank platform, the motor-carrying chain-hoist tracks, the dash assembly platform and the radiator platform. They then take the wheels, run on the wheels on roller frames over the pit where a workman caps the front-axle bracing globe, and then down a short incline onto the motor-starting drive for the rear wheels. Then the chassis is driven under its own power, through the door, D, and on the John R street track to the southward axle assembling line 189 inches per minute, and the body-and-top assembling line 144 inches per minute. The speed of the chassis-assembling line is 72 inches (6 feet) per minute.

The work is so divided among the assemblers that each operation is performed in 7 minutes and 36 seconds, turning out 300 complete chassis assemblies on each chassis-assembling line in 8 hours of working time, save in case of operations 1 and 2. . . .

. . . Operations 1 and 2 are on a side line, work moving from north to south, and this side line turns out 600 chassis frames with 4 mudguard brackets and rear springs in place in 8 hours, enough to supply two lines of automobile assemblers, work moving from south to north, each line turning out 300 automobile assemblies in 8 hours. The Ford Highland Park shops on June 11, 1914, were turning out 600 automobiles per day, and about 400 more per day were assembled at the various Ford branches, making about 1,000 new Ford automobiles assembled per day.

# 11. The Advent of Automation

One of the most momentous technological developments in history is the electronic computer, which has enhanced human capacity to store, retrieve, and transfer information on a scale and with a speed scarcely imagined a quarter of a century ago. Automation has been aptly called a new word for describing another phase of continuing technological progress in an era of mechanized continuous flow production. Automation would be inconceivable without the electronic data processor, which enables the feedback principle to be applied to a wide range of automatic machines and equipment. Some industries, notably chemical and petroleum refining, lend themselves more easily to automation than others, where technical difficulties arising from the final assembly of styled products with changing designs will probably continue to resist thoroughgoing automation. But this innovation has been successfully installed in office and clerical work, and promises to have a revolutionary effect on publishing and education. The following selection sums up the progress of the first decade of automation. In 1955, there were less than 1,000 computers in the United States; in 1966, there were 30,000.

SOURCE: Edgar Weinberg, "A Review of Automatic Technology," Monthly Labor Review, LXX (June, 1955), 637–44.

Automatic technology, automation, or automatization are terms widely and interchangeably used to describe the most recent phase of American industrial development. They cover the increasing use, both in offices and factories, of various types of laborsaving equipment having virtually continuous and, in some instances, self-regulating operation. Instead of small changes to achieve greater efficiency, as in traditional management practice, recent innovations often involve extensively replanning the flow of work and the layout of plants and offices, and completely redesigning products for greater automaticity in production. While these changes are hailed as the beginning of a new era, they are in principle a continuation of past trends. . . .

Today's technological developments carry forward the search begun in the eighteenth century for new mechanical ways of displacing man as a source of energy in production. The Industrial Revolution, the first phase of this movement, marked the transition from dependence on hand labor to the application of power-driven machinery. Many of the principles of automatic technology can be traced to such early developments as Oliver Evans' continuous flour mill, Babbage's calculator, Jacquard's card controlled loom, and Watt's automatic controls for his steam engine. The nineteenth century saw the steady improvement in speeds, capacity, and efficiency of machines, and their use in virtually every activity of the economy.

The 1920's ushered in the mass-production phase of industrial development. Ewan Clague, in the July 1926 *Monthly Labor Review*, described improvements in machinery and processes of that period as a "new industrial revolution . . . the most remarkable advance in productivity efficiency in the history of the modern industrial system." Machine operations in mass-production plants were made uniform, reduced to routine, and subdivided into simple tasks. The worker's job became a machine-paced operation on a highly standardized product, with mechanical conveyors employed to bring the work and carry it to the next step of a sequence. This type of specialization resulted in great increases in productivity but also in greater monotony for the operator of production machines and the man on the assembly line.

Automatic technology, starting with the cumulative accomplishments of the past, introduces the possibility of eliminating direct human intervention in operating, guiding, and feeding machines and in controlling processes. Instead of the worker, specialized mechanisms with capacity for elementary sensing, discriminating and counting, can now perform routine tasks of handling material and information with a high degree of reliability.

As this new movement progresses, job opportunities in more com plex control, service, distributive, and creative functions become relatively more important in total employment. Many less skilled jobs become obsolete. A growing awareness of the readjustment that may be required to conserve human values is accompanying these industrial changes. Automatic technology, wisely applied, a Norbert Wiener suggests, holds promise of "more human use o human beings."

## RECENT DEVELOPMENTS

Recent innovations leading toward more automatic technology in industry may be grouped in four categories: (a) automatic machinery; (b) integrated materials handling and processing equip ment; (c) automatic control systems; and (d) electronic computer and data-processing machines. The first two categories cover ex amples of advanced mechanization based on engineering principles already familiar in industry. The latter two encompass innovation largely developed out of experience during World War II in the new fields of electronics, control, and communication engineering.

The emergence of this technology is part of the general accelera tion of the nation's economic growth following World War II. The availability of the results of wartime research, large expenditures for new plant and equipment, and the continued need for a large volume of defense items have greatly stimulated the production of new types of equipment. Like Eli Whitney's system of interchange able musket parts manufacture, production principles found useful in speeding the output of arms are now used to good advantage in civilian industries.

*Automatic machinery.* Some types of specialized machinery which carries out a pre-set cycle of operations with almost no human intervention is found today in virtually all plants having a large output of standardized goods. New models of automatic glass making, textile-spinning, and papermaking machinery, printing presses, and wire-drawing machines are constantly being introduced.

The basic principles are often unchanged, but improvements in speeds and capacity may greatly reduce the labor required for a unit of output.

A recently developed automatic filling machine, for example, packages cans with 4 ounces of semi-solid baby food, "untouched by human hands," at the rate of 800 per minute. The worker's function is limited to manual pushbutton starting and stopping, observing and adjusting the performance to correct malfunctioning, and repair and maintenance of the mechanism. Such routine decisions as determining when a can is filled are made by tireless, highly accurate, specially designed devices built into the machine.

New models of automatic machines frequently incorporate devices to save labor in inspecting, gaging, and testing, as well as fabricating operations. Also, labor in servicing machinery is now economized by means of automatic lubrication systems which distribute a precisely measured volume of oil to bearings at regular intervals without direct human intervention.

The possibility of mechanizing an industry through intensive research on the redesign of the product as well as of the fabricating machinery is illustrated by new techniques of producing electronic parts. Previously, it has not been practical to devise laborsaving mechanisms for duplicating the complex hand manipulations of producing and assembling electronic components. According to a Bureau of Labor Statistics study, assembling operations employed, in January 1953, about 30 per cent of the work force in the electronics industry. With the tremendous civilian and military demand for electronics output, the need for time-saving automatic fabricating methods has become urgent.

A key development in the mechanization of electronics manufacture is the fabrication of the printed circuit board. Instead of hand-wired circuits, conducting patterns are now etched or stenciled on plates by means of specially designed machines. The results are a considerable economy in time and a high degree of uniformity of manufacture.

Another important development is the manufacture of equipment for attaching standard electronic components to printed circuit boards. Assembling these parts can now be done mechanically at significantly higher rates of speed than by manual methods. . . .

*Integrated materials handling and processing equipment.* As faster and larger automatic machines reduce the amount of labor directly engaged in fabricating operations, engineers are turning their attention to developing mechanical ways of saving labor in the movement and handling of materials. . . . The trend toward more elaborate processing of raw materials serves to make the moving of goods within plants increasingly more significant. Manual loading and unloading of goods in process, moreover, are often too slow to permit full utilization of the new high-speed production machinery.

The metalworking industries, notably automobiles and ordnance, provide some of the most striking examples of the integration of materials handling and processing to achieve continuous production. Indeed, the word "automation" was coined by D. S. Harder of the Ford Motor Co. to refer to "the automatic handling of discrete parts between progressive processing operations." Automation in this sense is now applied in the machining of engine blocks, pistons, ring gears, crankshafts, and 155-mm. shells. Like the assembly line of the 1920's, methods of materials handling used in the automobile industry are also being imitated by other metalworking plants producing large volumes of standardized goods.

A basic feature of this type of automatic production is the linking together of high-speed automatic machine tools so that a predetermined sequence of boring and drilling operations can be performed on a standardized part, such as an engine block, with virtually no direct human labor. Extensive use is made of specially built powered conveyors, or "shuttles," to transport the work from machine to machine; of pneumatic, hydraulic, and electrical devices to turn, load, position, and unload; and of timing mechanisms to synchronize the movement of parts being processed. Inspection after certain operations is also done automatically. The result is a continuous flow of production, except for brief interruptions for changing wornout tools and making repairs.

Integrated handling and processing equipment is also being introduced to save labor in the metal-forming and finishing departments of metalworking plants. Conveyors and chutes are now extensively used to move sand and heavy castings in foundries. "Iron fingers" automatically load and unload heavy presses and stamping machines. In one large plating plant, automobile bumpers pass continuously through a 31-step process, guided by a combination of shuttles and elevators. Operators at an electrical control panel check the process at numerous points.

Significant advances toward more automatic operations have also been made in the handling of bulk materials. New plants for processing such bulk materials as cake mix and grain are now built around a system of belt conveyors, gravity chutes, and pneumatic tubes to provide a continuous flow from raw material to finished product. A fertilizer plant studied by the Bureau of Labor Statistics, for example, combines several processing operations into a single automatic sequence, from loading to bagging, by means of automatic weighing hoppers, screw conveyors, and chutes.

Longer, faster moving, and larger capacity belt conveyors are increasingly used to reduce manual handling in transporting coal in mines and utilities, loading and unloading ships, and moving bulk materials at construction sites. . . .

In summary, increasing integration of materials handling and fabricating operations means fewer workers on jobs involving primarily physical strength. Greater use of machinery for these tasks, however, requires workers skilled in the repair and maintenance of costly equipment, engineers trained in designing new machinery and plant layouts, and management executives capable of directing technicians and coordinating mass production and mass distribution.

*Wider use of automatic controls.* With the large-scale use of automatic control devices in industry, a new phase of the long process of substituting mechanical for human energy begins. Hitherto, technological progress has been concerned primarily with the transfer of manual skills from man to machines, the worker remaining a controller and director. New developments involve the use of improved devices for such operations as sensing, measuring, comparing, and remembering, as well as operating in a predetermined manner. Control of machines by other machines or completely self-regulated production now becomes possible.

Although automatic control devices have long been used in the operation of the telephone system and industrial furnaces, their diffusion on a large scale was greatly speeded by new knowledge and experience gained during World War II. The collaboration of engineers, scientists, and mathematicians in designing servomechanisms for gun positioning, radar, and so forth, as Professors

Brown and Campbell of the Massachusetts Institute of Technology have pointed out, "soon focused attention on the essential principles that apply to all control systems."[1]

The basis for automatic control of industrial processes is the technique of "feedback." Briefly, feedback control exists when information about the output at one stage of a process is returned or fed back to an earlier stage so as to influence the process and hence change the output itself. This closed loop between input and output contrasts with open-loop controls where a human operator receives information about the results of a process, mentally compares it with the desired performance, and makes adjustments in the input, if necessary, to achieve the predetermined standard performance. Like the human nervous system, one scientist suggests, closed-loop systems have the remarkable ability to control the application of a substantial amount of force with a minimum expenditure of energy.

The operation of automatic control is exemplified by the simple closed-loop circuit used to control room temperature. In this familiar case, a sensing device of the thermostat measures the controlled variable, room temperature. The reading is then automatically compared with the preset desired value. If some deviation or error is detected, a signal is transmitted to the servomotor or starting switch of the furnace which operates until the desired temperature is reached and then stops. A new factor that alters the room temperature beyond the tolerance allowed sets off this self-regulating system anew.

Plants converting raw materials into finished products through some form of chemical processing are making increasing use of automatic control instruments. Self-regulation of the temperature, pressure, flow, and level of liquids and gases in these processes is often achieved by networks of control instruments. Materials handling in and out of processing tanks, pipes, and chambers is naturally continuous. The result is completely automatic production, from the input of raw material to the output of finished products.

Notable examples of whole plants built around automatic controls are found in the petroleum refining and chemical industries, including atomic processing, which have expanded their capacity fairly rapidly since the end of World War II. Other industries

[1] G. S. Brown and D. P. Campbell, "Control Systems," in *Scientific American* (September, 1952), p. 59.

where scientific experts believe advanced planning now aims at fully automatic plants are cement, beverages, paper products, telephone and telegraph, and electric power. Some industries, such as steel, make extensive use of instrument control in important steps of the processing.

As chemical processing is substituted for mechanical operations in other industries such as metal refining, the use of automatic controls no doubt will be extended. Improvements in measuring instruments also promise new applications. For example, a new gage employing radioactivity for continuous noncontact measurement of thickness makes possible more exact automatic control in coating paper, plastics, or rubber with abrasives, varnish, or adhesives.

An important objective of using automatic controls in many of these already highly mechanized operations is the finer adjustment and better quality of products made possible, rather than any large-scale saving of direct labor. Direct labor is already a relatively small proportion of the work force. A Bureau of Labor Statistics study of synthetic rubber plants, for example, indicated that workers directly engaged in process operation in 1949 comprised only about a quarter of total plant labor. Maintenance, administrative, engineering, and other overhead labor were the most important occupational categories.

The application of feedback controls to machine tools introduces the possibility of automatic production in industries other than those having continuous processes. While suitable for mass production of standardized parts, the automatic, though not self-regulated, materials-handling equipment and custom-built machine tools described earlier are generally not economical for job-lot production.

Tape control of machine tools provides a flexible method for producing small lots. With this type of automatic control, the tool is guided over the work without human intervention in response to a series of instructions previously recorded in code on such media as cards, paper tape, magnetic tape, or film. These instructions can be changed after each job. Punched-tape programming, for example, is being applied to standard precision-boring machines. . . .

*Electronic computers and data-processing machines.* As the economy grows in size and complexity, the work of information handling becomes increasingly important. Although mechanization of recordkeeping, accounting, and computing has advanced, the proportion of the labor force engaged in clerical and related work has continued to increase. Scientists and engineers in the past 10 years have therefore devoted considerable effort to developing new and faster tools in this field.

A major advance is the electronic computer or data-processing machine. The direct result of organized research for military purposes, the electronic computer applies principles of communication engineering to the tasks of counting and control. The broad stream of scientific research that produced radio and television also contributed to the development of this remarkable new tool.

Two general types of electronic computers are the analog and the digital. The analog, the first to be developed, is essentially a measuring device and is used to derive answers to engineering problems from the operations of a physical analogy of the problem. Analog computers allow engineers to study the operation and improve the design of a complicated process, without costly experimentation, by simulating its behavior. They are now widely used tools for such problems as designing guided missiles and analyzing the distribution network of utilities.

The digital computer operates as a counting rather than measuring device. Its principal feature is the use of electrical impulses to perform arithmetical operations at speeds far beyond human capabilities. The electronic computer combines several data-processing operations into one machine. The entire processing of data goes on automatically, without the manual transferring of data from one step to the next as in mechanical systems.

The high computing speeds and reliability of these machines have steadily been improved. According to the Stanford Research Institute, "figures can be handled electronically at more than 1,000 times the speed of conventional punched card equipment." A machine introduced in 1953 had 25 to 35 times the speed and capacity of the first large electronic computer produced by the same company in 1948.

Two types of digital computers may also be distinguished: the special purpose and general purpose. Special purpose computers consist of specially designed parts to perform a few fixed sequences of computing operations or programs. A large mail order firm, for example, uses a memory unit and computer to keep an up-to-the-minute inventory analysis, item by item, of 12,000 different lines. An airline employs a similar high-speed computer to handle seat reservations. Special purpose, high-speed computers are also used in air traffic control and to analyze unit demand for retail merchandise in department stores.

The general purpose computer can be used for a variety of operations not having a fixed built-in program. Instead, a new program must be developed in each application. Programming for the computer, however, involves time-consuming analysis of procedures and operations which is not subject to mechanization.

The first digital computers were developed for scientific and engineering research purposes in connection with military defense. Their ability to telescope tremendous series of computations taking months into a few hours' work has been of incalculable value in preparing ballistic tables, evaluating airplane designs, and solving problems in nuclear physics. New pathways in scientific research are open because mathematical computations for weather forecasts, interindustry economics, astronomy, seasonal trend analysis—too costly with conventional methods—are now practical.

The marketing and rental in 1953 of high-speed electronic machines specially designed for processing business data probably marked the beginning of a new era in office work. According to a survey made early in 1955, about a dozen large companies have installed data-processing machines and nearly 30 others may have machines installed in the near future.

Although many firms eventually expect to use the computers to obtain new information for management, the first applications are being made on tasks now being performed by slower methods. A large appliance company uses its electronic computer for preparing its payroll, scheduling materials, and controlling inventories. A utility prepares customers' bills. Insurance companies plan to use high-speed computers on premium billing, premium accounting, and actuarial computations.

The possibilities of savings in routine clerical labor appear to be substantial. A chemical company recently reports that its computer produces a financial report in 2 hours that formerly took 320 man-hours and prepares 1,200 manufacturing cost reports in 12 machine-hours, in contrast to the 1,800 man-hours formerly required. Although these comparative figures take no account of the long period needed for developing the complex instructions for the machine, there is little doubt that the electronic data-processing machine is a highly efficient tool for handling the ever increasing volume of information needed in business enterprises for making decisions.

## OUTLOOK

Although the general direction of technological change is toward greater automaticity, the actual time it will take each industry to adopt automatic equipment now commercially available depends on a wide variety of economic factors and hence is difficult to forecast. Piecemeal progress, with some industries and processes affected more than others, seems more probable than any abrupt changeover in a short period.

Fragmentary data on past experience with mechanization illustrate the gradualness of technological change. "One of the interesting results," Carroll D. Wright observed in his 1898 study of *Hand and Machine Labor*, after several decades of mechanization, "is the extent of the hand method of production, even at the present time." . . . Other studies revealed a similar pattern of gradual change, with variations from industry to industry depending on economic circumstances.

So far as the immediate future is concerned, a brief review of some general factors accelerating and retarding the spread of technological improvements suggests the likelihood of a fairly steady growth but no economywide revolution. A significant accelerating factor is the increasing supply of new equipment. . . .

The continued expansion of the chemical-processing and petroleum-refining industries may mean greater demand for automatic control, particularly in new plants. Progress may also occur in insurance and banking, Federal tax collection, patent processing, and postal service, where special committees are now studying ways of introducing electronic data-processing machines. In several large metalworking companies, separate automation departments have been charged to find new ways and areas for using laborsaving equipment.

Certain economic factors tend to retard the development of automation. Because of the high cost of the new types of equipment, automation is generally limited to plants producing a large volume of standardized goods of fairly stable design. Most goods therefore may continue to be produced on a mechanized but job-lot basis.

Because of the complexities, progress toward greater mechanization of assembly work is likely to be slower than in fabricating.

Another obstacle to rapid diffusion of automatic technology is the long time needed for designing and custom building the complex specialized machinery. A large scale electronic scientific computer, for example, took about 5 years of research and development and involved the production and assembly of thousands of components from nearly 300 manufacturers. A large insurance company required 2 years for analyzing its methods in order to install a data-processing machine.

Finally, internal factors within the modern corporation often create delays in introducing large-scale changes. The purchase of costly automatic equipment involves long-range planning and complex decision in the fields of corporate finance, marketing, and personnel. Conflicting interests of stockholders, executives, supervisors, and workers need to be resolved. Installing a high-speed electronic data-processing machine in a large company, for example, means changes in the duties and status of certain executives as well as workers, and their resistance to change may be an obstacle. In brief, the elusive and sensitive human factor may prove one of the important brakes on the rapid diffusion of the new technology.

## SOME BROAD IMPLICATIONS

To clarify the broad implications of the growth of automatic technology, it is useful to distinguish between man's role as a consumer and as a producer. Concerning his welfare as a consumer, it is clear that the per capita amount of goods and services consumed in any economy basically depends on the per cent of the population employed, average hours worked, and the output per man-hour. An increase in the annual rate of productivity growth of the private nonfarm economy . . . would . . . allow for some increase in leisure through shorter workweeks and longer vacations. In short, increased productivity as a result of technological change may be the source of higher living standards in the United States.

The implications of the new technology for man as a producer are more difficult to assess. Broadly considered, one probable effect will be to intensify the shifting of productive resources of workers, management, and capital among various activities of the economy.

In this process of change, some individual workers inevitably suffer losses as a result of displacement; others are benefited, as a result of up-grading. Employees in firms that do not adopt advanced techniques of production may become unemployed. Firms that are able to adopt cost-cutting equipment may gain a significant competitive advantage and expand their employment. The total extent of displacement as a result of technological changes will always be difficult to disentangle from other factors that cause economic unbalance.

The record of the past provides considerable support for believing that technological progress may be accompanied by high levels of employment. Carroll D. Wright in the 1890's used the phrase "expansion of labor" to describe the rise and growth of new industries providing new opportunities to offset displacement in older and declining industries. The shift of home activities to the factory, the growth of urban transportation and utilities, and the expansion of distributive, service, and government activities opened new opportunities in the past. In industries in an early stage of growth, such as rayon, autos, and chemicals in the 1920's, Dr. Solomon Fabricant found that productivity and employment both rose rapidly, the gain in total output offsetting the reduction in unit man-hour requirements.

In the future, some accommodation to job displacement, as automatic technology is gradually introduced, may come from a shorter workweek and new sources of industrial expansion such as atomic energy, aircraft, instruments, electronics, and other industries producing equipment for the new technology; industries catering to the leisure needs (travel, home repair equipment, and recreation); new products from industrial research and development; and public programs for highway building and school construction. If the progress of automatic technology is gradual, these industries may provide a source of new opportunities. Public and private policies that contribute to growth of the economy and to high levels of employment will be a major contribution in meeting the problems of job losses occasioned by greater use of laborsaving equipment.

The need for adequate measures to ease the hardships of displaced individuals, to train workers with new skills, and to adjust conflicting interests on the job are likely to be important issues of the transition. . . . They constitute a new framework for all groups having an interest in the labor market. Labor, management, and government agencies, responsible for education, vocational training, employment services, unemployment insurance, apprenticeship, wages and hours, and industrial relations, therefore, are likely to be increasingly concerned with the problems created by technological change.

One conclusion that follows is the ever increasing importance of information about the human aspects of technological change. Carroll D. Wright was aware of the pervasive influence of technology on labor problems when he initiated his pioneering studies of mechanization at the end of the last century. Today a sound basis for policies and programs for easing the transition to the new technology requires a comprehensive system of timely information about such subjects as productivity, employment, unemployment, labor turnover, occupations, consumption, production, and leisure. With broader understanding, automatic technology and greater productivity become the basis for enriching life in a free society.

# V. BUSINESS ENTERPRISE AND PUBLIC POLICY

## 12. Securities and Banking Reform

*Two landmarks in the federal regulation of business are the Securities and Exchange Act of June 6, 1934, and the Banking Act of August 23, 1935. Both were shaped by public demand for reforms in the securities markets and in the banking system after the Wall Street crash of 1929. The powers of control over all stock exchanges in the United States conferred on the Securities and Exchange Commission still stand as the broadest and strictest granted to any such government agency in the West. The Banking Act constituted the first thorough revamping of the Federal Reserve System since its establishment in 1913. As a result of this banking legislation, the management and control of the volume and flow of credit were placed in the hands of public authority.*

SOURCE: For I, *The Economist* (London), CXXV (December 12, 1936), 530–2; for II, *ibid*, Supplement (October 3, 1936), 12–14, 21–3.

### I

### CONTROLLING WALL STREET

The Securities and Exchange Commission is an integral part of the machinery of America's New Deal. Its historical background explains and even excuses many features which at first sight may appear extreme and anomalous to British observers. From Wall Street's earliest days, when share transactions took place under a buttonwood tree, up to quite recently, American securities law was a spasmodic hotch potch of civil and criminal statutes, enacted separately by individual States of the Union. The public attitude was one of complacent unconcern, until the devastating collapse of the boom of the nineteen-twenties brought the nation's entire credit, banking and business structures to the verge of catastrophe. Evolution thereupon became revolution, and from 1933 onwards the Federal Government assumed affirmative, full, and continuing control of security business. This control, it is generally admitted, has come to stay. Even if the Republican party had been returned to power at last month's elections, federal security regulation might have been curtailed, but would undoubtedly have remained.

The Federal Government's control has been embodied in three successively enacted laws. The Securities Act of 1933 (the so-called "Truth in Securities Act") has the fundamental purpose of enabling the public to make an intelligent appraisal of newly offered issues. It seeks to achieve this purpose by requiring initial full disclosure of corporate information. Both a "registration statement" and a full prospectus are demanded from those who issue new securities. The former must include a specified mass of information, must be signed by a majority of the issuer's Board of Directors, and must be filed with the Securities and Exchange Commission. Every offer for sale made thereafter by an issuer, underwriter or dealer must be accompanied by an unabridged and voluminous prospectus, whose sheer bulk has been said by a London banker to rival that of the Telephone Directory. Criminal and civil liability attaches to issuers, directors, and all officers, accountants and underwriters who sign the document if it contains a materially untrue statement, or omits a prescribed piece of information, or is guilty of any other material omission. In short, *caveat vendor* has definitely replaced *caveat emptor*. In practically every heading this statute is far more stringent than the corresponding British or Continental laws.

The second law, in which the Government's policy has found expression, is the Securities Exchange Act of 1934, which has three spearheads of attack. The first is the regulation of speculative credit; the second is the compulsion of continuing disclosure of company information and the abolition of "corporate" abuses; and the third, the regulation of market and trading practices. Its loan provisions are designed to prevent a recurrence of the situation in the last decade, when the nation's banking system threatened to become engulfed in the speculative maelstrom. These borrowing restrictions, which are administered by the Federal Reserve Board, limit the credit which may be extended on "margin" both to clients and to brokers and dealers. For margin borrowing, the minimum ratio of collateral is now 55 per cent of market value; and since last May this limit has been applied uniformly to loans on securities made both by brokers and by all commercial banks. This part of the Act has been bitterly criticised by brokers and investment houses who contend that the restrictions have punitively curtailed the volume of trading, "frozen the market," and expelled business to London. The Act also requires the periodic filing of detailed corporate balance sheets and income statements. It regulates proxy solicitation and insiders' personal security trading. Its market trading provisions deal broadly with all exchange activities. They bar manipulative devices such as "wash sales," "matched orders," market "rigging" and "jiggling," and the dissemination of market tips with misleading statements.

The third pillar in the edifice of control is the Public Utility [Holding Company] Act of 1935. This Act assumes drastic federal jurisdiction over utility holding companies. The latter are defined as units owning more than 10 per cent of the voting stock of a gas or electric company, and they comprise, in effect, the major segment of the industry, with its $13,000 millions of capital. This law is the outgrowth of a system of frenzied promotional finance which had previously juggled with operating companies like so many stock jobbing pawns, and had pyramided them in layers, sometimes a dozen deep. It regulates, inter alia, all financial activities within the different groups, and seeks to prevent the "milking" of underlying assets. The highly controversial "death sentence" clause in the Act provides for the (possibly) forced dissolution after 1938 of all companies beyond the "second degree," except those whose properties form a geographically and economically integrated system. The companies affected are, at present, refusing compliance with the Act's registration provisions and certain other of its affirmative stipulations, pending a bitter challenge of its Constitutional validity in the Federal Courts.[1]

The form taken by all of this legislation reflects the formidable difficulties imposed by the United States Constitution. England and the leading European nations enjoy central control over all

---

[1] Subsequently, the registration provisions were upheld by the Supreme Court in *Electric Bond and Share Co. v. S.E.C.*, 303 U. S. 419 (1938), and the constitutionality of the "death sentence" clause affirmed in *North American Co. v. S.E.C.*, 327 U. S. 686 (1946) and *American Power & Light Co. v. S.E.C.*, 329 U. S. 90 (1946). [Ed.]

company matters. They can, by passing national laws, exercise any necessary regulation uniformly, inclusively and by direct mandate. Under the present status of the American Constitution, however, federal control is barred, except over activities which are directly and demonstrably concerned with inter-state commerce, the postal system and taxation. The draftsmen of the Acts which have been described have consequently had resort, in some instances, to legal artifice and circumvention, and those administering their provisions have been similarly handicapped. For example, regulation of cardinal matters (such as current balance sheets, earnings and salary information, proxy solicitation, and market trading by "insiders") can—except when new capital is sought—be enforced only at the focal point of inter-state commerce which the Stock Exchange provides. But Stock Exchange listing facilities are not so indispensable as in England. The "sanctions" of the law, again, are not applicable to certain companies whose shares were traded on the Exchanges before the Acts were passed—the so-called "issues admitted to unlisted trading privileges." Legal difficulties have similarly limited administrative control of "over-the-counter" business outside the Exchanges, and have involved the Government in a bitter struggle in the Courts over its power to enforce the public utility holding company legislation. If control is to be extended in the future to investment trusts, some new constitutionally justified point of contact will need to be found, for the trusts do not usually desire facilities for dealing on the Stock Exchange.

Another fundamental departure in current American practice is the broad delegation of administrative responsibility and discretionary power to an executive Commission. In England, supervision by the registration authorities of the Board of Trade, at Bush House, is largely mechanical. In France, direct reliance is placed on formal penal provisions. In Germany, the somewhat lax supervision of conformity is effected by the Commercial Registrar Judge. By contrast, the United States Securities and Exchange Commission, which, with its staff of 750 employees, works in combination with the Federal Reserve Board, provides a highly flexible instrument of supervision and control. In the absence of such a continuing administrative body, capable of dealing with individual and varied phenomena, it may well be argued that wide, searching and insistent regulation cannot possibly be enforced. Indeed, the chief objection to it, as revealed by America's brief experience, may be the creation in the public mind of a false assurance of security. But America seems to be increasingly willing to accept this disadvantage as well as the danger of power delegation, as the price of efficiency and flexibility in control.

The extent of the power which has been delegated to the Securities and Exchange Commission may be appreciated by a brief recital of the Commission's powers under the various Acts. By virtue of the Securities Act of 1933 the Commission may (subject to review by the Federal Courts) issue stop orders against new offerings; investigate violations and conduct elaborate hearings; and promulgate all manner of rules and regulations applying to registration statements and prospectuses. The Commission prescribes the form in which corporate information is to be given. It specifies the detailed items to be shown in balance sheets and earnings statements, and even the methods to be followed in the preparation of accounts. It takes no responsibility, however, for the investment merits of the securities, or the prices at which they are offered.

In administering the Securities Exchange Act, the Commission licenses the Stock Exchanges and supervises their administration. It has broad powers to list and de-list issues. It keeps exchange trading and ticker "quotations" under continual surveillance and investigates price movements when any suggestion of manipulation is present. It has already proceeded formally against several firms and leading operators, including the far-famed Mike Meehan. The Commission has imposed sixteen important rules upon the Stock Exchanges, which are designed to bring trading under its direct control. It has direct jurisdiction over the operations of floor specialists and member firms—including their credit arrangements. It is about to limit professional floor-dealing activities as part of a broad long-term programme to divest the trading market of its speculative and manipulative elements.

Its powers in the domain of company accounting are similarly wide. It lays down, in detail, the way in which balance sheets and income data are to be drawn up, and it may even, on occasion, prescribe the method by which depreciation is to be calculated. It has jurisdiction over proxy solicitation. Within its absolute discretion, it may insist on the public disclosure of directors' and executives' salaries, "insiders'" personal transactions, and current commercial data. It issues licences to over-the-counter brokers and dealers, and is engaged on a codification of the principles of fair practice according to which they must function. Over and above all this, the Commission is given general "blanket" authority in making additional rules.

Finally, under the Public Utility [Holding Company] Act all acquisitions of securities and properties by holding companies and their subsidiaries, and all service contracts and borrowings between parent companies and subsidiaries, are made subject to the Commission's approval. As the Commission also administers the vital "death sentence" clause, the decisive nature of its powers needs no further emphasis. . . .

Inevitably, the net effect of recent security legislation is the subject of spirited controversy. "Wall Street," naturally, is bitterly resentful. In addition to complaining of the damage done to its business (reflected in the low price of Stock Exchange memberships), the financial community contends that the law has hindered capital financing, and that trading and margin restrictions have needlessly reduced activity and market liquidity. At the other extreme, complaints are heard that the teeth have been drawn from legislation which was originally drafted in more stringent terms, and that the S.E.C. is really acting "in cahoots" with the brokers and bankers. It is the present writer's opinion, however, that the social and economic benefits secured by the new law far outweigh its incidental disadvantages. Broadly, the "Truth-in-Securities" Act makes *seller* rather than buyer beware, it compels directors to direct, and it makes pertinent financial facts available to the investor. The results of the Holding Company legislation are somewhat obscured by its continued immersion in litigation and its possible emasculation. But the results of the Securities Exchange Act are more clear. Restriction of credit seems to provide the most effective check on speculative excesses by quantitatively controlling its main stimulating source. The "margins" already imposed have undoubtedly changed the basic structure of the stock market by reducing its so-called liquidity and widening the spread of quotations. But this former "liquidity" was largely mythical, and its alleged benefits were attained at a high cost of artificial gambling activity. The *investment* quality of the market has been thus accentuated, at the expense of its speculative forces. Even more important, a flexible means has thus been provided for preventing the nation's banking and credit system from becoming again dually involved in a stock market boom.

Unfortunately, the effectiveness of stock loan regulation has been vitiated by the antithetical fiscal policies which the Government has pursued. The enormously expanded credit supply, the Government's deficit financing and inflation of bank deposits, the artificial reduction of interest rates, and—above all—the capital gains and undistributed earnings taxes, have combined as an overpowering inflationary force on security prices. The result may well be that the investor will eventually lose his money on a "cash" rather than on a "credit" basis. But these factors only add to the importance of the Securities Exchange Commission. Without its restraining influence, the inflationary damage would be immeasurably more injurious. In the long run, the Acts may go far in combating the abuses inherent in the large-scale concentration of American wealth and the concomitant diversion of corporate ownership from control. That process, however, must, in the nature of things, be evolutionary.

## II

## BANKS AND BANKERS

Bank failures were no depression novelty in the United States. All through the prosperous decade of the '20's there was a continuous epidemic of bank failures. Starting with 1921, there was no year in which less than 354 banks failed, or less than $110 millions in deposits were impounded. The average annual rate throughout the nine years to 1929 was 627 bank failures, involving $169 millions of deposits. The figures reveal, however, what manner of banks they were that failed in such numbers. The average total of deposits per failed bank was only $270,000. . . . They were, in short, the smallest variety of rural bank and the cause was, in the main, the collapse of land values in and after 1921 and the slow deflation of agricultural pipedreams which occupied the whole of the '20's. The total number of banks in the country, which had been 30,812 in June, 1921, had fallen to 23,696 by June, 1930, but the banking facilities of the country had not been reduced in anything like the proportion that a bare comparison of these figures would suggest.

The fact that failures were largely confined to small banks in outlying districts does not, however, mean that all was well with the

American banking system. On the contrary, there were many grievous defects which the depression successively uncovered. . . . The real run on the American banks can be dated from the failure of the Bank of United States in New York in December, 1930. . . . From that time the tide of public suspicion mounted. Failures continued at an increasing rate and the size of bank affected was growing. Public uneasiness was reflected in the hoarding of currency; money in circulation increased from an average of $4,546 millions in 1930 to $4,957 millions in 1931 and to $5,699 millions by the end of 1932. President Hoover attempted to stem the flow. In October, 1931, he persuaded the banks to organise themselves for mutual defence in the National Credit Corporation, which was to derive funds by assessment on the sound banks and lend them, against sound security, to banks in difficulty. This failing, the Reconstruction Finance Corporation was set up in January, 1932, to lend Government funds, though still with the requirement of adequate security, to hard-pressed banks. The R.F.C. succeeded in slackening the pace of failures, though they continued throughout 1932 at the average rate of 40 banks and $2 million of deposits every day. Towards the end of the year the final collapse began. The first State moratorium was declared on October 31st; the Detroit banks closed on February 14, 1933, and within three weeks the bank "holiday" had spread to every State in the Union.

It is impossible to exaggerate the effect of this banking trouble in intensifying the depression. If reasons be sought for the greater severity of the depression in the United States than in Great Britain, this is undoubtedly the chief. A run by the public on the banks not merely reduces directly the circulating medium of the country, it also compels the banks to put every conceivable pressure on their debtors for repayment of loans and to dump securities on the Stock Exchanges. While such a deflation of credit is proceeding, the Government is powerless to reverse the downward sweep of all the economic indices. In the fiscal year 1931–32, the Federal deficit amounted to $2,473 millions and to that extent fresh funds were pumped into the system. But in the same period the total loans and investments of the banks of the country declined by $8,951 millions. Deflation of this nature imposes a creeping paralysis on the whole economic structure of a nation. Some idea of the baleful effects of banking instability can be gained from the fact that the total value of cheques drawn (excluding New York City) was in

1933 only 44 per cent of the 1929 level. The total of the British Metropolitan, County and Provincial clearings, in 1931, the worst year, was 95 per cent of the 1929 total.

## REOPENING THE BANKS

The utter collapse of the whole banking system of the country forced itself on President Roosevelt as his first and most urgent problem. His handling of this emergency, in his first days in office, has won universal praise. It is no detraction from this praise to say that his approach was purely psychological. He contrived to convince the public that only "sound" banks would be allowed to reopen, although, had the panic continued, there would not have been a sound bank in the country. Moreover, he induced the man in the street to believe that the Government was now behind the banks, although in fact no sort of guarantee was given. It is probably the case that a collapse so complete would in any case have been followed by a return of confidence. The obvious lunacy of attempting to convert all deposits into cash is apparent if once the public is given time to see it, and in economic fevers, as in physiological distempers, improvement follows on the crisis. Be that as it may, when the banks re-opened, deposits returned and the strain was lifted.

The Roosevelt Administration has taken measures to buttress the banking system other than the reversal of psychology which the President achieved at the time of the crisis. One of these was the creation, in June, 1933, of the Federal Deposit Insurance Corporation. Apart from a preliminary investment of capital by the Treasury, the F.D.I.C. is a purely mutual institution. Membership is obligatory for all members of the Federal Reserve system and optional for other banks. Funds are raised by assessment from all member banks, and are available to insure deposits—small deposits in full, larger deposits in part. Another buttressing measure has been the purchase by the Reconstruction Finance Corporation of preferred stock in a number of banks. The amount of money placed at the disposal of banks in this way amounted at the peak to $1,265 millions. This device had the virtue that it did not compel the banks to mortgage their soundest assets in order to get Federal help. Whether as a result of these measures, or for other reasons, bank failures have been very much reduced. From March 16, 1933 (the end of the "holiday") until the end of the year, there were 179 suspensions, involving $146 millions in deposits (approximately the *monthly* average in 1931); in 1934, the figures are 57 and $37 millions respectively; in 1935, 34 and $10 millions respectively. . . .

The Government's attentions were not, however, solely directed towards the underpinning of the banking structure. The long period of deflation had revealed a number of abuses, real or imagined, in American banking practice. A whole folk-lore of anecdote had grown up around the unpopularity of the banker, and the President himself, in his Inaugural Address, spoke of money-changers fleeing from the Temple. In the circumstances, reform was inevitable, and it was no less inevitable that the reform programme should take little account of the wishes of bankers themselves. Much of it, in fact, amounted to penal legislation. Thus, the Banking Act of 1933 enforced an immediate and complete divorce between banking functions and any form of security trading, whether the issue of new securities or dealing in existing issues. Plural bank directorships were prohibited, and many of the activities of banks were made subject to the control of the Federal Reserve (e.g. rate of interest payable on time deposits, volume of collateral loans).

Nobody would deny the need for a reform of some American banking practices. The actual measures adopted, however, have been disappointingly negative. They amount almost entirely to prohibitions of practices deemed unsound, and even then there has been a strong tendency to penalise the whole race of bankers for the sins of a few. Of encouragements to sound banking, there have been few indeed. This applies more especially, in foreign eyes, to the failure to provide even the legal framework for a system of branch banking. The Act of 1933 went no further than to permit national banks to open branches in States where the State law permits. Conditions in 1933 were such that the President could have carried any measure he proposed for banking reform, and it must be one of the severest indictments of his financial policy that he allowed prejudice against bankers, especially big bankers, to blind him to the needs of American banking.

## FEDERAL RESERVE POLICY

In the years before 1929, high claims were made for the Federal Reserve system. It was generally believed that the secret of credit stability had been discovered; and, indeed, the long period of comparatively stable prices, combined with steadily mounting production, appeared to offer strong testimony to the success of the system. This complacency was not seriously shaken by the events of the autumn of 1929, for though it was apparent that the period of steady prices and constant expansion of industry was over, a Stock Exchange panic had been overcome without the banking crisis which in pre-Federal Reserve days would have been almost inevitable. Accordingly, the policy pursued by the Reserve authorities throughout 1930 was a negative one. They had eased credit late in 1929, and were content to leave the volume of credit provided for the market at the level then attained. Member bank borrowings from the Reserve had fallen to a low level by March, 1930.

This Fabian policy was continued in the first half of 1931, although assistance was given to the market temporarily in the Bank of United States crisis in December, 1930. But in the second half of 1931 more drastic measures became necessary. The rising tide of bank failures was inducing a steady flow of currency into hoards. Moreover, after September, 1931, the flow of gold, which had been steadily inwards, was sharply reversed, and the imports of thirty-two months departed in nine months. These influences greatly increased member bank borrowings and restricted the money market. Between July and October, the Reserve bought some $650 millions of securities to ease the market, but in the last two months of the year the Reserve system itself began to feel the pressure of gold exports. As the law then stood, Federal Reserve notes could be backed by gold or "eligible collateral." But since the supply of eligible paper meeting the requirements of the law was limited, most of the backing was, perforce, composed of gold, and the minimum gold reserve percentage was, in practice, far above the 40 per cent specified by the law. Consequently, from November onwards, the Federal Reserve, far from being able to expand the credit structure still further, was compelled to sell the securities it had bought since July. These four months, from November, 1931, to February, 1932, were the period of severest deflation during the whole depression.

The restrictions on the Federal Reserve were removed by the Glass-Steagall Amendment to the Federal Reserve Act, approved on February 27, 1932, which, for a period of three years (since made permanent), permitted United States Government bonds to serve as collateral for notes. The Reserve immediately started buying securities. About $1,000 millions were bought between February and June, when the total was stabilised until the end of the year. There was plenty of banking trouble still to come, but (with the temporary exception of the final crisis of February and March, 1933) the basis of the credit structure was steadily expanded from this time onward.

The Roosevelt Administration has considerably altered the structure of the Federal Reserve system without changing the fundamental policy adopted by President Hoover in February, 1932. The chief changes in structure are contained within the Banking Act of 1935, although several other enactments have contributed. Two tendencies are clearly visible. In the first place, the Reserve system as a whole has been given greatly enhanced powers over the member banks and over the credit market generally. It can substantially regulate the interest rates paid by banks; it can restrict credit to banks which it believes to be financing speculation; it has increased powers over brokers' loans, both by regulating their source and by specifying the minimum cash margin to be demanded; finally, it can vary the minimum legal reserves required of members. But the second tendency is to concentrate these new powers in the Federal Reserve Board at Washington rather than in the twelve regional Federal Reserve banks. The officers of the regional Reserve Banks are now virtually appointed by the Board, while the open market operations of the whole system are regulated by an Open Market Committee on which the Board has a majority. Rediscount rates have always been more the concern of the Board than of the banks. The Board itself has been reconstructed. The two former political ex-officio members, the Secretary of the Treasury and the Comptroller of the Currency, have gone. The Board, now rechristened the Board of Governors, consists entirely of whole-time specialists appointed for fourteen-year terms. President Roosevelt has appointed the whole Board, which can therefore be taken as reflecting his views. But future Presidents will only be able to fill vacancies as they occur and to nominate one of the Governors as chairman.

Within the Federal Reserve system there has thus been a distinct centralisation of authority. But it should not be assumed that the Board of Governors is now the supreme authority in American banking. . . . First there is the Federal Deposit Insurance Corporation, with its own powers of inspecting and coercing banks. . . . Perhaps most potent of all, there is the Treasury, at once the largest debtor and the largest creditor of the banks, which controls a whole string of Government institutions granting credit to mortgage institutions, house owners, farmers, etc. It is impossible to say exactly where the balance of power in American banking now lies. The only certainty is that it does not lie with the individual member bank. . . .

## THE BANKS AND THE MARKETS

The insistent demand for a change which swept Mr. Roosevelt into office four years ago related to Reform as much as to Recovery. The most fervent desire of the American people was for work and wages, and the primary task of the incoming Administration was undoubtedly to hasten recovery. But there was also a nation-wide spirit of anger which clamoured for reform of the abuses of the system which had permitted the depression to happen. Those abuses centred in the securities exchanges of the country. It is true that the sternest disfavour was reserved for the bankers, but the link between the banks and the Stock Exchange is a close one in the United States, and it was for his misdeeds in the stock market far more than for his mistakes in the field of commercial banking that the name of banker was made a byword. It may be urged that the public, in large part, had only itself to blame. It had yielded to the temptation of speculation, had "plunged" on a gigantic scale, had proved itself only too ready to listen to the siren songs of the chart-readers and the economic prophets. All that is true, but it did not lessen the anger of the many thousands who had lost their life savings in the market to see the market professionals still, to all appearance, wealthy or to hear them blandly confess before Congressional investigating committees to practices which far outstepped the limits of ethics, even if they remained within the somewhat more obliging boundaries of the law.

There were, indeed, very grave abuses in the security markets in the years before the depression. There was, first of all, the close connection between the banks and speculation. The banks not only invested their own funds in securities, they not only poured money into the markets for the use of speculators, but, through their "security affiliates," they took the lead in peddling securities, often of doubtful merits, up and down the country. Secondly, there was far more profit being made by "those in the know" at the expense of the innocent investor than could be reconciled with a healthy state of the markets. And thirdly, all forms and varieties of rigging the market were rampant. In addition to the insistent clamour that arose after the crash for the reform of these abuses and the punishment of the guilty, the belief was also widespread that the depression had been caused by excessive security speculation, and that prevention of speculation would prevent future depressions. . . .

The Banking Act of 1933 imposed upon the banks a complete divorce from their security affiliates. Every financial institution which had hitherto been doing a combined banking and investment business had to choose one of the two and abandon the other. There is a great deal to be said in theory for a connecting link between the banking system of a country and the system by which capital is invested in industry. Historically it can be established beyond much question that the American banks were almost forced into the security business by the declining use being made by industry of banking accommodation, by the terrific demand from industry for capital and from the public for investments, and, finally, by the absence of a sufficient number of other financial institutions to serve the needs of the new issue market. There is thus quite a weighty academic case to be made out for security affiliates. But the abuses which had crept in during the later years of the boom swept away all these arguments. If security affiliates behaved as only too many of them did behave in these years, then it was both inevitable and proper that they should be suppressed. The effect on the market of their disappearance was regarded with apprehension in some quarters. It is true that if a very large demand for the services of the new issues market had arisen immediately after the Banking Act of 1933 was passed, the machinery of the market, stripped of its most important members, would have been unable to cope with it. It may still prove that the market is too narrow or too inadequately supplied with capital to deal with a period of real activity, but in the intervening years several new agencies for the origination of securities have been able to develop.

Congress has imposed further limitations on the use of banking funds in financing speculation. The most important of these provisions is that giving the Board of Governors of the Federal Reserve system the power to specify a minimum cash margin which must be put down for every security transaction. . . .

. . . The degree of regulation imposed since 1933 is certainly most onerous to the persons and institutions engaged in the market; Wall Street is tightly restricted by red tape. But the majority of people not directly interested in security trading would probably take a different attitude. The business of dealing in capital is manifestly affected with the public interest. Moreover, the first requisite of a free market, the approximate equality of bargaining power of all concerned, has never been realised; the shrewd insider has always had better information and greater acquaintance with manipulative technique than the private investor. This majority opinion would undoubtedly consider that some check on these abuses was worth a considerable interference with the freedom of the market. . . .

On the whole, therefore, this may be considered one of the more successful departments of the New Deal. One can sympathise with the attitude of the Wall Street brokers who see part of their livelihood taken away as retribution for practices which they did not consider to be sins and were, in any case, largely perpetrated by others. But regulation of their activity was long overdue, and if it has now come all in one crushing instalment the shock must be set against the freedom which they enjoyed throughout the years of booming markets.

# 13. The Broadened Reach of Antitrust

The Clayton Antitrust Act of 1914 was partly a response by anti-monopoly forces to the seemingly vague distinction which the Supreme Court made between "good" and "bad" trusts when it enunciated the "rule of reason" doctrine in the Standard Oil and American Tobacco cases in 1911. With the aim of establishing a clear-cut standard of public policy, Section 7 of the Clayton Act prohibited mergers through stock acquisitions where these had substantially anti-competitive effects. The law, however, did not forbid the intercorporate acquisition of assets tending toward lessened competition. When subsequent judicial interpretation virtually emasculated Section 7 as a preventative of new combinations, Congress passed the Celler-Kefauver Amendment of 1950, which extended the ban of Section 7 to the acquisition of assets. The first judicial test of the amendment arose in a case involving the proposed merger of the Bethlehem Steel Corporation and the Youngs-

*town Sheet and Tube Company. The decision rejecting the merger is notable for its subordination of purely economic factors to the public interest standard of Congressional policy intent. The opinion of the court was delivered by Judge Edward Weinfeld of the United States District Court for the Southern District of New York.*

SOURCE: *U.S. v. Bethlehem Steel Corporation et al.,* 168 Fed. Supp. 576 (1958), at pp. 581–9, 592, 615–18.

. . . The record before the Court reveals that generally there is no dispute as to the basic facts. The essential differences between the parties are as to the inferences and conclusions to be drawn from those facts and the interpretation of section 7 of the Clayton Act.

The Government's basic charge is that the proposed merger will substantially lessen competition in the iron and steel industry as a whole and in a variety of important products on a nationwide basis as well as in many areas of the country.

The defendants, while conceding they are in competition with one another in certain areas of the country with respect to certain products, deny that such competition is substantial. . . . Their essential position is not only a denial that the merger may substantially lessen competition, but on the contrary that it would have a beneficial competitive effect; that the expansion of steel capacity contemplated under the merger plan would stimulate competition both in the area of expansion and in other areas, and would enable Bethlehem to challenge the dominant position of United States Steel Corporation in the steel industry.

At the outset it is well to emphasize that the case does not involve any claim of violation or threatened violation of any provision of the Sherman Act. We are not dealing with issues of restraint of trade, monopolization or attempt to monopolize. The Government's attack on the proposed merger is grounded solely on section 7 of the Clayton Act, as amended in 1950, which provides in pertinent part:

> No corporation engaged in commerce shall acquire, directly or indirectly, the whole or any part of the stock or other share capital and no corporation subject to the jurisdiction of the Federal Trade Commission shall acquire the whole or any part of the assets of another corporation engaged also in commerce, where in any line of commerce in any section of the country, the effect of such ac-

quisition may be substantially to lessen competition, or to tend to create a monopoly.

We turn to the legislative history of the Clayton Act, to the circumstances which gave rise to its passage and to the 1950 amendment of section 7.

It is stating a fact of history to say that Congress felt that the Sherman Act passed in 1890 had proved quite ineffective in halting the growth of "trusts" and monopolies. Huge consolidations and mergers continued to be effected through the purchase of stock and "trusts" continued to flourish. The evils of corporate mergers and combines with their increasing concentration of power commanded the concerned attention of the nation. The "rule of reason" enunciated by the Supreme Court in 1911 in Standard Oil Co. v. United States, regarded by many as having weakened the Sherman Act, gave impetus to efforts to secure more effective means of preserving our free enterprise system. Political agitation for curbing the growing power of "trusts" and the concentration of economic power followed the Supreme Court ruling. In the national campaign of 1912 all major political parties denounced the monopolistic trends and their platforms carried planks for remedial legislation. The leadership in the efforts to strengthen the antitrust laws was assumed by Woodrow Wilson, who thereafter in a series of messages to Congress urged further legislative action. The Congress acted in 1914 by passing the Clayton Act. Its essential purpose was preventative—to check anticompetitive acts in their incipiency before they reached the dimensions of Sherman Act violations. In short, Congress contemplated a standard much less rigorous than that which had become required under the Sherman Act. As stated in the Senate Report on the bill:

> Broadly stated, the bill, in its treatment of unlawful restraints and monopolies, seeks to prohibit and make unlawful certain trade practices which, as a rule, singly and in themselves, are not covered by [the Sherman Act], or other existing anti-trust acts, and thus, by making these practices illegal to arrest the creation of trusts, conspiracies, and monopolies in their incipiency and before consummation.

This has been expressly recognized by the Supreme Court.

Despite the clear purpose of the original section 7 of the Clayton

Act, its objectives were not fully realized. This frustration was generally attributed to a number of factors. First, the statute applied only to acquisitions of stock and did not apply to acquisitions of assets, and even as to stock acquisitions it was interpreted so as not to apply where the stock was used to acquire assets. Second, it was generally assumed that original section 7 did not apply to vertical mergers. The inadequacies of the section, whatever the reasons, were further highlighted by pronounced post war merger activity which resulted in the elimination by large corporations of independent companies in industries which had traditionally been considered small business fields. Congress showed increasing concern with the sharp rise in economic concentration and with the prospect of even greater concentration in the light of the continuing merger trend. Further, the Columbia Steel case (*U.S.* v. *Columbia Steel Co.*, 334 U.S. 495 [1948]) brought home the limitations of the Sherman Act in merger cases. It was against this background that Congress amended section 7.

The 1950 amendment to section 7 expanded its sweep so as: (1) to prohibit the acquisition of assets as well as stock; (2) to broaden the area in which competition may be adversely affected by eliminating the test of whether the effect of the acquisition may be substantially to lessen competition *between the acquiring and the acquired corporation;* (3) to eliminate the prior test of whether the acquisition might restrain commerce "in any * * * community" and instead, to make the test whether "in any line of commerce in any section of the country" the acquisition may substantially lessen competition, or tend to create a monopoly; and (4) to cover vertical as well as horizontal mergers.

The Congressional reports illuminate the reasons which led to the amendment of section 7. A fair reading of both the Senate and House Committee Reports leaves no doubt as to its major objectives. As stated in those Reports they were . . . (1) to limit future increases in the level of economic concentration resulting from corporate mergers and acquisitions; (2) to meet the threat posed by the merger movement to small business fields and thereby aid in preserving small business as an important competitive factor in the American economy; (3) to cope with monopolistic tendencies in their incipiency and before they attain Sherman Act proportions; and (4) to avoid a Sherman Act test in deciding the effects of a merger.

Against the historical background of the Clayton Act and the 1950 amendment of section 7, we proceed to consider the issues.

In broad outline, the essential issues which the Court is called upon to determine, and as to which the Government has the burden of proof, are: the line or lines of commerce and the section or sections of the country in which the effects of the merger may be felt—in other words, the relevant market with respect to both products and geographic areas—and whether there is a reasonable probability that the merger may substantially lessen competition or tend to create a monopoly within the relevant market.

The contending positions of the parties can be understood only against the background and general pattern of the iron and steel industry, the making and distribution of steel and steel products, the nature, size and location of the companies in the industry, the nature of competition in the industry generally, and the relative positions of Bethlehem and of Youngstown. The parties are in irreconcilable dispute on what are the relevant markets both as to products and areas. The difficulty recognized by the Supreme Court "of laying down a rule as to what areas or products are competitive, one with another" is highlighted in this case. . . .

The iron and steel industry is a highly concentrated one. It is an oligopoly. Twelve integrated companies control 83% of the industry capacity. In all, as of January 1, 1957, the iron and steel industry consisted of 247 companies engaged in one or more processes of making steel products. There were 23 integrated, 61 semi-integrated, and 140 nonintegrated companies. In addition there were 12 producers of ferroalloys and 11 operators of merchant blast furnaces.

Integrated companies begin the manufacture of steel by mining the raw materials. They operate coke ovens, blast furnaces, steel making furnaces and rolling and finishing facilities. Semi-integrated companies do not operate blast furnaces which make pig iron. They purchase pig iron or steel scrap from which they manufacture steel. Nonintegrated companies purchase steel from integrated or semi-integrated companies and begin their manufacturing operations with the rolling of steel.

The 23 integrated companies own approximately 90% of the industry capacity for coke, blast furnace products, ingots and hot rolled products. The semi-integrated companies own over 9% of the industry capacity for ingots and hot rolled products. The output of these companies is measured in millions of tons. Their gigantic size becomes graphic when it is noted that 39 of these companies are included in the 500 largest American industrial companies and that 16 of the 39 are not fully integrated.

The twelve largest integrated companies and their percentage of the industry ingot capacity for 1957 are shown in the following table:

| Company | Per cent of industry capacity |
|---|---|
| United States Steel Corp. | 29.7 |
| Bethlehem Steel Co. | 15.4 |
| Republic Steel Corp. | 8.3 |
| Jones & Laughlin Steel Corp. | 4.9 |
| Youngstown Sheet & Tube Co. | 4.7 |
| National Steel Corp. | 4.6 |
| Armco Steel Corp. | 4.5 |
| Inland Steel Corp. | 4.1 |
| Colorado Fuel & Iron Corp. | 2.1 |
| Wheeling Steel Corp. | 1.6 |
| Sharon Steel Corp. | 1.4 |
| Ford Motor Co. | 1.4 |

This table demonstrates the high degree of concentration in the iron and steel industry and within the class of the integrated companies. As already noted, these twelve largest integrated companies had almost 83% of the ingot capacity. The six largest had almost 68%. The two largest, United States Steel and Bethlehem, had 45.1%. . . .

Bethlehem is the second largest company in the iron and steel industry; Youngstown is the sixth largest.[1] Bethlehem's steel ingot capacity as of January 1, 1958 was 23 million tons, representing 16.3% of the total industry capacity. Youngstown's ingot capacity was 6.5 million tons, representing 4.6% of the industry total. The combined capacity of the two companies would amount to 29.5 million tons, representing 20.9% of the industry. Both companies rank among the largest corporations in the United States. In 1957 Bethlehem was the ninth, and Youngstown the fifty-third largest industrial corporation in terms of sales. Bethlehem at the end of 1957 had total assets of $2,260 million while Youngstown had total assets of $636 million.[2]

[1] Youngstown's ingot capacity as of January 1, 1957 put it in fifth position for that year.

[2] In terms of assets the two companies ranked eleventh and fifty-second.

Bethlehem and Youngstown are fully integrated from the mining of iron ore through the production of pig iron, steel ingots and various finished steel products. Both companies are further integrated vertically into the manufacture and sale of oil field equipment and other fabricated products. Both operate oil field supply stores in the oil producing regions of the country. Bethlehem has carried its integration into a number of fabricating fields not occupied by Youngstown. Youngstown is a source of supply for independent fabricators who compete with Bethlehem in the sale of certain fabricated products. . . .

About 75% of the combined capacity of Bethlehem and Youngstown for the production of finished steel products is represented by products which both companies produce and sell in common. In 1955 the combined sales of Bethlehem and Youngstown of these common products amounted to approximately $1.5 billion. . . .

Much of the growth of both Bethlehem and Youngstown is attributable to mergers and acquisitions. Bethlehem was incorporated in 1904 as a consolidation of ten companies. Since its formation, it has acquired the properties of more than thirty independent companies. Its initial entry into each new steel producing location in various parts of the country has been achieved through the acquisition of other companies. Indeed, Bethlehem has never built a new steel plant in a new location. In addition to acquiring various sizeable steel companies, Bethlehem in later years has also acquired a number of small companies in the steel fabrication field.

Bethlehem, starting with an ingot capacity of 212,800 tons in 1905, has grown to an ingot capacity of 23,000,000 tons as of January 1, 1958. In 1920 Bethlehem held 6.3% of the industry ingot capacity. Following acquisitions in the 1920's Bethlehem by 1930 had reached 14.2%, and by 1958 had increased to 16.3% of the industry ingot capacity. Since its formation, 26% of the growth of Bethlehem has been due to acquisitions, 58% to enlargement of acquired facilities, and 16% to enlargement of Bethlehem's original facilities.

Youngstown, starting with an ingot capacity of 806,400 tons, has grown to an ingot capacity of 6,500,000 tons as of January 1, 1958. A substantial portion of this growth is attributable to mergers and acquisitions. Since 1901, 20% of the growth of Youngstown has been due to acquisitions, 52% to enlargement of acquired facilities, and 28% to enlargement of Youngstown's original facilities.

There is no real price competition in the iron and steel industry. The record in this case establishes that United States Steel initiates the price changes for steel products and that its lead is followed by all other steel producers. With few execptions, the mill price for each steel product does not vary significantly from company to company.

A principal form of competition in the steel industry is the assurance to buyers of continuing sources of supply. Although from the buyer's standpoint the total delivered cost is an important factor in determining from which steel company he will buy, it is not controlling. There have been recurrent periods of short supply of steel generally. Particular steel products have chronically been in short supply. An assured source of supply is extremely important; it is so important to a steel consumer that he regards a stable and continuing relationship with a supplier of greater importance than price. Equally important are multiple sources of supply. The consumer, to assure himself of a continuing supply in times of scarcity, will, in times of plenty, often forego buying from a nearby steel supplier and instead deal with a more distant supplier and willingly bear the freight differential.

Another consideration influencing the buyer's choice is the desire to purchase from a steel company which does not manufacture the same products to avoid dependency on a competitor for his raw material. The buyer also takes into account the services offered by the steel supplier, such as engineering assistance and delivery schedules.

Competition in the steel industry is sometimes reflected in the absorption of freight. When steel is plentiful, steel mills tend to reach out to distant markets and, in times of shortage, they tend to fall back from distant markets. When the supply of steel exceeds the demand a steel company will absorb more freight than it would otherwise absorb in order to reach a distant market. The following is a general illustration of how freight absorption works.

Steel products are sold f.o.b. the mill. When steel or a particular steel product is in short supply the customer pays the freight cost. When steel is plentiful the steel company may absorb the freight differential so that the total delivered cost to the customer is no greater than the amount he would have to pay to a steel company located closer to his plant.

This is the general picture of competition in the steel industry.

We now proceed to consider the issue of relevant market and the impact of the proposed merger in that market.

Section 7 of the Clayton Act proscribes those mergers which may substantially lessen competition or tend to create a monopoly "in any line of commerce in any section of the country." The ultimate question of whether a merger comes within the ban of section 7 requires a consideration of the relevant market. Like other sections of our antitrust laws, section 7 does not contain the word "market." It is clear, however, that "line of commerce" signifies a product market and "section of the country" refers to a geographic market. Equating the language of section 7 to the concept of market does not, however, mean that the section 7 market is the same as the market for purposes of other sections of the antitrust laws. Nor is the section 7 market necessarily the same as the economist's concept of market. Whatever difference there may be between legal scholars and economists in their respective definition of terms used in the antitrust laws, obviously the Congressional standard is controlling upon, and serves as the guide to, the Court.

The section 7 market can only be defined in the light of its overall objectives and with particular recognition that it is being defined for the purpose of determining the reasonable probability of a substantial lessening of competition and not for the purpose of determining whether monopoly power will exist as a result of the merger. As the House Committee Report states "[Section 7] is intended [to apply] when the effect of an acquisition may be a significant reduction in the vigor of competition, even though its effect may not be so far-reaching as to amount to a combination in restraint of trade, create a monopoly, or constitute an attempt to monopolize."

A horizontal merger can affect competition in at least two ways. It can have an impact not only on the competitors of the merged companies but also on the buyers who must rely upon the merged companies and their competitors as sources of supply. The purpose of section 7 is to guard against either or both effects of a merger— if the likely consequence is substantially to lessen competition or to tend to create a monopoly. The section 7 market must therefore be considered with reference to the two groups—(1) the competitors of the merged companies and (2) the buyers who would be dependent upon the merged companies and their competitors as sources of supply. While both impacts of a merger are interrelated and in an ultimate sense feed on each other, the major impact in some cases will be on the buyers and in other cases on the competitors of the merged companies. As the House Committee Report states:

> [The proscribed] effect may arise in various ways: [1] such as elimination in whole or in material part of the competitive activity of an enterprise which has been a substantial factor in competition, [2] increase in the relative size of the enterprise making the acquisition to such a point that its advantage over its competitors threatens to be decisive, [3] undue reduction in the number of competing enterprises, or [4] establishment of relationships between buyers and sellers which deprive their rivals of a fair opportunity to compete.

Where, as in this case, the companies proposing to merge sell numerous products from several plants which are not in the same immediate area, it is to be expected that there would be a difference of opinion on the question of relevant market. The defendants urge market delineations which the Government charges have been arbitrarily defined for the purpose of minimizing the true competitive picture and to distort the availability of each as an alternative source of supply. The Government instead advances its own markets which in turn the defendants charge exaggerate the true competitive relationship of the defendants to one another and in the industry.

The Government contends that a line of commerce is any product or group of products that has peculiar characteristics and uses, which make it distinguishable from all other products. . . .

The Government urges broad lines of commerce on an industrywide basis and also narrow lines based on individual products. The Government contends that the entire iron and steel industry is a line of commerce; that the products of the iron and steel industry in general have sufficient peculiar characteristics and uses to make them, as a totality, a separate line of commerce from the products of other industries. . . .

As noted, the Government does not confine its contentions to the broad industrywide lines of commerce. It urges that encompassed within the broad iron and steel industry line there are various steel products each of which constitutes a separate line of commerce. These additional separate lines of commerce advocated by the Government are: hot rolled sheets, cold rolled sheets, hot rolled bars, track spikes, tin plate, buttweld pipe, electricweld pipe and seamless pipe. The Government's position is that even though each of these products originates in the ingot and some of these products are made in mills which are capable of turning out other products, each is a separate line of commerce because each is physically distinct from the other, is used for different purposes, has different prices and markets, and is recognized as a different product by practice, understanding and usage in the trade. . . .

The Court is persuaded that the Government's position for determining lines of commerce by the peculiar characteristics and uses standard is sound and should be adopted. . . .

To sum up the Court's conclusions as to the impact of the merger, it is clear that the acquisition of Youngstown, by Bethlehem, would violate section 7 in that in each of the relevant markets considered the effect may be substantially to lessen competition or to tend to create a monopoly.

The proposed merger would eliminate the present substantial competition between Bethlehem and Youngstown in substantial relevant markets. It would eliminate substantial potential competition between them. It would eliminate a substantial independent alternative source of supply for all steel consumers. It would eliminate Youngstown as a vital source of supply for independent fabricators who are in competition with Bethlehem in the sale of certain fabricated steel products. It would eliminate Youngstown as a substantial buyer of certain fabricated steel products.

One final matter remains to be considered. The defendants urge earnestly that in considering the impact on competition of the proposed merger the Court take into account what they point to as its beneficial aspects. Any lessening of competition resulting from the merger should be balanced, they say, against the benefits which would accrue from Bethlehem's plan to expand the Youngstown plants thus creating new steel capacity in an existing deficit area and enhancing the power of the merged company to give United States Steel more effective and vigorous competition than Bethlehem and Youngstown can now give separately.

We pass for the moment the question of whether or not this contention is anything more than an expression of good intention and high purpose.

The substance of their argument is: the steel mills in and around the Chicago area lack sufficient plant capacity to satisfy demand in that area, especially for heavy structural shapes and plates; these have been in critical short supply for years and the lag has been supplied by distant steel producers at excessive freight costs and premium prices. The defendants contend that the situation will become more acute in the years ahead and that the shortage has already resulted in new steel consuming industries locating their plants in other regions of the country—a "kind of chain reaction [which] is a wasteful drag on the country's economic resources." The defendants say a remedy is sorely needed "and that the merger will unquestionably provide that remedy." In essence this summarizes their justification for the merger.

What is planned under the proposed merger is an expansion of the ingot capacity of Youngstown's two existing plants, one at Chicago and the other at Youngstown, by 2,588,000 tons, and a new plate mill and a new structural shape mill at Youngstown's Chicago plant with combined capacity of 1,176,000 tons. The plan also provides for a modernization program which would increase capacity to roll certain products at the Chicago and Youngstown plants. This part of the plan is unrelated to the structural shape and plate program.

It is undoubtedly easier and cheaper to acquire and develop existing plant capacity than to build entirely anew. Each defendant in urging the merger takes a dim view of its ability to undertake, on its own, a program to meet the existing and anticipated demand for heavy structural shapes and plates in the Chicago area. Youngstown claims it is without the know-how, the experienced personnel, or the requisite capital to enter into the structural shape and plate business. Bethlehem, acknowledging it has the know-how and the experience in that field, contends that the construction of an entirely new fully integrated plant in the Chicago area of 2,500,000 tons of ingot capacity is not economically feasible. It estimates that such a new plant would cost $750,000,000 (or $300 per ton of ingot capacity) as compared to $358,000,000 (or $135 per ton ingot capacity) for expansion of Youngstown's existing plants under the plan outlined above. Bethlehem also rules out as uneconomical the construction of a new plant in the Chicago area limited to structural shape and plate mills.

The defendants' apprehensions, which, of course, involve matters of business judgment and, in a sense, matters of preference, are not persuasive in the light of their prior activities and history, their financial resources, their growth and demonstrated capacity through the years to meet the challenge of a constantly growing economy.

Over the decades Bethlehem has grown through mergers and acquisitions; it has grown internally; it has not only maintained but bettered its position in a highly concentrated industry; it has never lacked the financial resources or the effective means required to expand and keep pace with the increased demands of our national economy.

From an ingot capacity of 212,800 tons in 1905 Bethlehem's capacity reached 23,000,000 by January 1, 1958. During the nine year period from January 1, 1948 to January 1, 1957, it expanded its ingot capacity from 13,800,000 tons to 20,500,000 tons, an increase of 6,700,000 tons or 48.6%. Over the five year period from 1953 to 1958 the percentage increase was 30.7%. The fact is that within one year of the commencement of this action to enjoin the merger, Bethlehem increased its steel capacity by 2,500,000 tons. The significance of this increase is apparent when it is noted that as of January 1, 1957 there were in the United States 84 companies with steel ingot capacity, of which 75 had a total capacity of less than 2,500,000 tons.

Youngstown no less than Bethlehem has demonstrated ability to keep pace with the demands of our growing economy. Youngstown expanded from an ingot capacity of 806,400 tons in 1906 to 6,500,000 tons by January 1, 1958. During the nine year period from January 1, 1948 to January 1, 1957 it expanded its ingot capacity from 4,002,000 tons to 6,240,000—an increase of 2,238,000 or 55.9%. Over the five year period from 1953 to 1958 its ingot capacity grew 31.4%.

Youngstown, too, has been a vigorous factor in the steel industry. Its position as No. 6 casts it in the role of one of the giants of that mammoth industry. Through the years it has carried on a regular expansion program. In 1955, without regard to the merger, it projected a comprehensive future development plan, part of which has already been put into effect. During the 10 year period, 1947–1956, Youngstown made capital expenditures of $353,000,000.

A fact not to be overlooked—indeed one to be underscored—is that no adverse factor justifies Youngstown's participation in the proposed merger. Indeed for a number of years the return on its invested capital was greater than that earned by either United

States Steel or Bethlehem. No financial stringency, present or threatened, justifies its absorption by Bethlehem.

The Court is not persuaded that the proposed merger is the only way in which the supply of plates and shapes in the Chicago area can be expanded. Other steel producers are capable of meeting the challenge. In fact both United States Steel and Inland are in the process of expanding their capacities in the Chicago area for structural shapes and United States Steel is also expanding its capacity for plates in that area.

In essence, the defendants are maintaining that a proposed capacity increase of 1,176,000 tons in the Chicago area for plates and structural shapes counterbalances a merger between companies which produced over 24,000,000 tons of ingots and shipped almost 15,500,000 tons of a great variety of finished steel products in 1955. It has already been noted that hot rolled sheets, cold rolled sheets and hot rolled bars are the three most important products of the iron and steel industry and that Bethlehem and Youngstown are substantial and important factors in the production of these key products. Plates and structural shapes are substantially less important in terms of tonnage than hot and cold rolled sheets and hot rolled bars. Assuming the relevance of the argument, the defendants have failed to establish counterbalancing benefits to offset the substantial lessening of competition which would result from the merger.

Not only do the facts fail to support the defendants' contention, but the argument does not hold up as a matter of law. If the merger offends the statute in any relevant market then good motives and even demonstrable benefits are irrelevant and afford no defense. Section 7 "is violated whether or not actual restraints or monopolies, or the substantial lessening of competition, have occurred or are intended."

The antitrust laws articulate the policy formulated by Congress. The significance and objectives of the Clayton Act and the 1950 amendment are well documented. In approving the policy embodied in these acts, Congress rejected the alleged advantages of size in favor of the preservation of a competitive system. The consideration to be accorded to benefits of one kind or another in one section or another of the country which may flow from a merger involving a substantial lessening of competition is a matter properly to be urged upon Congress. It is outside the province of the Court.

214    BUSINESS ENTERPRISE AND PUBLIC POLICY

The simple test under section 7 is whether or not the merger may substantially lessen competition "in any line of commerce in any section of the country."

Any alleged benefit to the steel consumer in the Chicago district because of reduced freight charges and an increased supply, cannot, under the law, be bought at the expense of other consumers of numerous other steel products where the effects of the merger violate the Act. A merger may have a different impact in different markets—but if the proscribed effect is visited on one or more relevant markets then it matters not what the claimed benefits may be elsewhere. . . . Amended section 7 as stated in the Committee Reports "* * * is intended [to prohibit] acquisitions which substantially lessen competition, as well as those which tend to create a monopoly * * * if they have the specified effect in any line of commerce, whether or not that line of commerce is a large part of the business of any of the corporations involved in the acquisition. * * * The purpose of the bill is to protect competition in each line of commerce in each section of the country." (Emphasis supplied.)

The merger offers an incipient threat of setting into motion a chain reaction of further mergers by the other but less powerful companies in the steel industry. If there is logic to the defendants' contention that their joinder is justified to enable them, in their own language, to offer "challenging competition to United States Steel * * * which exercises dominant influence over competitive conditions in the steel industry * * *" then the remaining large producers in the "Big 12" could with equal logic urge that they, too, be permitted to join forces and to concentrate their economic resources in order to give more effective competition to the enhanced "Big 2"; and so we reach a point of more intense concentration in an industry already highly concentrated—indeed we head in the direction of triopoly.

Congress in seeking to halt the growing tendency to increased concentration of power in various industries was fully aware of the arguments in support of the supposed advantages of size and the claim of greater efficiency and lower cost to the ultimate consumer. It made no distinction between good mergers and bad mergers. It condemned all which came within the reach of the prohibition of section 7. The function of the Court is to carry out declared Congressional policy. "Though our preference were for monopoly and against competition, we should 'guard against the danger of sliding unconsciously from the narrow confines of law into the more spacious domain of policy.' " The Court must take the statute as written.

The proposed merger runs afoul of the prohibition of the statute in so many directions that to permit it, is to render section 7 sterile. To say that the elimination of Youngstown would not result in "a significant reduction in the vigor of competition" in the steel industry is, in the light of its history, to disregard experience.

# VI. THE CONCENTRATION
# OF CORPORATE POWER

## 14. An Early Balance Sheet: The Industrial Commission

In 1898, a decade after President Grover Cleveland warned the nation of the rising dangers of combinations, the nonpartisan 38-member United States Industrial Commission was established to investigate the problems of labor, agriculture, and capital. In practice, it became an intensive survey of trusts and monopolies. Before going out of existence in 1902, the Commission published nineteen volumes of testimony, monographs, and reports. Its preliminary report, issued in 1900, recommended moderately closer supervision over industrial corporations engaged in interstate commerce. The voluminous testimony taken by the Commission constituted a storehouse of valuable material on the development of the industrial economy at the turn of the century. The Commission was one of the first public bodies of inquiry to make extensive use of the services of professional economists, university professors, and trained experts at a time when this was virtually unknown. While it is difficult to assess the influence of the Commission, it probably heightened popular interest in the growing size and power of industrial combinations.

SOURCE: U. S. Industrial Commission, *Preliminary Report on Trusts and Industrial Combinations. . .* , 56th Cong., 1st sess., House Document No. 476, Part 1 (Washington, D.C.: Government Printing Office, 1900), pp. 9–13, 16–20, 32–4.

## REVIEW OF EVIDENCE

### INTRODUCTION

This Industrial Commission has taken a mass of evidence regarding industrial combinations—facts regarding their organization and methods of work, opinions from all points of view regarding their effects, good and evil, upon business and society, and suggestions regarding legislation.

As, in the first instance, the most important task was to learn the facts regarding them, most of the witnesses summoned were either persons connected with the combinations—hence those inclined to see their favorable side—or their rivals, who were naturally led to see and speak of their evil aspects. An inevitable result has been that the evidence, even on questions of fact, has often been contradictory, and in some instances it has been impossible from the testimony so far taken to reach any positive conclusion. On the whole, however, a careful weighing of the evidence will lead to some conclusions regarding the nature of industrial combinations and their effects which seem fairly well justified. It should be kept clearly in mind through all the discussions that great capital or a great combination of capital has no necessary relation to monopoly, though it seems to be established that a virtual monopoly may at times be secured through the influence that comes merely from great capital.

## COMPETITION THE CHIEF CAUSE

Among the causes which have led to the formation of industrial combinations, most of the witnesses were of the opinion that competition, so vigorous that profits of nearly all competing establishments were destroyed, is to be given first place. . . . Many of the witnesses say that their organization was formed to make economies, to lessen competition and to get higher profits—another way of saying that competition is the cause without conceding that the separate plants were forced to combine. One or two witnesses simply mention the higher profits wanted or some [factor] like ambition, as when Chairman [John W.] Gates asserts that the American Steel and Wire Company was formed because its organizers "wish to be the wire manufacturers of the world."

The methods by which the combinations hope to effect savings so as to keep new competitors from coming into the field will be mentioned under the advantages of combination, but it may be noted that they usually assert that they expect the increased profits to come from savings and lessened cost of production, and not from higher prices.

## THE FORM OF ORGANIZATION

While the form of organization of the industrial combinations is not of so great importance, perhaps, as their effects upon prices and wages and society at large, it is nevertheless of consequence to see what legal form has been taken by those that from the point of view of their managers are most successful, especially if an effort is to be made to legislate regarding them.

The form of organization that has given them their name "trust" was the one started by the Standard Oil Trust in 1882, afterwards followed by the Whisky combination—the Distillers and Cattle Feeders' Trust—and by the Sugar Trust—the American Sugar Refineries Company. The plan of that organization was as follows: The stockholders of the different corporations entering the combination assigned their stock in trust to a board of trustees without the power of revocation. That board of trustees then held the voting power of the stocks of the different companies, and was thus enabled, through the election of directors, to control them absolutely. In place of the stock thus received the trustees issued trust certificates upon which the former holders of the stock drew their dividends, these being paid upon the certificates regardless of what disposition was made of the plants of the different corporations. Owing largely to hostile legislation and to the bitter feeling against the trusts above named, these trusts, after some adverse decisions of the courts, went out of existence, reorganizing as single corporations in most cases, and none at the present time remain.

A somewhat similar form of organization, however—the voting trust—is found at times. In this form of trust the holders of at least a majority of stock of a single corporation put their stock into the hands of trustees for the purpose of voting it, retaining for themselves all the privileges of drawing dividends and making transfers. Such a voting trust has been formed, it is claimed, in the case of the Pure Oil Company—an organization of the independent oil interests—for the sake of protecting a majority of the stock against purchase by the Standard Oil Company. The Standard had bought large blocks of stock before in another independent company with the probable purpose of securing control. It will be observed that the purpose of such a trust is not to unite various corporations under one management, but to secure in perpetuity an agreed-upon policy without danger of interference through sales of individual shareholders. Some profess to find danger in this form of voting trust, while others think it decidedly beneficial. It is, however, true that this form of trust may put the direction of a company into the hands of a comparatively few members, the trustees, who are in this way able to manage the affairs of the company and to secure it a permanent policy (whatever later wishes of stockholders may be) such as could not be secured under the ordinary corporate management with so great certainty. At any rate, as a form of corporate combination for the sake of securing monopolistic control, the voting trust does not seem to be now in vogue.

The form of organization that seems most common at the present time is that of the single large corporation, which owns outright the different plants. A combination of this kind is formed by the purchase of all of the plants of the different corporations or individuals who enter into it, the corporations then dissolving as separate corporations. Often payments for the plants are made largely in stock of the new corporation, so that many of the former owners maintain their interest in the business. The affairs are then managed entirely by the stockholders of the one corporation through their board of directors, elected in the ordinary way. It is usual for these larger corporations to choose a very liberal form of charter.

A third form of organization, which is in many particulars quite like the original trust form, is that which has been taken by the Federal Steel Company, by the Distilling Company of America, and others. In this form the central company, instead of purchasing the plants of the different corporations which it is proposed to unite, simply buys a majority of the stock, or possibly the entire stock of each one of the corporations. The separate corporations keep in separate corporate existence, but a majority of the stock being held by the one larger corporation, its officers, of course, elect the boards of directors of all the separate corporations, and in this way hold ultimately complete control. It is usually true that the separate corporations manage their own affairs practically independently, although they are furnished information regarding the workings of the other establishments in the combination through the central officers, and are doubtless largely directed in their policy in this way.

In the case of the Standard Oil Company, when the original trust was dissolved, there were issued to the holders of trust certificates proportional amounts of stocks of each of the constituent companies, and since the trustees themselves had held a majority of the certificates, they retained as individuals a majority of the stock in each one of the companies that had formerly been in the trust. The separate corporations were named as separate corporations, but the majority of the stock of all being held in the same hands, the directors of the different companies were largely the same men, and their affairs were managed in unison in substantially the same way as had been the case before. The new Standard Oil Company of New Jersey has recently been formed with the intention of transferring the stocks of the different corporations into the stock of the new company, so that when the transfer has been finally made, one single corporation, the Standard Oil Company of New Jersey, will own outright the property now owned by the separate companies which are commonly known and mentioned together under the name of the Standard Oil Company. This combination at present has no formal unity. It has a practical unity as great as it will have probably after the complete change into the New Jersey company is effected.

As most of the larger corporations have, within the last few years, been organized in New Jersey, it will be worth while to note the special advantages given by the corporation laws of that State. The advantages that seem to be brought out most clearly are:

First, taxation. The organization tax is considerably lower than that of most of the States, while the annual tax is fixed upon the amount of capital paid in, so that it is an absolutely certain quantity and can be determined by anyone, thus leaving no opportunity for corruption on the part of either the corporation itself or of State officials. The rate of the tax is moderate, and decreases as the amount of capital increases.

Second. Perhaps a greater advantage is to be found in the liberal form of the New Jersey charter. The amount of capital is unlimited, the period of organization is unlimited, the amount of indebtedness is not limited, the powers that are granted to corporations are also practically unlimited, with the exception that an ordinary business corporation is forbidden to engage in banking. The Federal Steel Company would have found it impossible to organize for the purpose of engaging in the various enterprises which it has undertaken had it incorporated in the State of Illinois or of Pennsylvania. The same thing holds also with reference to the American Steel and Wire Company.

Third. There is less liability on the part of the stockholders than in several other States.

Fourth. The directors has also less liability. In case of issuance of stock for property the judgment of the directors is conclusive as to the value of the property taken, unless there is evidence of fraud. Stock issued thus for property is considered fully paid up, and the stockholders can not be held further liable in case the property proves to have been taken at less than its cash value. The directors are not personally liable for the debts of the corporation if they fail to file reports or to conform with certain other requirements.

On the other hand, some of the witnesses, notably Mr. [James B.] Dill, called attention to the somewhat rigid provisions of the New Jersey corporation law regarding the making of reports and the keeping of a registered office in the State, where could be learned the leading facts regarding the corporation. It is the purpose of the registration companies, which act as representatives of most of the large corporations organized in the State, to secure the filing of the annual reports and to have the stock and transfer books of the corporation always kept up to date and accessible to stockholders who may wish to find out who their fellow-stockholders are and the extent of their holdings. It was, however, brought out in the evidence that these provisions with reference to registration offices are not fully carried out in practice by the attorneys and others who act as agents usually of the smaller corporations, while there are violations of the law probably in the case of a large majority of the small corporations as regards the filing of the annual reports.

The laws of Delaware and West Virginia were also explained at considerable length. They are even more liberal in some particulars, especially as regards taxation, than those of New Jersey. Neither of these States requires that shareholders' meetings be held within the State, while West Virginia does not even require a permanent office to be kept in the State, although it does insist upon the payment of an annual fee, and limits the capitalization to $5,000,000.

## OVERCAPITALIZATION

### GENERAL STATEMENTS REGARDING THE EVIL

During the past few years the total capitalization of the new industrial combinations has reached an enormous sum, well into the billions, and in many cases at least the nominal capitalization of the corporations far exceeds the cash value of their property. The impressions among different people regarding the effect of this overcapitalization vary. Some of the witnesses who have appeared before the Commission are of the opinion that the question of the capitalization of any corporation is of slight consequence. They think that if the amount of stock issued is only three or four times in par value more than the cash value of the plants themselves, no especial harm is done. If the plant shows that its earning capacity is sufficient to pay dividends on the large capitalization, the stock will hold its value fairly well, and the capitalization is justified. If the earning capacity of the establishment is not sufficient to pay dividends, this condition will show itself in the value of the stocks. While some individuals who are careless about their methods of doing business may be injured by the purchase of stock through misrepresentation, that is not a matter that concerns materially the general public. People who deal in stocks are likely at times to lose. The State, it is said, can not act as guardian for foolish individuals. It is not believed by these witnesses that overcapitalization has any effect upon prices which is injurious to the public.

Other witnesses believe that this overcapitalization is a serious injury to the public. Not merely do the misrepresentations of the promoters of these corporations, and perhaps also of the underwriters of their stocks, mislead prospective buyers of stock, but it is thought also that the attempt to pay dividends on the inflated capitalization seriously affects the prices of the products to consumers and the wages of employees. These witnesses are inclined to believe that possibly the chief evil of the great industrial combinations comes at the time of their organization, when private bankers and others acting as financial agents or underwriters, together with promoters, make huge profits from floating the new corporations, which will afterwards find themselves unable to pay dividends to stockholders and which must within a comparatively short time go through a process of reorganization to the great loss of those who have invested their money in good faith. Some of the witnesses are inclined to think that this overcapitalization has been so prevalent within the past two or three years that the result must inevitably be a financial crisis which will prove injurious to the public at large, aside from those who have foolishly, perhaps, invested their money in these stocks.

The position seems well taken that the methods of promotion and financiering are often decidedly against public interest and ought to be checked. The overcapitalization, too, is probably felt somewhat in increased prices at times. . . .

# PRICES

## RAW MATERIAL

The statement is frequently made that owing to the fact that a large combination becomes a principal buyer of raw material it has great influence in decreasing its price. Thus it is said that, as the chief purchaser of raw sugar, the American Sugar Refining Company is able to get a certain advantage. Mr. [Henry O.] Havemeyer concedes that the fact that he is a very large buyer gives him some advantage in selecting his markets. All seem to be agreed, however, that this advantage probably does not on the average amount to more than one-sixteenth of a cent per pound.

In the case of the American Tin Plate Company it was said that owing to the fact it was a very large buyer of steel it could at times get contracts at better rates than smaller buyers, although apparently it could not get any better rates than several other large buyers of steel doing different classes of business. Especially, however, does the fact that the directors of the American Tin Plate Company are in large part the same as the directors of the National Steel Company, that the business conditions of each are known to the other, and that their interests are closely allied, enable the Tin Plate Company at times to secure rather better rates from the National Steel Company than would be given by that company to an outsider. Similar statements are made regarding the American Steel Hoop Company, which is similarly associated with the National Steel Company.

Nearly all of the opponents of the Standard Oil Company who appeared before the commission testified that owing to the fact that the Standard had control of the main pipe lines and was the chief refiner of petroleum it could practically fix the price of crude oil, and had done so for many years, often to the detriment or even financial ruin of the producer. By virtue of its control over the pipe lines the Standard Oil Company, when in competition with smaller pipe lines in certain localities, had frequently put premiums upon the oil produced there, thus paying more than the regular market rate for it. Sometimes through this practice the competing pipe lines found themselves deprived of oil, were financially ruined, and were at length bought up by the Standard Oil Company, which then recouped itself by removing the premium, and perhaps making a general reduction in the price of crude oil. The opponents of the Standard Oil Company seem to be of the opinion that this payment of premiums has been almost altogether for the sake of forcing the competitors out of the business. The Standard Oil witnesses, on the other hand, asserted that the premiums were often, perhaps usually, and at present only, made because of the better quality of the oil from these special localities; but they also conceded that at times the Standard has paid premiums for the sake of forcing a competitor out of the business, and that under similar circumstances it would do it again.

It is charged also that where the Standard Oil Company has had exclusive control of the pipe lines in certain territory it has frequently held the price of crude oil so low that it could at length buy up the wells or the oil lands from the producers and owners, after which the price of crude oil would be raised again to a fair price. There can be little doubt that when a company is the owner of the only pipe line in any district, this gives it great control over the price of oil, and in consequence over the welfare of the producers themselves.

Owing to this control (which seems to be in the main conceded by the witnesses on behalf of the Standard Oil Company), some of the witnesses assert that the tables and charts of prices of crude and export refined oil, which show also the ratios or margins between them, misrepresent in many cases the real state of the business. If the prices of crude oil are fixed arbitrarily for the purposes of buying up oil territory, of buying out competing pipe lines, or of raising the cost to independent refiners, or if losses on refined export oil are recouped by raising the price of American refined, such figures can hardly be an indication of the real condition of the business. On the other hand, the testimony of Mr. [James W.] Lee in explaining the course of prices of crude oil over a series of years seems to show that he also believes that the amount of the output has, in spite of many arbitrary acts of the Standard, in the long run and on the whole been certainly a very important if not the chief cause in determining its variations in price.

It is asserted by the Standard Oil Company itself that its prices for crude petroleum, as of late years announced through the Seep Purchasing Agency, are fixed on the world demand and supply, and that in the main these prices have been fair to the producers.

It is probably true in general that the extent of the output has been the main factor in determining prices, though the fact of very many individual cases of arbitrary shifting of prices to a degree ruinous, in certain localities, to the competitors and to the producers, may also be considered established.

PRICES OF PRODUCT

*1. Control of output.* Several of the combinations, as appears from the testimony of their officers, control a large proportion of the entire output of the country. The American Sugar Refining Company was selling at the time of the testimony about 90 per cent of the output. The American Tin Plate Company was probably also, at the time when its representatives appeared, controlling something more than 90 per cent. The whisky combination has controlled at times as high as 95 per cent of the production of spirits, and has probably during most of the time for the past 12 years controlled more than 80 per cent of the output. Most of the iron and steel companies claim, on the other hand, that they make no attempt to control so large a percentage of the output, and that they make no approach to monopolistic power, but secure their advantages by bringing together different branches of the industry which insures them a steady supply of raw material or, on the other hand, a sure customer for part of the product. Thus the Federal Steel Company controls possibly some 30 per cent of the output of its main products, and carries the processes from the mines to the finished product. The National Steel Company controls about 18 per cent, and it also operates mines, fleets, and mills. In the case of the American Steel and Wire Company, however, the combination at the time of the testimony was selling from 75 to 80 per cent of the total output of steel rods, the same percentage of smooth wire, and 65 to 90 per cent of wire nails. Moreover, the American Steel and Wire Company has practically a monopoly of barbed-wire and woven-wire fencing through the patents which it holds, and not merely by virtue of its large capital. With the exception of the monopoly secured through these patents Mr. Gates, chairman of the company, thinks it does not control competition.

The proportion of refined petroleum produced by the Standard Oil Company has varied materially at different times, but during the past few years has, as stated by its own officers, increased gradually from 81.4 per cent in 1894 to 83.7 per cent in 1898. Opponents of the combination are inclined to put the figures as high as 90 or 95 per cent. The control of the crude petroleum field by the combination is much less, but is, nevertheless, considerable. It is not claimed, however, that the Standard fixes the price of crude petroleum by virtue of the fact that it is the greatest producer, but rather by the fact that it owns the pipe lines and is the chief buyer.

2. *Control of prices.* A manufacturer who controls so large a proportion of the product as do some of these combinations can, beyond question, to a considerable degree control the price. Throwing into the market a large amount of goods at one time tends to lower the price. Likewise, one who controls plants enough to supply the entire normal demand of the country can, evidently, by closing some of these plants, readily raise the price.

The custom has regularly been for some years for the Standard Oil Company to announce from day to day the price which it would pay for crude petroleum and the price at which it would sell refined petroleum. This price is generally accepted as the market price, and competitors follow.

Likewise, the American Sugar Refining Company first posts the prices for the day, and is then followed by its competitors, who post theirs. Generally they take the prices fixed by the American Sugar Refining Company; but at times, if they have a little surplus stock on hand, or if it is difficult for them to secure a customer, they will cut the price perhaps one-sixteenth of a cent per pound. One or two of the chief competitors seem to be forced to put their prices quite frequently at one-sixteenth of a cent below that of the American Sugar Refining Company. In spite of its control over the output it is said . . . that the American Sugar Refining Company has not . . . unduly restricted the output. It is probable that . . . had that company not been formed the competitive system would have ruined many established refineries, so that as many would have been closed as is now the case and the output would have been fully as small, probably even less. Practically all of the witnesses, both members of the combination and their opponents, concede that while there is a certain arbitrariness in fixing the prices it has been exercised in most cases only within comparatively narrow limits, and then mainly to meet competition or stifle it.

While prices may be kept at rates sufficient, by virtue of the economies of combination, to pay reasonable, even considerable, profits, though still largely excluding competition, any attempt, it is claimed by many witnesses, to secure extortionate prices defeats itself by provoking competition. Thus the whisky combination, in the days of the Distillers and Cattle Feeders' Trust and the Distilling and Cattle Feeding Company, in certain instances put up the prices to an excessively high point. The result was that numerous competitive distilleries were built, so that either the trust was forced to buy them out at high figures or else the competitors secured enough control of the market so that the prices were comparatively soon forced down.

It seems to be conceded by all parties that the whisky combination might, if it would adopt that policy, hold its prices at profitable rates, and at the same time so low that no one would care to compete, its present leading competitors being willing to buy whatever product they need for compounding purposes from the trust at a fixed price based upon that of corn.

The officials of the American Tin Plate Company recognize that their price is to be considered the American price, although they, with all of the other representatives of combinations, deny that they possess a monopoly, and show that there are some competitors in the field. The company fixes the price, which its competitors in the main follow, but its officers realize that if they push their profits too high they will simply call in competitors to so great an extent that it will hurt their own business and prevent their control of the conditions. The same argument is presented in general terms by several witnesses regarding the control over prices by the combinations.

In some cases, notably in the iron and steel and allied industries, there has been within the last year or two an almost marvelous increase in the demand for products of all kinds. In consequence, prices have advanced very rapidly. While it is probably true that the combinations have been able to seize the advantages of the situation better than could smaller manufacturers, there can be no doubt that the main increase in price has come from the most unusual demand. Mr. Gates testified that in his judgment the new output of steel cars, steel vessels, and steel frames for buildings and bridges constituted as large a tonnage as the total tonnage of the United States in iron and steel fifteen or twenty years ago. All the witnesses in those lines seemed to agree as to the increase in demand and as to the fact that it, with the corresponding increase in price of basic materials, was the chief cause of the increase in price of finished product. Hardly any of the companies could meet present demand and all were taking contracts for months ahead.

The fact, however, that in the main the great combinations fix the prices and their competitors follow would seem to show a certain element of monopoly. When they make a cut in the price the others must follow, and their action is substantially an arbitrary one. They, on the other hand, having so large a control of the market, need not follow the cut of a competitor in a comparatively small market, although, of course, they can not permit the competitor to widen his market materially, provided they wish to hold the control. So, on the other hand, this monopolistic element is shown by the fact that the increased price fixed at any time by a combination must be taken, at least temporarily, by most consumers, since the combination is, substantially, at the moment the chief source of supply, its competitors being utterly unable to meet the needs of the market. This is true in spite of the fact that if the prices are made unreasonably high, competitors would, in the long run, deprive the combination of its trade.

The success of great combinations as chief manufacturers depends, their officers claim, upon a cheaper cost of production than that which their competitors possess. If they can not effect this, the witnesses maintain that the combinations will comparatively soon lose their control, unless they can succeed in bringing some other element, like a patent, into the problem. On the other hand, it has been conceded by one or two of the witnesses that the fact merely that the combinations possess so large a capital and can exert so much power tends to frighten their actual or would-be competitors, and this enables them to secure or keep a certain element of monopolistic control, aside from the greater cheapness of production which they may or may not possess. Of course, this latter monopolistic element, depending upon the deterrent effect which their power exerts upon their competitors, is, these witnesses claim, comparatively slight. . . .

3. *Cuts in local markets.* From the standpoint of the competitors of the combinations, the greatest evil perhaps is not the fixing of prices too high, although assertions against the monopolies are not infrequently made on this ground, but rather that they cut

prices to an unreasonable extent in certain localities, and even to individuals at certain times for the sake of driving out their rivals. This practice has been most frequently charged against the Standard Oil Company. Doubtless, too, in order to get into new fields, the competitors will at times cut the price, and to hold its market the Standard follows, or makes still lower prices; or again, to prevent a competitor from entering a market which he seems to be threatening, a first cut is made by the Standard. Witnesses disagree as to the side which usually makes the first cut, and doubtless all depends upon the circumstances of the special case in question. The same policy has also been followed by the American Sugar Refining Company, at any rate in its earlier days, and of late since it has been competing against the new refineries of Arbuckle Brothers and Doscher.

The opponents of the Standard Oil Company do not hesitate to charge it with employing competitive methods which they consider dishonorable. They assert that persons are engaged to follow wagons of competitors to learn who their customers are, and that then they make lower offers to those customers; and it is still further asserted that at times the employees in the offices of rivals are bribed to disclose the business to the Standard Oil Company.

The Standard Oil Company denies authorizing or approving any such methods of learning its competitors' business, although it is acknowledged that it takes practically every honorable means of finding out what its competitors are doing in order that it may properly meet the competitors on their own field. The methods of competition charged, it is said, may rarely be followed by an over-zealous employee, but such action would be discountenanced in every case by the company. . . .

## SUMMARY OF ADVANTAGES AND EVILS

### I. ADVANTAGES

Those who advocate the formation of large industrial combinations claim that they possess over the system of production on a smaller scale by competing plants the following advantages:

1. *Concentration.* By closing individual plants less favorably located or less well equipped and concentrating production into

the best plants most favorably located a great saving can be effected, both in the amount of capital necessary for the production of a given product and the amount of labor required.

Another advantage of the concentration of industry is that the plants which are kept employed can be run at their full capacity instead of at part capacity, and can largely be run continuously instead of intermittently, so far as the combination happens to control the larger part of the entire output—a material source of saving in certain lines of industry. A still further advantage of this concentration comes in the selling of the product, from the fact that customers, being always sure of ready supply whenever it is wanted, more willingly buy from the large producer, and that there is less loss from bad debts. This readiness to buy from trusts, however, is denied, some witnesses holding that dealers prefer to buy from independent producers.

In certain lines of industry much greater economy can be practiced, especially in the way of using by-products to better advantage in a large establishment than in a small one. Much difference of opinion exists among witnesses in most lines of industry as to the size of plant that can secure the most economical division of labor and use of by-products, without making adequate supervision too difficult.

2. *Freights.* Where the product is bulky, so that the freight forms an essential element of the cost, much can be saved by an organization which has plants established at favorable locations in different sections of the country so that purchasers can be supplied from nearest plants, thus saving the cross freights, which, of course, must be paid where customers are supplied from single competing plants.

3. *Patents and brands.* Where different establishments, selling separate brands, are brought together into one combination, the use of each brand being made common to all, a great saving is often effected, since the most successful can be more efficiently exploited.

The control also of substantially all patents in one line of industry sometimes enables the combination to secure a monopoly which it could not otherwise secure.

4. *Single management.* The great completeness and simplicity of the operation of a single great corporation or trust is also a source of saving. Where each of the different establishments which are united had before a president, a complete set of officers, and a

separate office force, the combined establishment need have but its one set of chief officers, and subordinates at lesser salaries may take the places of the heads of separate establishments. In this way a material saving is often made in the salaries of the higher officials; while a considerable reduction of the total office force is also possible. It is likewise true that this same form of organization enables one set of traveling salesmen to sell all of the brands or all classes of goods for the separate establishments, and in that way much labor is saved. This is considered a great saving from the standpoint of the producer and consumer, but is likewise naturally considered an evil from the point of view of those who are thus thrown out of work.

The more complete organizations also will distribute the work among the different plants in such a way that to each is given the particular kind of product for which it is specially adapted, and in many cases changes in machinery and changes of workmen from one kind of product to another are avoided, a source often of great saving.

5. *Skilled management.* The bringing into cooperation of leading men from the separate establishments, each having different elements of skill and experience, makes it possible to apply to the business the aggregate ability of all, a factor in many instances doubtless of great advantage. To some degree there may be a finer specialization of business ability, each man being placed at the head of the department for which he is specially fitted, thus giving, of course, the most skilled management possible to the entire industry, whereas before the combination was effected only a comparatively few of the leading establishments would have managers of equal skill.

But this advantage, some think, is limited. The chief managers at the central office are likely to be large stockholders, and thus to have a strong direct interest in the success of the enterprise. This may hold also of many of the superintendents of departments. But others will be hired managers, and, it is claimed, a hired superintendent will not take the same interest in the establishment or be able to exert the same intelligent control as the owner of a comparatively small establishment. Moreover, minute supervision can not well be exercised in a very large combination.

6. *Export trade.* The control of large capital also, it is asserted, enables the export trade to be developed to much greater advantage

than could be done by smaller establishments with less wealth at their disposal.

## II. EVILS

Among the evils of the great combinations those most frequently mentioned are:

1. *Employees discharged.* When different establishments come together into one, it is often the case that certain classes of employees are needed in much less numbers than by the independent plants. This is specially true in the case of commercial travelers, and, also, perhaps in the case of superintendents and clerks in the offices. While this is generally admitted, it is considered by many to be an inevitable condition of progress and only a temporary hardship which, like that resulting from the introduction of a new machine, will ultimately result in a greater gain.

2. *Methods of competition.* The large establishments, by cutting prices in certain localities, while maintaining the prices in the main, have a decided advantage over the smaller competitors whose market is limited to the one field in which the prices are cut, and consequently can often succeed in driving their rivals out of the business.

Connected with this method of competition is also the use of unfair methods, such as following up rivals' customers, bribing employees of rivals to furnish information, etc.

The sudden raising and lowering of prices by the combinations, without notice and apparently arbitrarily to embarrass their opponents, is also considered a great evil.

3. *Increased prices.* When the combinations have sufficient strength, or for any reason get monopolistic control more or less complete, it is thought that they often raise prices above competitive rates, to the great detriment of the public.

4. *Speculation and overcapitalization.* Another evil often charged against these newer combinations is that the promoter, by virtue of misrepresentations or by the concealment of material facts, is frequently able to secure very large profits for himself at the expense of the people at large who buy the stocks, and that in this way undue speculation is encouraged.

Connected with this evil which comes with the modern method of promotion is that of overcapitalization. Stock is frequently issued to four or five, or even more, times the amount of the cash value of the plants that are brought into the combinations. These stocks then placed upon the market go into the hands of persons ignorant of the real value of the property, who afterwards are likely to lose heavily. Pools are sometimes made to control the stock market, or other of the common ways of disposing of the stock by unfair methods are employed.

At times also the officers and directors of the large combinations seem to have taken advantage of their inside knowledge of the business to speculate on the stock exchange in their own securities to the great detriment of the other shareholders.

5. *Freight discriminations.* Among the chief evils mentioned are those of freight discriminations in favor of the large companies, which many assert are the chief cause for the growth of the great combinations.

6. *Monopoly; its social effects.* The fact that an organization possesses a practical monopoly and can in that way direct its operations at the expense of its rivals, thereby preventing competitors from coming into the field, it is thought, takes away from the individual initiative of business men and prevents particularly the younger men from going into business independently. The formerly independent heads of establishments entering the combinations are also, it is said, reduced to the position of hired subordinates. By these means, witnesses claim, the trusts are in reality sapping the courage and power of initiative of perhaps the most active and influential men in the community. This evil is denied by many of the members of the large corporations, who think that within those corporations are found opportunities for the exercise of judgment and enterprise and for rising in life which do not exist outside.

# 15. The Imperatives of Concentration

Until recently, growth by merger and acquisition was the most effective way of winning a larger share of market power without seriously hazarding government antitrust action. The lifespan of the United States Industrial Commission (see above) came during the first great wave of the merger movement in the boom years 1897–1906, when more than 3,200 mergers of manufacturing and mining firms were recorded. A second massive wave occurred in the 1920's, when more than 1,250 mergers in mining and manufacturing resulted in the disappearance of more than 8,000 firms. A third wave of mergers that began after 1945 has not yet run its course. If any single trend has been discernible, it has been the shift from an emphasis on vertical and horizontal integration in the first wave to a stress on diversification since the 1920's. The following selection considers some of the major economic factors involved in mergers and acquisitions.

SOURCE: Federal Trade Commission, Report on Corporate Mergers and Acquisitions (Washington, D.C.: Government Printing Office, 1955), pp. 103–12, 114–17, 124–32, 135–43.

## ECONOMIC FORCES DISCERNIBLE IN ACQUISITIONS AND MERGERS

### 1. INTRODUCTORY STATEMENT

It is often said that, in both manufacturing and distributive trade, a successful concern cannot afford to stand still, but must continuously expand; that if stagnation, retrogression, and decay in either new or established businesses are to be avoided, there must be steady improvement in products and service and expansion to obtain the advantage of economies arising out of increased volume. It is often stated as axiomatic that this principle is equally applicable to both large and small business, and that failure of a firm in either size group to recognize and apply it in practice means that it will be outstripped by competitors.

Insofar as this principle is followed by both large and small business units, it becomes the justification for their efforts to expand, and, if necessary, to do so by diverting business from each other. A realistic approach to the problems faced by competitors of different size, however, requires recognition of the fact that opportunities to grow are not equally available to them. It is a fact that the ability to stay in a highly competitive market often determines the outcome as between large and small competitors. This ability sometimes turns upon the financial strength or the possession of one or more competitive advantages which enable large concerns to stay in the competitive struggle longer.

Smaller companies facing this greater economic power of large competitors often become discouraged or financially embarrassed, and are willing to sell to the highest bidder. The highest bidder often is a larger competitor to whom the acquisition may have numerous economic advantages, such as removal of a competitor and the acquisition of at least a part of his business, the acquisition of needed additional manufacturing facilities, or the acquisition of facilities more advantageously located to serve local areas, etc. Such acquisitions, though economically sound from the viewpoint of the acquiring company, may have the effect of fostering monopoly conditions through the elimination of competition in ways contrary to existing public policy and law.

The Sherman Act approached this matter only indirectly by declaring every contract, combination, or conspiracy to be illegal, and by making the efforts of persons to monopolize or combine with others to monopolize punishable as misdemeanors. These provisions do not adequately cover the varied market conditions and business relations that result in softening of competition in ways which may adversely affect the economy. Hence, many acquisitions and mergers fall short of being actionable under the Sherman Act. The movement of legislative theory, therefore, has been in the direction of laying a basis in law for applying sanctions to acquisitions, even though they reflect competition among acquiring firms, if their effect may be substantially to lessen competition or tend to create monopoly in some line of commerce.

Since the importance of adverse competitive effects often is dependent upon the relative size of business units involved and of the market affected, and large business units normally are owned and operated by incorporated companies, the trend in public policy and law is to apply sanctions with respect to acquisitions and mergers only where judged necessary with respect to corporations. In doing this, it is necessary to recognize that the same forces and circumstances of the business world are applicable to individuals and corporations, regardless of the size of the business units they conduct. It is further necessary to recognize that the imposition of sanctions respecting corporate acquisitions involves interference with the freedom of corporations in the exercise of property rights. These rights involve the freedom of initiative on the part of both the acquiring and acquired companies of all sizes to enter into, expand their operations in, or withdraw from fields of business as business judgment dictates. It is further necessary to recognize that there are many economic factors other than good management and the will to grow by improving products or services, or both, which determine the outcome of competition among large and small companies. Among these are the importance of control of raw materials or of productive facilities for component parts in manufacturing, or of control of the quality and cost of identified products sold under private or other brands in the wholesale or retail trades.

It is further necessary to recognize that there are many different types of both large and small companies, and many surrounding circumstances which may be involved in acquisitions and mergers. For instance, a small successful firm which has developed a new product or a new process for making an old product may decide to sell to a larger company which offers a high price in order to obtain the product, process, or know-how; independent concerns operating in a market area may find it profitable to sell out to some other company that wishes to acquire capacity in order to compete on a more favorable cost basis; small nonintegrated concerns which depend on larger integrated companies for their supply of some or all of their raw materials may sell out because they fear that a squeeze may be applied by the material supplier.

Also in every industry there normally are companies which are marginal or submarginal on the basis of their cost of producing goods and services. Such marginal companies may participate in acquisitions and mergers, either as the buyers or the sellers. Protection of their rights as acquirers attempting to remove their cost handicaps, or as sellers attempting to salvage something of their investment, is important. However, their protection against elimination as a result of lower cost competition cannot be defended unless some other consideration, such as the need of retaining their capacity in working order against possible national emergency, may condition the decision.

From this brief review of some of the circumstances under which corporate acquisitions occur, it is evident that fundamental property rights and freedom to exercise them in entering or withdrawing from business is involved whenever regulatory sanctions are involved. In general, from the viewpoint of overall efficiency and freedom of opportunity in the economy, the guiding principle in applying sanctions should be that unless some compelling considerations such as public safety, or some element of monopoly, such as substantial lessening of competition or tendency to create monopoly, or some unfair aspect of competition is present, the rights and freedoms of neither the acquirer nor the acquired should be abridged. The proper application of this principle further requires care to distinguish between protection of competition, which is in the public interest, and protection of competitors against competition, which may have adverse effects on efficiency in industry and trade, and thereby adversely affect the public interest.

Since the same forces and circumstances of the business world are applicable to individuals and corporations regardless of the size of their operations, it follows that many of the economic forces discernible in the largest acquisitions and mergers are the same as those present in the smallest market place dealings in the same or similar segments of industry and trade. The ultimate effects of small market place dealings on the economy as a whole, however, may be quite negligible, while those of a large acquisition may have important adverse effects. For instance, in manufacturing and mining, if the control of an adequate supply of raw material is important to avoid the necessity of depending on a competitor at a later stage in production, freedom from concern on this score is always at least as important to a small manufacturer as to an industrial giant, and often is more important, due to the smaller financial ability of the smaller concern. The principal difference then lies in the size of the provision that needs to be made to supply the need and the relative ability of the two concerns to finance the matter.

Similarly, in trade, if a small merchant wishes to expand his volume by acquiring additional store locations, thus setting himself up as an incipient chain-store organization, the two courses open to him are equally open to the largest chains. Both may expand by leasing or building one or more stores and stocking them, or both may acquire stores already in operation with which they may or may not already directly compete. The economic considerations entering into these decisions are quite similar although the size of the operations involved are radically different.

A further highly important consideration is that, regardless of the size of the competing units, two courses are open when competition brings them into collision. The first is continued competition in price, service, or quality of products, with possible decrease in profit to both. Pursued to its extreme, this may lead to bankruptcy for the weaker. Recognition of this by all parties often leads to stalemates in which no one presses the matter to its ultimate conclusion. A situation of balance then prevails. If the competing units are few and relatively large so that they exercise strong or dominant leadership in the relevant markets, such a live-and-let-live stalemate may be followed by rapprochements which may result in such modifications of competitive practices as will injure the public.

In the ensuing discussion of economic factors discernible in acquisitions and mergers surveyed by the Commission, the foregoing general considerations should be kept in mind. Because of the differences in the circumstances surrounding the operation of these factors in manufacturing and in purely distributive trade, special attention is given to certain large-scale production and marketing factors in the first two sections of the discussion, while in other sections dealing with financing, competition, taxation, and investment factors, a less clear line of segregation between manufacturing and distributive trades will be drawn.

## 2. LARGE-SCALE PRODUCTION FACTORS

*New capacity—purchases vs. construction.* Acquisition of new plant facilities to produce end products of the same kind already manufactured falls into two general categories: (1) increasing the capacity of existing plants, or (2) adding capacity advantageously located to serve new markets. Increasing the capacity of existing plants in turn may involve either adding capacity to produce products already manufactured, or adding capacity to produce some component or material used which previously was not produced in sufficient quantity to fully supply the acquirer's requirements for finished products. . . .

Such a desire to balance operations in existing facilities is an economic objective often evident in acquisitions and mergers involving acquiring and acquired companies or properties of all sizes. Even a small local feedmill may find that both the demand for its products and its grinding and mixing facilities have outgrown the grain storage capacity of its mill so that the provision of new capacity by construction or purchase becomes desirable. If there is a local elevator adjacent to the mill and that capacity becomes available for purchase, several important economic questions immediately present themselves for consideration. Among these are: (1) How the cost of constructing the new capacity needed will compare with the cost of acquiring the already existing facility; (2) if the storage capacity of the existing facility is materially greater than the mill's immediate need, does the expanding demand for the mill's end products warrant an expenditure for facilities in excess of present needs; (3) pending such possible expansion of the market for end products, does the management feel that it would be advantageous to enter into the commercial storage and marketing of grain in order to employ the surplus elevator capacity not immediately needed in its milling and mixing operations; and (4) whether the prospect of profit from operations in storage and marketing is sufficient to warrant the risk involved in making the investment required in the purchase. Consideration may also be given to the possibility of beginning the manufacture of kinds of feed or other products not previously produced and of expanding marketing operations to distribute them.

Thus, the relatively small matter of balancing the operations of existing facilities in a local feedmill in order to obtain full utilization of existing equipment may involve a long list of economic considerations. It also may involve consideration of marketing factors such as the feasibility of expanding into new markets with both old and new products. But whatever the considerations, the decisions based thereon are for the acquirer to make within the framework of existing public policy and law.

*Acquisition of contributory producing capacity.* In some industries, notably automobiles, household electrical appliances, and various types of machinery manufacturers, many producers have pursued the policy of manufacturing only a part of their requirements of components and, in some instances, they may manufacture none at all. Independent parts manufacturers generally prefer to manufacture for several customers in order to avoid too great loss in volume if any one account is withdrawn. If now a manufacturer of finished products who has previously been a buyer decides to increase his own manufacture of components, and does so by acquiring the facilities of the previously independent parts manufacturer, the acquisition may have distinct effects on third parties. These effects, however, may vary widely. If the facilities acquired have previously been employed exclusively in production for the acquirer, the acquisition may have little or no effect on third parties. If, however, some part of the production of the acquired facility was previously sold to others, the fact that the supplier has now become captive may adversely affect the interests of those whose open market supply is thereby curtailed. The potential severity of these effects will be greatest if the acquirer and those who may lose a source of supply are competitors in the sale of end products. Even here, however, the nature and severity of possible effects will vary widely with the number, the availability, and the satisfactoriness from a cost viewpoint of alternative sources of supply. If there is no competition in the sale of end products between the acquirer and third parties whose supply of components is affected, and numerous equally satisfactory sources of components are available, there may be no adverse effects at all, even though the acquired company has previously served both the acquirer and others. If, however, the acquirer absorbs more of the acquired company's production than was previously used, and alternative sources are not available to others, some adverse effects are to be anticipated. The adverse effect may be no more severe than the inconvenience of finding another supplier. If, however, alternative sources are not readily available, the effect on those unable to find ready suppliers may be enforced curtailment of their operations regardless of whether their end products compete in any way with those of the acquiring company. The severity of effects on third parties, therefore, may range from none at all to the imposition of severe operating difficulties entailing financial loss, or even bankruptcy for those who lose sources of supply.

*Acquiring added capacity to produce end products.* If, in contradistinction to the production of component parts, the facilities acquired have previously been producing consumer products directly competitive with those manufactured and marketed by the acquirer, effective competition between the two parties obviously is wholly eliminated from the market, even though the brand names of both parties may be continued. The acquiring company now controls the production and marketing policy governing what previously were competing products. Under these circumstances, statements by the acquirer that both brands will be kept on the market and that all previous customers will continue to be served has little value in determining what long-run competitive effects may be. The extent to which consumer interest may be adversely affected depends on whether numerous equally satisfactory substitute brands of equal quality and price are available from other suppliers. These considerations again bring third parties and the nature and extent of their competition, as well as the consumer interest, into perspective in the economic effects of acquisitions and mergers.

*Diversification of products.* From the viewpoint of production economics, diversification of products may be highly desirable as a means of increasing efficiency in the utilization of either, or both, production and distribution facilities. Such diversification, however, may have marked effects on competition. These results may be either short run or long run, or both, in an entire industry, or in a particular subbranch of an industry in which the diversification occurs. In some respects competition may be increased in some segments of the line or lines of industry or trade affected by the diversification, while in other segments it may be decreased. Many circumstances, some of which may tend either to nullify or supplement each other, are important for consideration. Among these are size of the interest diversifying; whether the diversification is accomplished by internal growth and construction of facilities by the diversifying interest, or whether it is accomplished by acquisition from others of facilities already existing; and finally, if the diversification is by acquisition, whether the acquiring interest has previously stood in the position of supplier of raw or semifinished products either to the acquired facilities or to others.

Among the benefits which may accrue to the diversifying company may be the profitable utilization of byproducts or even of more profitable use of a part of the diversifier's principal product, if the latter previously has been sold to others for further processing. There also may be more continuous and efficient use of facilities in seasonal industries if the manufacture of the newly added products can be done in the off-season for principal products previously made. Spreading the production and selling costs and overheads over a large total volume of production, consisting of both old and new products, may also be an important factor.

Diversification by acquisition of existing facilities rather than by construction of new ones may have distinct economic advantages to the acquiring company. Among these is the fact that the acquisition of existing plants producing branded products, which already have consumer acceptance, may give the acquirer a market position immediately without the promotional expenditures which would be necessary to establish that position competitively. Such acquisition also has the advantage of augmenting the acquirer's labor, management and, in some instances, research personnel by taking over the ready-made staffs of the acquired facilities without the expense and effort of competitively assembling, organizing, and training new staffs.

And finally, an acquisition may remove what otherwise would be a competitor in the field. In considering whether such removal is economically significant in a particular acquisition, the size of both the acquiring and the acquired companies is important. Size, how-ever, is only one of a number of relevant factors to be considered. If there still remain in the market many other uncontrolled independent sources of supply to whom third parties, including both other producers and ultimate consumers, may turn for equally satisfactory supplies of the same or close substitute products, acquisition may have no adverse effects. This, further, often hinges upon the degree of integrated control over both raw and finished products residing in one or both of the parties to the acquisition and in other independent competitors.

In numerous basic materials industries a few large companies often are both the dominant producers of finished and semi-finished products and, in addition, have already become, or are continuing to become, increasingly important in the production of consumer goods. Each new integration by a supplier of raw materials, or semi-finished products, casts him in a dual role of supplier at an earlier stage and a competitor of those supplied at a later stage of the production chain. In such cases, each subsequent level at which the primary producers diversify in competition with those to whom they supply raw or semi-finished materials, constitutes a separate segment of the market in which third parties affected are multiplied by each new diversification step taken by the suppliers. It becomes necessary in all such cases to define relevant market segments and to consider separately the competitive effects in each segment.

*Diversification under varying conditions of market control.* The fact that diversification by both construction and acquisition have been going on for many years yields a body of experience upon which to judge the effects in various segments of the market for particular products marketed under known production and marketing circumstances. . . .

. . . Wherever such diversification results in cost savings due to more efficient use of materials, manufacturing and distribution facilities and overall management, it has economic justification from the viewpoint of the diversifier. This is equally true of integrations and diversifications by companies of all sizes and at all levels in which they operate. Offhand condemnation of diversification, even when accomplished through merger, on a per se basis therefore cannot be justified from an economic viewpoint. To the extent, however, that diversification increases the size and enhances the stature of the diversifier in his market, it may carry with it enhanced economic power, the mere possession of which may produce economic results inconsistent with established public policy.

A by-product of the exercise of such integrated power is that weaker, semi-integrated and nonintegrated companies are subjected to economic pressures to move in the direction either of themselves integrating with each other as a defensive move, or of selling out to some already integrated producer. Thus an acquisition, whether it represents new diversification on the part of the acquirer or merely an extension of control in a field in which the acquirer is already engaged, may bring into operation a whole chain of economic forces affecting several segments of the market for products ranging from raw materials to finished goods.

The extent of the economic forces brought into play in the various market segments, however, varies greatly with the market position and the economic power of the acquirer. In manufacturing acquisitions, it is necessary to consider the position and stature of the acquirer in the market. If there are many producers, none of whom exercises dominant leadership in the acquired segment, or in the industry as a whole, the acquisition of a single competitor may have little significance, especially if there is opportunity for new competitors to enter. If, however, there are only a few large companies producing materials or component parts, which both potential new and present competitors must have for their operations, both the number of and the strength of the cumulated economic forces brought into effect by acquisitions and mergers, are more numerous and potentially more injurious to competition.

*Specialization in plants.* Economic considerations underlying specialization in plants are much the same as those underlying diversification. In fact such specialization often is a part of diversification. In the basic materials industries, specialization at the source of production takes the form of separation of processes whenever volume is sufficient to warrant devoting an entire plant or building to a given process. In steel, for instance, such specialization with respect to blast furnace, blooming mill, rolling mill, and finishing mill facilities in adjacent buildings to facilitate the routing of materials for processing is a part of good plant engineering and layout, and has become an established feature in the industry. Further diversification into finished steel products and even into consumer products presents to the steel producer similar advantages in plant specialization.

As the production of basic sizes and shapes moves forward for further fabrication, the flow of material sub-divides for further processing. This means that the volume of material to be moved into each successive operation becomes progressively smaller. Also, if the mills producing the basic sheets, shapes, etc., are not adjacent to consumption centers for component parts, it often is more advantageous for a diversifying steel producer to ship semi-finished materials to the consuming center for fabrication in order to thereby minimize transportation costs. Such savings are substantial whenever the fabricated products become more bulky in proportion to their weight than the materials from which they are manufactured. This often leads even the largest integrated steel companies to locate such facilities as wire and wire-products mills, or pipe and tube mills near consumption centers rather than near the mills at which the basic steel products are produced.

The same considerations have caused independent component-part manufacturers to set up their facilities near consumption centers. The manufacture of automobile bodies, refrigeration cabinet components, and stampings and assemblies for other machinery and household items has developed quite naturally near the factories which assemble them into consumer products. If now either the consumer goods manufacturer using such independently manufactured components, or a supplier of the materials used in their fabrication, decides to enter the field, he faces the problem of whether to build a new facility or to buy an already existing one. If he builds a new facility, he is in effect setting himself up as a new competitor in the field. If he can buy an existing one, he has the advantage of simply replacing an existing competitor, and may also have the further advantage of acquiring most or all of the customers and business previously served by the acquired company.

Situations of this kind often are further complicated by the fact that large consumers of component parts already are set up to manufacture a part of their requirements. Some such large manufacturers have found it advantageous to provide facilities of their own only to the extent to which in their judgment they will with certainty be able to employ them at full capacity. Where this is done, independent parts manufacturers are relied upon to supply any additional components that the large manufacturer of consumer products may require. The independent parts manufacturer, therefore, becomes the supplier only of excess requirements, the volume of which the consumer goods manufacturer may be unable definitely to forecast.

This shifts to the independent parts manufacturer the risk of changes in volume of production which arise from changes in demand for products at the consumer level. Loss of a large contract by such an independent parts manufacturer may mean the difference between profitable and unprofitable operation or even may lead to bankruptcy. Consequently, as already noted, independent parts manufacturers generally find it advantageous to serve as many different consumer goods manufacturers as their facilities will permit. In case of loss of an important customer, the facilities of an independent parts manufacturer may become available for purchase in the open market. The result is that when either a raw material producer or a consumer goods manufacturer finds it desirable to expand his production of component parts, he frequently finds some facility already in operation available for purchase.

## 3. LARGE-SCALE MARKETING FACTORS

*Tendency to integrate control of production and marketing.* The history of mass production is replete with the efforts of manufacturers to establish greater control over the marketing of their products in volume at wholesale and retail. In automobiles and farm machinery, such controls are established by the manufacturer performing the wholesale distribution of his products, which he sells only to or through franchised dealers. For most lines, however, the volume that a dealer can sell, or the characteristics of the product itself, make it unsuitable to serve as a sole line handled by wholesalers or retailers. Other means of control of wholesale and retail distribution are sought by manufacturers of such lines. In some cases, this takes the form of the manufacturers making forward acquisitions into wholesaling, or into retailing, or into both fields. In other cases, wholesalers may integrate backward into manufacture, or retailers may integrate backward to assume both the wholesaling and the manufacturing function. Such acquisitions generally have varying combinations of beneficial and adverse competitive effects at each of the market levels affected.

At the wholesale level, several trends in distribution are discernible. Some of these are of long standing while others are comparatively new. In the food trade, for instance, the inroads made by chain stores on the business of independent retailers, and the tendency of both chains and supermarkets to deal directly with manufacturers in the purchase of both manufacturer-owned and private brands, began years ago to make inroads upon the trade previously served by old-line grocery wholesalers. Many old-line wholesalers who survived did so by becoming wholesale purchasing and merchandising service organizations for voluntary chains. Some of the largest wholesalers had already developed their own brands which often were produced by independent processors. Also, old-line wholesalers took a leaf from the chain store book in developing private brands of their own, and finally, some private brand-owning wholesalers acquired processing facilities of their own in order to maintain the quality and volume production of their brands. Paralleling this development in the wholesale field, some retail chains and large supermarkets pursued a similar policy of acquiring or controlling production in various industries, such as meat packing, bread, biscuit, and cracker baking, food canning, and frozen food packing. . . .

## 4. STABILITY THROUGH PRODUCT DIVERSIFICATION

Acquisitions offer opportunity for quick attainment of the recognized economic advantages accruing from product diversification both in production and distribution. Such diversification may occur in a single industry or line of trade, or it may involve acquisition in several different industries or lines of trade. In any case, the acquisitions involve the combining under a single management of two or more economic functions previously performed by independent business units. Corporate control through acquisitions of such previously independent units becomes the means of accomplishing for the acquirer the dual economic benefits of diversification and attainment of volume without further competitive struggle in highly competitive industries and lines of trade. . . .

In general, such diversification, both as to products and their territorial distribution, occurring in any industry or line of trade offers the possibility of coordinating and stabilizing both the acquirer's manufacturing and distribution. Attaining this through a combination of vertical and horizontal acquisitions of already exsting important concerns engaged in both processing and wholesaling offers the possible further advantage of removing both actual and potential competition. By contrast, to develop new facilities by construction might well require at least an equal expenditure of capital funds which would sharpen competition. The relative competitive advantage of expansion by acquisition versus expansion by competitive capital expenditure, therefore, is an economic consideration strongly tilting the scale in favor of growth by acquisitions rather than by new competitive entry.

This important consideration applies to both horizontal and vertical acquisitions where the acquiring company is already operating at one or more levels in a given industry or line of trade. Its operation is to be noted in the vertical acquisitions by which the large integrated steel companies have extended their vertical forward integration and control in such fabricating fields as steel drums, bridge and structural steel fabrication and erection, oil-field equipment and other lines as a means of utilizing increasing proportions of their basic steel production which likewise has been expanded, often at earlier dates, by horizontal acquisitions at the raw and semifinished steel manufacturing levels.

But one need not go back to these historical developments in the steel industry, which have been extensively publicized in the past, to find examples in which greater stability results from acquisitions. The same is also true of diversification of the type commonly referred to as "conglomerate" in which the products of several industries are added to the acquirer's diversified line or lines.

Such conglomerate acquisitions may be in wholly unrelated lines of products, as in the case of Avco Manufacturing Corp., which, beginning in 1945, has put together by acquisitions the following diversified lines:

1945:
| | |
|---|---|
| Crosley Corp. | Radios, household appliances and broadcasting |
| New Idea, Inc. | Farm machinery |
| 1947: Nashville Corp. | Electric ranges |
| 1950: Bendix Home Appliances, Inc. | Household laundry equipment |
| 1951: Horn Manufacturing Co. | Farm equipment |
| 1953: | |
| WLTV, Atlanta (through Crosley division) | Television station |
| Ezee Flow Corp. | Fertilizer application equipment |

These acquisitions added a wide variety of consumer goods including radios, household electrical appliances, refrigerators, automatic washers, dryers, kitchen equipment, radio stations, farm machinery and fertilizer equipment to Avco's earlier lines of aircraft engines and equipment, industrial tools, heating boilers, etc.

In the textile field, Burlington Mills Corp. presents a somewhat similar set of acquisitions which, while horizontal within the broad industry classification of textile products, are also conglomerate within that industry in that its acquisitions have successively resulted in Burlington's adding cotton, woolen, worsted and mixed fibre fabrics and knit goods to its original line of rayon products, the manufacture of which it began in 1923. The present Burlington Mills Corp. was organized in 1937 to take over the rayon hosiery, knit goods and broadloom fabrics manufacturing properties and good will of the previously existing Burlington Mills Co. Since 1937, the company has acquired more than two dozen entire companies, or assets representing parts of companies, until at the end of 1953 it operated 76 textile plants in 46 cities in the States of North Carolina, Virginia, Tennessee, Alabama, Georgia, West Virginia, Pennsylvania, California, Maryland, Florida, and in three foreign countries, Canada, Colombia and Mexico. Its products include knitted and woven fabrics of rayon acetate, nylon and other synthetic fibres, also cotton, wool and combinations of natural and artificial fibres. Its woven and knitted fabrics include dress goods, lingerie, suitings, shirtings, automotive and industrial fabrics, upholstery, drapery, bedspreads, curtains, men's and women's hosiery, ribbons, and other narrow fabrics. In addition, the company's business is integrated from the purchase, spinning, and throwing of yarns to fabric dyeing and finishing and the sale of its products in either greige or finished condition.

## 5. LARGE-SCALE FINANCING

From a financial viewpoint, if two companies of unequal size have shown equal rates of earnings on their investments in the past, the larger one will normally be able to command greater financial resources in the form of cash, bank credit, and the ability to float new securities than the smaller one. Size, territorial and product diversification, and past earnings record all are factors in this matter. If, in addition, the stocks of the larger company are registered and are dealt in publicly, that fact provides a more definite basis for establishing the market value of securities at any given time than is available to smaller, less well-known companies, even though they may have shown long periods of sustained growth and earning power. The larger companies, therefore, normally have what might be characterized as a differential advantage in the command of financial resources.

Regardless, however, of how great a potential acquirer's command over financial resources may be, that command alone is by no means the only consideration entering into his decision to buy. More importantly, the acquisition must offer other advantages, some of which have already been touched upon. Among these are whether it offers opportunity for savings in cost and increase in profits commensurate with the income realizable from a like amount of capital invested in some other way; whether it provides facilities enabling entry into new markets, or new facilities to serve old markets more advantageously; whether it provides facilities to manufacture materials previously bought, or whether it provides opportunity for more effective utilization of management, production and distributiton facilities and organization. From the acquirer's viewpoint, therefore, not mere possession or command of necessary financial resources, but whether, on balance, the acquisition offers greater present or both present and future opportunity for enhancement of the acquirer's competitive position, power, control of the market and profit than the expenditure of a like amount of capital in some other way, becomes the controlling consideration.

To the seller, however, lack of command of financial resources greater than local markets for unregistered securities or local bank loans can supply may be a highly important consideration causing the selling company to take the initiative in seeking a buyer. But added to this there also may be other, often personal considerations. For instance, owners and executives of closely held corporations of all sizes may wish to convert their holdings into cash for investment elsewhere, or ageing executives who have failed, for various reasons, to develop junior executives to succeed themselves, may wish to withdraw and so adjust their estates as to provide income for themselves and their families without future responsibility of management. These considerations, as well as the need for funds to modernize or expand the business, may cause local owners and executives to wish to convert family holdings into the securities of a larger company for which there is a more ready market, as well as to obtain the financial support of the larger company in the raising of funds needed in the local business. . . .

Another aspect of the command of larger financial resources by large companies is that where cash purchases sometimes amounting to millions of dollars are involved, investment bankers and other sources of capital often are called upon, and through them the investing public is drawn upon for funds. This introduces a whole chain of contributors of both capital funds and services which may include brokers, investment bankers, insurance companies, investment trusts and private investors without whose assistance in varying respects and to varying degrees few cash acquisitions, even of moderate size, are consummated. The functions performed by these interests vary from the purchasing and selling services of brokers . . . to the loaning of cash and the complete investment services provided in underwriting the sale of securities to the investing public for cash. . . .

## 6. COMPETITION FACTORS

*Production facilities.* Various lines of industry and trade often are described as having overcapacity to produce and distribute commodities and services. As so used, the term "overcapacity" is of extremely variable meaning. In order to be meaningful, it must be further defined in terms of volume of products or services in relation to effective consumer demand. Volume must in turn be defined in terms of full-time employment of available facilities for one or more shifts daily. Likewise, effective consumer demand must be further defined in terms of the quantity consumers within a specified market area will buy at a given price level, taking into consideration also the availability of satisfactory substitutes at competitive price levels. Based on wearing quality, a $30 suit may be a satisfactory substitute for a $50 suit, but based on style and finish, it may not be a fully satisfactory substitute. The capacity of existing tailoring shops producing in both price classes at the rate of one 8-hour shift 5 days a week may be inadequate to supply the consumer demand for either, but the addition of a second shift may result in production of more suits than wearers in the market served will buy at either price level. Furthermore, the alleged overcapacity to produce at the 2-shift rate may disappear if the number of potential customers is increased by distributing over a wider market area or by lowering the prices of both price classes.

Two extremes of expansibility of markets in relation to capacity to produce are to be noted. The first has to do with products for which consumer demand is inelastic and saturated. For such products the term "overcapacity" may describe a condition of positive ability to produce at minimum costs more than the market will absorb at any price that will cover costs. At the other extreme are products the consumer demand for which is highly elastic, so that even a relatively small reduction in price may cause what was overcapacity at the old price level to disappear.

The more usual situation lies somewhere between these two extremes, so that opportunity exists for members of the industry to experiment with both price and extension of territorial areas served in an attempt to obtain more complete utilization of their producing and marketing facilities. Such experimentation is the very essence of competition in a free-market economy, and when one competitor increases the utilization of his capacity his success in this respect tends to idle the capacity of some of his competitors.

The existence of overcapacity for an industry as a whole, or for some producers operating in a local area, creates a reserve of capacity upon which other producers may draw by acquiring rather than constructing new capacity of their own. Among those who may make such acquisitions, even in an overbuilt industry, are some who may find their capacity inadequate, some who may wish to acquire capacity to serve some local market more advantageously, some who wish to integrate their operations vertically to utilize a larger part of their production in further processing, and some who wish to expand their operations by absorbing the facilities and volume of competitors in order to avoid further competitive collision in the market place. . . .

*Elimination of competitors.* Every acquisition of existing hitherto independently owned and managed properties results in the elimination of any direct competition which may have existed between the parties, as well as forestalls any potential competition which might have developed later between the two had the acquirer constructed his own new facilities. This is true regardless of the size of the acquiring and acquired units. Furthermore, the size of the market affected generally is also a function of the size of the business units involved. . . .

*Mergers of smaller companies to compete more effectively.* Whenever a small number of outstandingly large companies set the pattern of competition in a highly competitive industry, and there is a wide difference in size and relative economic power of the leaders and a similarly small number of lesser competitors, the existence of dominant leadership tends to foster mergers among the smaller companies as a means of competing on a more equal basis with the dominant leaders. This is especially true if the combined producing facilities of both large and small companies are adequate to supply consumer demand. Under these conditions, further acquisitions and mergers among lesser companies means added concentration and control by progressively fewer competing interests. This fact must be balanced against the possibility that, if acquisitions and mergers among the smaller companies are not permitted, they may be unable to continue to compete with each other and with the dominant leaders, while if their merging is permitted they may be able to do so. The price of their assured continuance then is greater concentration in the industry. This presents a distinct dilemma in attempting to evaluate the competitive effects of their merging.

The automobile industry is an outstanding instance of such a situation. There is a wide difference in size between the three dominant companies and the largest of their smaller competitors. Capital requirements to create a new make and establish its nationwide distribution and consumer acceptance on the basis of service are extremely large. Resolution of the dilemmas presented by the Nash-Hudson, Kaiser-Willys, and Studebaker-Packard mergers involved a decision as to whether the public interest would be best served by permitting the independents to merge in an attempt to strengthen their competitive positions, or by proceeding against their mergers to force them to continue to compete, with the possible eventual disappearance of at least some of them through total withdrawal or bankruptcy. It was resolved in favor of permitting them to merge on the basis that the mergers would strengthen the ability of the combining companies to compete with the big companies which already firmly set the pattern of production and distribution in the automobile industry.

Similarly in the farm machinery industry, the acquisition by Massey-Harris Co. (Delaware) of Racine, Wis., of the properties and business of Harry Ferguson, Inc., of Detroit, Mich., as a result of the merger of Massey-Harris Co., Ltd., of Canada—the parent company of Massey-Harris Co. (Delaware)—and Harry Ferguson

Co's. of England under the name of Massey-Harris-Ferguson, Ltd., of Canada, was approved. . . . Prior to the acquisition, Massey-Harris Co. (Delaware), was the smallest of the eight long-line American farm machinery manufacturers. Its dealer organization offered ready-made outlets for Ferguson system implements which previously had been competitive with the implements of all eight full-line companies. The acquisition by Massey-Harris Co. (Delaware) was approved on the basis that the overall effect of the acquisition would be to preserve the Ferguson competition in the domestic market and thus strengthen rather than weaken competition among the eight large American companies producing long lines of farm machinery in the United States.

Three of these four approved mergers occurred in the automobile industry and the fourth was in farm machinery. In each of these industries, a few very large companies set a pattern of competition in production and nationwide distribution through franchised service retailers. In each, the smaller existing firms have been having difficulty in maintaining the volume necessary to compete effectively. Furthermore, the difficulties faced by a new company attempting to enter the field competitively are such as to make the attempt extremely hazardous. Paradoxical as it seems, it may be found that under such circumstances, the most practicable way to preserve for the future some measure of competition may be to permit further consolidations among existing smaller companies, in the hope that they may thereby be able to achieve the volume necessary to enable them to support national dealer distribution.

The more usual situation is one in which there are numerous competing firms ranging in size from large to small among which horizontal acquisition may occur. Some of these may be the result of efforts of smaller companies to strengthen their positions vis-a-vis their larger competitors who have in the past strengthened their positions in the same manner. If in addition there are no strong bars to entry of new competitors, the criteria involved in deciding whether to question any given horizontal acquisition or merger then are different. The decision then hinges upon whether the particular acquisition under consideration results (a) in immediate elimination of competition between the acquiring and the acquired companies; (b) if it does, how substantial is the competition eliminated; (c) what are the immediate effects in lessening competition generally in the industry; and (d) what are the probable future effects with respect to a substantial lessening of competition or tending to create monopolistic control. Each of these questions needs to be considered against the production and marketing environment in the relevant market affected by the acquisition. Where multiple acquisitions are involved, each likewise must be considered in relation to its relevant market area; the overall effect of the series in relevant segments of the market must be considered, and a judgment formulated as to the extent to which the public interest may be adversely affected.

## 7. TAXATION

In numerous instances the representatives of both acquiring and acquired companies have pointed out in discussions with members of the Commission's staff that tax savings possible under the terms of the various revenue acts under which business has operated in recent years often are factors in acquisitions. . . .

The basis for tax savings as a motive in the minds of managements of both acquiring and acquired companies is found in the more favorable rates on capital gains as compared with the rates applicable to operating profits of corporations and the personal incomes of individuals; the provisions governing the determination and payment of estate taxes; the provisions covering tax-free exchanges of stock, and the provisions governing the carrying forward of operating losses as tax credits against future earnings if the losing corporation should subsequently get itself into a position to earn profits.

For instance, the carrying forward of past losses of the surviving corporation was an important factor in the Kaiser-Frazer merger with Willys-Overland regarding which it was stated early in the negotiations that:

> Tax motivation was strong in the dickering between the two concerns. In these post-war years Willys has been making money steadily; its net income for 1952 was over $6 million. And, of course, it had to pay heavy taxes. In contrast, K.-F. lost $30 million in 1949, $13 million in 1950, $12 million in 1951, and over $5 million in the first 9 months of 1952—despite substantial military business to supplement its auto-making. So it had a big tax credit which could be carried over to reduce levies if it should—through a merger—get in a position to earn money.[1]

[1] *Wall Street Journal* (February 28, 1953), p. 2.

. . . Willys-Overland, in becoming the earning asset in the merger, obtained Kaiser-Frazer's past losses for tax credits against its future earnings. . . .

These are outstanding examples of the advantages to be gained by merging companies which have in the past shown profits with a company which has had heavy losses in such a manner that the losing company becomes the surviving corporation. This possibility offers such opportunity that promoters of such deals have been advertising publicly their desire to acquire companies having past losses. Other income tax provisions, such as lower rates on capital gains, provisions covering tax free exchanges of stock, and heavy inheritance taxes on the sale of family-held corporations are all matters closely watched and taken advantage of by both corporations and individuals, as occasion arises in connection with acquisitions and mergers.

## 8. INVESTMENT OF SURPLUS CAPITAL

Corporations with unused cash available face the question of how to put that capital to profitable use. If such funds represent unused working capital or surplus which the management wishes to keep liquid against possible future operating needs, they may be invested more or less temporarily in the securities of other companies without any particular interest in participating in the managements of the companies whose securities are purchased. Such temporary investments by corporations of otherwise idle funds in the voting or nonvoting securities of noncompetitors without desire to participate in management of the company whose securities are bought are likely to be no more significant in their effects on the economy than investments made by individual in stocks for the income they may yield. Investments in either the voting or the nonvoting securities of competitors likewise may have only similar significance, although there is always a stronger possibility that they may be the first step toward acquisition.

The appearance in corporation balance sheets of considerable amounts representing acquisitions of the nonvoting securities even of competitors, therefore, normally has only contingent significance so far as ultimate control of other companies is concerned. In fact, if such investments are in the nature of pure investments they assume importance as a step leading to ultimate acquisition only where, subsequent to the investment, the company invested in falls into financial straits, so that further investment representing control may become part of an operation to salvage the investment already made.

In addition to the possibility that an investment may thus be converted into a salvage move, there always is basis for legitimate question as to whether such conversion was wholly adventitious, or whether the investment might originally have been made with the possibility of eventual acquisition in view. This contingency with respect to claimed investments in nonvoting securities, therefore, cannot be wholly ignored; it may ultimately prove to be the stepping-stone leading to eventual acquisition of control of a competitor. The conditions under which the claimed investment holding was acquired, therefore, need to be examined. For instance, if the holding was acquired in liquidation of past due accounts arising out of the fact that the acquirer stood in the position of supplier of raw materials to the acquired company which, in turn, competed with the supplier in the sale of further processed products made therefrom, the existence of such a holding may indeed be such a first step to ultimate acquisition of management control of a weaker troublesome competitor. If, however, no supplier-customer relationships exist, and a corporation acquires an important part of a competitor's outstanding nonvoting securities of any kind, the contingency that such acquisition may be a first step toward acquisition of outright control is even more to be suspected. . . .

## 9. CONCLUDING COMMENT

[These are] some of the numerous economic forces and considerations which underlie and motivate both large and small acquisitions. . . . No attempt has been made either to enumerate all possible forces or to cover comprehensively all of the myriad of combinations in which they may appear in different acquisitions and mergers.

Broadly, the forces involved are those which underlie the considered decisions by business executives. Those which are basic have to do with the efforts of business managements to attain the advantages of scale in production and distribution so diversified as to products and as to distribution services performed as to level out peaks and valleys due to seasonal changes, changes in consumer demand, or shifts in the market for their products. These are the forces which are relied upon to keep a free economy vital and active.

Collaterally, however, there are numerous combinations of these and other forces which affect the pattern and the quality of competition relied upon to keep the economy vitally efficient. The purpose has been to indicate some of the more important ways in which combinations of these economic forces operate, and the varying importance which attaches to them under the diverse market circumstances which constitute the economic environment in which acquisitions and mergers occur. . . .

It has long been recognized that the growth of large business units in both production and distribution carries with it great economic power due to the scale of operations and the scope of markets affected. Experience further abundantly demonstrates that when managements already possessing great power decide to exploit fully the economic forces available to them through acquisitions and mergers, their decisions and actions may have such adverse competitive effects on third parties and on the economy as a whole as to bring them into question as a matter of broad public policy.

Decision as to whether the public interest is adversely affected requires consideration of the effects of particular acquisitions against the competitive marketing setting in which they occur. This requires economic evaluations and determinations of consequences in which the controlling factor is not whether the acquisitions are such as are dictated by prudent business judgment on the part of one or both of the parties involved, but rather whether, even though they can be so defended from the viewpoint of the parties, they have such adverse effects on third parties and competition generally as to transgress public policy. This involves economic judgments of a high order, which in turn require consideration of factors other than the business prudence of the decisions of the parties to acquisitions and mergers. . . .

# VII. THE IMPACT OF WAR

# 16. The Civil War and Economic Development

*Since the publication of The Rise of American Civilization (1927), by Charles and Mary Beard, historians have been concerned with the stimulating effects of the Civil War on American economic development, especially in the industrial sector. Over the past decade, differing interpretations have been based on the long-range influence of the war on economic policy and institutional change, as distinguished from the more immediate results of the Northern mobilization effort. At present, most historians are inclined to believe that the Civil War accelerated an economic process which was already under way by 1860, and that the war period itself was not the matrix of a new industrial order. Nevertheless, the war is still regarded as a turning point, as it was in the following excerpt written more than fifty years ago. It is a succinct presentation, with an approach remarkably fresh for its time, whose generalizations have proved surprisingly durable.*

SOURCE: T. W. Van Metre, "Internal Commerce of the United States," in Emory Johnson et al., History of Domestic and Foreign Commerce of the United States (2 vols., Washington, D.C.: The Carnegie Institution of Washington, 1915), I, 254–5, 257–9, 263–5. Reprinted with the permission of The Carnegie Institution of Washington.

## ECONOMIC DEVELOPMENT, 1860 TO 1900

The Civil War marked a notable turning-point in the economic history of the United States. National development since 1860 has been shaped to a large degree by fundamental political and economic changes that occurred during the war—changes which were, for the most part, the effect of various expedients resorted to by the Federal Government to enable it to bring the struggle for the preservation of the Union to a successful issue. To crush the military strength of the South the Federal authorities adopted the expedient of the abolition of slavery and, to the surprise of both the North and the South, "the cause of the conflict ceased before the conflict itself," and the country emerged from the war freed of the greatest obstacle to its social homogeneity. To secure revenue for the prosecution of the war, the duties on imports were raised between 1861 and 1866 to an unprecedented point, and when Congress failed, after the return of peace, to reduce the tariff schedules to their old level, manufacturing interests found themselves protected by a tariff so high that foreign competition was largely eliminated. To secure needed aid in financing the costly struggle, Congress established the national banking system, which gave more uniformity to the currency and brought the financial centers of the country into closer relation. The anxiety to connect the Atlantic and Pacific coasts by rail led the Federal Government to adopt the practice of granting large subsidies to the builders of great transcontinental railway lines. The stimulation which the war gave to manufacturing and transportation in the North and the shrewd manipulation of the money market during the years of the national crisis made possible the accumulation and concentration of large quantities of capital funds under the control of a small number of persons.

It was inevitable that such radical changes would modify the course of industrial progress. Because of the importance of slavery as the underlying cause of the war, there has been a natural tendency to regard its abolition as the most striking and significant net result of the great conflict, but it is to be doubted whether the emancipation of the Negro had as great an effect on subsequent economic development as the other innovations, which were so obscured by the turmoil of the war that they received but little attention and were regarded as being of much less significance. The complete transformation in the tariff policy of the nation permitted the growth of manufacturing to an extent that likely would have been impossible had the war not occurred; the construction of the transcontinental railroads had an immeasurable effect on the development of the great region west of the Missouri River; the concentration of capital provided the means by which industrial enterprises could be carried out on a gigantic scale; the establishment of a uniform currency and a better banking system accelerated the growth of industry and trade. It is in these changes that is found the explanation of much of the economic history of the United States since the Civil War.

The period from 1860 to 1900 was one of development and exploitation. The years prior to the Civil War had been marked by the advance of the political authority of the United States to the Pacific Ocean, and at the same time the nation had enjoyed an era of notable agricultural, industrial, and commercial prosperity, especially in the States east of the Mississippi River. However, the tremendous possibilities of the country were only beginning to be realized in 1860 and, remarkable as was the development before that year, it was completely eclipsed by the amazing progress made during the latter part of the century. An abundance of unoccupied land of rich and varied natural resources, favorable climatic conditions, a complete absence of checks on individual initiative and enterprise and of restrictions on internal communication and trade, and the encouragement afforded to industry by the liberal policies of the Federal Government all combined to create exceptional economic opportunities. Labor, capital, and transportation facilities alone were needed, and as these increased the wealth production of the United States multiplied with great rapidity. The extension of the railway system permitted the constant growth of agriculture and rendered accessible the mineral and forest products in which the land abounded; cheap and plentiful raw materials from field, mine, and forest made possible a rapid increase of manufacturing. European immigrants, eager to share in the wealth of the new world, poured in to recruit the labor force necessary for the industrial conquest; and the invention and application of labor-saving machinery of every description greatly increased the effectiveness of the effort of each individual. All parts of the country participated in the material progress. The South recovered from the state of prostration in which it was left by the ravages of the disastrous war, and became more prosperous and flourishing than ever; the Northern States east of the Mississippi increased their agricultural production and also became one of the greatest manufacturing and mining districts in the world; on the prairie lands west of the Mississippi a new cereal kingdom was founded; the western plains were converted into live-stock ranches; and the forests, orchards, and grain-fields of the Pacific States proved to be greater sources of wealth than were their mines of gold and silver. . . .

The growth of agriculture, which had been one of the most conspicuous features of the development of the United States before 1860, proceeded on a still greater scale after the war. Within two decades the country assumed the leading place among the nations of the world in the production of grain and live-stock, maintaining at the same time its supremacy as a producer and exporter of cotton and tobacco. The chief reasons for the great increase in the farming industry were the existence of an enormous area of fertile land, the application of machinery to the cultivation of the soil, and the fact that foreign and domestic markets expanded to a degree sufficient to absorb the greatly augmented annual production.

West of the Mississippi River in 1860 lay wide areas of rich soil yet untouched by the plow. In 1862 the Homestead Act was passed, by the provisions of which farms were granted without charge to persons who would settle on the land and maintain a residence for at least five years. The opportunity to secure a comfortable home on such easy terms was eagerly seized by thousands of people. During the twenty years between 1860 and 1880 the Federal Government gave away 65,000,000 acres of land to various individuals; the "frontier" disappeared before the advance of the sturdy "home-steaders"; and much of the western prairie was transformed into grain fields. In the western section of the Northern Central States, where the greatest agricultural development took place, the population increased 4,000,000 in the twenty years following 1860. In the rest of the region west of the Mississippi the increase was but little less rapid, and by 1880 the wave of westward migration had swept across the continent. During the remainder of the century the West continued to fill up very rapidly. The less desirable grain-land was occupied, large tracts of arid soil were irrigated and added to the cultivated area of the country, and wide sections of the western plains were fenced off and converted into sheep and cattle ranches. In 1860 the total number of farms in the United States was 2,044,-077, comprising 407,212,538 acres of land. By 1880 the number of farms doubled, with a total added area of 130,000,000 acres, and by 1900 there were 5,739,657 farms, with an acreage of 841,201,546, while the value of farm property advanced during the forty years from $7,980,493,000 to $20,514,001,000.

This addition of 400,000,000 acres to the agricultural domain of the nation would have been impossible had it not been for the rapid growth in the use of agricultural machinery and the consequent transformation in the methods of farming. Not only did the improved methods of agriculture make possible the cultivation of a much larger quantity of land, but they added greatly to the productivity of each unit of land and labor, thereby cheapening the products of the farm for the consumer without curtailing the profits of the farmer.

Before the Civil War broke out, the application of machinery to agriculture had spread to a considerable extent. The withdrawal of a large part of the labor-supply to recruit the armies greatly stimulated the use of labor-saving devices while the war was in progress, and after the return of peace the practice was continued on a still more extensive scale. Improved cultivators, seeders, reapers, threshers, and other machines, and the substitution of horse-power and steam-power for manual labor multiplied the productive capacity of a single man more than twelve-fold in the half century between 1830 and 1880. The value of farming implements in use increased from $246,000,000 in 1860 to $407,000,000 in 1880 and to $761,-000,000 in 1900.

Of no less significance was the improvement of the mechanical devices and the processes by which raw products of the farm were handled, transported, and converted into commodities ready for the consumer. The roller process of manufacturing flour made the spring wheat of the Northeast superior to winter wheat as a breadstuff. The devices for separating cotton seeds from the fiber were greatly improved. The methods of slaughtering live-stock and of packing and transporting meats were revolutionized. The marketing of the annual product of agriculture was made possible only by the use of unique devices by which the various commodities could be handled and transported in a safe, speedy, and economical manner.

The most striking feature of the new agricultural era was the rapid expansion of the exportation of farm products, especially of cereals. The development of the grain-raising industry subsequent to 1860 gave rise to an annual product far in excess of domestic needs, and it was fortunate for the farming interests and for the country as a whole that it was found possible to dispose of the large yearly surplus abroad. The exportation of grain in large quantities began during the Civil War, when the grain States lost temporarily one of their most important domestic markets. After the close of the war the internal grain trade quickly surpassed its former proportions; but, rapidly as the home market expanded, the increase of the volume of production was considerably greater, and of the entire amount of wheat raised in the country between 1870 and 1900, nearly a third was sent abroad for consumption. The exportation of cotton, which had constituted the most important part of the foreign trade in agricultural products for several decades before 1860, was almost completely stopped while the war was in progress, but after 1865 it soon regained and surpassed its former volume. More than two-thirds of the cotton raised in the United States between 1865 and 1900 was exported. For the last quarter of the nineteenth century the United States was the chief source of supply of food products for nations of western Europe, as well as the chief source of supply of raw materials for some of their most important industries. The increase in the volume of exports to Europe created and maintained a balance of trade by which abundance of new capital was obtained for use in the United States. Thus the growing foreign market not only made possible the rapid agricultural progress, but furnished the means of creating and expanding many other lines of industry.

Among the various products grown on the farms of the United States after 1860 the cereals held by far the most important place. The advance in cereal production is shown by Table 1.

The cereal crop of 1899 constituted nearly half of the total value of all the crops raised in the country and almost a third of the total value of all farm products of that year. . . .

Table 1. Cereal Production in the United States, 1860, 1880, 1900

| | | Production | | | |
|---|---|---|---|---|---|
| All cereals | Corn | Wheat | Oats | Rye | Barley |
| bushels | bushels | bushels | bushels | bushels | bushels |
| | | Census Year—1860 | | | |
| 1,242,000,000 | 839,000,000 | 173,000,000 | 173,000,000 | 21,000,000 | 16,000,000 |
| | | Census Year—1880 | | | |
| 2,699,000,000 | 1,755,000,000 | 459,000,000 | 408,000,000 | 20,000,000 | 44,000,000 |
| | | Census Year—1900 | | | |
| 4,435,000,000 | 2,666,000,000 | 659,000,000 | 943,000,000 | 26,000,000 | 120,000,000 |

The most significant feature of the economic history of the United States between 1860 and 1900 was the rise of manufacturing. Previous to this period the country had been primarily agricultural. . . . The inability to dispose of surplus farm produce abroad had led in the early twenties to the adoption of a system of protective tariffs to encourage manufacture. When resulting expansion of manufacturing industries and the removal of foreign restrictions on the entry of American agricultural products had brought relief to the agricultural interests, the necessity of encouraging the growth of manufacturing at a faster rate than would have occurred under normal conditions had been obviated and the practice had been discontinued. The result had been a tendency in the United States to invest capital in all varieties of industry. Consequently economic development before 1860 had been in the main symmetrical. Agriculture had maintained the lead because physical conditions gave it a peculiar advantage; ship-building and shipping had grown steadily, reaching a point of maximum development just at the opening of the war; manufacturing, too, had increased largely, but the increase had not been due, after 1846 at least, to any conditions tending to give it an unnatural advantage in the competition for capital.

This situation the war abruptly changed. In the first place, the armies demanded large quantities of clothing, arms, wagons, and other military supplies and the manufacture of these articles was greatly stimulated. In the second place, one of the most important sources of profits of the northern shipping interest, the carrying trade between the Southern States and Europe, was suddenly cut off, and though the export trade of the North Atlantic ports expanded somewhat, the increase was not nearly enough to overcome the reduction in the total foreign trade occasioned by the loss of southern exports and the decrease in imports. The changes which occurred in New England after the enactment of the tariff of 1824 were repeated on a larger scale. Capital hitherto invested in foreign trade was invested elsewhere, many sailors entered the navy or engaged in other occupations, and the tonnage of the merchant marine of the United States engaged in foreign trade fell more than 1,000,000 tons, almost 45 per cent, between 1861 and 1866. And finally, the imposition of heavy tariffs while the war was in progress greatly enhanced the profits to be derived from manufacturing by insuring a domestic market free from foreign competition.

Had Congress, after the close of the war, reduced the tariff schedule to the level of 1860, it is probable that a flood of foreign imports, similar to that following the war of 1812, would have swamped many of the new manufacturing plants, and the subsequent economic history of the United States would have more nearly resembled that before the war. But the southern influence which had been able to compel the tariff compromises after 1830 was absent in 1865, and the northern sentiment against protection was unable to muster sufficient strength to counteract the powerful influence brought to bear upon Congress to make the war tariffs a permanent part of the national program. The result was inevitable. Manufacturing almost immediately became the dominant industry, because it promised the largest returns on investments. The value of the manufactured products of the United States increased 124 per cent between 1859 and 1869, exceeding the value of the total products of agriculture for the latter year by $2,250,000,000. The decline of the merchant marine engaged in foreign trade has continued unchecked to the present day, and though agriculture, for reasons given before, has continued to expand wonderfully, its growth was far less rapid than that of manufacturing.

The rapid rise of manufacturing between 1860 and 1900 is shown in Table 2.

Table 2. Growth of Manufacturing in the United States. Decennial Censuses, 1860 to 1900

| Census year | Capital invested | Wage-earners employed | Value of products |
|---|---|---|---|
| 1860 | $1,009,855,715 | 1,311,246 | $ 1,885,861,676 |
| 1870 | 2,118,208,769 | 2,053,996 | 4,232,325,442 |
| 1880 | 2,790,272,606 | 2,732,595 | 5,369,579,191 |
| 1890 | 6,525,156,486 | 4,251,613 | 9,372,437,283 |
| 1900 | 9,817,434,799 | 5,308,406 | 13,004,400,143 |

Of course, the radical change in the tariff policy was not alone responsible for the great industrial expansion. The growth of manufacturing in the United States would have been impossible without a corresponding growth of the domestic market for manufactured commodities, and the mere fact that foreign competition was largely excluded was not the cause of the expansion of the domestic market. Indeed, the elimination of competition permitted such high prices that without the influence of other important factors in the industrial evolution of the country the effect of the policy of seclusion might have been to arrest rather than to hasten development. The enormous increase of agriculture throughout the entire country, and particularly in the West and South, was the chief factor in the creation of a large home market for manufactured goods of every description. Furthermore, great natural resources offered an apparently unlimited supply of raw materials and cheap fuel. The self-sufficiency of the nation enabled it to carry out a program of industrial independence that could have been attempted in but few other countries. Furthermore, in manufacturing as in agriculture, acting as both cause and effect, there was a steady evolution in methods of production. Growing dependence on steam and electricity as sources of motive power, discoveries of new processes, invention of mechanical devices of every description and improved means of transportation and communication were all potent factors in this epoch of progress.

# 17. World War I

After the United States entered World War I in April 1917, there were no sharp increases in output over the preceding two years of prosperity induced by Allied war orders, and the return to peace in November 1918 did not entail an extended industrial reconversion effort. Nevertheless, in the economic sense World War I persisted until 1920, when a business decline which began in the summer of that year inaugurated one of the deepest and fast-moving recessions in American history. The following excerpt is from an account which was the first to challenge the accepted view that pent-up consumer purchasing power sustained a postwar boom in 1919–1920. The war was too short to generate considerable purchasing power. The major sources of demand which staved off an immediate slump were government deficit spending, an exceptionally favorable balance of payments, and an easy money policy.

SOURCE: Paul E. Samuelson and Everett E. Hagen, After the War: 1918–1920; Military and Economic Demobilization of the United States—Its Effect upon Employment and Income, prepared for the National Resources Planning Board (Washington, D.C.: Government Printing Office, 1943), pp. 2–5, 6–8, 10–11, 13, 15, 21–2, 24–5, 27, 30, 32–4, 37.

We had been in the conflict for only 19 months, but the American people were tired of war and eager to enter upon the peace. For even prior to the formal declaration of war in April 1917, we had been the arsenal for those who were later to become our allies,

and the war had unsettled and disturbed us, although it had preserved and heightened our prosperity. The days before 1914 were
far enough away to seem Utopian in retrospect, so that one could
speak glibly of a return to "normalcy." Those with more accurate
memories might have known that in 1914 there were signs that
the world was about to enter upon a depression period and that,
but for the World War, the Wilson administration might have had
to face the same type of problems which were to become acute
only two decades later.

The social and economic unrest of the closing years of the last
century had been temporarily banished by the wholly fortuitous
outpourings of the gold mines of the Rand and the Klondike. The
trust movement and financial manipulations of the first decade of
the century could not provide lasting prosperity any more than
could the get-rich-quick speculative activities of the "New Era"
of the twenties. But a rising immigration had created a tremendous
demand for housing and for all the facilities which an expanding
urban population must have, and investment was sustained at a
high level with only one interruption in more than a decade. By
1914, however, a decline seemed imminent.

The war pushed all of these vital trends into the background.
England, France, and Russia provided an insatiable demand for
our durable products. Some payments were made in cash, but more
of the purchasing power was created by security sales and by loans
distributed largely to private individuals by investment bankers
acting as agents for foreign governments. These debt-financed expenditures provided brisk demand leading to a great upswing in
production and employment. We did not have to curtail domestic
consumption in order to send goods abroad; nor did the external
demand leave domestic consumption unchanged. On the contrary,
the increase in foreign demand expanded domestic incomes and increased both our purely domestic production and our purely domestic consumption. Led by the prices of farm products, and
pulled upward by the increase in purchasing power, prices in general began to rise, and after them, but with a lag, wage rates.

Our entry into the war added our own military demands to that
of our Allies. The proceeds of short-term borrowings and of Liberty
Loans were paid out for war materials, enhancing civilian incomes
and civilian demand. By 1917 the inflation of total demand brought
us to the limits of our productive capacity. Unemployment sank

to a minimum, and persons who normally would not seek work were drawn into the labor force. But the customs and habits limiting the gainful employment of women still held sway. Fewer than a million women above the normal number joined the labor force, and even these did so for only a relatively short time in 1918. The 4 million men drawn into the armed forces by the latter part of 1918 were not fully replaced by new workers, and total output fell. Production for war could be increased only at the expense of production for civilian use. Before the Armistice, 9 million persons— almost one-fourth of the civilian labor force—were engaged in war production. Enlarged consumer demand for a reduced output of consumer goods drew prices still higher. While War Industries Board controls checked the prices which had risen fastest, and held them during 1918 at double the 1913 levels, other prices caught up with them.

As cessation of hostilities brought military demand to an end, the problem of economic demobilization might have been expected to occupy the minds of the people. With war demand for the services of 13 million persons about to disappear, their transfer to peacetime occupations might have been expected to receive attention second in importance only to the effort previously devoted to economic mobilization. True, the problem was different in nature. During the mobilization for war, controls had been necessary to prevent excessive demand from siphoning production into undesired channels; now, the root-cause of inflation demand was ceasing to operate. Yet even on the facile assumption that the sole necessity was to let things snap back into place, concern might have been expected lest income fall and suffering result during the rough passage from war to peace.

There existed another problem, more fundamental, but much more obscure. The United States had comparatively recently developed as a full-blown industrial world power. Behind her was a century of tremendous growth. During the nineteenth century, when effective demand fell off, one had only to sit back and wait for the market to "grow up to" the conditions of supply. Even then the waiting was sometimes a long, misery-creating process, as in the great depressions of the seventies and the nineties. . . .

The demand for goods during the war and the intense economic activity generated by it differed only in degree from those created by the historic bursts of private debt creation. Like the transient war boom, each historic wave of private investment had come to an end, and the closing of outlets for savings had ushered in depression. . . .

At the time of the armistice, in addition to contractual agreements for troop maintenance, transportation, medical facilities, and the like, the War Department had $6 billions of manufacturing contracts outstanding. One-third of them were for goods on which production had already been completed. Of the remaining $4 billions, $2½ billions were canceled within 4 weeks. Typically, cancellation included provision for subsequent acceptance of a quantity of goods equal to a month's production at the current rate. Attempts by the War Industries Board and the Department of Labor to arrange for consideration of the welfare of the community concerned, before cancellation of each contract, were overridden in the interest of speedy termination. During the winter and spring, production on most War Department contracts tapered to the vanishing point. On December 12, Congress by joint resolution directed the United States Housing Corporation, whose work was just getting into swing, to suspend work on all buildings not more than 70 per cent completed.

Certain other types of war work in process (e.g., for the Navy) went on for some time, and the United States Shipping Board Emergency Fleet Corporation, caught in midstride, continued operation on a large scale. Shipping Board monthly expenditures declined very gradually throughout 1919. Deliveries of ships reached their peak, not during the period of hostilities, but in May 1919. Fewer than 500 ships, of less than 3 million deadweight tons, had been delivered by the end of October 1918. Despite cancellations where feasible, almost three times as many ships, with well over twice the tonnage, were delivered during the subsequent two years. Because of the delayed termination of these and other activities, some war production was carried on long after the armistice. These continuations reveal, however, not a planned gradual transition but rather the impossibility of checking immediately a great war program in full swing. . . .

The haste with which war production and the armed forces were demobilized is not surprising, considering the temper of the times. More surprising is the complete failure to consider the consequences of the rapid disgorging of manpower. The abrupt reduction in scale of operations by war plants whose contracts had been canceled occurred at the same time that the first 2 million members of the armed forces were being returned to civil life. Yet neither the Federal nor the State and local governments had planned in advance to initiate a compensating program of useful work projects to cushion the transitional shock. Nor had any other program been adopted. This was laissez faire with a vengeance; the Government created the disturbance in the economic system, then ignored its results. . . .

But the bottom did not drop out of the market. Consumer buying continued, so that wholesale prices steadied and in March turned upward. Automobile output and employment in furniture manufacturing, both of which had been sharply curtailed before the armistice, began to rise before the end of 1918. Employment in clothing, in textiles, and in silk and rayon rose early in 1919. Output of the nondurable goods industries as a group declined until February 1919, but in March it held at the February level and in April began to rise.

In spite of rises in activity in automobile and furniture production, total employment in the durable goods industries declined until May, primarily because of the termination of war contracts. Thereafter it increased. The total volume of industrial output rose in June and again in July. . . .

Ominously, the rise in prices which had begun in April 1919 accelerated in the latter part of that year, and amid a nation-wide outcry about the "high cost of living" we reached the hectic climax of the boomlet in early 1920. The prices of the goods and services which make up the low-income consumer's budget had risen between 10 and 15 per cent each year since war broke out in Europe in 1914. After a slight drop in early 1919, they rose so rapidly that by June 1920 they were 25 per cent above the wartime peak. Wholesale prices also soared again, to unprecedented levels. . . . In May 1920 they were one-fifth above the wartime high. Speculation in securities, in land, and in commodities accompanied and fed the rise in prices.

While prices soared, a moderate increase in employment and production continued. As was to be expected, business conditions were uneven; some industries were unusually active, while for others demand was dull. The volume of retail and wholesale trade in some lines had increased sufficiently by the third quarter of 1919 so that mills and factories began to fall behind in deliveries. . . . By the end of the first quarter of 1920 industrial output as a whole was 20 per cent and factory employment 13 per cent above the lows of early 1919. These magnitudes of change may not seem large as percentages, but in terms of output of goods and the employment of human labor they are exceeded only in the transition from severe depression to prosperity. Hence they testify to the reality of the 1919 distress.

Economic activity, having risen, did not move along on an even keel. Industrial output turned down rather sharply in April 1920, even while prices were still rising. Unnoted, unemployment slowly increased. Then, like a leaking toy boat which suddenly floods and sinks, prosperity vanished. At mid-year wholesale prices and raw materials prices collapsed. To many persons the termination of Government support for the price of wheat (at $2.26 per bushel) seemed to be the act which scuttled the ship. Actually the causes of decline lay deeper. The recession in economic activity remained gradual until fall, then turned to a rout. By the beginning of the new year output and employment were far below the 1919 lows. The year of 1921 was a year of severe depression. Then began a steady climb to the prosperity plateau of 1923–29, when prosperity was sustained by the unprecedented housing boom; by the expansion of installment sales, and of the automobile industry with all its satellites; by the increase in debt-financed local and State public works, especially roads and schools; and by the flow of American credit to foreign countries to finance their purchases of our goods. When these influences had run their course, economic activity again collapsed, and we entered the depression of the 1930's. . . .

In spite of the hasty demobilization of the armed forces and the abrupt cancellation of war orders wherever possible, it was impossible to wind up the war quickly. *Economically* the first World War lasted until 1920. This is to be emphasized in explaining why a severe depression did not develop in the first 6 months of 1919. The conditions which prolonged the flow of war expenditures have been discussed. Demobilization itself, plus the $60 bonus per man, required large expenditures. Cancellation of war contracts typically permitted delivery of added output equal to 1 month's production. With multiple shifts and overtime eliminated and with hours shortened in some cases, production of the permitted added quantity of goods was often spread over several months. Many projects for one reason or another could not be terminated quickly; shipbuilding is an example. After November 11, 1918, the United States extended $2 billion in loans to the Allies, practically all of which was spent for goods and services within this country.

Because of these and similar expenditures after the armistice, Treasury expenditures reached their wartime peak, not during hostilities but in December 1918, with January 1919 as the second highest month. . . . Though monthly expenditures declined irregularly during 1919, they remained huge by pre-war standards. Pre-war Federal expenditures reached a yearly peak of $760 millions in 1915. Monthly expenditures exceeded this figure in every month of 1919 through August.

Even more significant than the huge expenditures was the huge net governmental contribution to the nation's purchasing power after the armistice. Full appreciation of that contribution, and of its sharp decline during 1919, is basic to an adequate analysis of economic developments. Budgetary deficits will serve as a rough measure of the Government's contribution to the income stream. . . . For December 1918 and January 1919 they were higher than those of any war month. They were more than double any pre-war year's total expenditures and were fantastically in excess of any annual deficit dreamed of before the war. They contributed greatly to the maintenance of effective demand. These deficits were at a yearly rate of $20 billion in the last quarter of 1918, and of $11 billion, $6 billion, and $3 billion in successive quarters of 1919. It was not until the quarter beginning October 1919 that the Treasury operated without a deficit. . . .

First, it must be remembered that the stimulus to national income from governmental expenditure is not immediate, ceasing at the moment that spending ceases. The direct recipients of Government disbursements hold funds for some time before spending. After individuals do finally spend part of what they have received the new recipients take some time before they in turn spend. For part of the funds received by business enterprises the lag is even longer than for income received directly by individuals, since dividends are paid only quarterly, semiannually, or annually. This explains the statistical fact, true of the period between the two wars as a whole, that investment and offsets to savings in a given year exert some 60 per cent of their income-stimulating effects in that year and 40 per cent in the succeeding year. The soldiers' bonus paid out in the summer of 1936 contributed to price increases well into 1937. Similarly the reduction in Federal deficits early in 1937 as a result of social insurance taxes was felt only in the late summer and fall of that year. In the same way the purchasing power created by the Government month by month in 1918 and in the first half of 1919 stimulated buying many months later, although with taper-ing effect in the latter part of 1919 and in 1920. When the deficit reaches a peak and then declines, the contribution to the national income, direct plus indirect, reaches its greatest magnitude some time later. It is probable that, though the Treasury deficit reached its peak in December 1918, Government support to production and income reached its maximum during 1919.

Second, it is a mistake to think that the Government's contribu-tion to employment and effective demand is correctly measured by the deficit alone—that only the difference between expenditure and receipts is important. The level at which revenue and outlay bal-ance is of considerable importance, even if there is no deficit. If Government taxation and expenditure have the result of discourag-ing private investment, the stimulating effect of a high level of Government activity may be counterbalanced in whole or in part by a decline in private activity. Under the conditions prevailing in the period following the armistice, it seems certain that there was no such negative effect, no matter what may be thought to be the case at other times. Throughout the latter half of 1918 and the first half of 1919 the level of Federal expenditure was high, both com-pared to the pre-war period and to the years which were to follow. This high level of Government activity was in itself a sustaining force. . . .

The huge dollar volume of exports did not diminish after the armistice. Instead it increased. . . . During the war our exports had consisted largely of agricultural commodities. In the immediate post-armistice period the upward surge of exports likewise consisted of cotton and food for a cold and hungry Europe. . . . The United States Government was advancing huge sums for the purchase of foodstuffs and other necessaries, and private credit was readily avail-able here. During the war inflation and depreciation of European currencies had far exceeded that in the United States. With the coming of peace and the removal of wartime exchange controls the American dollar became undervalued in terms of foreign currencies. This created a powerful incentive to buy the relatively cheap Amer-ican exports, and at the same time tended to limit our imports from abroad. As a consequence the bulk of the European buying in 1919 was in the United States. The net flow of purchasing power into this country increased materially from 1918 to 1919. It then tapered from $3.3 billion in the latter year to $2.8 billion in 1920 and $1.6 billion in 1921. . . .

To understand the boom and its extravagances it is necessary to appreciate the speculative excesses which developed during 1919 and reached their culmination in early 1920. . . .

Credit conditions paved the way for the excesses of the boom. The establishment of the Federal Reserve system at the beginning of the European war had made it possible for the existing volume of monetary reserves to support a much heavier superstructure of bank credit. During the war an inflow of gold in payment for exports had enlarged the credit base. By the end of the war individual demand deposits had increased from the pre-war figure of $18.5 billion to some $30 billion; yet Federal Reserve bank reserve ratios were still well above the legal minimum of 40 per cent.

It was obvious throughout 1919 that bank credit was being extended in considerable volume to finance speculative activity, but the hands of Federal Reserve officials were tied. The Federal Reserve system was bound to maintain rediscount rates at their low level to facilitate the marketing of the Victory Loan by the Treasury. From time to time the Federal Reserve Board warned member banks that the funds of the system were not to be used in support of speculation. But whatever tightening of the market such vague warnings may have caused was promptly offset by action of the Treasury. The use by the Treasury of the "bond purchase fund" to support the price of Government securities had the effect of supporting the price of other securities as well and of maintaining low interest rates and easy credit conditions. . . .

Speculative activity became apparent during the first half of 1919. As the price rise got under way speculation increased. The prices of stock market securities turned upward and the volume of activity on the stock exchanges skyrocketed. In the speculative activity of 1915 the monthly average number of shares traded on the New York Stock Exchange was 19.4 million. By 1918 it had dropped slightly below normal to 12 million. In 1919 it catapulted to over 26. Call loan rates touched 7 per cent in February, 15 per cent in June, 18 per cent in July, and 30 per cent in November;

yet so great were the short-run paper profits expected from appreciation in price of securities that speculation was not discouraged.

Increased activity in trading became more marked by the middle of 1919 than the increase in manufacturing output. Heavy dealing and rapidly mounting prices were reported from the produce exchanges. As one not untypical example, on July 23 live hogs brought $23.50 per hundredweight at the Chicago stockyards—the highest price ever recorded. The volume of commodity loans by commercial banks increased; it was clear that they were for the purpose, not of moving commodities through the channels of trade, but of withholding them. Loans were also needed because transportation bottlenecks caused delay in disposing of goods.

At the same time that security and commodity speculation was rampant a nation-wide land boom developed. Both farm and city real estate began to change hands with greater and greater rapidity and at higher and higher prices. Because securities and real estate could be purchased on very small equities, the balance of the purchase price being financed by bank credit, this speculation did not siphon funds from the commodity markets. Instead it created an illusion of high prosperity and enormous demand, and so stimulated still more forward buying of commodities.

During 1919 . . . the value of business inventories increased by $6 billion, an increase almost twice that of any other year of the decade to follow, and almost four times that of any other year except 1923. Two-thirds of the change . . . was due to increase in the physical volume of stocks held, one-third to the increase in prices which both resulted from and stimulated the speculative fever. The largest increase was in wholesale and retail inventories. . . .

Forward buying increased demand and bid up prices. The expectation of continued increase in prices caused added speculative buying. The price structure was lifting itself by its bootstraps. Amid this hysteria of speculation we reached the peak of the boom in the first half of 1920. . . .

As inventories grew, earlier in the year, worry began to manifest itself among the more cautious that inventories might become so large as to endanger the price structure. Consumers became more vociferous in their denunciations of the "high cost of living," and fear arose that it would be impossible to pass on ever-increasing raw-materials prices to the final buyer. . . . Federal Reserve warnings and the repeated raising of rediscount rates caused many banks to apply some pressure upon their borrowers; to repay bank loans some stocks of goods held in the hope of still higher prices had to be placed upon the market. Retailers and jobbers suddenly realized that they did not need the goods they had demanded so desperately a few weeks previously. Cancellations snowballed in volume; huge backlogs of orders vanished from the books of manufacturing corporations. The fall in agricultural prices from mid-year on was catastrophic. It was clearly the pricking of a speculative bubble, for no readjustment of real supply and demand could have produced so extreme an effect. The fall in wholesale prices continued until July 1921, when the Bureau of Labor Statistics index stood 43 per cent below its May 1920 level. . . .

Only housing construction, among the private sources of demand, might conceivably have continued its support to income. But lumbering and other enterprises in the none-too-competitive building materials industry were eager to take advantage of the rising demand. So were construction workers. . . .

The construction industry faced an added difficulty. By late 1919 even the resources of the Federal Reserve system were strained. Little additional credit extension was possible. The interest rate earned upon money loaned for stock market use and the attractiveness of other kinds of speculation was so great that mortgage money became almost unobtainable. Here, as at so many times in our history, speculation inhibited income-producing economic activity. In April 1920 the construction boom reached its peak. By July it was one-third below, and by September 50 per cent below the April peak. Thereafter it fell off rapidly until at the end of the year it was below any month since March 1919.

Thus the reversal of fiscal policy, the decline in our favorable foreign balance, and the collapse of housing construction acted with the reaction from the speculative boom to bring depression. The recession continued gradual until fall, partly because of the continued plant construction mentioned above, partly perhaps because of the respending of income created by the previous export boom. In the autumn the decline to deep depression accelerated.

# VIII. THE PROMOTION OF ECONOMIC GROWTH AND STABILITY

## 18. The Employment Act of 1946

*The Employment Act of 1946 affirmed continuous federal respon-sibility both in prosperity and recession for creating policies aimed at maintaining a strong and stable economy with high levels of production, employment, and purchasing power. It wrote into law the proposition that within reason men can influence and direct their economic en-vironment, and that, as President Harry S Truman put it, "intelligent human action will shape our future." To a considerable degree, as the following review indicates, the measure was a result of the fears and uncertainties inherited from the depression-stricken 1930's. In December, 1967 the national economy rounded out the eighty-second consecutive month of the longest period of business expansion in American history.*

SOURCE: *Economic Report of the President . . . 1966. . . .* (Washington, D.C.: Government Printing Office, 1966), pp. 170–82.

### THE EMPLOYMENT ACT: TWENTY YEARS OF POLICY EXPERIENCE

THERE were great expectations and not a few qualms when the Employment Act was signed into law on February 20, 1946, following enactment by heavy bipartisan majorities in both houses of Congress. This year, which marks the 20th anniversary of that enactment, is a suitable occasion to review our experience under the Act, to take stock of where we stand today, and to con-sider the challenges ahead.

277

## THE ACT AND ITS BACKGROUND

The legislation of 1946 set forth the following declaration of policy:

The Congress declares that it is the continuing policy and responsibility of the Federal Government to use all practicable means consistent with its needs and obligations and other essential considerations of national policy, with the assistance and cooperation of industry, agriculture, labor, and State and local governments, to coordinate and utilize all its plans, functions, and resources for the purpose of creating and maintaining, in a manner calculated to foster and promote free competitive enterprise and the general welfare, conditions under which there will be afforded useful employment opportunities, including self-employment, for those able, willing, and seeking to work, and to promote maximum employment, production, and purchasing power.

In making this declaration, the Congress recognized that the billions of independent spending and saving decisions of a free economy could well result in levels of total demand either short of full employment or in excess of productive capacity. Furthermore, it took the view that Government policies could play a constructive role in improving the stability and balance of the economy.

The Act was a product of the experiences of the Great Depression and World War II. The Depression shook but did not destroy the faith in an automatic tendency of the economy to find its proper level of operation. In the early 1930's, public works and other anti-depression programs were justified as temporary "pump priming," to help the private economy get back on its track after an unusual and catastrophic derailment. And the departure from orthodox fiscal principles was made with regret and without complete consistency. The Government expenditures explicitly designed to combat depression necessarily increased budget deficits; but this implication was veiled by financing these outlays through an "extraordinary" budget. Meanwhile, taxes were raised, and salaries and housekeeping expenditures cut in the regular budget, thereby reducing the overall stimulation of Government measures.

The relapse of the economy in 1937 into a sharp decline from a level still far below full employment gave rise to conflicting interpretations. To some, it proved that pump priming and Government deficits had undermined the confidence of the business community and thereby only worsened the situation. Others, however, concluded that it pointed to the need for larger and more sustained fiscal and monetary actions to revive the economy. In drawing this conclusion, economists were buttressed by the writings of J. M. Keynes, who offered a theoretical explanation of the disastrous depression. The Keynesian conclusions received additional support during World War II because they offered a satisfactory explanation of why the high deficit-financed defense expenditures of that period not only wiped out unemployment but went beyond to create inflationary pressures.

Memories of the disastrous 1930's were very much in the public mind as World War II was drawing to an end. Many active proponents of "full employment" legislation in 1945 and 1946 feared a relapse into depressed levels of economic activity like those of the 1930's, once military spending ended. They looked toward Federal public works spending as a peacetime replacement—at least, in part —for the wartime defense outlays.

The opponents of "full employment" legislation had several reservations and objections. Some feared that it would mean a statutory blessing for perpetual budgetary deficits, soaring public expenditures, and massive redistribution of income from upper to lower income groups. There were doubts that Government actions could and would on balance raise employment; and there were fears that these actions would lead to regimentation and would jeopardize the free enterprise system. The proponents of legislation, on the other hand, argued that the Act would merely provide a setting essential to the proper functioning of the free enterprise system because a depressed economy heightened social tensions, discouraged innovation and initiative, dulled competition, and undermined confidence.

The legislation which finally emerged from this discussion wisely abstained from diagnosing depression as the disease and public works as the cure, but instead concentrated on establishing the principle of continuing Government responsibility to review and appraise economic developments, diagnose problems, and prescribe appropriate remedies. And it placed major responsibility squarely upon the President, who was asked to discuss his execution of that responsibility in an Economic Report to be transmitted to the Congress at the start of each year.

The Act also established two agencies—the Council of Economic Advisers in the Executive Branch and the Joint Committee on the

Economic Report (later named the Joint Economic Committee) of the Congress—with interrelated but separate responsibilities. These institutions have each filled a vital and previously missing role in their respective branches of Government—they have provided a coordinated overview of the economic impact of the entire spectrum of Government tax, expenditure, monetary, and other activities. To maintain the emphasis on advice and coordination, the Joint Economic Committee was not given any substantive legislative responsibility nor the Council any policy-executing duties. Both agencies have participated actively in the counsels of Government; both have conscientiously striven for a thoroughly professional economic competence and approach in their respective reports and recommendations; and both have contributed to the public understanding of economic issues. . . .

Today's economic policies reflect the continuing impact of the Employment Act in all the years since its inception. And our accumulating experience is certain to be reflected in the policies of the future. This chapter reviews the development of policy in the past 20 years and outlines the present relationship between economic analysis and economic policy.

## AVOIDING DEPRESSIONS AND BOOMS

The Congress proved wise in its decision to state goals broadly and to concentrate on continuing review, analysis, and proposals, since the specific problems that actually arose were somewhat different from those which many supporters of the Employment Act had anticipated.

Although an important part of the impetus for the Employment Act derived from the prolonged depression of the 1930's and the resulting fear of stagnation in the American economy, this problem did not prove to be the primary challenge to economic policymaking under the Act. Indeed, immediately after World War II, excess-demand inflation proved to be the key problem. Subsequently, policy was focused on the age-old problem of limiting the size and duration of cyclical swings. Only much later and in a much different and milder form did stagnation arise as a live issue.

Thus, much of our experience under the Act consisted of policy actions to combat recession—lest it turn into depression—and to contain excess demand pressure—lest it generate inflationary boom.

## COMBATING RECESSIONS

A series of relatively short and mild recessions required Government attention in the postwar period. The problem of cyclical declines was not unexpected by the framers of the Employment Act, nor was it new to the American economy. In the period between 1854 (the beginning of the business cycle annals of the National Bureau of Economic Research) and World War II, we had experienced 21 periods of recession or depression. Our postwar record is blemished by 4 additional periods of contracting economic activity—1948–49, 1953–54, 1957–58, and 1960–61.

Compared with the previous cyclical record, the postwar recessions have been far shorter, considerably milder, and substantially less frequent. Postwar recessions ranged in duration from 8 to 13 months; the average duration of previous declines had been 21 months, and only 3 had been shorter than 13 months in length. Measured by the decline in industrial production from peak to trough, postwar recessions ranged in magnitude from 8 per cent to 14 per cent. By comparison, in the interwar period, the declines ranged from 6 to 52 per cent; three of the five contractions exceeded 30 per cent and only one was less than the 14 per cent maximum of the postwar period. During the past 20 years, the economy has spent a total of 42 months, or 18 per cent of the time, in periods of recessions, far less than the 43 per cent applicable to the 1854–1939 era.

*Discretionary policies.* This improvement in the postwar record of the economy was aided by the deliberate discretionary steps taken by the Government to modify the impact of business downturns and thereby to prevent cumulating declines into depression. The speed and force of these actions—in both the fiscal and monetary areas—varied among the recessions. Thus, in 1949 little new fiscal action was taken, partly because inflation was viewed as a key problem even during the decline, and partly because Government measures taken the previous year were expected to have a considerable impact on the economy: the tax reductions of 1948 were supplying large refunds, and large expenditure increases were forthcoming under the recently enacted Marshall Plan. The Federal Reserve did act to reduce reserve requirements in a series of steps during the spring and summer of 1949, reversing a two-year rise in short-term interest rates.

In 1953–54, as military outlays declined and aggregate activity retreated, the principal expansionary influence came from previously scheduled reductions of corporate and personal income taxes. But some new action was taken to reduce excise taxes and to speed up expenditures. All three major instruments of monetary policy—reserve requirements, the discount rate, and open market operations—were used to encourage the expansion of credit-financed expenditures. Meanwhile, the Administration planned larger fiscal steps that might be taken if the recession seemed likely to be prolonged. Significantly, in 1954, the bipartisan character of expansionary fiscal policies was established for the first time, as the Republican Administration of President Eisenhower adopted measures that had previously been linked to the New Deal and Keynesian economics.

In 1958, the recession was considerably deeper than its two postwar predecessors and both the Eisenhower Administration and the Congress were more vigorous in taking action. An important concern of earlier years—that business confidence might be disturbed by Government recognition of a recession—seemed insignificant since the sharp recession was obvious to all.

Several important measures were taken. The benefit period for unemployment compensation was temporarily extended. Grants to States under the Federal highway program were enlarged and accelerated, and other programs in the budget also were expanded or rescheduled to provide an earlier stimulative effect. The Government also acted to spur housing activity by financial operations in the mortgage market and by altering terms on Government-guaranteed home mortgages. The important measures were launched near, or after, the trough of the recession. Thus, in retrospect, policy helped most to strengthen the early recovery rather than to contain or shorten the recession. Nevertheless, in view of the general recognition that the Government would be running a substantial deficit in any case, these additions to Federal otulays were a significant reflection of changed attitudes toward the role of fiscal policy.

Monetary policy also played a constructive role in the 1957–58 recession, once the monetary authorities moved to ease credit 3 months after the peak in economic activity. Thereafter, Federal Reserve actions contributed to a revival in housing and other investment by promoting a sharp reduction in interest rates, both short- and long-term.

The first fiscal measures to deal with the 1960–61 recession were aken with the inauguration of President Kennedy in January 1961, when the recession had just about run its course. Nevertheless, improvements in the social insurance system, rescheduling of Federal expenditures, and expanded programs (including defense and space) were an important stimulus to the recovery during 1961. In contrast to the delay in taking fiscal measures, the Federal Reserve reversed a tight money policy early in 1960, prior to the downturn.

Not all discretionary changes in taxes or expenditures have contributed to economic stability. Indeed, some steps taken to pursue national security or social goals had destabilizing economic impacts, which were not always appropriately offset. Previously scheduled payroll tax increases took effect in 1954, 1959, and 1962, and drained off purchasing power in recession or in initial recovery. In 1953, defense outlays declined and triggered a recession before offsetting expansionary policies were adopted.

*Structural changes for stability.* On the whole, discretionary fiscal and monetary actions made a distinct positive contribution in limiting declines. Even more important in this respect was the strengthened inherent stability of the postwar economy.

In large measure, this can be traced simply to the greater size of the Government relative to the total economy: that is, the increased importance of Government expenditures—both purchases of goods and services and transfer payments. Government outlays do not participate in the downward spiral of recession; because of its borrowing capacity, the Federal Government—unlike businesses and households—can maintain its spending in the face of declining income receipts. Although State and local governments do not have equal immunity from the need to tighten their belts, they have been able to maintain their growing spending programs relatively unaffected during the mild postwar recessions.

The increased relative importance of Government outlays is shown in Chart 1. Social insurance and national defense have added especially to the postwar totals of Federal outlays. State and local outlays have been rising rapidly in an effort to catch up with neglected needs and to keep up with the desires of a wealthier society for improved public services.

The contribution to the stability of the economy resulting from a high level of Government expenditures, insulated from revenue declines, has been augmented by the cushions to private purchasing power provided by the built-in fiscal stabilizers.

When private incomes and employment decline, purchasing

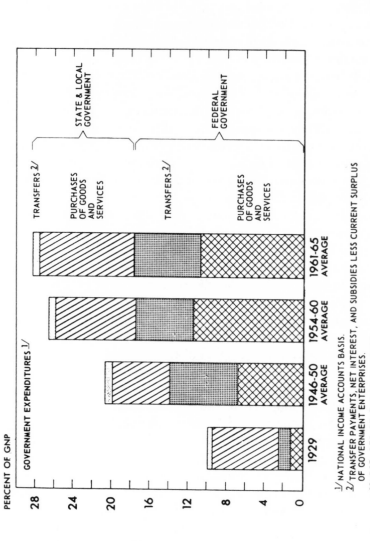

Chart 1.   Role of Federal and State and Local Governments in the Economy

power is automatically supported by both a decline of Federal revenues and an increase in unemployment compensation payments. Transmission of the virus of deflation is thus impeded. During postwar recessions, the progressive Federal personal income tax has not had to demonstrate its full stabilizing effectiveness because of the mildness of dips in personal earnings. There have, however, been sharp declines in corporate incomes; the Federal Treasury has shared about half of the drop in profits, thereby helping to bolster dividends and to cushion cash flow, and hence investment outlays.

A number of improvements in our financial structure were developed in the 1930's to assure that financial collapse and declines in economic activity would not generate a vicious downward spiral as they did after 1929. These important financial mechanisms include Federal insurance of private deposits; the separation of commercial and investment banking functions; the Federal Reserve's increased ability to provide banks with reserves in time of crisis; and the joint work of the Federal Reserve and the Securities and Exchange Commission to reduce harmful speculation in the stock market. The very existence of these structural changes has contributed to stability by improving confidence.

With the help of the more stable structure of the economy, recessions in the postwar era have been limited to declines in investment spending (and, in 1953–54, Federal outlays). Consumer incomes have not declined significantly, and hence households have maintained their spending in recession. With the nearly two-thirds of GNP represented by consumer expenditures insulated from decline and with a solid foundation of public outlays, declines in private investment have not cumulated. In contrast, the Great Depression generated a decline of consumer outlays of 40 per cent from 1929 to 1933, and the shrinkage of consumer markets aggravated and reinforced the collapse in investment spending.

### CONTAINING INFLATIONARY PRESSURES

The desirability of price stability was clearly recognized in the legislative discussion of the Employment Act. But few considered the danger of postwar inflation nearly as great as the opposite danger of relapse into depression. The legislation itself emphasized the objectives of using resources fully and attaining high employment. It did not explicitly label price stability an objective of policy, although this was implicit in the Act and fully reflected in the policies of every Administration. Nevertheless, concern has been expressed at times that policies for "maximum employment" might allow demand to press too hard on available resources, thus biasing the American economy toward inflation.

In the wartime environment, inflationary pressures of excess demand had been suppressed by direct controls on prices and by rationing. It turned out, however, during the years immediately following World War II that these measures had served partly to postpone—rather than to eliminate—significant demand pressures. Substantial backlogs of demand emerged in the 1946–48 period. Consumers and businesses possessed large accumulations of liquid assets to finance the rebuilding of their depleted stocks of household appliances, machinery, and equipment, and their houses and plants.

Thus, contrary to expectations, the initial years of the postwar era were marked by excessive rather than inadequate demand. In this environment, living standards of consumers, the productivity of labor, and the capacity of businesses rose rapidly. But so did the price level, with a jump of 31 per cent in consumer prices from June 1946 to August 1948. Automatic fiscal stabilizers helped to contain the growth of private after-tax incomes, and were reflected in budgetary surpluses during the period. The economic policymaking machinery set up under the Employment Act may have moderated pressures to cut taxes drastically. Meanwhile, monetary policy was tied to a policy of supporting Government bond prices and was not free to combat inflation.

During the Korean war, however, the Government acted vigorously to counter inflationary tendencies close to their source. The March 1951 Federal Reserve-Treasury "accord" unleashed monetary policy. Selective controls on consumer instalment credit and on home mortgages were instituted. The enactment of three large increases in income and profits tax rates in 1950 and 1951 is one of the better examples of timely fiscal policy. These actions reflected, in part, recommendations by the Council of Economic Advisers and hearings and reports of the Joint Economic Committee.

Right after the outbreak of hostilities, prices had risen sharply in a flurry of consumer and business buying and, as a result, prices and wage ceilings had been imposed early in 1951. Once the restraining influence of over-all fiscal and monetary policies was fully felt, there was little pressure on the ceilings, and the economy was ıble to meet the peak defense demands of the emergency without ınflationary strain. The immediate postwar period and the early months of the Korean war are the two blemishes of clearly excessive demand on ɔur postwar record. Apart from these two intervals, wholesale prices ɪave shown a net increase of only 2 per cent in the postwar era. In 1956 and 1957, the only other periods of marked price increases, ɔver-all demand was not generally excessive. That inflation raised ɪew issues. . . .

## EVOLVING PROBLEMS AND POLICIES

During the postwar era, the American economy has remained ʾree of the malignant diseases of depression and run-away inflation. And the rate of economic growth has considerably exceeded its long-term average. The objectives of the Employment Act, however, have not always been fully met. In particular, experience has demonstrated that the avoidance of depression did not guarantee the achievement of "maximum employment" and the avoidance ɔf excess-demand booms did not assure the maintenance of price stability.

### INADEQUATE DEMAND IN EXPANSION

The strength of private demand in the early postwar years and then again immediately after the Korean war led to a reassessment ɔf the tasks of stabilization policy. After a decade of postwar experience, suspicions arose that the typical problem would be to contain rather than to stimulate private demand.

Any such conclusion was soundly refuted by the facts of the ensuing years. With the backlogs met, and with a marked decline in the rate of family formation, private demand weakened in the late 1950's. The economy's performance weakened correspondingly because Government did not act to compensate. Thus, while unemployment had averaged 4.2 per cent of the civilian labor force in the first postwar decade, it remained above that level every month between late 1957 and October 1965, averaging 5.7 per cent.

The problem of inadequate demand in expansion, which became the primary focus of fiscal action in the 1960's, was a new challenge to policymaking under the Employment Act. In the first postwar decade, each time the economy advanced or rebounded from a recession, it reached the neighborhood of full employment. The policymakers had been ready in the early postwar years to deal with noncyclical problems of submerged prosperity or stagnating production. They had seen maximum employment as a moving target which could be maintained only through a substantial growth of output. Both the Council of Economic Advisers and the Joint Economic Committee had given these issues repeated attention in the late 1940's and early 1950's. But until the late 1950's, no experience had been encountered to distinguish the problem of full employment from that of cyclical prosperity.

Then came a sequence of disturbing events: the 1957–58 recession followed a year of slow advance; the 1960–61 recession began from a peak far below full employment; and the expansion that began in 1961 seemed to be running out of steam after little more than a year.

During the initial years of this period, Government policy maintained vigilance against excessive buoyancy of demand when that was no longer the problem. Restrictive fiscal and monetary actions choked off the recovery of 1958–60. The shift to an expansionary fiscal policy by the Kennedy Administration early in 1961 was designed primarily to initiate a thriving recovery. A determined policy strategy to assure complete recovery was first formulated when the economy faltered in 1962.

The combination of fiscal stimuli to consumer demand and direct tax incentives to investment, together with monetary actions permitting an ample rise in credit, promoted a vigorous and sustained expansion after 1963. The inherent strength of both consumption and investment demand appeared in a new light, once the Revenue Act of 1964 exerted its invigorating influence.

### INFLATION AT LESS THAN FULL EMPLOYMENT

Another problem encountered at times during the postwar era has been the tendency of prices to rise even in the absence of overall excess demand pressures. This tendency reflects structural characteristics of the American economy. The economy is not made up of fully competitive labor and product markets in which large numbers of buyers and sellers interact and respond passively to prices. On the contrary, in many industries both unions and businesses exercise a considerable degree of market power. As a first result, wages and prices are both somewhat rigid in a downward direction.

To the extent that prices rise more readily in response to excess demand than they decline in the face of excess supply, the price level is given an upward bias, which can become particularly acute if there are sharp shifts in demand among various sectors of the economy. Secondly, because of market power, some firms augment increases in costs originating elsewhere and unions can escalate their wage demands if prices begin to rise. Third, firms can use a strong market position to widen margins in a period of prosperity even if there are no upward pressures on their costs. Fourth, in the nature of the collective bargaining process, key wage bargains in some industries may tend to establish a pattern applied elsewhere. In particular, if the industries with key wage bargains happen to have excess demands and very strong profits, the pattern will tend to pull wages upward more rapidly throughout the economy.

An important, broadly oriented study by the Joint Economic Committee analyzed the workings of these important influences in the 1956–57 inflation. In that period, excess demands that were present in machinery and equipment, automobile, and metals industries led to price increases that were not offset elsewhere. Large wage settlements in these industries with high demand and high profits had pattern-setting effects on many other contracts, thus adding to costs on a broad front.

Rising prices that originate from such a process can affect expectations, jeopardize the stability and balance of an expansion, and create inequities and distortions just as readily as demand inflation. But measures to restrain these price increases by reducing over-all demand will enlarge unemployment and impair the productivity record so important to cost-price stability over the longer run. Policies to improve the operations of markets, increase resource mobility and accelerate technical change can help to increase the economy's resistance to rising prices. But in a world where large firms and large unions play an essential role, the cost-price record will depend heavily upon the responsibility with which they exercise the market power that society entrusts to them.

The need for responsible private action was brought to public attention in the Economic Reports of President Eisenhower's second Administration. Through the major innovation of the guideposts in the Kennedy and Johnson Administrations, this need has since been focused and developed into a national policy to enlist the force of public opinion to maintain cost-price stability. The emergence of such a policy has been all the more important in recent years because of the balance of payments problem that has persisted alongside the domestic need for more expansion.

Two decades of economic analysis and policy experience have shaped the development of a revised economic policy. By some, current policy has been labeled the "new economics." It draws heavily on the experience and lessons of the past, and it combines both new and old elements. Current policy represents a coordinated and consistent effort to promote balance of over-all supply and aggregate demand—to sustain steady balanced growth at high employment levels with essential price stability.

This approach to policy has several key aspects, not entirely novel by any means. First, it emphasizes a continuous, rather than a cyclical, framework for analyzing economic developments and formulating policies. Stimulus to demand is not confined to avoiding or correcting recession, but rather is applied whenever needed for the promotion of full-utilization and prosperity. Second, in this way, it emphasizes a preventive strategy against the onset of recession. Third, in focusing on balance of the economy, this policy strategy cannot give top priority to balance in the budget. When private investment threatens to outrun saving at full employment, a Government surplus is needed to increase total saving in the economy while restrictive monetary policy may also be called for to restrain investment outlays. When, as in recent years, private saving at full employment tends to outrun actual private investment, the balance should be corrected by budget deficits and expansionary monetary policy. Fourth, it considers the budget and monetary conditions in the framework of a growing economy, recognizing that revenues expand and thereby exert a fiscal drag on demand unless expansionary actions are taken; similarly, it recognizes that money and credit must expand just to keep interest rates from rising. Fifth, this strategy emphasizes the use of a variety of tools to support expansion while simultaneously pursuing other objectives. Manpower policies, selective approaches to control capital outflows, as well as general fiscal and monetary measures, are all part of the arsenal. Sixth, it calls for responsible price-wage actions by labor and management to prevent cost-inflation from impeding the pursuit of full employment. Finally, it makes greater demands on economic forecasting and analysis. The job of the economist is not merely to predict the upturn or the downturn but to judge continuously the prospects for demand in relation to a growing productive capacity.

THE NATURE OF CYCLICAL INSTABILITY

An industrial economy is vulnerable to cumulative upward and downward movements in activity, so evident in our long-term record. While they can have diverse specific causes, these cyclical fluctuations can be explained as the result of imbalances between the rate of growth of productive capacity and the rate of growth of final demands that make use of productive capacity.

During periods of prosperity, a considerable part of the nation's output is used to increase productive capacity through investment in plant and equipment and business inventories. If demand keeps pace, sales expand and the new capacity turns out to be profitable. Businessmen find that their decisions to increase capacity have been validated and they continue to pursue expansionary investment policies. If, on the other hand, inventory stocks are built up far in advance of need—on the basis of overly optimistic sales forecasts or as an inflation-hedge—businessmen will subsequently wish to cut back their rate of accumulation. Similarly, if outlays for business fixed investment add to productive capacity faster than demand expands, overheads on new capital cut into profits, inducing business firms to trim their capital outlays. Even if businessmen continue to add somewhat to their productive capacity, the mere decline in the rate of expansion can mean an absolute reduction in the demand for capital goods and for output to go into inventories. Payrolls and purchasing power are thereby curtailed and a decline in total demand can result. Thus a slowdown in economic activity is converted into a definite downturn—a recession or depression.

Imbalance can arise because businessmen in the aggregate invest too much and overbuild, creating more capacity than the economy can—even at best—put to productive use. Or alternatively it can stem from "underbuying," a growth of final demand too slow to make use of even moderate additions to capacity. In principle, cyclical movements can also be triggered by overbuilding of new homes and consumer durables.

Overbuilding of inventories—partly encouraged by expectations of rising prices—was probably the key factor in the first postwar downturn, which occurred in 1948. That experience demonstrated that a situation of high total demand could deteriorate rapidly into recession without any change in the basic underlying factors in the private economy or any restraining shift in public policy. In 1953, the sharp decline in defense outlays reduced final demands and precipitated recession; productive capacity became temporarily excessive and investment spending declined. In 1956–57, rapid growth of productive capacity was associated with an investment boom; meanwhile, final demands grew very slowly. It is not possible to deliver a clear verdict on whether more vigorous growth of final demand would have justified the high investment levels then obtaining. But with the slow growth of demand that actually occurred, there was an abrupt decline in plant and equipment spending as well as inventory investment in 1957. In 1959–60, the rate of expansion of capacity (including inventories) was not excessive measured against the capabilities of the economy; the failure of the economy to support that growth of capacity must be attributed to "underbuying," the inadequate expansion of final demand, in an environment of restrictive fiscal and monetary policies.

In the future as in the past, policies to avert recession cannot wait until imbalances develop and the signs of a downturn are clear. The fact that economic activity is rising cannot be an assurance of continued growth if the expansion is too slow to match the growth of productive capacity. Nor can a strong level of investment be relied on to sustain expansion if it threatens an excessive growth of productive capacity. Recognizing these tasks, Government must apply its fiscal and monetary policies continuously to sustain and support a balanced expansion, sometimes by moderating the strength of an excessive investment boom, sometimes by adding to the strength of lagging final demand. The best defense against recession is a policy to sustain continued expansion. In a free economy, fluctuations in private demand will inevitably occur, and the Government will not always have the wisdom or the ability to counteract them. Continued expansion cannot be guaranteed, but recurrent recession need not be accepted as a necessary fact of economic life.

# 19. Adapting the "New Economics"

*Although John Maynard Keynes formulated the complete body of his economic thought by 1936, his ideas on fiscal and monetary policy were not widely accepted by American economists until some two decades later. A development of momentous significance was the process* by which President John F. Kennedy incorporated some aspects of Keynesian doctrine into government policy for stimulating business expansion. A first step was the 7 per cent investment tax credit of 1961–1962 which encouraged larger private outlays for machines and equipment. A second step was Kennedy's proposal for planned deficits, even at the crest of the business cycle, in order to maintain a healthy rate of economic growth. This approach was embodied in the tax reduction bill passed by the House of Representatives two months before Kennedy's death, and finally enacted in February 1964. Chairman Walter W. Heller of the Council of Economic Advisers, a professor of economics at the University of Minnesota, is credited with having persuaded Kennedy of the usefulness of Keynesian ideas for making national economic policy.

SOURCE: Economic Report of the President . . . 1964. . . . (Washington, D.C.: Government Printing Office, 1964), pp. 32, 34–7, 39, 41–8.

## ECONOMIC EXPANSION AND FEDERAL POLICY

The American economy has recorded nearly 3 years of solid expansion since early 1961. But it urgently needs the tax cuts now pending to complete the climb back toward full employment and ful production that began 3 years ago. . . . After examining the role of Federal fiscal and monetary policy in achieving this record, this [excerpt] discusses the economic situation at the end of 1963; the prospects for 1964; and the broad outlines of policy that can complete the return to full employment.

## REVIEW OF THE EXPANSION

By April of this year [1964], the present expansion will have become the second longest peacetime expansion of this century—exceeded only by the prolonged climb out of the depths of the Great Depression. . . . The $100 billion expansion since early 1961 has eclipsed the brief 1958–60 expansion in both extent and duration, and has achieved in its first 11 quarters a greater increase in total real output—16 per cent—than was achieved in the 13 quarters of the 1954–57 expansion. With early enactment of the pending tax bill it has every prospect of continuing throughout 1964 at an accelerated pace.

### EXPANSION OF DEMAND

While all major components of demand have contributed to the expansion of the past 3 years, much of the advance has come from

Table 1. Changes in Real Gross National Product in three Postwar Expansions

| Component | Annual rate of change[1] (Percent) | | | Distribution of total change[1] (Percent) | | |
|---|---|---|---|---|---|---|
| | 1954 II to 1957 III | 1958 I to 1960 II | 1961 I to 1963 IV[2] | 1954 II to 1957 III | 1958 I to 1960 II | 1961 I to 1963 IV[2] |
| Total gross national product | 4.1 | 5.3 | 5.4 | 100.0 | 100.0 | 100.0 |
| Federal Government purchases | -3.3 | -.6 | 5.6 | -10.9 | -1.2 | 11.4 |
| State and local government purchases | 4.9 | 4.5 | 4.7 | 10.6 | 8.4 | 8.8 |
| Residential construction | .9 | 7.8 | 11.0 | .8 | 6.0 | 8.2 |
| Business fixed investment[3] | 5.3 | 4.1 | 6.8 | 13.3 | 7.4 | 11.1 |
| Business inventory change | [4] | [4] | [4] | 10.1 | 17.2 | 12.0 |
| Personal consumption expenditures | 4.6 | 4.9 | 4.1 | 70.5 | 60.5 | 48.9 |
| Net exports | [5] | [5] | [5] | 5.7 | 1.9 | -.5 |

[1] Based on data in 1963 prices.
[2] Preliminary estimates by Council of Economic Advisers for latest quarter in current expansion.
[3] Includes producers' durable equipment and nonresidential construction.
[4] Inapplicable because inventory changes were negative in the trough quarters.
[5] Not shown because of small numbers on which changes would be based.

NOTE. Detail will not necessarily add to totals because of rounding.

SOURCE: Department of Commerce (except as noted).

rising Federal, State, and local purchases of goods and services. Federal purchases in constant dollars rose by 16 per cent from the first quarter of 1961 to the fourth quarter of 1963 and accounted for 11 per cent of the total increase in demand. As Table 1 indicates, this contrasts sharply with the two previous expansions, when declining real Federal purchases detracted from the increase in gross national product. State and local purchases rose by 13 per cent in constant dollars over the recent period, accounting for 9 per cent of the total demand increase.

A second major source of demand strength in the present expansion has been private nonfarm residential construction. In contrast to the experience of the two previous expansions, housing expenditure has risen fairly steadily since the beginning of 1961. From the first quarter of that year to the fourth quarter of 1963, it rose 33 per cent in constant dollars, accounting for 8 per cent of the total increase in GNP.

The unusually vigorous expansion in government expenditures and residential construction has been supplemented by a sustained increase of business investment in producers' durable equipment and nonresidential construction. Measured in constant dollars, it rose by 20 per cent from the first quarter of 1961 to the fourth quarter of 1963. Although this percentage rise is larger than that in total GNP, it is disappointing by past standards. Business investment typically has risen faster than GNP in expansions, just as it has fallen faster in recessions. During the 1947–57 period, the rate of business fixed investment consistently exceeded 10 per cent of GNP in constant (1963) dollars; in the current expansion, the ratio has remained close to its recession low of 9 per cent.

The pace of inventory accumulation has been moderate by comparison with some periods in the past and has been usually steady since mid-1962. After jumping from a $4.3 billion annual rate of liquidation at the recession trough to an $8.1 billion rate of accumulation in the first quarter of 1962, inventory investment has fluctuated moderately around an average value of $4.4 billion for the last half of 1962 and the whole of 1963.

Despite the notable strength of the demand for automobiles . . . total personal consumption outlays have remained between 92 and 94 per cent of after-tax personal income, as they have in every year since 1950. The rise in consumption outlays from the first quarter of 1961 to the fourth quarter of 1963 amounted to 12 per cent in constant dollars, and accounted for about half the over-all increase in GNP.

This strong, sustained advance in real output in the past 3 years has been accompanied by an unusual degree of price stability. As in nearly all periods of expansion, there has been some upward drift in the prices of final purchases. But the price rise of the past 3 years has been well below that in other periods of comparable output gains. Of the 20 per cent increase in current-dollar GNP from the first quarter of 1961 to the fourth quarter of 1963, 16 per cent consisted of a rise in constant-dollar output, and only 4 per cent of a rise in prices. Only in the short expansion of 1958–60 was the price rise comparably small.

The average annual rate of increase in the consumer price index over the first 34 months of the current expansion amounted to a very moderate 1.2 per cent. Considering the availability of new products and quality changes not fully reflected in the index, there has been little, if any, real erosion of the purchasing power of the consumer's dollar. The wholesale price index, which is a better measure of the international competitiveness of American products, has not risen since the recession trough in early 1961.

In this environment of sustained increases in output and comparative price stability, gains in real income have been significant and widely diffused. The moderation of money wage increases has served the nation's balance of payments well without serving labor ill. Money wages have not had to push ahead rapidly in order to keep pace with consumer prices. Employee compensation per nonfarm worker, adjusted for the mild rise in consumer prices, increased by 7 per cent from the recession trough to the last quarter of 1963.

The farming sector of the economy has also shared in the advance. Net income per farm, adjusted for changes in prices paid by farmers for cost-of-living items, rose by 9 per cent from early 1961 to 1963.

The rise in disposable personal income adjusted for price increases—the best measure of the after-tax economic gains of individuals—amounted to 13 per cent from the recession trough to the fourth quarter of 1963. On a per capita basis, the rise was 8 per cent.

In previous business expansions corporate profits characteristically have risen rapidly in the early quarters of recovery and then levelled off or declined because of a sharp diminution in the rate of gain in productivity. In the current expansion, the rate of increase in GNP per worker has been better maintained than in the past. As a consequence, profits after taxes increased $10 billion, or 52 per cent, from the recession trough to the fourth quarter of 1963. Because of the advantageous shift of corporate earnings from profits to depreciation allowances permitted by the 1962 liberalization of the Internal Revenue Service's depreciation guidelines, the sum of corporate profits after taxes and capital consumption allowances provides a more useful comparison over time for most companies. This total rose $17 billion during the expansion. . . .

These continued gains in both labor and profit incomes could not have been consistent with price stability without the excellent productivity record during the past 3 years. A high rate of productivity increase is the surest means of reconciling the aspirations of all for higher incomes with the maintenance of a stable price level and improvement in the balance of payments.

#### UNEMPLOYMENT AND UNUSED POTENTIAL OUTPUT

Although the expansion brought rising levels of economic welfare to most Americans during the past 3 years, it was marred by continuing excessive unemployment. The 16-per cent increase in demand from the first quarter of 1961 to the fourth quarter of 1963 brought about a 4-per cent increase in civilian employment; but even so, in the last quarter of the year 5.6 per cent of the civilian labor force was unemployed. Moreover, lack of job opportunities kept many potential workers out of the labor force, while others held jobs well below their capabilities.

In the first year of recovery substantial progress was made in cutting unemployment. The over-all seasonally adjusted rate dropped from 6.7 per cent in 1961 to 5.6 per cent in 1962. Reductions were largest among those workers most affected by the 1960–61 recession; the unemployment rate fell 1.5 percentage points for nonwhites, 2.1 points for semiskilled and unskilled workers, and 1.9 points for manufacturing workers. However, during 1963, no further progress was made. The monthly unemployment rate varied within narrow limits about an average of 5.7 per cent.

Excessive unemployment is the most obvious symptom and one of the worst consequences of a level of demand that falls short of the nation's potential output. During 1963 the Council of Economic Advisers carefully re-examined its measure of potential GNP. This concept, fully discussed in the Council's January 1962 Report, defines "potential" as the output that would be produced if unemployment were at the interim-target level of 4 per cent. For the period to date, the earlier conclusion still holds: the level of constant-dollar GNP needed to maintain the unemployment rate at 4 per cent has been growing at an average rate of about 3½ per cent a year since mid-1955, when the unemployment rate was close to 4 per cent.

. . . The cumulative effect of actual output growth at a rate less than 3½ per cent after mid-1955 had produced a gap of $50 billion (1963 prices) between actual and potential output by the first quarter of 1961. The rapid recovery in the first year of expansion lowered this gap to $30 billion by the first quarter of 1962, but since that time expansion in output has just about kept pace with the growth in potential. As a consequence, unemployment has failed to decline to a tolerable level, and a gap close to $30 billion between actual and potential output remained in the fourth quarter of 1963.

Merely avoiding recession or even maintaining a rate of expansion comparable to that of the last 8 quarters will not close the gap or eliminate excessive unemployment. Only a significant acceleration of expansion can enable the nation to make full use of its growing labor force and productive potential. The choice of appropriate fiscal and monetary policies to achieve this goal is one of the problems challenging the Federal Government in 1964.

## MAINTENANCE OF THE EXPANSION

Two years ago, many observers who noted that postwar expansions had become successively shorter wondered if this trend would continue. Although that anxiety has long since been allayed, there is some fear now that, simply because of its duration, the current expansion must be approaching its end. If this were true, we would face much higher unemployment and greater wasted potential instead of a return to fuller use of our available resources.

The fact is that over-all business fluctuations have no fixed rhythms, and recessions are not in any scientific sense inevitable.

There are, it is true, certain systematic features of the economic process leading to the onset of recession. During periods of prosperity, a larger part of the nation's output is used to increase productive capacity through investment in plant, equipment, and business inventories. If over-all demand rises rapidly enough to justify the added capacity, incentives for further growth of capital are maintained, and the expansion of economic activity continues. But when the growth of demand does not keep pace, business firms curtail further additions to capacity by trimming their investment outlays. The reduction in investment, in turn, reduces employment and income, thus converting the initial slowdown in the growth of demand into an actual decline in general economic activity—a recession.

While individual recessions have their own features and their own proximate causes, reversals from expansion can typically be traced to a failure of demand to keep pace with the expansion of capital facilities. There have been many occasions in the past when timely Federal policy actions could have maintained the balance between demand and capacity and thereby changed our economic history. It is vital that such opportunities be seized in the future.

FEDERAL POLICY AND FULL EMPLOYMENT

To comply with the mandate of the Employment Act of 1946 "to promote maximum employment, production, and purchasing power," the Federal Government must adjust its programs to complement private demand. Given the magnitude of its expenditure commitments, its revenue collections, its public debt management obligations, and its money and credit responsibilities, the Government inevitably exerts a powerful impact on demand. It is, therefore, a first principle of responsible Federal economic policy to try, insofar as possible, to adjust this impact in a way that promotes expansion and price stability.

The instruments of fiscal policy—Federal taxes, transfer payments, subsidies, grants-in-aid, and purchases of goods and services—are the Government's most powerful tools for promoting expansion. Federal purchases of goods and services are themselves a component of demand, and indirectly they affect the other components. Through their impact on employment and income, they influence the level of consumption. By increasing sales and profits, they encourage investment expenditures. Similarly, taxes, transfers, and subsidies affect consumption and investment through their obvious effects on disposable incomes, after-tax profits, and incentives. Federal grants-in-aid finance many State and local expenditure programs.

These fiscal policy tools, while powerful, can at present be used by the Executive with only limited flexibility. Major expenditure programs must be related to a variety of domestic and international objectives as well as to the requirements of economic efficiency. They are therefore sometimes difficult to reconcile with income and employment goals in the annual budgetary process. Moreover, under our constitutional system, legislation needed to implement fiscal policies is the prerogative of the Congress. The Congress has demonstrated its ability to enact tax and expenditure legislation quickly in time of emergency, and the Executive Branch does have some flexibility in the timing of expenditures. This limited flexibility was used to good advantage in 1961. But without legislation to establish in advance specific rules designed to facilitate flexible fiscal policy—such as those requested by President Kennedy in 1962—tax and expenditure policies cannot be adjusted with sufficient speed to cope with the swift changes in private demand that bring recession or inflation. Greater flexibility would be desirable. However, the main function of fiscal policy must continue to be the provision of a good supporting framework for expansion.

### THE FULL-EMPLOYMENT BUDGET

The Federal budget on a national income and product accounts basis gives the most comprehensive picture available of the revenue and expenditure activities of the Government as these affect private demands and the level of economic activity. This budget includes the receipts and expenditures of the Federal trust fund accounts, as well as those in the administrative budget, but excludes credit transactions. Unlike the administrative budget, it records corporate tax liabilities at the time they accrue rather than when collections are made. These and other differences between the administrative budget and the national income and product accounts budget are outlined in the January 1962 Report of the Council of Economic Advisers.

Federal policy decisions determine budgeted expenditures and a set of laws governing tax rates and transfer payments. The actual surplus or deficit position of the budget depends partly on the planned levels of expenditure and the rates incorporated in the tax structure, and partly on the general strength of private income and demand. Since both receipts and expenditures are affected by the level of private demand, the budget serves as an automatic stabilizer, moving into deficit in a recession and toward a surplus in recovery. . . .

The economic impact of a given budget program is best measured by its surplus or deficit at full-employment income levels. The surplus in the full-employment budget is too large when the Government demand contained in the budget, and private investment and consumption demands forthcoming from after-tax incomes, are insufficient to bring total output to the full-employment level. The actual budget will then show a smaller surplus or larger deficit than the full-employment budget.

If the fiscal structure is biased in this direction, it can be corrected either by expanding Government purchases to employ idle resources in satisfying public needs; or by expanding private business and personal after-tax incomes through reduced tax rates or increased transfer payments to employ idle resources in satisfying the demands of the private sector. When the budget is too expansionary, the combination of public and private demands will eventually exceed productive capacity, and excessive upward pressure on prices will develop. In this event, sound fiscal policy calls for lowering expenditures or raising tax rates, or both.

The appropriate size of the surplus or deficit in the full-employment budget depends on the strength of private demand and its responsiveness to fiscal policy. The budget must counterbalance private demand. The weaker the underlying determinants of private demand, the more expansionary the budget should be; the stronger these determinants, the more restraining the budget should be.

Whether a given budget is too expansionary or restrictive depends also on other Government policies affecting private spending, of which monetary policy is the most important. Other things being equal, a strongly expansionary monetary policy permits a larger surplus by strengthening business investment, residential construction, and other expenditures that are sensitive to the cost and availability of credit.

### FISCAL POLICY IN A GROWING ECONOMY

In a growing economy, periodic budget adjustments are required to maintain adequate expansion of total demand. The volume of tax revenues rises as incomes grow if tax rates remain unchanged. At present tax rates, the revenues that the Federal Government would collect at full employment increase by more than $6 billion a year. If program needs do not require expenditures to grow at the same rate, tax rates must be reduced, or a growing full-employment surplus will result, with increasingly restrictive effects on the economy.

In the past this very process has been a major factor in slowing expansions and precipitating downturns. Thus the consequences of excessive potential surpluses have been large actual deficits, unemployment, and inability to achieve steady growth.

To avoid these consequences, an appropriate expansion-promoting fiscal program would call for tax and expenditure policies that prevent a constrictive rise in the full-employment surplus. . . . The experience of the past 10 years has illustrated the tendency of the full-employment surplus to build up to expansion-retarding levels as the economy grows. The tax reductions of 1964 will be a giant step to remove a burdensome fiscal restraint *before* the economy levels off or goes into a recession, and to provide a framework for continued vigorous growth.

THE ROLE OF MONETARY POLICY

Establishing a suitable fiscal framework is not the only step the Government can take to promote full employment. The ability of the economy to maintain expansion in both its actual and its potential output is significantly affected by the monetary and debt management policies of the Federal Reserve System and the Treasury Department. Expenditures on long-lived assets, such as residential and commercial buildings, business plant and equipment, and to a lesser extent consumer durables, are particularly sensitive to cost and availability of credit, which are heavily influenced by monetary and debt management policies.

The choice of monetary policies must be related to the character of private demand, to the type of fiscal policy being pursued, and to goals with respect to the balance of payments. In the light of these considerations, various combinations of fiscal and monetary policies are appropriate to different conditions in the economy.

When aggregate demand is generally deficient and investment and consumption are expanding too slowly to provide jobs for all those seeking employment, expansionary monetary policy normally can and should accompany expansionary fiscal policy. Likewise, when excessive aggregate demand threatens to cause inflation, a tight monetary policy may be called for in conjunction with a fiscal program that permits full-employment Federal revenues to rise relative to expenditures.

Under some circumstances, however, it may be appropriate to operate monetary policy at seeming cross purposes to fiscal policy in order to restrict or expand the share of output devoted to investment. In general, an easier monetary policy will permit a higher sustainable rate of investment and capacity growth. Together with a slightly restrictive full-employment budget, such a policy mix may raise the growth rate of potential output while keeping total demand within noninflationary bounds. Alternatively, if investment is so large relative to consumption and Government purchases as to threaten a rapid buildup of excess capacity or serious bottlenecks in capital-goods industries, the need may be for monetary restraints on investment and stimulus to consumption through a tax reduction.

A partially offsetting mix of fiscal and monetary policies also becomes appropriate when, as now, the nation's balance-of-payments deficit is excessive at the same time that domestic expansion needs to be stimulated. In this case, however, it is useful to differentiate among types of monetary policies. Efforts can be made—as they have been in the current expansion—to use the various tools of monetary and debt-management policy to keep the cost and availability of long-term credit favorable to domestic expansion, while maintaining short-term interest rates at a level necessary to restrain short-term capital outflows. Meanwhile, other more direct measures to deal with the balance-of-payments problem need to be pushed vigorously to correct the basic causes of the deficit and in the process provide more scope for monetary policy in promoting domestic expansion.

Against the background of these general considerations, an understanding of the problems and possibilities of Federal policy in the maintenance of expansion can best be gained by examining the experience of the past three expansions.

FEDERAL POLICY IN THE EXPANSIONS OF 1954–57 AND 1958–60

The recovery from the 1954 recession was aided by a substantial tax cut and by the fact that materials shortages and controls during the Korean conflict had limited the buildup of capacity to produce civilian goods. The result was a period of rapid expansion in late 1954 and early 1955, centering first in inventories, automobiles, and housing. This was followed by a remarkable boom in fixed investment from the third quarter of 1955 through the third quarter of 1957.

The absence of price-wage restraint in the 1955–57 period contributed to a widespread inflation despite the lack of any general excess of demand over capacity output. Excess demand was confined to the durable goods manufacturing industry, where orders strained capacity in many lines. But sharp price and wage increases in this sector were imitated in other industries that did not share similar demand pressures.

Indeed, the lack of real output increases in early 1956 prompted predictions of recession. Despite the capital goods boom, total output levelled off at that time as automobiles, residential construction, and Federal purchases all declined. But defense outlays increased sharply from mid-1956 to mid-1957, and capital goods purchases remained strong. By the time the investment boom had run its course, total demand had not grown sufficiently to use fully the added capacity that had been created. Federal outlays levelled off early in 1957 and then declined, just at a time when expansionary policy was needed to avoid a downturn. And the Federal Reserve, which had been tightening money and credit conditions throughout most of the expansion, raised the discount rate in August 1957, just as the downturn in production was beginning.

The entire expansion of 1958–60 was characterized by price stability, ample productive capacity, and excessive unemployment. Wholesale prices were virtually steady throughout the expansion. The capacity utilization rate in manufacturing had dropped to 73 per cent in the 1958 recession, nearly 20 points below its peak level in the fourth quarter of 1955. Except for brief periods of rapid inventory accumulation before and after the lengthy steel strike of 1959, the utilization rate never regained much more than half this loss. Consequently the recovery of investment expenditure was weak. The unemployment rate fell only to 5.0 per cent, and that for only 1 month. The average unemployment rate from January 1959 to May 1960 (when the peak of the recovery was reached) was 5.4 per cent.

Yet Federal policy was restrictive and wholly inappropriate to a period of insufficient demand. The full-employment surplus was allowed to rise drastically from a $4½ billion level in 1958 to more than $12 billion in 1960. The expenditure line was held firmly while the only tax-rate changes made were increases in social insurance and excise tax rates. The turnaround from actual deficit to actual surplus was even more striking. Between the third quarter of 1958 and the first quarter of 1960, there was a swing of nearly $20 billion (annual rate) from a $10.7 billion deficit to an $8.2 billion surplus. At a time when private investment demand was depressed by excess capacity, this fiscal restraint was clearly inconsistent with continued expansion. If it had not been for a slow rise throughout the period in the share of disposable income consumed, it is doubtful that this shortest of all recent recoveries would have lasted even as long as it did.

The restrictive fiscal policy of 1958–60 was accompanied early in the expansion by a shift toward monetary restraint that became progressively more severe and by late 1959 resulted in the tightest monetary and credit conditions of the postwar period. Treasury bill yields rose by 3½ percentage points from mid-1958 to the end of 1959. Long-term Government bond yields increased by a full percentage point during the same period. The sector most adversely affected by this monetary tightness was housing. Private housing starts, which had risen strongly during the period of monetary ease immediately following the 1958 recession, fell by one-fourth from the beginning of 1959 to the middle of 1960. This reduced the demand for building materials and, through its effect on incomes earned in the construction industry, the demand for consumer goods. The combination of fiscal and monetary tightness contributed to a halt in the expansion of business investment expenditures and led to a downturn after only 25 months of expansion.

FISCAL POLICY IN THE PRESENT EXPANSION

When the new Administration came to office in early 1961, the 1960–61 recession was near its trough. The unemployment rate was close to 7 per cent, and the rate of capacity utilization in manufacturing had fallen to 77 per cent. The economic task of first priority was to end the unnecessary waste of resources.

The fiscal program adopted by Congress and the Administration lowered the $12 billion full employment surplus of 1960 to $6 billion by 1962. This reduction was accomplished through both tax reductions and expenditure increases.

The expenditure increases of the 1961–62 period, undertaken to bolster our defense and space programs and to provide for unmet civilian needs, were highly stimulating to the economy. Total Federal expenditures increased by $10 billion (annual rate) between the first quarter of 1961 and the first quarter of 1962, making a major contribution to the 8.8 per cent rise in GNP during the first recovery year. Increases in Federal expenditures continued beyond the initial recovery year. From the first quarter of 1961 to the fourth quarter of 1963, Federal purchases of goods and services in current prices increased by $11½ billion at annual rates, or 21 per cent. Total Federal expenditures, which include transfer payments, subsidies, interest, and grants-in-aid as well as purchases of goods and services, increased by $19½ billion, or 20 per cent, over the same period.

Two tax reduction measures—the new depreciation guidelines announced by the Treasury in July 1962 and the investment tax credit enacted by the Congress in the Revenue Act of 1962—were adopted to stimulate lagging private investment. . . . Their net effect was to raise the annual cash flow to corporations by $2.5 billion in 1963 and to increase the after-tax rate of return on new investment projects. These measures contributed to the rapid rise in plant and equipment outlays that occurred after the first quarter of 1963. Since there are substantial lags in the investment decision-making and spending process, their full effects have not yet been realized.

In early 1963 the Administration proposed a program of tax reduction and revision designed to move the country toward full employment. Failure to enact this key part of the fiscal program by mid-1963 led to a rise in the full-employment surplus when a reduction was needed. By the fourth quarter of 1963, with output still about $30 billion short of potential and an unemployment rate of 5.6 per cent, the full-employment surplus was $9 billion, and the actual budget deficit, on a national income and product basis, fell close to zero. However, early enactment of the tax bill and enactment of the President's budget for fiscal 1965 will bring a sharp and needed reduction in the full-employment surplus. The tax and expenditure program will give a bigger fiscal stimulus in calendar 1964 than in any of the past 3 years and will provide a strong, fresh impetus to the expansion.

### MONETARY POLICY IN THE PRESENT EXPANSION

The fiscal policy of the 1961–63 years was complemented by a monetary policy designed to encourage an expanding economy while also defending the balance of payments. Actions were taken to raise short-term interest rates and to maintain them at levels that would reduce outflows of funds to money markets abroad. Within the limits established by this policy, the Federal Reserve provided money and bank credit to support the expansion and generally avoided placing upward pressure on long-term rates.

In attempting to pursue both its domestic and its balance-of-payments objectives, the Federal Reserve used its policy instruments flexibly. In February 1961 it began to supply a portion of new bank reserves through the purchase of longer-term securities. Meanwhile the Treasury concentrated its new offerings of securities largely in short maturities to exert upward pressure on short-term interest rates. In the autumn of 1962 the Federal Reserve reduced reserve requirements on time and savings deposits, thereby releasing reserves for seasonal growth in money and credit without purchasing short-term securities in the open market.

A particularly important factor that exerted upward pressure on short-term rates but held long-term rates down was the two-step change in Regulation Q in January 1962 and July 1963, which permitted banks to pay higher interest rates on time and savings deposits. These steps accelerated the flow of savings into commercial banks, which in turn invested heavily in mortgages and State and local securities, thereby putting downward pressure on mortgage and other long-term yields. At the same time commercial banks began to issue negotiable time certificates of deposit in substantial quantities, which in effect added to the supply of short-term securities and helped to push up short-term interest rates.

In July 1963 the Federal Reserve increased the discount rate from 3 to 3½ per cent, largely to reinforce efforts to raise short-term interest rates for balance-of-payments reasons.

Analysis of the results of Federal Reserve actions on the growth of deposits and bank credit is especially difficult for this expansion period because of the changes in Regulation Q. The recorded growth in money supply—at an average rate of 2.8 per cent a year during the expansion—understates the degree to which monetary policy provided a stimulus to the economy, since many business firms and individuals were induced to shift idle balances from demand to time deposits in order to take advantage of the higher interest rates.

On the other hand, the increase in time deposits—at an average rate of 15.2 per cent a year—exaggerates the expansionary stimulus from monetary policy. The interest-rate increases on commercial bank time deposits raised their attractiveness relative to direct holdings of securities or deposits at other financial intermediaries. Thus, while bank credit expansion was particularly rapid, part of it reflected lending that otherwise would have occurred through nonbank financial institutions or directly through the securities markets.

# IX. AGRICULTURE IN AN INDUSTRIAL SOCIETY

## 20. The Postwar Agricultural Crisis

The immediate origins of the farm problem that overtook the United States after 1920 lay in the expansion of staple production during World War I and in the subsequent erosion of the overseas market for surplus agricultural commodities. The plight of the wheat farmer was especially acute, for reasons cited by Secretary of Agriculture Henry C. Wallace in the following special report. An Iowa farm journal editor who was brought into the Cabinet by President Warren G. Harding, Wallace was strongly sympathetic to the farmer, but his advanced position on agricultural policy found no support in the administration. Wallace based farm relief on the idea of parity through increased commodity prices, accomplished through a government export corporation that would dispose of the surplus abroad and thus restore the farmer's purchasing power. This proposal, suggested by George N. Peek in his influential pamphlet Equality for Agriculture (1922), was later incorporated into the McNary–Haugen bill.

SOURCE: Henry C. Wallace, "The Wheat Situation," Yearbook of the Department of Agriculture, 1923 (Washington, D.C.: Government Printing Office, 1924), pp. 95–6, 98, 102, 110, 118, 120–2, 126, 130–1, 133, 145–7, 149–50.

The farm price of wheat is down nearly to pre-war level and the purchasing power of a bushel is far below. The farm price August 1, for the first time since the beginning of the war, fell below the average for the corresponding month in the period 1909–1913, being 84 cents, compared with 91 cents. Since August prices have risen and are now slightly above the pre-war level. The November 1 average farm price was 95 cents. If the seasonal price movement for this year 1923–24, parallels that of last year, prices will continue to rise slightly, reaching the highest point of the season in the early spring.

The purchasing power of a bushel of wheat is more significant than the price of wheat. Although the average farm price of November 1 was above the 1909–1913 average for November, it is equivalent to only about 60 cents per bushel in the pre-war period. A suit of clothes which cost the farmer in North Dakota 21 bushels of wheat in July, 1913, cost him 31 bushels in 1923, and a wagon which then cost him 103 bushels would now cost him 166. The cost of nearly everything the farmer buys is necessarily very high because freight rates and industrial wages which enter not only into the cost of manufacturing but also the cost of transportation are far above their level before the war. With the November farm price of wheat only 107 per cent of the pre-war average price, the wholesale price of all commodities which is generally taken as a measure of the price level was 153 per cent in October.[1] On the basis of this price level the average farm price of wheat should have been about $1.35 per bushel for November to give wheat pre-war purchasing power at wholesale prices.

The low price and purchasing power of wheat directly affects the income of about 2,000,000 farmers. In large areas of North Dakota, South Dakota, Kansas, Nebraska, Montana, Idaho, and Washington farmers depend almost entirely upon wheat for their cash income. According to the census of 1919, 80 per cent of the farmers in North Dakota, 76 per cent in Kansas, and 66 per cent in South Dakota grew wheat. A farm survey in the Palouse district of Idaho and Washington for the three years 1919–1921 showed that approximately 80 per cent of the cash income of the farmers in that district was derived from wheat; and, in 1922, 78 per cent of the income of farms surveyed in Sheridan and Daniels Counties in Montana was from wheat. As a direct source of cash income the wheat crop of the United States is more important than the corn crop, a large part of which is fed to livestock. In five years ending with 1922 farmers sold on the average 711,000,000 bushels of wheat and 544,000,000 bushels of corn. Moreover, a large part of the corn sold is from one farmer to another for livestock feed. Many wheat farmers produce other commodities than wheat, but the prices of many of these, such as oats, barley, and rye, are below pre-

[1] A one-year base for an individual commodity is not satisfactory. The index of the price of wheat is therefore based on the 1909–1913 average.

war prices. The specialized wheat farmer, as a rule, does not produce, or produces only for home use, the commodities such as corn, butter, eggs, cotton, and wool, which are now selling at relatively high prices.

The low price and purchasing power of wheat is far-reaching in its effects, for not only the wheat farmer but practically all classes of business men whose income depends to any extent upon the prosperity of the wheat farmer are adversely affected. . . .

. . . Changes in international, commercial, financial, and political relations, as well as the increase in quantity and improvement in quality of wheat produced by competing countries, have increased the difficulty of selling our surplus wheat. . . .

Decrease in consumption of wheat flour in this country has contributed to the large exports of the war and post-war periods. The war appeal to save bread, aided by high prices, formed food habits which have remained with us. The pre-war custom of serving bread free with every a la carte order in restaurants, hotels, and dining cars was abandoned during the war period and has not been generally revived. "Free bread" is undoubtedly consumed more liberally than bread at the rate of two slices with a nickel order of bread and butter. At the rate of a cent and a half per slice, the cafeteria patron pays between 25 and 30 cents for a pound loaf of bread. In hotels, restaurants, and dining cars, where the charge for an order of bread and butter may be as high as 20 cents, the consumption of bread has been materially reduced.

The retail price of bread in cities has not fallen with the price of wheat and flour. A pound loaf of bread in Minneapolis which cost 5.3 cents in 1913–14 cost 9 cents in 1922–23, whereas a barrel of flour which cost $4.43 in 1913–14 cost $6.89 in 1922–23. Allowing 280 loaves of bread to the barrel of flour, the margin between the price of the flour and that of the bread produced from it increased from $10.40 to $18.30. Doubtless a narrowing of the margin between the prices of flour and bread would lead to more liberal use of bread and to some increase in the per capita consumption of wheat flour, with a consequent reduction in the surplus of wheat.

The increase in the cost of transportation from the farm to consuming centers is a very important factor in the present situation. The rates from country shipping points to primary markets are about 45 per cent above the pre-war rates. For example, the rate from Larimore, N. Dak., to Minneapolis in 1913 was 7.2 cents per bushel; the present rate is 10.5. From McPherson, Kans., to Kansas City the rate was 7.6 cents per bushel in 1913 as compared with the present rate of 11.4. Export rates in general have been increased more than 45 per cent. In 1913 the export rate from Chicago to New York amounted to 7.8 cents per bushel; to-day it is 13.5 cents, or 73 per cent aboue the pre-war rate. The export rate from Mc-Pherson, Kans., to Galveston was 15.6 cents in 1913; the present rate is 27 cents, or 73 per cent above the 1913 rate.

War conditions caused freight rates to be raised, reaching the high point in 1920. Unfortunately the highest rates of the period were put into effect after prices had begun to fall. It was no more burdensome to pay 19.8 cents for transporting a bushel of wheat from Chicago to New York while the price was $2.20 and above than it was to pay 7.8 cents before the war when the price was about $1 at Chicago. Since 1920 prices of wheat have fallen nearly to the pre-war level, whereas freight rates remain 45 per cent and more above pre-war rates.

Relatively high freight rates from producing regions of the United States to the seaboard are a serious handicap in competition with other countries in the markets of the world. . . .

The indebtedness of farmers in various parts of the United States, especially in the West, has grown to burdensome proportions. There are a number of causes which account for this situation. Land values in the Middle West rose sharply during the war and some land was purchased by farmers at inflated prices. The number of farmers, however, who bought land during these years is not as large as usually thought. Surveys that have been made indicate that from 10 to 15 per cent of the farms in the United States changed hands during the years 1916 to 1920. It should also be noted that a great many farmers who purchased at exorbitant levels have already lost their land. Still other farmers who did not buy land marked up the value of their land and other property, placed too much reliance upon this new and fictitious wealth and incurred liabilities in excess of their normal earning capacity.

Frequently the scale of farm operations and expenditures was materially expanded to meet the demand for increased production as well as to reap the benefit of war prices. In many parts of the dry-land wheat regions an extraordinary series of crop failures was experienced during the years 1917 to 1921. Farm operations in these years were conducted at maximum costs, and instead of profiting by high prices farmers piled up additional debts. The financial situation in these dry-land wheat regions became, in fact, so serious that Federal funds to the amount of $8,500,000 were provided in 1918, 1921, and 1922 for seed and feed loans to enable farmers to continue their operations.

The degree to which farm debt has been increased is shown to some extent by the census. The average mortgage debt per owner-operated farm, which in 1910 ranged from $1,960 to $2,364 for the principal wheat regions, about doubled by 1920. These census figures do not include the mortgage debt on farms operated by managers and tenants. In addition to the farm mortgage encumbrance, a substantial part of farm indebtedness is represented by personal bank, and merchant credit, for which separate data are not available.

The evidence does not indicate that the total volume of farm indebtedness is in itself of alarming dimensions. Its significance lies more especially in its distribution. In some parts of the more specialized wheat regions the burden of farm debt is much heavier than in others. Within every community there are farmers who have very little or no debt, while others are very deeply involved. The situation on the average appears to be most serious in the semi-arid regions where wheat farming is conducted as a specialized industry and under conditions of high crop risk. On the other hand, many farmers in the better wheat regions purchased land at inflated prices or incurred other heavy liabilities during the war and are now carrying burdensome debts.

When price deflation came in 1920, farmers who had accumulated large debts were seriously embarrassed. While the majority of them have been successful in tiding over their financial difficulties, a substantial number have not. This situation is brought out in a special inquiry made by the Department of Agriculture in the spring of 1923. Reports were secured from 15 States covering the period January, 1920, to March, 1923. Out of over 68,000 owner farmers included in this survey 4 per cent lost their farms through foreclosure or bankruptcy, 4.5 per cent lost their farms without legal proceedings, and a little over 15 per cent had been spared such loss up to March, 1923, only because of the leniency of their creditors. Out of almost 26,000 tenant farmers, 7.2 per cent lost property through foreclosure or bankruptcy, 7.8 per cent lost property without legal proceedings, and 21.3 per cent retained their property merely as a result of the leniency of creditors.

According to this survey, the losses of farms and farm property were relatively most numerous in the Great Plains region. Applying the results obtained from these reports to the 1920 census figures for owners and tenants, it was estimated that the percentage of farmers who since 1920 had lost farms or other property ranged from 8.9 per cent of all farmers in Kansas to 28.3 per cent in Montana.

The seriousness of the situation is further reflected in the records of the bankruptcy courts. While the total number of bankruptcy cases among farmers is not large, it must be remembered that farmers as a rule do not resort to the bankruptcy courts when forced to give up property to creditors. The significance of the record lies, therefore, in the increase and distribution of such cases rather than in their absolute number. The records of the Department of Justice show that during the three pre-war years 1912–1914 an average of 5.5 per cent of all bankruptcy cases were farmers, while in 1922 the percentage was 14.4. The resort by farmers to bankruptcy courts was especially pronounced in the more specialized wheat regions. In the western winter wheat region farmer bankruptcy cases in the pre-war years averaged 8 per cent of all cases; in 1922 this percentage had increased to 25. In the spring wheat region the percentage increased from almost 22 per cent of all cases in the pre-war years to 48.9 per cent in 1922. The increase in bankruptcy among farmers in the Pacific Northwest States is also marked, particularly in Idaho, where almost 47 per cent of all cases put through the bankruptcy courts in 1922 involved farmers. The percentage of bankruptcies among farmers in 1922 was especially high in Iowa, Kansas, Nebraska, Colorado, North Dakota, South Dakota, Montana, and Idaho, ranging from 32.6 per cent of all cases in Nebraska to 78.5 per cent in North Dakota. Preliminary reports indicate that bankruptcies of farmers for the fiscal year ending June 30, 1923, will materially exceed those of 1922.

Further illustration of the financial distress of farmers in various parts of the West is found in the accumulation of delinquent farm taxes. Tax payments in some sections are in arrears from one to four years. In some of the wheat-growing areas of Kansas, for example, delinquent taxes since 1917 have increased in volume several hundred per cent.

The movement of population from country to city is in this connection very significant. In 1922 there was a net shift of 1,120,000 persons from farms to city, or about 3.6 per cent of the rural agricultural population at the beginning of the year. This cityward movement is a result of attractive urban wages, on the one hand, and inadequate returns in agriculture, on the other. From a survey of vacant farmhouses it appears that the percentage of all inhabitable farmhouses not occupied in the United States increased from 4.7 per cent in 1920 to 7.3 per cent in 1922. This abandonment of farmhouses was high in various sections of the country, but especially so in several States of the Great Plains region and the Pacific Northwest.

The cost of the principal factors in the production of wheat advanced during the war less rapidly than the price of wheat, and a margin of profit was realized by farmers who obtained fairly good yields.

With the break in general prices in 1920 wheat declined much more rapidly than the cost of production. While the price of wheat is now slightly above the pre-war level, the factors of cost are relatively much higher. This difference between wheat prices and production costs has resulted during the last few years in heavy losses to wheat farmers generally, and has borne down with special weight upon those who accumulated large debts during the war.

Practically all costs which enter into the production of wheat are considerably higher than before the war. Average monthly farm wages for the United States on July 1, 1923, were 59 per cent above the 1913 level. Day wages at harvest time had increased even more. In Kansas the day wage in harvest was 82 per cent above 1913. This fact is of special importance in commercial wheat-producing regions where the bulk of the harvest labor is supplied by day hands. Interest charges which farmers must pay have increased with the accumulation of debts. Wholesale prices of the more common farm implements were this season from 45 to 59 per cent higher than in 1913, and retail prices were considerably higher. Threshing rates in various sections of the wheat territory ranged this fall from 7 to 15 cents per bushel, or 50 per cent more than in 1913.

The burden of taxes in many regions has become excessive. Taxes on farm lands in Kansas increased 171 per cent between 1913 and 1921, in South Dakota, 129, and in the eastern 20 counties of Washington, 237 per cent. With the exception of South Dakota, taxes in these States have continued upward since the war. It should be observed that a substantial part of public funds is expended for local improvement purposes, such as roads, and that from 80 to 90 per cent of such taxes in Kansas and South Dakota, for example, are levied by local government units. The remedy for high taxes in some regions, therefore, rests in large measure with farmers themselves. No doubt the ready market for tax-exempt securities also accounts in part for some of the ill-advised expenditures in local improvements. . . .

The cost of producing wheat varies widely between individuals as between regions. The average cost for the total production, as shown by some investigations, covers the cost of a little more than half of the crop, and a wheat price which only equals this cost will not permanently maintain the industry. To place wheat growing on a stable basis, the price for wheat must be sufficiently high to yield satisfactory returns on the bulk of the production. This price wheat farmers have not received during the last several years.

The spread between the price paid to the producer of wheat and the price paid by the consumer of bread has widened very materially since 1913.

The retail price of a 16-ounce loaf of bread in Washington, D.C., has increased from 5.45 cents in September, 1913, to 9 cents in September, 1923. This advance in bread prices has not benefited the farmer. The portion received in 1913 by the wheat grower for the wheat equivalent of flour used in baking the Washington loaf was about one-fifth of the retail price of bread; in 1923 it amounts to less than one-sixth. While the wheat grower's portion of the retail price of bread has increased during this period less than one-third of a cent, the margins above have increased a total of 3¼ cents.

The margins between the mill and the retailer are, therefore, of most interest to the consumer, but the margins between the farm and the terminal market are of special concern to the farmer. According to the best available evidence the margins for the services of local and terminal handling agencies as well as those of transportation agencies bear down heavily upon the wheat grower.

The Department of Agriculture has made an analysis of the operations during 1921–22 of 40 country elevators in north central Kansas. The gross margin of these elevators ranged as high as 9.6 cents per bushel, and averaged a little better than 4 per cent of the terminal selling price. The transportation costs to Kansas City averaged about 12½ cents per bushel or a trifle over 10 per cent of the terminal price.

The operating cost of these 40 Kansas elevators varied from 1.9 cents to 7.4 cents per bushel. This wide variation in operating expense is largely due to the variation in the volume of grain handled by the several elevators. The tendency for costs to decline with increase in volume of grain handled is quite marked.

The information at hand suggests the need of reducing both local and terminal margins in the marketing of wheat. A reduction of the country elevator margin can be effected in considerable measure by increasing the volume of grain handled by each elevator. This would necessitate a reduction in the number of elevators at points where there are two or more competing elevators. It should not be overlooked, however, that in the case of privately operated elevators the increased volume thus obtained might to some extent at least be offset by lower prices resulting from decreased competition.

Such investigations as have been made indicate that the cooperative farmers' elevator efficiently operated is an effective factor in reducing local buying margins. . . .

Under the stimulus of war prices and in response to the demand for large food supplies, the production of wheat was increased enormously during the years of the war. The initial rise in price following the declaration of war in 1914 encouraged the expansion of our wheat area. This large acreage, together with a favorable season, caused the wheat crop of 1915 to be the largest we ever harvested. Other countries also secured large crops that season, and as a result the price of wheat dropped to practically the pre-war level and remained low through the crop year 1915–16. A marked decline in wheat plantings followed, and with the heavy abandonment in 1917 the acreage harvested that year fell to a point slightly below the pre-war average.

With the bottling up of the Russian surplus the Allies had to depend upon overseas countries, especially North America, for their wheat. The price of wheat advanced sharply in the fall of 1916 and continued to rise through the forepart of 1917. After the United States entered the war, measures were taken to regulate the price of wheat, and minimum prices were fixed for the 1917, 1918, and 1919 crops. Under continuous appeals for production of food, the production of wheat rose from an average of 690,000,000 bushels in the period 1909–1913 to 968,000,000 in 1919, an increase of 40 per cent, and the wheat area expanded from an average of 47,000,-000 acres to 75,000,000 in 1919.

In order to provide land for wheat, rye, oats, tame hay, and some other crops, of which there was an increase, the corn acreage was materially reduced, and a large amount of pasture and meadow land in the older regions and wild grass land in the newly settled regions was drawn into cultivation.

When general deflation of prices began in the summer of 1920, wheat prices broke sharply and have continued to decline into the present season. As a result substantial reductions have taken place in both acreage and production of wheat. Nevertheless, the crop for 1923 is 781,000,000 bushels or 13 per cent greater than the average before the war, and the acreage is about 24 per cent larger. The corn acreage which was replaced by wheat has now recovered most of this loss, but is still slightly under the pre-war average. While there has been some reduction in cultivated crops, the total crop area of the country is still between 30,000,000 and 40,000,000 acres larger than before the war.

The States included in the Corn Belt, western winter wheat region, spring wheat region and Pacific Northwest, contain over 85 per cent of the 1923 wheat acreage and are, therefore, of special importance. Winter wheat accounts for the major portion of our expansion in production. Of the 28,500,000 acres increase in total wheat area during the war about 22,000,000 were winter wheat.

In the Corn Belt wheat increased 7,000,000 acres and displaced about 3,000,000 acres of corn. Although substantial adjustments in crop acreages have been made since 1919, the wheat area is still almost 2,900,000 acres over the average before the war and the corn acreage is about 1,722,000 acres below. Some lands in the Corn Belt have also been returned to pasture and meadow.

The largest addition to the winter wheat area was made in the Great Plains States of Nebraska, Kansas, Colorado, Oklahoma, and Texas. By 1919 the wheat acreage in these States had been expanded by over 13,450,000 acres. . . .

## SUMMARY AND CONCLUSIONS

The wheat industry of the United States is in a period of serious depression. A great many farmers have already lost their farms or other property and the financial condition of others is critical. This condition of things has resulted from the decline in wheat prices, the relatively high level maintained in the prices of other commodities and services, and also from the maladjustments which exist in the wheat industry itself.

Present low prices are caused by the large world supply of wheat, for which there is not an effective demand at higher price levels. The total world crop outside of Russia is estimated at 3,400,000,000 bushels, which exceeds the production of last year by 300,000,000 bushels and the pre-war average by 500,000,000, excluding Russia. Both importing and exporting countries whose production fell during the war are resuming rapidly the position they previously held as wheat producers. Moreover, the evidence indicates that competition in wheat production will increase very materially. Russia is gradually restoring her agriculture and is already exporting some bread grains. Argentina, Australia, and especially Canada are selling abroad large amounts of wheat and will in all probability continue to expand their wheat exports. These countries enjoy material advantages over the United States in the production of wheat. So long as the United States produces a surplus, the prices of American wheat will be determined largely in the markets of the world and American farmers as exporters of wheat must be prepared to meet the keen competition of foreign producers for these markets.

Although wheat prices have dropped to pre-war levels, prices of manufactured commodities and of services remain high. The costs which enter into the production and marketing of wheat are so high that, at present prices for wheat, the farmer can not continue to pay them and remain in business. Taxes, machinery, wages, freight rates, and prices of food and clothing are out of proportion to the price of wheat and the earnings of the wheat farmer.

A number of factors within the wheat industry itself also have contributed to the present wheat crisis. Lands on which wheat can not under present economic conditions be grown profitably have been brought into cultivation in some regions. This fact coupled with the dependence placed upon wheat as a cash crop accounts for the losses of some farmers. Furthermore, high prices and the appeal for larger food supplies during the war induced many farmers to expand unduly their farm operations and to incur liabilities which since the break in wheat prices they have been unable to carry. The financial distress which has come as a result of these various causes is considerably aggravated by losses which are due to inefficient farm management. Many farmers are growing and marketing wheats which do not fulfill the highest market requirements and consequently fail to yield maximum net returns. On some farms, furthermore, excessive emphasis on wheat carries with it an unsatisfactory seasonal distribution of farm labor with resulting heavy expenditures for hired help. The financial difficulties of many, in short, would be reduced if their farm business were operated along more efficient lines.

It is important to bear in mind that the solution of present agricultural difficulties depends quite as much upon the efforts of farmers themselves as upon any Government action. There are fundamental and far-reaching adjustments in production and marketing which farmers themselves must make as a part of a long-time program. A survey of the situation indicates that well-considered action in a number of directions will bring wheat farmers a substantial measure of relief.

A large number of wheat producers are on the verge of bankruptcy. Many of them are, no doubt, beyond the point where further credit extensions would benefit them. On the other hand, a larger number can and should be saved by the renewal of loans or by additional credit on reasonable terms. Where a large volume of personal credit exists and the mortgage status of the farm permits, outstanding short-time loans should be funded into long-term mortgage loans at lower rates of interest. In this connection full advantage should be taken of the facilities afforded under the Federal Farm Loan Act. Moreover, the new credit facilities provided in the Federal intermediate credit banks should be utilized to reduce the cost of personal credit to the farmer. In this bankers should lend a willing hand even where such action does not increase their immediate profits. The constructive country banker will readily see that in the long run such action benefits him as well as the farmer.

To meet successfully foreign competition in some markets in which exchange rates and opportunities for exchange of commodities favor purchases of wheat from other sources, easy credits on American purchases may be necessary. The War Finance Corporation should make special efforts to finance the exportation of wheat in line with the joint resolution of Congress, January, 1921, reviving the activities of that corporation. . . .

Prices paid at terminal markets reflect quite accurately the variations in quality of wheat; prices paid at country points frequently do not. Farmers must know the quality and grade of their wheat in order intelligently to bargain for the best market price. Wheats of high gluten content usually command premiums at terminal markets. While the Federal grades for wheat through subclass specifications indicate broadly the gluten content, the only practicable method of measuring it requires extensive laboratory equipment. It is desirable, therefore, that State authorities, in cooperation with the Federal Government, undertake to determine and make available as early as possible in the harvest season information in regard to the gluten content of wheat in the important wheat-producing areas. Wheats may vary widely in gluten content within local areas; farmers should, therefore, have individual tests made of their wheats by the agencies set up for this purpose.

Concerted and coordinated action in the form of producers' organizations should improve the production and marketing of wheat. Higher returns may be obtained by standardizing the production of wheat in conformity with market demands, and substantial economies may be made in the cost of wheat marketing. Cooperative organizations efficiently managed will contribute to this end and their development should, therefore, be still further encouraged.

The movement of farmers into other occupations which is now under way will help to restore the balance between agriculture and other industries. Every farmer who is not able to make a living where he is should review carefully his own possibilities, but should not make a blind move into other types of farming or into city occupations. There are, however, thousands of farmers skilled in the industries of the city who will doubtless turn to their former occupations for relief.

The adjustments that have been indicated are part of a long-time program for agriculture and must be made in considerable measure through the efforts of the farmers themselves. Yet all of these means will not go far toward promptly restoring the purchasing power of the farmer's dollar, which has been unreasonably reduced by the rapid deflation which agriculture was least able to resist.

Since the immediate difficulty in the present situation is the maladjustment in price ratios, what is most needed right now is some way to restore the proper ratios either by increasing the prices of farm products or by reducing the prices of other commodities.

The prices of farm equipment, food, clothing, and building materials, as well as farm wages, are influenced by the costs of mining, transportation, and manufacturing, and by the ability to adjust production to that limit of supply which can be sold in the domestic market at a price to yield a profit.

One of the largest elements in the production cost of manufactured products as well as in transportation cost is the wages of labor. Wages have remained high since the war. The immigration and Adamson laws, together with the policies of organized labor, have been potent factors in maintaining wage scales. On the other hand, the domestic market for the products of the manufacturing industries makes it possible for them to continue production at a profit even with high wages for industrial labor. Under these conditions organized industry can maintain high prices in the domestic market and dump surpluses in foreign markets at low prices.

The question may be raised whether protection to labor and industry shall be withdrawn in order that the inflow of foreign labor and manufactured products may reduce the prices of the products which farmers buy to the level of farm products or whether some better remedy should be sought. The better and more practical alternative may be to try to improve prices of farm products of which we have an exportable surplus and which are, therefore, unduly depressed. Abundance of work at good wages gives assurance of good demand for farm products, but justice requires that the farmer be helped so far as possible and proper to secure relatively good wages for his labor. Indeed, industry and labor can not hope long to enjoy a disproportionately high price level for their products for the simple reason that farmers constitute about 30 per cent of the purchasers of such products and if the farmers' ability to buy is materially lessened for any length of time, both industry and labor suffer through lessened demand and prices will be forced lower.

Cooperation among farmers has been suggested as a means of attaining the end sought. While cooperation is to be encouraged as one of the best means of improving marketing methods and reducing marketing costs, as well as of improving the quality of farm products, it does not appear possible, and certainly not within a short period of time, to organize the producers of the great staples of American agriculture so effectively as to give them that control over supply which is necessary substantially to influence price.

The sale or gift of a substantial part of our surplus wheat to countries which are not able to buy, and which would, therefore, take out of the ordinary channels of trade and competition the wheat sold or given, would unquestionably have a helpful effect upon domestic prices of wheat, provided larger tariff protection were given. Before such sale or gift could be consummated, however, more than two-thirds of this year's wheat crop will have passed out of the hands of the farmers.

Inasmuch as the first step looking toward increasing the domestic price requires the disposition of the surplus over and above domestic needs, and inasmuch as the facts presented in the foregoing pages indicate that the world production of wheat will probably be over-large for another year or so, the suggestion that the Government set up an export corporation to aid in the disposition of this surplus is worthy of the most careful consideration. Such a corporation necessarily would need rather broad powers. It would not be necessary that it should undertake to handle the entire crop, and it could probably carry on its activities in cooperation with existing private agencies. If it should be found necessary to arrange for the sale of the surplus exported at a price much lower than the domestic price, the loss so incurred would properly be distributed over the entire crop.

The prime duty of such an export corporation would be to restore, so far as possible, the pre-war ratio between wheat, and other farm products of which we export a surplus, and other commodities. Its activities would therefore expand or contract according as the relative prices for farm products varied with other commodities, and it would cease to function as pre-war ratios become fairly well restored.

# 21. The Federal Government Underwrites Agriculture

The persistence of agricultural surpluses, combined with the further collapse of farm prices in the early years of the Great Depression, posed a need for fresh policies to stabilize and raise the price level. One of the first important measures of the New Deal was a crop restriction program which offset losses to participating farmers by compensating them for taking acres out of production. As the following selection indicates, the first twenty years of federal crop controls and price supports reveal policy inconsistencies, but the central objective of protecting farm income against the vagaries of changing demand and economic instability remains the same. Since the innovative legislation of the New Deal, the federal government has been committed to a policy of intervention in the farm economy in order to provide minimal guarantees for commercial agriculture, on the premise that a prosperous agriculture is essential to a strong economy.

SOURCE: Murray R. Benedict and Oscar C. Stine, *The Agricultural Commodity Programs: Two Decades of Experience* (New York: The Twentieth Century Fund, 1956), pp. xv–xxiii, xxv–vii, xl–iii. Reprinted by permission of The Twentieth Century Fund.

The economic disturbances created by World War I and the agricultural depressions of the 1920s and 1930s led to a marked change in the attitudes of farmers and the general public with respect to the role of the federal government in dealing with the problems of farmers. . . .

Though the broad objective was that of improving farm incomes generally, most of the specific programs undertaken related to particular farm commodities, rather than to farms as economic units. Several reasons lay back of that emphasis: one, a commodity approach was considered more practical and more generally satisfying to farmers than one oriented to individuals or to the industry generally; two, the commodities and areas involved were those in which political pressure for direct and quick action was most vigorous and vocal; and, three, it was argued that if prosperity and stability could be achieved in respect to these important farm commodities, the aid thus given would strengthen the agricultural industry generally and help to some extent in the effort to revive economic activity throughout the national economy.

The policies and procedures adopted departed sharply from earlier attitudes and earlier methods of providing government aid, though most of the types of agricultural aid initiated previously were continued and strengthened. The new departures can best be described as an abandonment of the earlier policy of nonintervention in agricultural business affairs and a step in the direction of a managed and planned agricultural economy.

But neither of these changes was clearly defined or perhaps even fully accepted by those responsible for making them. In the early stages, especially from 1933 to 1935, much of the program was regarded as temporary: an emergency measure for getting agriculture into better balance with the rest of the economy, with an underlying assumption that once that was accomplished principal reliance would again be on the functioning of uncontrolled production and marketing processes.

However, the idea of continuing government intervention soon came to be widely accepted. The Soil Conservation and Domestic Allotment Act of 1936 and the Agricultural Adjustment Act of 1938 constituted a more specific recognition of the need for a continuing program to strengthen agriculture's position in an economy in which the returns to other groups were becoming less and less subject to the free play of competitive forces. Nevertheless, the free market structure and individual decisions in the production process continued to be the dominant features of American agriculture.

Government intervention has been a modifying influence rather than a substitute for earlier patterns of activity. State trading and direct government price fixing have not had any large part in the thinking of farm and congressional groups, except in wartime and even then only to the extent deemed necessary for successful prosecution of the war. However, the maintenance of high-level price supports does result in government price fixing and heavy involvement of the government in trading operations. Though that is true, it should be noted that state trading has been limited to a relatively few commodities. The agricultural markets generally have continued to be free and competitive.

Moreover, it is an oversimplification to say there was no government intervention before the 1930s. There was intervention but, without implying that the steps taken were inappropriate, the emphasis was largely negative. The government specified what could not be done, not what must be done. Much of the earlier legislation sought and obtained by the farm groups and by the general public was of that nature. Federal inspection of the slaughter of meat animals, the pure food laws and the campaign for the elimination of bovine tuberculosis were measures for the protection of consumers. The Packers and Stockyards Act, commodity exchange regulation, and the development of grain grading and federal licensing of warehouses were intended to protect farmers from exploitation, not to prescribe in detail how and by whom such businesses might be conducted. Some of these earlier programs were in the nature of aids to be used, rejected or ignored by the farmer as he might choose; among them were such services as crop and price reporting, agricultural research and extension education, and disease and pest control.

Though the new programs went considerably farther in the direction of government guidance or control they never were extended to all of American agriculture and, for the most part, rigorous and compulsory controls were applied in a somewhat gingerly way even to the crops and areas where these techniques were regarded as most appropriate and acceptable. The traditional preference of farmers, and of the American public generally, for freedom to produce, process, sell or buy with a minimum of government interference was still very strong though farmers were coming to be more and more skeptical of the merits of a completely unregulated, competitive system for agriculture—the more so since many types of business and most labor groups were clearly moving toward self-imposed or governmental restraints on competition.

## EFFECTS OF DEPRESSION AND WAR

The depression decade did not provide a favorable setting for the expected reversion to freer trading and unregulated production. The long period of substandard prices and business activity tended instead to enlarge and consolidate the areas and types of control. The 1940s provided economic opportunities for relaxation of controls but at the same time brought into effect price guarantees and other measures that farmers were reluctant to relinquish, even when prices and incomes were at highly satisfactory levels. These measures in turn operated to inhibit the types of readjustment that would have made possible a retreat from intervention on the part of the government without creating price and income problems that many of the farm groups were unwilling to face.

The result was a continuance of extensive government participation in the production and marketing processes relating to some commodities, notably cotton, wheat, tobacco, rice and some of the dairy products, and almost complete reversion to pre-1930s marketing and pricing procedures for a large part of the agricultural industry, including such major segments as beef cattle, hogs, poultry and most of the minor perishable crops. . . . The issues are still in controversy. Strong political groups are seeking to reverse the drift toward greater reliance on competition and unregulated prices while other strong political groups, and economic forces, are working in the direction of removing or modifying some of the governmental restraints and guarantees now in effect. The outcome almost certainly will not be a return to the marketing and production policies of the pre-1930s era. In keeping with the almost worldwide trend toward increased protection of the individual against the vicissitudes of price and income declines that are beyond his control, it seems clear that some form of price and income support will be retained at least for the politically important crops.

The principal subject of controversy is the level of such supports, not whether supports shall or shall not be provided. No important political group advocates complete abandonment of safeguards against disastrously low prices for farm products. One school of thought would look to the maintenance of price floors, allowing considerable leeway for automatic adjustments to determine the actual level of prices received, while the other favors the maintenance through positive government action of "satisfactory" prices, together with strong controls on production which would adjust it to approximately the amounts that can be sold at the prices specified.[1] There is also controversy over the methods by which either of these types of support shall be made effective. Nonrecourse loan programs, government purchases, export subsidies, supplementary payments, acreage and marketing controls, and even reliance on general monetary and fiscal policies, are advocated or opposed.

For some few products, notably fluid milk, a continuing program of regulated marketing without subsidy but with federal or state control seems to have become well established over much of the country. This differs from similar procedures developed prior to 1933 mainly in that Secretary's orders or state legislation bring all producers and handlers into the system whereas participation was on a voluntary basis before the government programs were initiated. In some of the state-controlled markets the prices to consumers are also established by the control agencies, but the prices so established do not appear to differ greatly from those arrived at in the federally controlled markets or where no government control exists. For a few of the minor crops, including some of the perishables, similar programs have been developed and have achieved some

[1] Or, alternatively, procedures for letting products flow onto the market at lower prices with government payments making up the difference. There are, of course, many variants of these positions, which, for the sake of simplicity, are here stated in somewhat extreme form.

standing but they do not appear to be so well established or so generally accepted as those in the fluid milk markets.

## FARM PRICE POLICY NOT SETTLED OR CONSISTENT

Thus it is apparent that farm price-support policy in the United States is far from being settled or consistent. Further modifications and changes of direction can be expected in the years ahead. The direction of change will no doubt be considerably influenced by the nature of the supply-demand balance that develops as a result of government action and natural forces. If demand continues strong, as in the past fifteen years, and if weather conditions should prove less favorable, prices might be high enough to reduce the pressure for government intervention and encourage a return to increased reliance on traditional production and marketing procedures.

On the other hand, any serious setback in business activity or a continuing surplus will undoubtedly sustain or strengthen the demand for government action to support farm prices. In that event, the controversial issue will probably be whether to support prices in the market and attempt to deal with a continuing problem of excess stocks or to supplement returns to farmers by means of direct government subsidies (as is currently being done in Britain) or, alternatively, to introduce more rigorous and coercive controls on production. A third approach which seems to be emerging is that of attempting to speed the transfer of production resources out of agriculture, by means of "soil-bank" retirements of crop land not needed currently and encouragement to farm manpower to move into other and presumably more profitable types of employment.

Whatever direction is taken, it seems clear that agriculture will not be left so completely at the mercy of chance fluctuations in demand and supply as it was before the 1930s. Almost certainly some provision for the retention of price floors will be continued whether these be at high or lew levels. There will probably be some device for absorbing and later releasing redundant supplies that arise from temporary upsurges in yield and production. In addition, the government seems firmly committed, on a bipartisan basis, to a vigorous effort to maintain substantially full employment and high demand and to reopen where feasible the external markets for U.S. farm products. . . .

Most of the commodity programs relate to three quite different sets of conditions: (1) a period of deep depression with a heavy excess of production, very low prices and acute distress in the farm areas; (2) the war period when prices and production were high and when the principal emphasis was on increased production rather than on curtailment; and (3) a postwar period of general prosperity and relatively high farm prices when, however, production was beginning to outrun consumption, giving rise to fears of another depression in agriculture despite unprecedentedly high levels of employment and national income, and when the need for extensive readjustment in the kinds and amounts of production was beginning to be apparent.

The devices used fall roughly into six categories: (1) attempts to create an improved system of marketing based on producer-controlled cooperative marketing agencies; (2) holding operations designed to stabilize the flow of nonperishables onto the market; (3) efforts to cut back and hold down farm production with a view to bringing supplies into better adjustment with demand; (4) measures designed to transfer buying power from consumers or the Treasury to the farm groups; (5) marketing agreements intended to stabilize the industry and strengthen prices; and (6) efforts to hold prices up to the high levels achieved during the war and postwar years by means of government loans and purchases. Included with these were various supplementary programs having for the most part similar or related objectives. Among them were such measures as export subsidies, the food stamp plan, incentives for increased production in the war years, and soil conservation payments made for the purpose of transferring income, adjusting production and building up soils.

For some of the commodities, several or even most of these devices were used or tried. For others only one or two were considered appropriate and workable. For a few, principally the beef cattle industry, no large-scale program was undertaken, excepting emergency purchase of cattle in the drought areas in the 1930s.

## COTTON AND THE COTTON PROGRAMS

In the period here under review extensive and important changes were occurring in the cotton-producing areas. Some resulted from the specific programs undertaken by the government, others from forces that would have affected the industry profoundly even if there had been no direct intervention by the government. The two together brought about more significant readjustments and shifts in cotton production than had occurred in the nearly three quarters of a century between the close of the Civil War and the launching of the New Deal programs.

In the decades just prior to 1930, a cotton surplus was beginning to develop. It became more evident and serious as a result of the sharp reduction in cotton consumption in the early years of the depression. The first efforts to deal with it through the Farm Board's Cotton Stabilization Corporation were palliative and had no very significant effect on the industry. The failure of that program, however, contributed to the adoption of the more vigorous and positive programs of the succeeding years. It had become apparent that, without rigorous controls, the industry would produce more cotton than could be sold at prices that would sustain any acceptable level of prosperity in the cotton areas of the Southeast. From the time of the Civil War that region had been in a state of almost chronic depression because of the heavy reliance on cotton, the low price of that commodity and the underemployment of its labor.

The government's cotton program in the early years involved vigorous efforts to cut back acreage and production. These were soon supplemented by loan programs designed to maintain prices at levels well above those that would have prevailed in the absence of acreage controls and loans. These methods proved moderately effective so long as the loan rates were not put so high as to prevent movement of the cotton. Cash receipts from the sale of cotton were increased substantially and, in addition, sizable government payments were made to the growers. Cotton acreage was cut back some 20 per cent in 1933 and was further reduced in later years. By the early 1950s the acreage grown was not much more than half as large as in the late 1920s and early 1930s, but about as much cotton was being produced as before.

The program was considerably modified from 1936 on as a result of the invalidation of parts of the Agricultural Adjustment Act of 1933. That action eliminated the rigorous and relatively effective acreage and production controls established under the 1933 act and the supplementing Bankhead Cotton Control Act. In 1937 a sizable increase in acreage and a large yield resulted in the production of a 19-million-bale crop. This was far more than the market would absorb at prices comparable with those that had been maintained under the programs of the earlier years.

The Commodity Credit Corporation then became the major factor in preventing a new and serious price slump. It acquired nearly a third of the crop and also took over substantial quantities from the 1938 crop. Most of this accumulation was carried over under loan or in government ownership until the end of World War II. The operation was similar in nature to the acquisitions of the Farm Board's Cotton Stabilization Corporation but on a larger scale and with more adequate and more flexible financing which made possible a much longer period of withholding and liquidation.

The upsurge of production in 1937 led to congressional action to reestablish provisions for rigorous controls on acreage and for quotas on marketings, these being now more broadly applicable than the specific legislation for cotton and tobacco in the earlier legislation. Plantings were held in check during the war years by the strong demand for other farm products and the shortage of labor, but little progress was made in liquidating the large carry-over from the late 1930s. In the early postwar years unexpectedly strong demand coupled with a very moderate level of production led not only to a rapid reduction of stocks but to a sharp increase in price. By 1948, nearly all of the CCC inventories and loan commitments had been closed out. However, the high level of price support maintained, declining prices for competing products and record yields gave rise to a substantial increase in production and a new buildup of excess stocks, mostly in the hands of the Commodity Credit Corporation. The industry was again faced with the prospect of a period of heavy carry-overs and glutted markets.

The gloomy outlook of early 1949 and 1950 led to the reimposition of acreage controls in 1950. This coupled with lower yields and a sharp increase in demand in the summer of 1950 led to a severe shortage of cotton supplies throughout the world in 1950–51. Prices went to all-time highs and it became necessary to ration supplies to domestic mills and to foreign buyers. However, the tight supply situation was short-lived. Acreage controls were abandoned for the 1951 and 1952 seasons and production increased substantially. No serious disposal problems arose until 1953, but from then on through 1955 the size of cotton holdings in the hands of CCC or under loan to it became a matter of serious concern.

Acreage and marketing controls were reimposed in 1954 and

1955 and the situation appeared for a time to be stabilizing. However, the August 1, 1955 carry-over was up to 11.1 million bales, about the same as the heavy stock held in 1945, which was approximately equal to a full year's domestic consumption and exports. On top of this, the yield in 1955 was phenomenally high (over 400 pounds per acre, which was more than double the customary yields of the early 1930s). . . .

## WHEAT PROGRAM ONE OF THE MOST TROUBLESOME

The wheat program was originally conceived in terms similar to those relating to cotton. The underlying problem here also was one of heavy oversupply, large accumulations and low prices. The original plan of curtailing acreage was largely inoperative during the middle 1930s because of very severe droughts that reduced production even more than was contemplated by those in charge of the program. Except for some build-up of excess stocks in the late 1930s, the problem did not become serious until well after the close of World War II. Heavy war and postwar demand made full production and a considerable expansion of acreage desirable. Demand was sufficiently strong to absorb at good prices all that could be produced.

When the wartime and reconstruction demand eased off in the late 1940s, the true nature of the problem began to emerge more clearly. A considerable downward adjustment of wheat acreage was undoubtedly needed but the wartime guarantees, based on price relationships of the pre-World War I period, overpriced wheat in comparison with other farm products. Costs of production had been reduced much more than for most other farm commodities. Furthermore, the lands shifted into wheat production had few alternative uses and reversion to grass and livestock involved very heavy costs to the growers.

The price supports guaranteed in the war period and continued thereafter provided strong incentives for continuing to produce wheat on a scale comparable to that of the war and early postwar years. Consequently, there was strong resistance to the making of needed adjustments and extensive political support for the positions taken by the grower groups. At the same time, yields continued high and even increased, thus tending to offset such adjustments in acreage as were made. The result was a continuing build-up of stocks in the hands of the Commodity Credit Corporation and increasing concern as to how these stocks were to be liquidated. Acreage controls were instituted in 1954 and 1955 but high yields caused production still to be somewhat in excess of requirements for bread use, exports, and normal feed and seed use. The unbalance on the production side had been reduced but not eliminated. The problem of liquidating a billion bushels or more of CCC-owned wheat still remained.

It was complicated by rapid recovery in the agricultural economies of the major wheat-consuming countries and similar oversupplies in competing wheat-exporting countries. Heavy subsidies on U.S. exports were being provided by way of the International Wheat Agreement and some wheat was being made available for disaster relief abroad, but the liquidation and adjustment problems still were among the most perplexing ones facing government administrators as of the end of 1955. . . .

Nevertheless, the continuing overstimulation of wheat production in areas particularly prone to drought was creating a danger to wheat producers themselves as well as a perplexing problem for the government and its administrative agencies. Price guarantees could not provide much help to the farmer whose wheat crop failed. The fixed level of price support was in fact likely to increase income instability rather than to lessen it. As of 1955, no considerable progress had been made in the solution of this difficult problem. Wheat acreage still was excessive, inactive stocks were high and the prospects of a receptive foreign market for the excess were not bright. The cost of the program had been high, some $2 billion between 1930 and 1953, with other large losses already incurred or in prospect. . . .

## THE COMMODITY PROGRAMS AS A WHOLE

There are few broad generalizations that can safely be made about the numerous and diverse commodity programs undertaken by the federal government during the past two decades. One is that no one type of program can be applied to all commodities or even to any very large group of them. Each major commodity, and many of the minor ones, has so many peculiarities of its own that any program designed to improve its position needs to be carefully and specifically worked out to fit the existing conditions.

The lack of such product differentiation was one of the principal defects of the system of postwar guarantees established during the war years. A separate and more flexible arrangement for the greatly expanded industries like dried milk, dried eggs, potatoes and wheat would have led to more rapid adjustment and to large savings in public expenditure. This is not to say that such individual crop legislation could practically have been undertaken in the war period. It obviously could not. It does point up the fact, however, that generalized legislation applying to a number of commodities should be very carefully scrutinized in periods when more deliberate consideration is possible.

Though extremely difficult politically, some regional and type differentiation is needed even for various parts of what is ordinarily considered a single commodity. For example, it is not logical to apply the same percentage cuts in acreage to the spring wheat area, where overproduction is only moderate or perhaps nonexistent, as to a region of substantial overproduction like the hard winter area or the Pacific Northwest. The problems of the cotton-producing areas of the Southeast and of the western states are also sufficiently distinct to warrant some differentiation of programs. Similarly, the difficult adjustments facing the butter-producing areas may warrant special treatment.

Among the major crops, acreage controls and marketing quotas are more practical and effective for crops like cotton or tobacco, which must be processed, than for crops like corn and oats, which may be used on the farms where grown.

Most of the programs now in operation were developed as a means of dealing with two of the most uncharacteristic periods in the nation's history, one a prolonged and severe depression, the other a period in which war requirements were dominant. The time seems now to have arrived for devising more carefully considered and specialized programs designed to meet the needs of farmers, and of the general public, under a different set of conditions. During the years in which the existing programs were taking shape, considerable progress was made in adapting them to the problems of this diverse and complex industry, but there still is much to be done in developing a well-balanced and constructive long-term program that will give to agriculture an appropriate share of the national income and at the same time take due account of the national interest and of our changing position in international affairs.

In general, the trend toward more detailed specification by the Congress of the procedures to be followed and the price relationships to be maintained has tended to increase the difficulties of administration and to introduce more rigidity than is desirable from the standpoint of the public and of the industry. For example, greater freedom of action at the administrative level would have made possible more realistic handling of the cotton surplus of the late 1930s, the oversupply of potatoes, dried milk and dried eggs in the postwar period, and the heavy accumulations of butter, cheese, wheat and cotton which have created such perplexing problems in recent years.

There has been some relaxation of the extreme rigidities of the early postwar years, but as yet no clear and comprehensive policy has emerged. Excessive preoccupation by the Congress with detailed and specific provisions relating to particular crops and enterprises tends frequently to inhibit or retard readjustments that would be in the long-time interest of both farmers and the public. It also precludes or de-emphasizes the much needed effort to work out and popularize consistent and constructive over-all policies relating to the place of agriculture in the national economy, and the amounts and kinds of public aid that should be provided for it.

During the 1930s the laws passed left room for considerable administrative discretion in determining the kinds of aid to be given and the levels of price support to be maintained. Few would contend that the decisions made were always wise and appropriate, but, on the whole, an extremely difficult and complex situation was dealt with imaginatively and with a high sense of responsibility. The trend since then has been for the Congress itself to take on more and more of the task of specifying the procedures to be used and the levels of support to be provided instead of delegating this authority under appropriate general directives.

The division of responsibility between the Congress and the administrators of the programs obviously presents difficult problems. Too much delegation, especially if not carefully and continuously

supervised by the Congress, can open the way to excessive bureau-
cratic power, discrimination in favor of or against certain groups,
and so on. The Supreme Court has long exercised a restraining influence on such delegation of powers and has frequently checked
the drift in that direction as being in excess of the limitations set
up in the Constitution. Nevertheless, as the economy has grown
more complex, an increase in the amount of delegation of functions
formerly considered specifically legislative has come to be generally
recognized as inescapable.

Federal Reserve Board and Treasury management of monetary
policies and Interstate Commerce Commission regulation of railroad rates are cases in point. These have long been recognized as
too complex or too fast-moving to be handled adequately by direct
congressional action. No similar degree of discretion has been permitted for the administrators of such agencies as the Commodity
Credit Corporation, except in the 1930s, a period in which much
of the most forward-looking and realistic action for the betterment
of conditions in agriculture occurred.

Agriculture's position in an economy which is becoming more
and more rigidified by growth in the size and power of other organized groups is a difficult one. Its tendency to overexpand production and to defer needed adjustments when put on a price basis
that it regards as equitable is well recognized and extremely difficult
to deal with. How to determine what is an equitable balance between farmers and other groups in an economy which has become
so highly organized is, of course, difficult in the extreme, but some
guiding principle is required even if only a policy of trying to amel-
iorate the hardships inherent in an industry that is so highly competitive.

An approach entirely in terms of prices is clearly inadequate.
Stable prices in agriculture may mean very unstable incomes. Furthermore, if production is not to be guided and adjusted by price
changes, some other form of guidance must be provided. Thus the
problem is that of somehow channeling into agriculture a reasonably
adequate share of the total national income without at the same
time maintaining it as an overexpanded and relatively inefficient
part of the economy. The other alternative appears to be to undertake to shift enough resources out of agriculture so that it will obtain in the market, in most years, a return comparable in real terms
with those achieved by other groups.

# 22. The Continuing Agricultural Revolution

Since about 1940 there have been fundamental changes in the organization of agriculture that comprise another stage in the American farm revolution of the past century or more. The more recent changes have been generated partly by the more complex mechanisms of the market and by the character of government farm programs which tend to benefit the large commercial grower rather than the small family farm. These shifts have also been produced by technological factors which have enhanced the contributions of powered mechanization, chemical fertilizers, nutrients, and pesticides. A high rate of attrition is continuing among the operators of small family enterprises who cannot afford the sizable capital investment for modernizing their operations. The steady trend toward more extensive operations, marked by the rising importance of the corporate producer, has raised questions about the long-term survival prospects of small growers.

SOURCE: For I, *Economic Report of the President . . . 1960. . . .* (Washington, D.C.: Government Printing Office, 1960), pp. 87–8, 100–6. For II, *ibid.*, 1961 (Washington, D.C.: Government Printing Office, 1961), pp. 93, 96–100, 105–6.

## I

### CHANGES IN FARM POPULATION

The farm population has declined by about 34 per cent since 1910 (Table 1). The decrease in the number of persons living on farms was rather gradual until World War II, but since then net migration has proceeded more rapidly. While the farm population has been dwindling, the total population of the United States has been growing, so that the proportion living on farms has declined substantially. Fifty years ago, one out of three persons lived on a farm; at present, one out of eight is a farm resident.

The decline in farm population since 1950 has been much greater among persons 18 to 44 years of age than among other age groups. Because of this, farm people 45 years old and over now outnumber, for the first time, farm persons who are 18 to 44 years of age. The

Table 1. Farm Population, 1910–59

| Year | Farm population[1] Number (millions) | As percent of total population[2] |
|---|---|---|
| 1910 | 32.1 | 34.9 |
| 1920 | 32.0 | 30.1 |
| 1930 | 30.5 | 24.9 |
| 1940 | 30.5 | 23.1 |
| 1950 | 25.1 | 16.5 |
| 1953 | 22.7 | 14.3 |
| 1956 | 22.4 | 13.3 |
| 1959 | 21.2 | 12.0 |

[1] As of April 1.
[2] Based on thousands of persons.

SOURCES: Department of Agriculture and Department of Commerce.

total number of males on farms slightly exceeds the number of females, except in the age group 25 to 44 years.

The net migration of persons from farms in the past four decades has been substantially larger than the decline in the farm population, as farm families have continued to contribute to the growth of the total population. During the 1930's, as a result of the depression, the rate was considerably less than in the 1920's; but World War II caused a record increase. The annual average migration was very high in the years 1950–53, owing in part to the Korean conflict, declined somewhat until 1956, but rose again in the following three-year period (Table 2). Since 1920, net migration from farms

Table 2. Net Migration from Farms, 1920–59[1]

| Period[2] | Annual average (thousands) | Percentage change (annual average) |
|---|---|---|
| 1920 to 1930 | −630 | −2.0 |
| 1930 to 1940 | −383 | −1.2 |
| 1940 to 1950 | −952 | −3.5 |
| 1950 to 1953 | −1,190 | −4.9 |
| 1953 to 1956 | −474 | −2.1 |
| 1956 to 1959 | −753 | −3.5 |

[1] Includes persons who have not moved but whose residence is no longer classified as a farm.
[2] Years beginning April 1 and ending March 31.

SOURCE: Department of Agriculture.

has totaled nearly 27 million persons; however, the farm population has declined by only 11 million, from 32.1 million to 21.2 million. The continuing migration from farms to urban areas has contributed to the increase in the nonagricultural labor force and to the growth of towns and cities.

The employment status of persons 14 years old and over living on farms has changed significantly since 1950 when, out of nearly 9.5 million such persons employed, nearly 70 per cent worked in agriculture. The number of employed farm residents has since declined by almost 2 million, and less than 60 per cent, or 4½ million, now work in agriculture. During the past decade, the number of persons who live on farms but are engaged in nonagricultural activities increased, and, as a percentage of the farm-resident labor force, rose from 29 per cent in 1950 to 38 per cent in 1958. Participation in off-the-farm employment among employed farm residents is more common for women than for men. . . .

Despite less favorable weather, output on the nation's . . . farms in 1959 slightly exceeded the record volume attained in 1958 and was 25 per cent above the 1947–49 average. Crop production was virtually unchanged, while livestock production increased slightly. The corn harvest increased by 560 million bushels, to a new high of 4.4 billion, and cotton output rose by 3.2 million bales, to 14.7 million. These gains offset a decrease of 330 million bushels in wheat and sizable declines in oats, barley, and soybeans. Production of hogs, broilers, and eggs increased substantially while milk production declined somewhat.

## OVERPRODUCTION AND EXCESS STOCKS

Food and natural fiber production in 1959 was so great that it exceeded, once again, the absorptive capacity of domestic and foreign demand. As a consequence, carryover stocks, already excessive, continued to grow. . . .

The stock of 121 million tons of five grains expected to be on hand by the summer and fall of 1960 exceeds by 70 million tons the estimated size of reserves required to meet the initial needs of defense emergencies and all but the worst weather contingencies. Cotton stocks also are much in excess of a desirable carryover.

The major part of total stocks is in Government hands and constitutes a burden on the Federal budget. This ties up sizable amounts of Federal funds: during the fiscal year 1960, Commodity Credit Corporation investment in inventory and loans may at times reach nearly $10 billion, and by June 30, 1960 it is expected to be about $9 billion. Expenditures during the year for storage, transportation, and interest will exceed $1.25 billion, and substantial losses will be incurred as those commodities are disposed of in domestic and export markets.

## MAGNITUDE OF OUTPUT

As Table 3 indicates, United States agricultural output increased slowly during the three decades preceding World War II, and then advanced steeply during the two decades from 1940 through 1959. Output was particularly large in 1958 and 1959 when, for the first time, annual grain production exceeded 200 million tons; this is 80 per cent more than the average annual production during the decade before World War II. Production in 1959 of all kinds of meat, including poultry meat, exceeded 16 million tons, a rise of nearly 80 per cent since the 1930's. Cotton and tobacco production have increased less rapidly.

The more than 200 million tons of grain and 16 million tons of meat currently produced in the United States compare with an estimated 125 million tons of grain and 7 million tons of meat produced in the Soviet Union in 1957–58, and with a total of 107 million tons of grain and 14 million of meat produced in the 17 member countries of the Organization for European Economic Cooperation (OEEC), Yugoslavia, and Spain. Yet the population of the Soviet Union is 30 million more than that of the United States, and the population of the 19 European countries is almost twice the United States total. Production per capita in the United States, averaging 2,325 pounds of grain and 185 pounds of meat, compares with 1,200 pounds of grain and 70 pounds of meat in the Soviet Union, and 625 pounds of grain and 80 pounds of meat in the 19 European countries.

## GROWTH IN PRODUCTIVITY

The growth in United States farm output has been achieved through an extraordinary increase in production per unit of labor

## Table 3. Output of Farm Products, 1910–59

| Product group | 1910–19 average | 1920–29 average | 1930–39 average | 1940–49 average | 1950–59 average[1] | 1958 | 1959[1] |
|---|---|---|---|---|---|---|---|
| | Million short tons | | | | | | |
| Crops: | | | | | | | |
| 14 major food and feed crops | (2) | 150 | 136 | 180 | 208 | 253 | 250 |
| 8 grains | 123[3] | 129 | 112 | 148 | 168 | 205 | 203 |
| 3 root crops[4] | (2) | 19.9 | 22.1 | 23.7 | 25.9 | 29.3 | 30.1 |
| 3 oil-bearing crops[5] | .7 | .9 | 1.9 | 7.4 | 13.5 | 19.4 | 17.6 |
| 29 commercial vegetables | (2) | (2) | (2) | 13.1 | 17.0 | 18.2 | 17.3 |
| 15 fruits | 8.4 | 10.6 | 12.6 | 15.9 | 16.9 | 17.6 | 18.2 |
| Cotton | 3.1 | 3.2 | 3.2 | 2.9 | 3.3 | 2.8 | 3.5 |
| Tobacco | .6 | .7 | .7 | .9 | 1.0 | .9 | .9 |
| Livestock products: | | | | | | | |
| Red meat and poultry[6] | (2) | (2) | 9.3 | 12.6 | 14.9 | 15.9 | 16.7 |
| Beef and veal | 3.6 | 3.7 | 3.8 | 5.2 | 6.8 | 7.3 | 7.4 |
| Lamb and mutton | .3 | .3 | .4 | .5 | .3 | .3 | .4 |
| Pork, excluding lard | 3.7 | 4.2 | 4.0 | 5.5 | 5.4 | 5.3 | 5.9 |
| Poultry | (2) | (2) | 1.0 | 1.5 | 2.3 | 3.0 | 3.1 |
| Milk | (2) | 46.9[7] | 51.6 | 58.0 | 60.6 | 62.6 | 62.2 |
| Eggs | 1.8 | 2.2 | 2.3 | 3.3 | 3.9 | 4.0 | 4.1 |
| | 1947–49=100 | | | | | | |
| Index of total output | 64 | 70 | 73 | 95 | 112 | 125 | 125 |
| All crops | 73 | 78 | 76 | 95 | 106 | 118 | 118 |
| All livestock and products[8] | 64 | 72 | 78 | 100 | 118 | 125 | 128 |

[1] Preliminary.
[2] Not available.
[3] Excludes grain sorghums, which probably average 1 million tons.
[4] Potatoes, sweet potatoes, sugar beets.
[5] Soybeans, flaxseed, peanuts.
[6] Dressed weight of slaughter.
[7] 1924–29 average.
[8] Meat animal component is based on live weight production on farms.

source: Department of Agriculture.

341

and per unit of land (Table 4). Production per man-hour on farms in 1958 was more than three times the 1930–39 average. The increase in the last ten years was about 80 per cent, a growth rate of 6 per cent per year, or from 2 to 3 times the increase per year in nonfarm output per man-hour. Production per man-hour has increased much faster in crop production than in animal husbandry, since high mechanization and the heavy use of fertilizer in crops have had no equivalent counterparts in livestock production.

The national average production of crops per acre increased by 15 per cent from 1946–48 to 1956–58. In view of the very large acreage devoted to farming and the wide variation in latitude and climatic conditions under which farming is carried on, this over-all productivity increase is most significant. Underlying it is an even more rapid rise in yields per acre of such important crops as wheat, corn, and cotton, which have been pushed in recent years to levels twice those in the decade prior to World War II. There is as yet no sign of a halt in the uptrend in yields per acre.

Although the increase in productivity has been less for livestock than for crops, livestock output per man-hour, per animal, and per dollar of total capital has shown sizable gains, especially since the 1940's.

Because, as described below, increasing quantities of resources other than labor and land have been employed in agriculture, productivity has risen less rapidly in terms of total input than in terms of labor and land. The ratio of output to total input is estimated to have increased at an annual rate of about 2 per cent during the last ten years, and to have been more than 50 per cent higher in 1959 than in the 1930's. This increase in efficiency is the composite result of greater precision in apportioning and coordinating factors of production, the use of improved crop varieties and hybrid animals, a reduction of losses by plant and animal protection, and—most important of all—the increased managerial skill of farm operators.

## CHANGES IN TYPES AND RATES OF INPUT

The changes in technology and management in agriculture leading to the remarkable growth in output per man-hour and in output per acre of land have involved extensive shifts in the mix of factors of production. By 1958, labor input had been reduced to scarcely

Table 4. Indexes of Productivity in Agriculture, 1910–58

[1947–49=100]

| Output ratio | 1910–19 average | 1920–29 average | 1930–39 average | 1940–49 average | 1950–58 average | 1958 |
|---|---|---|---|---|---|---|
| Per man-hour of farm work: | | | | | | |
| All farm output | 46 | 51 | 57 | 85 | 143 | 188 |
| Livestock and products | 72 | 75 | 74 | 92 | 126 | 144 |
| Crops | 46 | 50 | 55 | 85 | 146 | 203 |
| Per acre: | | | | | | |
| All crops[1] | 80 | 80 | 77 | 96 | 106 | 126 |
| Corn | 72 | 74 | 65 | 93 | 116 | 143 |
| Wheat | 84 | 83 | 79 | 101 | 116 | 162 |
| Cotton | 64 | 57 | 68 | 93 | 123 | 163 |
| Per unit of capital: | | | | | | |
| Livestock production per breeding unit[2] | (3) | 76 | 86 | 96 | 114 | 125 |
| Farm output per unit of assets used | (3) | (3) | (3) | 97 | 100 | 108 |
| Per unit of total input[4] | 73 | 74 | 80 | 95 | 109 | 123 |

[1] Aggregate index computed from variable yearly weights.
[2] Live weight of farm production of meat animals plus output of livestock products, per head of breeding stock.
[3] Not available.
[4] Aggregate farm output per unit of total input.
SOURCE: Department of Agriculture.

half that used in 1930–39 (Table 5). Much labor has been replaced by capital. Investment in labor-saving machinery has increased greatly, and purchases of petroleum fuels have multiplied several times. The 1958 inputs of mechanical power and machinery, including fuels, were more than 2.5 times the inputs in the decade prior to World War II, owing in part to the substantially faster increase in farm wage rates than in prices of farm machinery and motor fuels.

A second important factor has been the increase in the application of purchased plant nutrients to crops and pastures. Commercial fertilizer applied in 1958 was 5 times the 1930–39 average. In addition to intensive application to cotton, truck crops, root crops, soybeans, and irrigated pasture, the use of fertilizer in the production of feed crops has increased rapidly in recent years. According to the latest Census of Agriculture data, the amount of nitrogen used on corn, oats, and barley in 1954 was 3 times that in 1947. A comparatively stable cost has encouraged this larger use of fertilizer. For instance, the 1959 price of $1.06 per unit of 20 pounds of pure nitrogen, in the form of anhydrous ammonia, differed little from the average for the last 25 years. The marginal return for expenditures on fertilizer appears to have continued high. For 1954 it is estimated to have been $3.00 per dollar spent on fertilizer for corn, $2.27 for soybeans, $1.55 for grain sorghum, $1.62 for barley, $1.44 for oats, and $2.26 for wheat. Since then, it appears to have been reduced somewhat, as prices of those commodities have declined.

Another input factor that has contributed to the expansion of output is the application of supplementary sprinkler irrigation in subhumid and humid climates, which is being used increasingly in connection with nitrogen fertilizer. Also, such inputs as commercial mixing of feed, pesticides and other materials, the services used in livestock production, selective weed-killing chemicals, and related items used in crop production have been rising rapidly.

When all inputs are combined, their total traces a slowly rising long-term trend. During the last few years, however, withdrawal of land from use by the Soil Bank and continued reductions in labor inputs have brought some declines in total inputs.

Indicative of the changing mix of inputs is the shifting proportion between those which are "paid" and "unpaid." The former refer to current cash costs, the latter to farm family labor and owned capital including land. Paid inputs increased by two-thirds

| Item | 1910–19 average | 1920–29 average | 1930–39 average | 1940–49 average | 1950–58 average | 1958 |
|---|---|---|---|---|---|---|
| | | | | 1947–49=100 | | |
| **Aggregate inputs:[1]** | | | | | | |
| Total | 88 | 94 | 92 | 100 | 102 | 101 |
| Farm real estate | 95 | 96 | 94 | 97 | 105 | 105 |
| Farm labor | 140 | 139 | 129 | 113 | 79 | 66 |
| Mechanical power and machinery | 35 | 47 | 50 | 78 | 133 | 137 |
| Fertilizer and lime | 22 | 29 | 31 | 77 | 147 | 166 |
| Feed, seed, livestock services[2] | 23 | 37 | 38 | 88 | 119 | 141 |
| **Paid vs. unpaid inputs:** | | | | | | |
| Paid | 58 | 70 | 70 | 93 | 112 | 117 |
| Unpaid[3] | 134 | 133 | 126 | 108 | 90 | 82 |
| Labor | 148 | 149 | 139 | 115 | 79 | 64 |
| Capital | 96 | 90 | 91 | 88 | 120 | 128 |
| | | | Short tons | | | |
| **Concentrate feeds:** | | | | | | |
| Supply per animal unit | (4) | 0.81[5] | 0.78 | 0.91 | 1.14 | 1.36[6] |
| Fed per animal unit | (4) | .69[5] | .64 | .73 | .80 | .87[6] |

[1] Proportion of total inputs:

| | Farm real estate | Farm labor | Mechanical power and machinery | Fertilizer and lime | Feed, seed, livestock services | Miscellaneous |
|---|---|---|---|---|---|---|
| 1940 | 14.4 | 56.4 | 9.5 | 1.6 | 5.4 | 12.7 |
| 1958 | 14.9 | 29.6 | 21.7 | 5.5 | 11.6 | 16.7 |

[2] Nonfarm inputs associated with farmers' purchases.
[3] Farm operator and family labor plus inputs of real estate and other capital owned by farm operator.
[4] Not available.
[5] 1927–29 average.
[6] 1957–58 feeding season.
SOURCE: Department of Agriculture.

345

from 1930–39 to 1958; unpaid declined by one-third. The increase in paid inputs, reflecting greater commercialization in farming, makes agriculture increasingly sensitive to the prices of goods and services that farmers buy—prices that recently have been rising.

## CHANGING ORGANIZATION OF AGRICULTURAL RESOURCES

The rapid increase in productivity in agriculture has been a major factor in releasing resources for use in the industrial economy. Only 8½ per cent of the civilian labor force is now engaged in agricultural production on the farm; the remainder is available to the nonfarm economy.

High productivity in agriculture, reducing labor needed for farm production, was achieved as profound structural changes in agricultural resources took place. The number of farms declined from 6.7 million in the 1930's to 4.6 million in 1959 (Table 6). The average size increased by approximately 100 acres. Yet the total acreage of cropland declined slightly. Moreover, in 1959 only 69 per cent of cropland was actually used for harvested crops; of the other 31 per cent, much is reserve capacity. Even so, at present yields per acre, the number of acres used for harvested crops is too great relative to the effective demand.

The number of tractors, trucks, and automobiles on farms increased from 5.8 million in the 1930's to 12.2 million in 1959, or from less than 1 per farm to nearly 3 per farm. The value of the inventory of machinery and motor vehicles increased from $3.1 billion in 1940 to $18.4 billion in 1959.

## II

Agriculture in the United States consists of two parts that are becoming more and more distinct: (1) commercial farm enterprises and (2) noncommercial holdings, many of which are little more than farm living units. Each is composed of numerous types. Commercial farms vary in area under operation from small vegetable farms to very large western cattle ranches; noncommercial units comprise backyard cow-and-garden farms, farms of retired and semi-retired people, part-time farms, and others.

The distinctions between the two broad parts are real and mean-

| Item | Unit | 1910–19 average | 1920–29 average | 1930–39 average | 1940–49 average | 1950–59 average[1] |
|---|---|---|---|---|---|---|
| Farms: | | | | | | |
| Number | Millions | 6.5 | 6.5 | 6.7 | 6.0 | 5.1 |
| Cropland per farm | Acres | 69 | 72 | 72 | 78 | 92 |
| Grazing land per farm[2,3] | Acres | 37 | 53 | 66 | 89 | 111 |
| Cropland: | | | | | | |
| Total | Million acres | 447 | 470 | 477 | 470 | 472 |
| Harvested[4] | Million acres | 332 | 350 | 335 | 344 | 323 |
| Idle, fallow, soil improvement | Million acres | 42 | 52 | 74 | 60 | 81 |
| Pasture | Million acres | 73 | 68 | 68 | 66 | 68 |
| Grazing land: | | | | | | |
| In farms[2,3] | Million acres | 240 | 347 | 442 | 535 | 570 |
| Not in farms[2] | Million acres | 607 | 592 | 502 | 413 | 350 |
| Manpower: | | | | | | |
| Family workers | Millions | 10.1 | 9.7 | 9.4 | 8.0 | 6.4 |
| Hired workers | Millions | 3.4 | 3.4 | 2.9 | 2.4 | 2.1 |
| Man-hours used in farm work | Billions | 23.3 | 23.3 | 21.7 | 18.9 | 13.0 |
| Power and machinery: | | | | | | |
| Horses and mules | Millions | 25.9 | 22.9 | 16.8 | 11.9 | 4.9 |
| Tractors | Millions | (5) | .5 | 1.1 | 2.3 | 4.2 |
| Trucks | Millions | (5) | .5 | .9 | 1.5 | 2.6 |
| Automobiles | Millions | .6 | 3.1 | 3.8 | 4.3 | 4.2 |
| Combines | Millions | (5) | (5) | (5) | .4 | .9 |
| Livestock on farms: | | | | | | |
| Grain consuming | Million units | 140 | 152 | 147 | 168 | 164 |
| Per farm | Units | 22 | 23 | 22 | 28 | 32 |
| Roughage consuming | Million units | 87 | 86 | 85 | 89 | 92 |
| Per farm | Units | 14 | 13 | 13 | 15 | 18 |
| Units of production[6] | Millions | 124 | 138 | 136 | 167 | 176 |

[1] Preliminary.
[2] Averages for census years, except 1958 and 1959.
[3] Permanent pasture and woodland pasture; excludes cropland pasture.
SOURCE: Department of Agriculture.
[4] Census concept of land area.
[5] Less than 50,000.
[6] Based on concentrate feed.

ingful for any attempt at weighing the economic and social problems of agriculture. Commercial and noncommercial agriculture differ in economic status, in the nature of their problems, and in the trends they exhibit. Commercial farms outnumber the noncommercial holdings in a ratio of almost two to one; the two groups together total roughly 3.7 million units, most of them family operated.

Commercial agriculture produces more than nine-tenths of all farm output, earns the major part of all net farm income, and holds most of agriculture's proprietary assets. Aggregate statistical measures, which seldom distinguish between commercial and noncommercial agriculture, must therefore be interpreted as pertaining chiefly to the commercial portion. Because of the differences in the economic performance of the two types of farms and their changing relative numbers, a conversion of aggregate totals into averages per farm tends to be misleading.

Since commercial agriculture contributes so much of all market supplies of farm products and absorbs even more of the capital resources used, its problems are essentially those of commodity markets. National concern with adjustment problems of underdeveloped and underemployed human resources in agriculture is associated with low income farms—those in noncommercial agriculture and the smallest-sized fringe of commercial agriculture. . . .

## INCREASING IMPORTANCE OF COMMERCIAL FARMS

The proportion of all farms that are operating on a commercial scale, and the share of such farms in the national output of farm products, are increasing. Also, commercial farms are employing an increasing percentage of all persons engaged in agriculture. Hence commercial farming represents a growing part of United States agriculture as a whole. In 1959, the Census of Agriculture reported that about 2.1 million commercial farms had sales of $2,500 or more. This number was almost the same as in 1950 and 1954, and was 56 per cent of all farms reported in 1959. Comparisons of this relative proportion with earlier censuses are complicated by a new definition of a farm introduced in the 1959 Census. In that year, approximately 232,000 units then in existence which would have been counted as farms according to the 1954 definition were excluded by the more restrictive new definition. If, for purposes of comparison, the 1954 definition is applied to the 1959 Census, commercial farms with sales of $2,500 or more would have constituted 52.5 per cent of all farms in 1959, a gain of 14 per cent from 1950 (Table 7).

Moreover, within the 2.1 million commercial farms having sales of $2,500 or more, those with sales of $10,000 or more have increased as those with sales of less than $10,000 have decreased. In 1959, 800,000 farms were in the larger category—64 per cent more than in 1950. Those with sales of $2,500–$5,000 decreased by 30 per cent, and those in the $5,000–$10,000 class decreased by 9 per cent.

Above-average growing conditions during 1959 contributed somewhat to the increased number of farms achieving a higher sales volume. Although expenses of production have been rising gradually, so that gross sales are not an exact measure of relative net income, it nevertheless seems likely that more and more commercial farms have succeeded in increasing their business to a volume that improves the chances of returning a satisfactory net income to the farm family. The 10-year increase of almost two-thirds in the number of farms having sales of $10,000 or more is evidence that this is true.

All these data apply to commercial farms selling farm products valued at $2,500 or more during the Census year. They omit those farms selling less that $2,500 of products that are technically classed as commercial owing to lack of any other sizable income. This classification of farms was chosen both because farms selling less than $2,500 of products are clearly inadequate as sources of farm income, and in order to facilitate statistical comparisons between Censuses.

## DECREASE IN NUMBER OF SMALL FARMS

According to the Census of 1959, there were 1,639,000 farms in the United States which sold less than $2,500 worth of farm products. This number included 348,000 so-called "midget" commercial farms—those for which the small volume of sales of farm products nevertheless was the primary source of family income. It also included 883,000 part-time and 405,000 part-retirement farms. The total of 1,639,000 was 44 per cent of all farms, as enumerated according to the new definition.

Table 7. Number of Farms, by Economic Class, 1950, 1954, and 1959

| Economic class | Number of farms | | | | Percent of total farms | | | Percentage change in number of farms, 1950 to 1959[1],[2] |
|---|---|---|---|---|---|---|---|---|
| | 1954 definition | | | 1959 (new definition)[1] | 1954 definition | | 1959 (new definition)[1] | |
| | 1950 | 1954 | 1959[1] | | 1950 | 1959[1] | | |
| | Thousands | | | | Percent | | | |
| Total farms | 5,382 | 4,782 | 3,936 | 3,704[3] | 100.0 | 100.0 | 100.0 | −26.9 |
| Sales $2,500 and over (commercial) | 2,087 | 2,101 | 2,065 | 2,065 | 38.8 | 52.5 | 55.8 | −1.1 |
| Sales $2,500 to $4,999 | 882 | 811 | 617 | 617 | 16.4 | 15.7 | 16.7 | −30.0 |
| Sales $5,000 to $9,999 | 721 | 707 | 654 | 654 | 13.4 | 16.6 | 17.7 | −9.3 |
| Sales $10,000 and over | 484 | 583 | 794 | 794 | 9.0 | 20.2 | 21.4 | 64.0 |
| Sales less than $2,500 | 3,295 | 2,681 | 1,871 | 1,639[3] | 61.2 | 47.5 | 44.2 | −43.2 |
| Commercial | 1,619 | 1,226 | (4) | 348[3] | 30.1 | (4) | 9.4 | (4) |
| Noncommercial | 1,676 | 1,455 | (4) | 1,291[3] | 31.1 | (4) | 34.8 | (4) |
| Part-time | (4) | (4) | (4) | 883 | (4) | (4) | 23.8 | (4) |
| Part-retirement | (4) | (4) | (4) | 405 | (4) | (4) | 10.9 | (4) |
| Miscellaneous | (4) | (4) | (4) | 3 | (4) | (4) | .1 | (4) |

[1] Preliminary.
[2] Based on 1954 definition.
[3] Not comparable with data for 1950 and 1954.
[4] Not available.

NOTE. The number of farms in this table is as reported in the Census of Agriculture. The total is smaller than that estimated annually by the Department of Agriculture because of adjustments for underenumeration.

SOURCES: Department of Commerce and Department of Agriculture.

All the farms omitted in the 1959 Census because of a more restrictive definition were small farms—those with less than $2,500 of sales. When these omissions are added, in order to make comparisons with data of earlier Censuses, the number of small farms becomes 1.9 million, a substantial reduction from the 2.7 million of 1954 and 3.3 million of 1950 (Table 7).

These reductions in numbers of small farms doubtless reflect some amelioration of the problem of low-income farms. Progress has been made in either enlarging the production resources on small farms, or in supplementing the farm income from sources off the farm. Yet also evident in recent trends is a gradual disappearance of units that have qualified as farms only by virtue of sideline "backyard" farming, a time-consuming occupation yielding minimum returns to labor.

On the other hand, the Conservation Reserve has probably shifted a number of farms of sizable acreage into the small-farms category, because of the small value of products now sold from their idled acreage.

## DECLINE IN TOTAL NUMBER OF FARMS

The total number of all farms reported in the 1959 Census, according to preliminary data, was 3.7 million. By use of the same definition as in 1954, the number in 1959 would have been reported as 3.9 million, compared with 4.8 million in 1954 and 5.4 million in 1950 (Table 7). This 10-year decrease amounts to no less than 27 per cent, and occurred, as noted above, exclusively in small farms —those selling less than $2,500 worth of farm products per year. While a later revision of these Census data may increase the reported number of farms slightly, owing particularly to the inclusion of idled Conservation Reserve farms, it is unlikely that the basic changes as shown will be affected significantly.

## INCREASE IN ACREAGE AND ASSETS OF FARMS

Year by year, commercial agriculture has become an increasingly technical enterprise demanding a high degree of managerial skill and requiring a larger acreage and investment base. Not only does the inventory of farm equipment and machinery on a typical farm now make it possible for each farmer to till more acres, but the accompanying heavy capital investment makes a larger acreage mandatory if efficiency in operation is to be achieved. The modern commercial farm uses capital in the same manner—and in larger amount per person employed—as do nonfarm manufacturing enterprises.

Between 1950 and 1959, the number of farms in every size class below 500 acres decreased (Table 8). The percentage reductions

Table 8. Number of Farms, by Acreage Groups, 1950, 1954, and 1959

| | Number of farms | | | | Percentage change[2] | |
| | | 1954 definition | | 1959 (new defini- | | |
| Size in acres | 1950 | 1954 | 1959[1] | tion)[1] | 1950 to 1959[1] | 1954 to 1959[1] |
|---|---|---|---|---|---|---|
| | Thousands | | | | | |
| Total farms | 5,382 | 4,782 | 3,936 | 3,704 | −27 | −18 |
| 0–10 | 485 | 484 | [3] | 241 | [3] | [3] |
| 10–49 | 1,478 | 1,213 | [3] | 811 | [3] | [3] |
| 50–99 | 1,048 | 864 | 658 | 658 | −37 | −24 |
| 100–139 | 579 | 491 | 394 | 394 | −32 | −20 |
| 140–179 | 523 | 462 | 378 | 378 | −28 | −18 |
| 180–219 | 275 | 257 | 226 | 226 | −18 | −12 |
| 220–259 | 212 | 206 | 189 | 189 | −11 | −8 |
| 260–499 | 478 | 482 | 471 | 471 | −1 | −2 |
| 500–999 | 182 | 192 | 200 | 200 | 11 | 4 |
| 1,000 and over | 121 | 130 | 136 | 136 | 12 | 5 |

[1] Preliminary.
[2] Based on 1954 definition.
[3] Not available.
NOTE. The number of farms in this table is as reported in the Census of Agriculture. The total is smaller than that estimated annually by the Department of Agriculture because of adjustments for underenumeration.
Detail will not necessarily add to totals because of rounding. Virtually all the farms excluded from the 1959 Census (new definition) because of more restrictive definition were smaller than 50 acres in size.
SOURCE: Department of Commerce.

were greatest for the smaller farms; the number having 50–99 acres was reduced by 37 per cent, and the 100–139 acre group by 32 per cent. Farms above 500 acres in size increased in number—to 336,-000 in 1959 from 303,000 in 1950.

The quantity of assets other than land used in agriculture has risen substantially—generally faster than have land assets. From 1940 to 1960, when improvements on land raised the physical real estate assets in agriculture by 22 per cent, the amount of machinery employed increased by 151 per cent. Although livestock inventories increased by only 19 per cent, all other assets combined—primarily crop inventories and demand deposits in banks—increased by 46 per cent. Total production assets in agriculture increased by 30 per cent during the 20-year period. These are estimated quantities, valued at constant (1947–49) prices (Table 9).

Table 9. Production Assets Used in Agriculture, 1940, 1950, and 1960

| Kind of asset | 1940 | 1950 | 1960 | Percentage change 1940 to 1960 | 1950 to 1960 |
|---|---|---|---|---|---|
| | Billions of dollars, 1947–49 prices | | | | |
| Total production assets | 83.3 | 95.9 | 108.6 | 30 | 13 |
| Farm real estate | 58.2 | 63.4 | 71.1 | 22 | 12 |
| Livestock | 12.9 | 13.1 | 15.4 | 19 | 18 |
| Machinery and motor vehicles | 4.1 | 8.6 | 10.3 | 151 | 20 |
| Other[1] | 8.1 | 10.8 | 11.8 | 46 | 9 |
| | Dollars, 1947–49 prices | | | | |
| Per farm[2] | 13,118 | 16,979 | 23,921 | 82 | 41 |
| Per farm worker | 7,347 | 9,625 | 14,707 | 100 | 53 |

[1] Includes crop inventories held for livestock feed and the portion of demand deposits owned by farmers estimated as being held to meet farm production costs.

[2] Based on number of farms as reported by the Department of Agriculture, according to 1954 Census definition.

SOURCE: Department of Agriculture.

As the number of farms has decreased, real production assets per farm have increased considerably. Valued in constant dollars, assets per farm advanced 82 per cent between 1940 and 1960. Assets per farm worker increased even more: their average doubled during the 20 years, to $14,700 in 1960, valued in 1947–49 dollars. Valued in 1960 dollars, farm assets per farm worker in 1960 averaged $21,-300, considerably more than the average investment of $15,900 per employee in manufacturing in the same year. Data on average assets per farm pertain to all farms, commercial and noncommercial, as reported by the Department of Agriculture according to the pre-1960 Census definition; they doubtless overstate the rate of increase, but underreport the present average size, of assets held on commercial farms alone. . . .

## CHANGES IN LOW-INCOME FARMS

On the 1.6 million small farms reported in the 1959 Census (Table 7), the income earned from farming alone is low by any standard. Persons living on those farms can be divided into three groups: (1) those of working age who receive an income from non-farm sources that is satisfactory, either of itself or when combined with the net income earned on the farm; (2) those past working age whose income status depends in large measure on retirement income available to them, derived from social security, private retirement plans, or private investments; and (3) those of working age who depend principally for their income on the operation of units with very small economic resources.

This third group faces more serious economic problems than do the other two, and from the standpoint of the national economy it represents a pool of human resources that is partially wasted. This group is a principal focus of the Rural Development Program. Since 1955 that program has coordinated and directed the efforts of various departments and agencies of the Federal Government, in cooperation with State and local organizations, toward rural betterment. In addition to five departments of the Federal Government, the Small Business Administration has been particularly active in assisting development of low-income areas.

The primary objective of the Rural Development Program is to build up local economic resources of low-income areas and to provide job opportunities for rural people. In some low-income areas where local resources are inadequate or have not been developed sufficiently to alleviate serious underemployment or unemployment, regional decreases in population are taking place. The 1960 Census of Population shows that within the national pattern of geographic shifts in distribution of the population, resulting primarily from internal migration, a number of localities previously designated as low income have increased their population in the last decade, some at more than the national average rate, others at less than the national rate. Usually these increases reflected new opportunities that developed for local employment. In other low-income localities the resident population remained constant or declined.

The Atlantic Coast and Piedmont regions were the main ones with above-average population gains. There, vigorous industrial de-

| | Population[1] | | | | Percentage change 1950 to 1960[2] | |
| | Total | | Nonmetropolitan | | Total | Non-metro-politan |
| Area classification | 1950 | 1960 | 1950 | 1960 | | |
|---|---|---|---|---|---|---|
| | Millions of persons | | | | | |
| Total population | 150.7 | 178.5 | 66.2 | 72.6 | 18.4 | 9.7 |
| Low-income farming areas[3] | 34.8 | 36.6 | 29.8 | 30.7 | 5.2 | 3.2 |
| By income: | | | | | | |
| Moderately low-income | 12.3 | 13.1 | 10.7 | 11.3 | 6.4 | 5.6 |
| Substantially low-income | 8.4 | 9.2 | 7.1 | 7.6 | 10.2 | 7.3 |
| Seriously low-income | 14.2 | 14.4 | 11.9 | 11.8 | 1.3 | -1.3 |
| By location: | | | | | | |
| Appalachian Mountain and border areas | 12.1 | 12.1 | 9.7 | 9.5 | -.5 | -1.9 |
| Southern Piedmont and Coastal Plains | 9.6 | 11.1 | 8.1 | 9.0 | 15.2 | 11.8 |
| Southeastern Hilly areas | 3.4 | 3.4 | 3.2 | 3.1 | -.6 | -3.0 |
| Mississippi Delta | 2.3 | 2.4 | 2.2 | 2.2 | 3.7 | 1.8 |
| Sandy Coastal Plains[4] | 2.2 | 2.1 | 2.2 | 2.1 | -6.3 | -6.3 |
| Ozark-Ouachita Mountains and border | 1.9 | 1.9 | 1.7 | 1.6 | -2.1 | -5.0 |
| Northern Lake States | 1.8 | 2.0 | 1.4 | 1.6 | 9.9 | 8.4 |
| Northwestern New Mexico | .3 | .5 | .3 | .5 | 58.1 | 58.1 |
| Cascade and Rocky Mountain areas | 1.0 | 1.2 | 1.0 | 1.2 | 16.7 | 16.7 |

[1] As of April 1.

[2] Based on actual number of persons.

[3] For description of areas, see *Development of Agriculture's Human Resources—A Report on Problems of Low-Income Farmers*, House Document No. 149, 84th Congress, 1st Session.

[4] Plains of Arkansas, Louisiana, Oklahoma, and Texas.

NOTE. Detail will not necessarily add to totals because of rounding.

SOURCES: Department of Commerce and Department of Agriculture.

velopment or expanded military installations contributed to growing local employment. Regions in which the population decreased were primarily those of the upper Appalachian and the South Central areas extending from eastern Oklahoma and Texas to Mississippi.

The decade of the 1950's lowered, in general, the population density in the rural low-income areas relative to the rest of the country. As indicated by Table 10, the total population of the nation increased by 18.4 per cent from 1950 to 1960, while the increase in the low-income farming areas was only 5.2 per cent. In the areas with serious social and economic problems, the increase was a mere 1.3 per cent. The nonmetropolitan population of the nation as a whole increased by 9.7 per cent, but in all low-income farm areas it increased only 3.2 per cent. In the serious problem areas, the nonmetropolitan population actually decreased by 1.3 per cent. . . .

While notable improvement made it possible for a number of areas to retain their local population during the 1950–60 period of high level performance of the economy, there is still a problem of underemployment in many areas, i.e., an excessive potential supply of labor and a need for more opportunities for employment, particularly off the farm.

# X. AMERICA IN THE WORLD ECONOMY

## 23. The United States as an International Creditor

*Although net indebtedness to foreign investors was steadily reduced after 1900, it was not until World War I that the United States became a creditor nation. The immediate cause of this historic transition was the massive liquidation of British and French investments in the United States by the European Allied governments in order to finance their purchases of American war goods, food, and other supplies. When the United States entered the war in April 1917, the net debt of approximately $3.7 billion she had owed in 1914 no longer existed, and within two years, largely as a result of American government loans to the Allies, the United States was the world's leading creditor nation and the financial center of the world had shifted to New York. In the following decade America became the principal source of capital for overseas investment, with important consequences for her international economic relations.*

SOURCE: Hal B. Lary and associates, *The United States in the World Economy*, U. S. Department of Commerce, Bureau of Foreign and Domestic Commerce, Economic Series No. 23 (Washington, D.C.: Government Printing Office, 1943), pp. 89–92, 100–5, 122–3, 169–75, 183, 197–8.

ONE of the most striking features of the balance of payments of the United States in the interwar period was the movement of capital, both short- and long-term, which for magnitude of the sums involved and abruptness of changes in direction has not been surpassed in the experience of any nation.

During the first post-war decade, long-term capital from the United States furnished a large and, until 1928, increasing annual supply of dollar purchasing power to foreigners. These large capital outflows enabled this country to maintain a substantial export surplus without serious disturbances in the balance of payments. During the same period, moreover, American short-term capital was employed to a substantial extent in the direct financing of export trade, principally through the medium of the banker's acceptance, which grew steadily in importance.

The decade of the thirties was marked, first, by a net export of capital from the United States in 1931–33 (accounted for by short-term capital alone, since the net movement of long-term capital was inward), and, beginning in 1934, by a capital inflow of unprecedented proportions. The world-wide desire for liquidity and the severe banking crises both in this country and abroad were chiefly responsible for the capital withdrawals in the early period. Repatriations and redemptions of dollar loans and, after 1934, flight capital from abroad, were the primary components of the inward movement.

In the period 1919–30 the United States provided $11,600,000,-000 to foreigners by way of subscriptions to new foreign issues and new direct investments abroad—an annual average of about $965,-000,000. During the same time, American short-term assets abroad increased by somewhat more than $1,000,000,000. This outflow was offset in part by amortizations and retirements of about $3,300,-000,000 and net purchases by foreigners of foreign securities in an indeterminable but relatively small amount. The movement of American long-term capital was then sharply reversed as, with the virtual cessation of foreign lending after 1930, annual amortization receipts and continued foreign purchases of foreign securities in this market far outweighed such new lending as took place. A net return flow of United States long-term capital to the extent of $1,200,000,000 was recorded for the period 1931–39; in addition, American investments abroad suffered large declines in value through operating losses in direct investments and defaults in foreign dollar obligations. Moreover, after 1931 there was a continual withdrawal of American short-term capital from abroad, the amount outstanding declining from almost $2,000,000,000 at the end of 1930 to $600,000,000 at the close of 1939.

The movements of foreign capital to and from the United States during the interwar period were also of great magnitude and were more consistent in direction than movements of American capital.

In most years foreigners were net purchasers of outstanding American securities, such purchases amounting to over $2,000,000,000 for the 21-year period. Likewise, foreign short-term capital moved to the United States during most of the period, with the notable exception of 1930–33, when foreign dollar balances were drawn down to the phenomenal extent of about $2,700,000,000. Beginning in 1934, the inflow of flight capital resulted in rapidly increasing foreign balances in this country and at the end of 1939 they were placed at $3,300,000,000, an increase of 575 per cent from the amount reported as of the close of 1933. . . .

American lending in the decade following World War I included two rather distinct classes of loans. In the first place, large sums were loaned to countries, most of which were normally creditor nations, whose capital shortage was of a temporary nature, having resulted from relief and rehabilitation needs after the war and from the release of pent-up demand that had accumulated during the years of the conflict. Subsequent developments showed that many of these countries did not require long-term loans at all but did need large supplies of foreign exchange to tide them over a very critical period. The currency stabilization loans also resulted more from a need for foreign exchange than for capital in the pure sense, if the two concepts can be distinguished in logic or in practice.

Most of the foreign loans of the United States, especially in the period 1924–28, were contracted specifically for the purpose of long-term capital investment. Such loans were made to countries which, with the notable exception of Germany, had been typically debtor nations, although some, such as Canada and Japan, were in a transition stage. On the other hand, loans directed to alleviating immediate shortages of foreign exchange or for currency-stabilization purposes were confined almost solely to European countries.

The course of events in the United States during the 13-year period following the first World War is probably unique in the history of capital-exporting nations. Although the transition of the country from debtor to creditor status was not so abrupt as is sometimes supposed, the rapidity with which it acquired foreign investments is unparalleled in the experience of any major creditor country in modern times.

Conditions in the early post-war years were peculiarly appropriate for a great outflow of American capital. Of the many factors facilitating this movement, the following were of particular importance:

1. Through the Liberty Loan campaigns a wide public market for securities had been built up in the United States.

2. The publicly offered foreign loans of the war period—particularly the large and, as it proved, "safe" issues of the Allied Nations —had begun to acquaint the investing public with foreign bonds.

3. Western Europe, which before the war had been an exporter of capital, was in the position of needing outside funds to purchase immediate necessities, stabilize currencies, and make permanent, or capital, improvements of both a public and private nature.

4. At the same time, the capital markets of the western European creditor countries were partly or completely closed to foreign issues, and it became necessary for borrowers in other countries to turn to the United States for their capital needs.

New issues for foreign account floated in the United States market provided the vehicle for most of the capital export in the twenties. With the exception of 1923, the net amount of new foreign security issues increased every year from 1919 to 1927. Over $1,000,-000,000 was made available to foreigners in this way in 1927 and again in 1928. The rising trend in foreign issues continued until the middle of 1928, over 70 per cent of the flotations in that year having occurred in the first six months. From this time the decline was precipitous and except for a spectacular but very temporary recovery early in 1930 foreign capital issues thereafter were unimportant in the United States balance of payments. . . .

Extension of American enterprise to foreign areas, usually termed direct, or entrepreneurial, investment, also provided an important source of dollars during the interwar period. It is estimated that $3,500,000,000 was furnished in this manner during the years 1919 to 1931, with the largest amount, $602,000,000 being invested in 1929, the peak year of the domestic boom. These estimates . . . include public offerings of American and semi-American corporations for foreign purposes as well as investments made directly by American corporations without recourse to the capital market.

Direct investments include all foreign enterprises controlled by American corporations or individuals or in the management of which Americans have an important voice. Extension of American industry to foreign countries, although not nearly so new a phenomenon as foreign security underwriting, like the latter became of much greater importance during the post-war years. In view of the varied nature of the enterprises constituting direct investments, both regarding their form and the manner of their establishment, and the unreliability of available data, a systematic and accurate appraisal of the influencing factors is impossible. The following account must be couched, therefore, in very general terms.

With respect to form of ownership, direct investments may be divided into three groups. First are the direct subsidiaries and other affiliates of American corporations whose chief field of operations is in the United States. The far-flung holdings of the Standard Oil Co. (New Jersey), Ford Motor Co., General Motors Corporation, and International Business Machines Corporation are well-known examples. Such investments are adjuncts to the domestic business of the parent company and are usually financed by the parent company without recourse to the capital market.They may represent enterprises organized and developed by the American company, or they may have been purchased as going concerns from foreign owners. Extension of industry through foreign subsidiaries and branches has been the most important form of direct investment.

Next in importance are American corporations organized for the specific purpose of operating abroad. Although this form of investment is much more common in British than in American experience, to illustrate the importance of this type of American investment mention need be made only of the American & Foreign Power Co., Inc., International Telephone and Telegraph Corporation, Cerro de Pasco Copper Corporation, International Railways of Central America, and the various companies operating sugar properties in Cuba or copper mines in Chile. This form of investment is sometimes combined with the first: American & Foreign Power Co., for instance, is a subsidiary of Electric Bond and Share Co., while the Chile Copper Co. and the Andes Copper Mining Co. are subsidiaries of the Anaconda Copper Mining Co. Most companies of this type, however, have been financed by public offerings of their own securities in the domestic market.

American holdings in such companies as Dome Mines, Ltd., International Nickel Co. of Canada, Ltd., Compañía Swift Internacional, S. A. C., and others illustrate the third form of holding— direct ownership by American individuals of stock of foreign corporations. The controlling shareholders were usually also the founders of the corporations, but Americans frequently purchased foreign securities publicly offered in the United States or procured large blocks of securities directly from abroad, either privately or on foreign exchanges.

Subsidiaries of American companies operating abroad are generally organized under the laws of foreign countries, or they may be incorporated in this country. Various legal and taxation problems apparently determine the exact form of the investment.

Foreign enterprises also may be classed in three groups on the basis of the purpose of the investment. The first of these groups that may be distinguished comprises what is generally referred to as branch plants though broadly it includes foreign sales subsidiaries as well as manufacturing plants. Such enterprises are established either to substitute for, or to facilitate, exportation of goods manufactured in this country. Although theoretically such developments may indicate greater marginal efficiency of capital abroad, practically they have been induced by tariffs, uncertain exchange conditions, nationalism and accompanying "buy-at-home" movements, patent legislation, transportation costs, and similar considerations. Most American investments in foreign manufacturing concerns are in countries well advanced industrially. Tariffs, especially the British imperial preference scheme, have been particularly important in this development.

The second of these groups includes American enterprises organized to develop foreign natural resources and raw materials. Often the object is to provide an assured source of raw materials for the parent company in the United States. The rubber plantations of the tire-manufacturing companies and the bauxite mines of the Aluminum Co. of America may be mentioned. Again, greater profits are anticipated from foreign enterprises than from similar domestic investments. American investments in Canadian mining and Caribbean agriculture are conspicuous examples of this incentive.

The third general type, like the others, is motivated chiefly by the possibility of greater profit from foreign enterprise, though it is not dependent on the location of a particular mineral deposit, soil, or climate. Investments in public utility systems, railroads, banks, insurance companies, and theaters are typical examples.

The rapid growth of American direct investments abroad in the twenties may be accounted for by various factors, all of which are essentially products of the prosperity and economic expansion of the decade. More than 40 per cent of the increase from 1919 to 1929 was accounted for by public issues of American corporations for foreign purposes. This type of financing was resorted to especially for investments in Canada and Latin American countries; in the latter, issues of sugar, public utilities, and mining companies accounted for most of the total. These investments were possible for much the same reasons as was general foreign security underwriting. As a matter of fact, flotations of domestic corporations for foreign purposes are ordinarily included in the statistics of new foreign issues. It is not surprising, therefore, that such issues became prominent in 1925 with the beginning of the boom in foreign underwriting. Unlike foreign bonds, however, they continued at a high level through 1928 and 1929, reaching a peak of $252,000,000 (net of refunding and discounts) in the latter year. These companies, unlike most foreign borrowers, were able to issue stocks and take advantage of the 1928–29 stock-market boom.

Most of the direct investments not financed by public issues were made from the ample funds of American corporations, whose undistributed earnings during the period 1922–29 averaged more than $2,500,000,000 a year. The expansionist psychology that possessed American business in the twenties had its influence, and the resulting pressure for markets and assured foreign sources of supply was of great importance. Hence, the course of new direct investments was not so closely linked with vagaries of the bond market as were new foreign issues. When financed from accumulated earnings, such investments obviously are not dependent on the money market. American corporations operating solely abroad by having recourse to both the bond and stock market have usually been able to raise funds for foreign purposes so long as there was an active market for new corporate issues of either type.

The outflow of capital on direct investment account reached peaks in 1928 and 1929 of $558,000,000 and $602,000,000, respectively. Although these figures must be considered as rough estimates, it may be recalled that in those two years the great public utility systems of the American & Foreign Power Co. and the International Telephone and Telegraph Corporation were undergoing rapid expansion, the Ford Motor Co., Ltd., began construction of its huge new plant at Dagenham, England, and General Motors Corporation acquired a controlling interest in Adam Opel A. G. of Germany. Many other similar transactions combined to swell the large totals of those years.

Substantial amounts of capital were placed abroad through direct-investment transactions in 1930 and 1931 and doubtless in subsequent years also, although the available annual data do not substantiate this opinion. American direct investments abroad declined from $7,500,000,000 at the end of 1929 to $7,000,000,000 at the end of 1940, a reduction of only $500,000,000. The declines in Mexico and Cuba alone, accounted for chiefly by operating losses, reorganizations, and revaluations, amounted to over $600,000,000, or more than equal to the estimated net amount of new direct investment during the 11-year period. Operating losses were undoubtedly large in other countries as well in the early thirties, and the exchange rates used in converting foreign currencies in 1940 were in general much lower than those prevailing in 1929. If the aggregates are correct, it follows, therefore, that net outflows of fairly substantial amounts occurred, at least after the worst phases of the depression. For instance, the foreign activities of American petroleum companies were considerably expanded during the decade. However, the outward movement of funds in these years was small as compared with that of the preceding decade and did not form an important source of dollar exchange to foreign countries.

The following features of significance for the future may be noted: (1) American direct investments abroad continued to increase when the more formal type of foreign lending was at a standstill; (2) continuing American interest and supervision over the operation of the enterprises is required, that is, American control over how the funds "loaned" to the foreign country are spent; (3) such investments have not been confined to countries that are normally debtors but have been distributed throughout the world; (4) direct investments have created an international business community which may help in laying the basis for closer international economic cooperation in the future; and (5) this type of investment provides an avenue for exporting American technical and managerial services, which, if the interests of the debtor countries are properly safeguarded, aids tremendously in the industrialization of those countries and thus increases their productivity and raises their standard of living.

In addition, this form of investment has other advantages from the point of view of the "borrowing" country. First, most direct investments are of an equity character; unlike external bonds they do not carry contractual service obligations payable in foreign currencies. This has a twofold advantage to debtor countries, especially those that produce raw materials and are therefore particularly subject to the swings of the business cycle. For one thing, a business depression usually means that the foreign-owned enterprise will have little or no profit to remit and hence will not put a strain on already overburdened exchanges. It may even result in inward remittances; the owner of the property, if necesary, will probably furnish funds to keep it going in anticipation of a business revival. Here, however, the possibility of disinvestment must be recognized, for in times of depression, a parent company may withdraw funds provided by depreciation charges, which ordinarily would be used to maintain or build up the property. Moreover, such profits as do accrue are payable only in the local currency, and the owner rather than the borrower must therefore stand the loss in the event of currency depreciation. This feature is an additional protection to the currency of a debtor country in times of stress.

Secondly, unlike foreign lending through public issues, direct investments are not a monopoly of mature creditor countries but are distinctly a two-way affair. An individual company may be in a position to expand abroad long before the capital markets of its country are capable of absorbing foreign issues. Firms in Canada and the United States, for instance, were making direct investments across the border while borrowers in both countries were still raising funds in Europe by means of public subscriptions. Then, too, some American subsidiaries abroad, particularly in Canada, establish subsidiaries in a third country—a move that obviously strengthens the international position of the second country, especially when the public in that country is permitted an investment interest in such enterprises. The foreign subsidiaries of the Ford Motor Co. of Canada, Ltd., and Imperial Oil, Ltd., are examples, and many others could be cited.

Further, it has been historically true, although it need not have been so, that direct investments have been more productive than foreign bond issues, for through development of foreign natural resources and addition to industrial capacity they have strengthened the general economic position of the debtor countries. The profit motive of direct investments has operated to insure this outcome, whereas foreign loans floated in the United States have been largely those of governmental entities not limited by profit considerations in their expenditure of borrowed funds.

Data available on foreign direct investments in the United States during the interwar period are so fragmentary that estimates of annual movements cannot be made with any confidence. Apparently, however, these investments increased substantially over the period, their value in 1939 being estimated at $2,000,000,000. Roughly approximated, the growth resulted in a demand for dollars ranging around $25,000,000 to $50,000,000 annually. The demand came chiefly from the United Kingdom, Canada, and the Netherlands, direct investments by those countries at the end of 1939 amounting to $847,000,0000, $476,000,000, and $216,000,000, respectively.

The motives underlying the investments of other countries are not different from those of American investments abroad. Canadian railroads have extended their systems into the United States, and foreign owners of trade-marks, patents, and manufacturing processes have set up subsidiaries to manufacture such varying products as whisky, dessert powders, soap, and rayon yarn. Other important foreign investments have been in the industrial-chemical and machinery fields. British insurance companies have long been important operators in this country, particularly in marine risks, and one of the leading petroleum companies in the United States is foreign-controlled.

Many of the investments represent enterprises of long standing, dating from the period when the United States was a debtor nation. Land companies, principally Dutch and British, founded in the past century, are still in operation in some western States. Of 205 foreign-controlled industrial enterprises in existence at the end of 1934 for which the dates of establishment are available, 21 were established before 1900, and the same is true of 47 of a total of 129 United States branches or affiliates of foreign insurance companies.

The prosperity of the twenties, high protective tariffs, and the repeal of prohibition were specific factors influencing the establishment of foreign direct investments in the United States from 1919 to 1939. . . .

In addition to the important direct role of capital movements in the balance of payments, changes in the international investment position of the United States resulting from these movements, and from other factors, also had significant influences through their effects on the interest and dividend items. . . .

During World War I, largely as a result of loans floated for the account of the British and French Governments and the liquidation of foreign holdings of American securities, the international investment position of the United States underwent a swift change. A net debtor status of approximately $3,700,000,000 in 1914 was transformed into a net creditor status, excluding intergovernmental debts, of the same amount by the end of 1919.

The rapid expansion of American assets abroad in the following decade, accompanied by a smaller growth in foreign claims on the United States, further increased this country's net creditor position to approximately $8,800,000,000 at the end of 1930 (Table 1). As a

Table 1. International Investment Position of the United States
in Selected Years (Excluding War Debts)
(In billions of dollars)

| Item | End of the year | | | |
|---|---|---|---|---|
| | 1919 | 1930 | 1933 | 1939 |
| United States investments abroad: | | | | |
| Long-term: | | | | |
| Direct | 3.9 | 8.0 | 7.8 | 7.0 |
| Portfolio | 2.6 | 7.2 | 6.0 | 3.8 |
| Total long-term | 6.5 | 15.2 | 13.8 | 10.8 |
| Total short-term | .5 | 2.0 | 1.1 | .6 |
| Total long-and short-term | 7.0 | 17.2 | 14.9 | 11.4 |
| Foreign investments in the United States: | | | | |
| Long-term: | | | | |
| Direct | .9 | 1.4[1] | 1.8[1] | 2.0 |
| Portfolio[3] | 1.6 | 4.3[1] | 3.1[1] | 4.3 |
| Total long-term | 2.5 | 5.7 | 4.9 | 6.3 |
| Total short-term | .8 | 2.7 | .5 | 3.3 |
| Total long- and short-term | 3.3 | 8.4 | 5.4 | 9.6 |
| Net creditor position of the United States: | | | | |
| On long-term account | 4.0 | 9.5 | 8.9 | 4.5 |
| On short-term account | −.3[4] | −.7[4] | .6 | −2.7[4] |
| On long- and short-term account | 3.7 | 8.8 | 9.5 | 1.8 |

[1] 1929 data.
[2] 1934 data.
[3] Includes miscellaneous investments.
[4] Net debtor position.
NOTE. All data for 1919 and the data for 1929 in foreign long-term investments in the United States are from unofficial estimates; other data are as estimated by the Department of Commerce.

result of the extensive liquidation of foreign-owned assets, particularly short-term, in the ensuing three years, and despite a reduction of $2,300,000,000 in American investments abroad during the same period, the net creditor position of the United States on international investments reached what was probably an all-time high— approximately $9,500,000,000—at the end of 1933. The decline in American investments abroad continued to the end of the period under survey, a reduction of $3,500,000,000 being recorded from the end of 1933 to the end of 1939. Concurrently foreign capital again moved in heavy volume into the United States. As a result, this country's net creditor status was drastically reduced to only $1,800,000,000. . . .

The years 1930 to 1933 constitute a period of transition during which the international trade and financial relations of the United States underwent a striking transformation under the impact of the great depression. However obscure the causes may have been, the general effects of the depression on economic activity throughout the world were abundantly clear. Industrial output declined abruptly, the index of industrial production for all countries (excluding the U. S. S. R.) falling from 100 in 1929 to 87 in 1930, to 75 in 1931, and to a low of 64 in 1932. Prices of industrial products, after stubborn resistance, also declined substantially. The effects on primary production, particularly agricultural, were expressed not so much in curtailed output as in an accentuation of the secular decline in prices and growth of unused stocks. Total stocks of primary commodities, according to the League of Nations world index, had risen by 30 per cent from 1925 to 1929 and grew by another 23 per cent to the middle of 1932.

Reflecting the combined influence of dwindling industrial output and falling prices in general, national incomes at home and abroad declined drastically. Business anticipations, after reluctantly abandoning early false hopes of a brief and mild recession, gave way to deepening gloom.

The physical volume of world trade was fairly well maintained in foodstuffs and raw materials, which declined by only 11 and 18.5 per cent, respectively, from 1929 to 1932, but the quantity of manufactured products decreased by more than 40 per cent. In terms of dollars, the fall in world trade was swift and deep, from 100 in 1929 to 81 in 1930, 58 in 1931, and 39 in 1932. To be sure, part of this decline, particularly after September 1931, reflected the depreciation of the exchange values of foreign currencies vis-à-vis the dollar; but for a world indebted to the United States in terms of its own currency, the measure is pertinent. As was inevitable under such circumstances, the pressure on debtor countries, as well as on internal debt structures, became intolerable, producing widespread defaults and serious credit and monetary disturbances.

The strains produced by the depression would have been severe in any event, but they were enormously aggravated by the disproportionately heavy fall in business activity in this country. It has indeed been asserted that the depression was essentially of United States origin. While the initial causes of the depression were too complex for any such ready allocation of responsibility, the charge has much to support it in that the American economy responded to the original disturbances with especial severity and thereafter appeared to be the chief drag on world recovery. The disparity was of the greatest significance in the evolution of the United States balance of payments after 1929 and exercised a powerful influence on world economic, financial, and commercial history in the thirties.

The foregoing reference to the greater severity of the depression in the United States is based solely on the extent of decline from the peak year 1929. Whether or not the depression was absolutely more severe in the United States than in other countries is a different and more doubtful matter. Many foreign peoples probably suffered more acutely because of their initially lower living standards. With respect to the influence on variations in international transactions, however, it is the degree of change in basic economic activity, and not the absolute level, that is of primary concern. On this point, the evidence is clear that economic activity declined more swiftly after 1929 and fell to a lower level in the United States than in foreign countries as a group. . . . As reflected in monthly figures, production both in this country and abroad began to level off in the middle of 1929 and to fall in the last quarter. By the final quarter of 1930 it was 26 per cent below the 1929 average in the United States as compared with a decline of some 13 per cent abroad, and by the last quarter of 1931 the decrease from 1929 was about 40 and 21 per cent, respectively.

The low points were reached in the summer of 1932. In the three-month period from June through August industrial production in the United States was off by 51 per cent as compared with the 1929 level, whereas output abroad had fallen by some 31 per cent. Then came an upturn in the autumn, which proved to be a definite revival in foreign countries but which was interrupted in the United States by a renewed decline at the end of the year. It was not until the second quarter of 1933 that production in this country again turned strongly upward.

Although the sharper fall in industrial production in the United States than abroad is a valid and basic consideration for purposes of this study, to speak of the trend in foreign countries as a group is a broad generalization—one which became increasingly unreal in later years as wide divergencies appeared. The two major areas where industry was most depressed were (1) the United States and Canada and (2) Germany and several smaller neighboring countries, particularly Austria, Czechoslovakia, and Poland. Even in these other countries, however, the decline in industrial production was not as precipitous as in the United States. The heaviest stage of the depression in Germany and other Central European countries did not set in until after external pressure on their banking and monetary structures had become irresistible. In most other industrial nations the decline in production did not exceed 20 per cent on the average during the worst year, and in some countries, notably the Scandinavian, it was far less. . . .

The downturn in domestic business in the fall of 1929 was immediately followed by a sudden and prolonged drop in United States purchases from other countries. From a total of $4,400,000,000 in 1929, imports fell more than $1,300,000,000 in 1930 and an additional $1,000,000,000 in the following year. It was not until 1933 that a slow and labored increase began. The physical volume of imports followed, as usual, a course closely paralleling the decline in industrial production, but the fall in total value was accentuated by the exceptional weakness of prices of raw materials, which made up such a large proportion of the aggregate.

Part of the decline in imports was undoubtedly caused by the new and heavier duties embodied in the tariff of 1930, but how large a part is difficult to say. Several general facts suggest that the restrictive effect of the new duties was relatively far less than that of the depression. For one thing, the fall in quantity of imports was somewhat less than that of industrial production. Moreover, the drop in imports subjected to heavier duties was not impressively greater than that in other commodities. Nevertheless, the unfortunate consequences of this additional barrier to trade at a time when foreign countries were already undergoing a heavy loss of gold to the United States should not be minimized.

The decline in United States exports started earlier than the decline in imports and proceeded somewhat more gradually in the early stages of the depression. Because of the larger totals involved, however, the absolute decline of $1,400,000,000 in 1930 was slightly greater than that in imports, reducing the export surplus to $782,-000,000, as compared with $842,000,000 in 1929. Further sharp declines in exports of $1,400,000,000 in 1931 and $800,000,000 in 1932 reduced the surplus to less than $300,000,000 in the latter year.

The reaction of exports to the depression was similar to that of imports in certain respects. Shipments of crude materials, including the important item of cotton, were well maintained on a quantity basis, falling by only 5 per cent from 1929 to 1931 and increasing slightly above the 1929 level in 1932. But prices sagged as sharply as those of similar import classes and were chiefly responsible for the fall of more than $600,000,000 in the value of crude material exports from 1929 to 1932. The greater part of the decline in exports was in finished manufactures, which fell by 75 per cent, or more than $1,900,000,000 from 1929 to 1932, and was far more the result of smaller quantities than of lower prices. This behavior, at least in the early stages of the depression, can be explained largely by the high income elasticity of demand for many leading export manufactures, but also by the resistance to price declines manifested by finished goods. Later, however, depreciation of foreign currencies and restrictive commercial policies abroad became increasingly strong barriers to United States exports. . . .

Initially, service transactions appear to have resisted the depression much more strongly than merchandise trade. Whereas from 1929 to 1930 exports fell by 27 per cent and imports by 30 per cent, both receipts and payments on all other current transactions fell by only 10 per cent. This difference is attributable to various special factors affecting service transactions: The resistance of ocean freight rates to adjustment; the expectation of the traveling public that only a brief slump was in prospect; and, of particular importance in receipts from abroad, the contractual nature of interest on international indebtedness. By 1931, when interest obligations began to be broken through default, the fall in service transactions became almost as precipitous as that in merchandise trade.

For a brief time after the collapse of the stock market in October 1929 a revival in the outflow of American capital seemed possible. An undue interest in speculative stocks had been a major force interfering with bond flotations, and the end of the boom tended to render conditions more favorable for such issues. Both domestic and foreign bond flotations in the American market showed definite signs of revival in the first half of 1930. Domestic corporate issues were higher in the first and second quarters, in fact, than at any time in the twenties. Foreign dollar issues did not recover so sharply but moved well above the 1929 low. There was thus some basis for hope that a renewal of American lending might help to reverse the unfavorable turn in world business conditions.

Such hopes were quickly disappointed. Any benefits that may have ensued from the small upturn in new foreign flotations were quickly submerged by the rising tide of the depression. The discouragement to further lending was reinforced by strong political disturbances and uncertainties in Latin America and Europe, and by the second half of 1930 new foreign flotations began a swift decline from which they never recovered. The sharpness of the fall in long-term issues was tempered somewhat by a continued outflow of American short-term funds. This outflow, however, was on a lower scale than in previous years, and much of it consisted of special credit arrangements improvised in an effort to bolster the reserve positions of other countries.

Provision of American capital in the form of direct investments abroad also declined precipitously after 1929. This outflow is estimated at not more than $300,000,000 in 1930, or at about half the 1929 rate, and further declined to near the $200,000,000 level in 1931. Thereafter new investments of this type sank to insignificant amounts.

The brief upturn in foreign-bond flotations in the first half of 1930 accounted for a slight increase in net outflow of long-term capital to approximately $300,000,000 for the year. Thereafter the net movement was sharply reversed as new American investment abroad declined while the inflow of foreign long-term capital continued. The larger part of the inflow was, more accurately, the return flow of American money previously placed abroad. This consisted in part of contractual amortization payments on foreign dollar bonds, which in 1930 amounted to some $300,000,000 but subsequently declined with the beginning of a wave of defaults. In addition, there was heavy repatriation of outstanding foreign securities as buyers abroad, who had concentrated on American stocks during the boom of 1928 and 1929, turned their interest chiefly to repurchases of foreign issues.

The fall in purchases of foreign goods and services and the virtually complete cessation in new investment abroad resulted in an extraordinarily rapid and severe shrinkage in the supply of dollars currently made available to foreign countries. . . . The amount of dollars paid out or transferred in this manner dropped from a level of about $7,400,000,000 for the three years 1927 to 1929 to a mere $2,400,000,000 in 1932 and 1933—a reduction of 68 per cent over a span of only three years.

This drastic decline in United States purchases from foreign countries and in the world supply of dollars must rank as one of the most severe disturbances to the world economy during the period, directly depressing business activity abroad and producing foreign-exchange problems of unparalleled dimensions. This does not imply that the origin of the world depression was exclusively or chiefly in the United States and that the behavior of foreign economies was merely a passive and forced reaction. Unfavorable economic and political conditions abroad, superimposed on the already over-borrowed position of many countries, presented a grave deterrent and ultimately a prohibitive barrier to further investment of American capital. Moreover, it would be difficult to divide responsibility between this and other countries for the disastrous fall in prices, particularly of primary goods, which were an important element in the decline in value of imports. Finally, the depression and other disturbances abroad in turn reacted most unfavorably on business activity in the United States.

In a study of these complex relationships, attention might first be centered on the shrinkage in foreign payments to the United States as the disturbing element and then directed to the effects on the domestic economy. In fact, however, the abrupt fall in dollars supplied was by far the more active disturbance, and conditions in the United States were primarily responsible for the decline, at least with respect to current transactions. The principal considerations supporting this conclusion may be summarized as follows:

1. The curtailment and eventual stoppage of the outflow of American capital, which had accounted for 20 per cent of the total supply of dollars in 1927 and 1928 and 14 per cent in 1929, was alone sufficient to create serious problems of readjustment.

2. The decline in economic activity in the United States was sharper and deeper and revival was longer delayed than in foreign countries, which, in conjunction with the new tariff of 1930, produced a particularly severe and prolonged decline in United States imports.

3. Fixed payments due the United States for service on war debts and foreign dollar bonds aggregated about $900,000,000 in 1929, and the contractual amounts due in years immediately following were probably of about the same magnitude. The volume of dollars supplied foreign countries and available for other purposes, if these obligations were to have been met in full, declined from $6,500,-000,000 in 1929 to $1,500,000,000 in 1932—a fall of 77 per cent in three years.

4. With few exceptions, foreign currencies were under pressure vis-à-vis the dollar throughout the greater part of the depression—a position leading to a steady drain of gold and exchange reserves of foreign countries to the United States. By contrast, the dollar was under pressure only during brief periods (specifically during the several months following the United Kingdom's departure from the gold standard and again for a short time before, and in anticipation of, the depreciation of the dollar). Moreover, this pressure emanated from an outflow of short-term capital, which produced a temporary but heavy exodus of gold from the United States, rather than from the position on current and long-term capital account. The movements of short-term funds and gold . . . were partly offsetting, but the prevailing condition is indicated by the fact that the net reduction in foreign gold reserves and dollar balances through payments to the United States and through liquidation of American short-term credits was in the order of $2,600,000,000 during the 4 years 1930–33.

5. Finally, the pressure generated by the shortage of dollars was reflected in the reactions of foreign countries to the resulting strains in their balance-of-payments positions. . . .

Following the revival that started in most countries in 1932–33, world economic activity again moved strongly upward, although, broadly expressed, the subsequent expansion did little more than restore in a very uncertain and unequal way the level of output attained before the great depression. World industrial production, as measured by the League of Nations index (1929 = 100), had fallen to 63.8 in 1932 but recovered to 77.7 in 1934 and thereafter advanced swiftly to 103.7 in 1937, or to a point slightly above the pre-depression level. The recession beginning in late 1937, however, brought an 11-point reduction in the index for 1938, from which there was only an incomplete recovery by the beginning of the war in 1939. Primary production, of course, had not declined in keeping with the collapse of industry in the early thirties, nor did it rise so spectacularly in later years. But economic conditions in primary producing countries, through changes in prices and unsold stocks, were strongly affected by changes in the principal consuming markets in industrial areas. . . .

Whatever hopes there may have been in the late thirties of achieving a durable balance in this country's international position were, of course, illusory and futile because of the imminence of the second World War. Any discussion of such matters as equilibrium, disturbances, and adjustments in international transactions in the years immediately preceding the war is likely to appear unrealistic or irrelevant. As political and military crises in Europe increased and the probability of war became more apparent, the flow of capital and gold to the United States assumed even more tremendous proportions than during the earlier stages when they were primarily related to the monetary difficulties of the gold bloc.

Other developments in the late thirties not primarily related to the approaching war, however, demonstrated once again the peculiar instability characteristic of the balance-of-payments relations of the United States. The rise in business activity in this country, which appeared to assume the proportions of a major boom during 1936, leveled off in the following year. In the fall of 1937 industrial production began the sharpest drop on record, and by the end of the year most of the increase from the middle of 1935 had been wiped out. The decline then became more gradual and was halted in May of 1938, after which there came another sharp rise that carried back to and slightly beyond the mid-1937 peak by the end of 1939.

The drop in domestic business activity in the latter part of 1937 was immediately followed by a sharp decline in imports, accentuated in agricultural products by the abundant American harvests which followed the end of the drought. In the second quarter of 1938 imports aggregated only $454,000,000, compared with $858,-000,000 in the second quarter of 1937—a reduction by almost one-half in 12 months' time. During the full year 1937 imports were

$1,100,000,000 lower than in the preceding year, a fall of 37 per cent, and total payments on current account were lower by $1,250,-000,000.

In sharp contrast to this behavior, exports and other current receipts items declined by only about $250,000,000 in the aggregate from 1937 to 1938. In consequence, the balance on current account changed sharply from a small excess of payments to a heavy excess of receipts, amounting to almost $1,000,000,000 in 1938. The shift in the balance on current account beginning toward the end of 1937 did not immediately give rise to an increase in gold imports, being offset by the outflow of capital which occurred at that time. By the summer of 1938, however, capital was again moving inward in large volume, and the influx of gold was resumed in doubly heavy amount.

Maintenance of exports at a high level despite the drastic fall in imports reflected the relatively light effects of the 1937–38 recession on most foreign countries. There was a mild recession in the United Kingdom and a somewhat more severe set-back in two of the former gold-bloc countries, France and Belgium, and in Canada, attributable both to the influences engendered by the decline in the United States and to various special factors more or less peculiar to each country. Production in the Scandinavian countries, on the other hand, was well maintained, and in Germany, Japan, and most other countries industrial activity decreased only slightly and temporarily at most and appears to have been little affected by events elsewhere.

Failure of the 1937–38 recession in the United States to have more perceptibly serious international repercussions may be attributed in part to the fact that the decline in domestic business activity, although extremely severe, was arrested in fairly short order. Vigorous anti-depression action by the Government, including an increase in public works outlays and an expansion of the credit base, were probably the primary factors in checking the downswing; but maintenance of relatively good export markets was also a stabilizing influence. As a result, import demand again improved slightly in the second half of 1938, although it was not until after the outbreak of the war in Europe the following year that the value of imports again moved close to the 1937 level.

The major reason, however, that the recession produced only mild effects on other countries appears to be that they resorted little or not at all to deflation as a means of adjustment to the pressure on their balances of payments. On the contrary, the tendency was definitely in the opposite direction. Most countries, including many dependent on primary production, at least took measures to offset direct effects on the volume of internal credit produced by the drain on their gold and exchange reserves and endeavored to maintain easy money conditions. A still more important influence was the increasing flow of public expenditure abroad on armaments. In the war economies, of course, production was maintained at forced draft, while by the latter part of 1938 military outlays in the United Kingdom, France, and other countries had become substantial enough to have a stimulating effect.

# 24. An Era of Transition

Over the past decade the position of the United States in the world economy has been affected by the emergence of the European Common Market, which since its establishment in 1958 has become the major world trading area, and by an increasing sensitivity to growing deficits in America's balance of payments. The gold drain over a nine-year period since 1958 has sharply reduced American gold reserves and raised the possibility of a dollar crisis that could disrupt the world monetary system and international trade. The sizable and continuing build-up of deficits in the balance of payments had not diminished by late 1967, when there were still fears that a wholesale demand by overseas holders of dollars for conversion into gold might precipitate a liquidity crisis and a devalued dollar. American gold losses may be diminished if enough member nations of the International Monetary Fund ratify a world currency reform, approved at Rio de Janeiro in September, 1967, under which "special drawing rights" for the settlement of payments deficits were proposed as a monetary reserve asset to supplement gold.

SOURCE: *Economic Report of the President . . . 1963. . . .* (Washington, D.C.: Government Printing Office, 1963), pp. 91–5, 98–103, 113–15.

The international economy has undergone a remarkable transformation in the past decade. For many years after World War II, import quotas, discriminatory trade practices, and exchange restrictions on all forms of international payments characterized the bulk of international transactions. Though further progress needs to be made, much of this restrictive legacy has now been swept away. This transformation culminated in the formal acceptance by the major European countries in early 1961 of the currency convertibility requirements of the International Monetary Fund. It is a notable achievement and has far-reaching implications for the U.S. economy and U.S. economic policy.

Among the factors facilitating this development has been a massive redistribution of the world's gold and foreign exchange reserves. At the end of 1948, the United States held 71 per cent of the free world's monetary gold stock; by June 1962, the U.S. share had fallen to 40 per cent. During the same period, Western Europe's share grew from 15 per cent to 44 per cent. In addition, foreign official holdings of liquid dollar assets rose by nearly $9 billion. This redistribution ended the excessive concentration of reserves which had been brought about by the political upheavals in Europe in the 1930's, World War II, and the requirements of postwar reconstruction. In achieving balance of payments surpluses which rebuilt reserves, continental European countries gained greater freedom of action to promote economic expansion and to reduce restrictions on international transactions.

The redistribution of reserves was brought about partly through deficits in the international payments of the United States, which led to large transfers of gold and liquid dollar assets to Europe. These U.S. payments deficits have persisted beyond the point where they improve the distribution of the world's monetary reserves. Indeed, continuing large payments deficits by the United States could create doubts about the stability of the dollar and threaten the efficient operation of the international payments system. As a result, the U.S. Government has had to pay close and constant attention to the net financial outcome of its transactions, and those of its citizens, with the rest of the world. Important measures have been taken to improve the payments position of the United States, and domestic economic policy has been framed with attention to the balance of payments and the position of the dollar. . . .

The relaxation of many restrictions on trade and payments and the redistribution of world reserves have not been the only factors transforming the world economy. The progress of the European Economic Community (EEC) toward a rapidly growing, unified, tariff-free market encompassing six European countries—and possibly more in the future—has already profoundly altered world economic relationships. The EEC offers a domestic market broadly comparable to the United States and an import market even larger. Liberal access to this market will be vital to future foreign trade; exclusion by restrictive import tariffs or other barriers could seriously affect the trade and economic development of many countries of the free world. . . .

It is now generally acknowledged that the responsibility of the industrial nations for providing capital and technical knowledge to other countries for economic development requires more than the occasional and sporadic efforts made before the mid-1950's. Systematic economic development of the low-income parts of the free world—within a span of time that is very short by historical standards—has become a major objective of western foreign policy. Carrying out this gigantic task will require considerable transfers of capital and technical skill. It will result in large shifts in the structure of world production and trade, and will require substantial adjustments in both advanced and developing countries. . . .

These developments have one common characteristic: they bring countries economically closer together. They tend to integrate the free world economy. Markets will become more unified, competition will be keener, and differences among nations in techniques of production will diminish. Substantial progress toward our foreign economic objectives will be made, but new challenges for economic policy, national and international, will arise. . . .

## U.S. INTERNATIONAL TRANSACTIONS

### THE UNITED STATES AS WORLD TRADER, INVESTOR, AND BANKER

The United States is by far the largest producing nation in the world, accounting for more than 40 per cent of total industrial production of the free world. Its 188 million inhabitants place it fourth among nations in population, and its unequalled level of per capita income makes it the world's largest domestic market and largest source of savings.

*As trader.* The basic purpose of our foreign trade is to exchange goods produced efficiently in the United States for goods which we can produce relatively less efficiently or not at all. International trade lowers costs and raises standards of living both at home and abroad. Foreign trade accounts for a much larger part of transactions of the U.S. economy than is generally appreciated. Even though our merchandise exports are only about 4 per cent of total gross national product (GNP), they amount to nearly 9 per cent of our total production of movable goods. For some products, overseas demand is exceptionally important; it provides over half the market for such diverse U.S. products as rice, DDT, and tracklaying tractors. Imports by the United States provide materials essential for production and also permit Americans variety and diversity in their consumption. Crucial products like nickel and cobalt come almost entirely from foreign sources.

U.S. exports and imports are a major part of world trade. In the first three quarters of 1962, U.S. merchandise imports were nearly 14 per cent of total world imports. For some countries and some commodities, of course, the U.S. market is far more important than this average share implies. For example, U.S. coffee imports are usually over half of total world imports of coffee.

U.S. citizens pay large sums for services provided by foreigners— transportation of goods and persons, food and lodging for American tourists and businessmen traveling abroad, interest, dividends, and profits on the funds of foreigners invested in American enterprise or securities. In addition, the United States spends overseas nearly $3 billion (gross) a year for its own military defense and, indeed, for the defense of the entire free world. This expenditure is made in part directly by the U.S. Government and in part by more than one million U.S. servicemen and their dependents stationed abroad.

The United States is also a major supplier of goods and services, accounting in 1961 for nearly 18 per cent of total world exports of merchandise, for nearly one-fourth of world exports of manufactures, and for nearly one-third of world exports of capital goods. It is a principal exporter of many agricultural goods, especially cotton, wheat, tobacco, soybeans, and poultry, and it exports large amounts of military equipment to its allies—some on a grant basis, some for cash payment.

The very size of the United States in the world economy lends to its economic activity and its economic policies special importance and interest abroad. Its rate of unemployment, economic growth, and commercial and financial policies are closely charted and carefully watched throughout the world.

*As saver and investor.* A nation as large and wealthy as the United States is naturally an important source of savings for the entire world, and national savings move abroad both as private investment and as official foreign aid. Its advanced technology invites emulation abroad, and the profitability of duplicating American technology draws American savers and investors beyond domestic borders. Its need for foreign resources to supply American production attracts private U.S. development capital. In addition, the United States has accepted heavy responsibility for the economic development of emerging nations, which require public as well as private capital.

Private long-term investment abroad by U.S. residents has risen markedly in the past decade, from an annual average of $0.9 billion in 1952–55 to $2.5 billion in 1958–61. Much of this increase has gone to Europe.

The U.S. Government provided $3.2 billion to foreign countries and international lending institutions in the first three quarters of 1962—in the form of development loans, Export-Import Bank export credits, sales for local currencies, commodity and cash grants, technical assistance, and contributions to international institutions. This was 12 per cent more than in the corresponding period in 1961. U.S. foreign aid to the developing nations has risen markedly since 1954, and under new programs, notably the Alliance for Progress in Latin America, U.S. economic assistance is expected to continue to be high. Total aid expenditures are, however, still below those reached in the late 1940's under the Marshall Plan to assist European recovery.

Both private investment outflows and government aid are appropriate for a high-output, high-saving country such as the United States, and both are expected to yield considerable economic and political returns in the long run. Government and private lending and equity investment add substantial amounts each year to the net foreign assets of the United States, which have risen steadily in the past decade. . . . But in the short run, both also aggravate the U.S. balance of payments deficit. To reduce the impact of the foreign aid program on the balance of payments, a large part of foreign aid expenditure has been tied to the purchase of goods and services in the United States. In the first three quarters of 1962, 76 per cent of government grants and capital outflows resulted in no direct dollar outflow, compared with 64 per cent two years earlier. Recent changes in the tax treatment of earnings on foreign investments . . . were designed to achieve more equitable tax treatment between U.S. investment at home and abroad. They should reduce the outflow of investment funds to the extent that these funds were attracted by various tax privileges available in several other countries, and should also increase the repatriation of foreign earnings. Thus these changes should improve the U.S. payments position, at least in the short run when improvement is crucially needed.

Though foreign aid and investment absorb only a small part of U.S. savings, the United States is providing a substantial part of the total flow of savings across national boundaries, especially of the flow to the developing nations. The Development Assistance Committee (DAC) of the 20-nation Organization for Economic Cooperation and Development (OECD) estimates that the United States in 1961 supplied 57 per cent of official foreign aid and 44 per cent of private long-term investment flow from DAC members to the less developed countries.

*As banker.*   Since the end of World War I, and especially in the past 15 years, the U.S. dollar has emerged as the principal supplement to gold as an international store of value and medium of exchange. The important position of the United States as a market for goods and as a source of goods and savings, its well-developed, extensive, and efficient financial markets, and its long-standing policy of buying gold from, and selling it to, foreign monetary authorities at a fixed price have all made the U.S. dollar an attractive form in which to hold international reserves. Foreign monetary authorities hold more than $12 billion—over one-quarter of their total gold and foreign exchange reserves—in liquid dollar assets, mostly in the form of U.S. Treasury bills and deposits in American banks. In addition, foreign private parties hold $8 billion in dollar assets, and international institutions nearly $6 billion.

These large outstanding claims on the United States indicate the importance attached by the rest of the world to the dollar as an international currency, and the significance of the United States as an international banking center. For a number of years, the deficit in the U.S. balance of payments was financed to a large extent by increases in foreign dollar holdings which enabled foreign governments and nationals to acquire earning assets and at the same time add to their liquid resources. In recent years, about one-fourth to one-half of our over-all deficit has been settled in gold, but the growth in dollar holdings abroad has continued on a significant scale. The rise in dollar holdings has been an important element in the growth of international liquidity.

But these large balances also make the dollar peculiarly vulnerable. A decline of confidence in the dollar, resulting in widespread conversion of dollars into gold, would create a serious problem for the international payments system and for the economic progress of the free world. Therefore, satisfactory progress in reducing the U.S. payments deficit is essential at this time. . . .

## EXTERNAL IMPACT OF U.S. ECONOMIC EXPANSION

*Structure of the world economy.* Virtually no economic event can occur anywhere without affecting trade flows and capital movements throughout the world economy. These repercussions can rarely be traced completely or precisely, but they are nonetheless real and important and cannot be ignored in the formulation of economic policies. The prominence of the U.S. payments deficit since 1958 has focused attention on those economic factors, at home and abroad, which most influence the international transactions of the United States. Because of their size and variability, U.S. exports warrant special attention.

About two-thirds of U.S. exports go to countries outside Europe. Typically, the ability of these countries to import depends directly on their foreign exchange receipts from their own exports, from capital inflow, and from foreign aid. Without such receipts, most non-European countries are unable to allow their citizens to import. As their receipts fluctuate, so do their purchases from the United States. The share of their markets captured by American goods depends upon a variety of factors—historical business relationships, the availability and terms of financing, and the competitiveness of American products.

Most countries in Europe are in a quite different position. Their large and growing gold and foreign exchange reserves indicate that they need not gear their imports and other foreign expenditures so closely to their receipts. On the contrary, their reserves provide an ample cushion for considerable deviation between foreign exchange receipts and expenditures. European imports are therefore, at least in the short run, more closely related to their domestic economic activity and to competitive conditions than to actual or prospective foreign exchange earnings.

The United States is an important supplier both of foodstuffs and of industrial materials to Europe (Table 1). These exports are closely related to the level of European economic activity and of consumption. The United States is also an important exporter of capital goods to Europe, and U.S. sales of such goods have been growing rapidly in recent years. Because the demand for capital goods reflects the prospects for growing markets, not simply large markets, continuing economic growth in Europe is of great importance for an early solution to the U.S. balance of payments problem.

The close dependence of other countries of the free world, and particularly of the less developed countries, on large and steady foreign exchange earnings to finance needed imports gives them, as well as the United States, a special interest in economic developments in Europe. The heavy dependence of many countries on exports of primary products for exchange earnings with which to purchase needed imports makes their development programs especially vulnerable to fluctuations in import demand either in Europe or in the United States. A recession or slowdown in economic activity in either of these major industrial regions reduces the export earnings of the other countries of the free world both by lowering the sales of their goods and by weakening the prices they receive. The network of world trade by major trading areas in 1961 is shown in Table 2.

These complex world-wide relationships must be taken into account in assessing the ultimate impact of changes in U.S. domestic economic activity on the U.S. balance of payments. Economic expansion in the United States, reducing and eventually closing the gap between actual and potential output, would have important repercussions throughout the world economy and significant "feedback" effects on the U.S. balance of payments. Because of the sheer size of the United States in the world economy, changes in its trade and investment outflows affect significantly its own international transactions receipts. The complexity of the feedbacks makes it impossible to trace with great precision the impact of higher economic activity on the U.S. payments position. But there is good reason to believe that the adverse impact, even in the short run, would be far less than is frequently assumed. Furthermore, vigorous prosecution of programs aimed specifically at improving the balance of payments and maintaining price stability should enable the United

Table 1. Commodity Composition and Destination of United States Exports, first 3 quarters of 1962
(Millions of dollars)

| Commodity group | Total exports | European Economic Community | Other Western Europe | Destination Canada | Japan | Rest of world |
|---|---|---|---|---|---|---|
| Total exports | 14,571 | 2,712 | 2,054 | 2,868 | 1,059 | 5,878 |
| Food and beverages | 2,747 | 566 | 572 | 305 | 204 | 1,100 |
| Industrial supplies and materials | 5,250 | 1,170 | 739 | 951 | 538 | 1,852 |
| Agricultural | 887 | 226 | 180 | 55 | 131 | 295 |
| Capital equipment | 4,862 | 751 | 561 | 1,154 | 267 | 2,129 |
| Machinery | 3,693 | 621 | 460 | 846 | 242 | 1,524 |
| Transportation equipment | 1,168 | 131 | 100 | 308 | 26 | 603 |
| Consumer goods, nonfood | 1,026 | 117 | 126 | 279 | 19 | 485 |
| All other | 687 | 108 | 56 | 178 | 31 | 314 |

NOTE. Detail will not necessarily add to totals because of rounding.

SOURCE: Department of Commerce.

385

## Table 2. Origin and Destination of Free World Exports, 1961
### (Billions of dollars)

| Exports from ↓ / Exports to → | Total exports[1] | United States | Canada | Japan | European Economic Community | Other Western Europe | Rest of World[2] |
|---|---|---|---|---|---|---|---|
| Total exports[1] | 110.4 | 14.3 | 5.3 | 4.6 | 29.1 | 25.4 | 31.6 |
| United States[3] | 18.7 | .... | 3.6 | 1.7 | 3.5 | 2.7 | 7.2 |
| Canada | 5.6 | 3.2 | .... | .2 | .5 | 1.1 | .9 |
| Japan | 4.0 | 1.1 | .1 | .... | .2 | .3 | 2.3 |
| European Economic Community | 30.9 | 2.2 | .3 | .3 | 11.9 | 8.9 | 7.3 |
| Other Western Europe | 21.2 | 1.7 | .7 | .2 | 5.8 | 6.3 | 6.5 |
| Rest of world[2] | 29.9 | 6.1 | .6 | 2.2 | 7.2 | 6.1 | 7.7 |

[1] Excludes some trade which could not be allocated by destination.
[2] Excludes Soviet bloc.
[3] Excludes "special category" exports of $1.8 billion.

NOTE. Detail will not necessarily add to totals because of rounding.

SOURCE: United Nations.

States not only to avoid an adverse over-all effect but to strengthen its payments position.

*Effects of domestic expansion on foreign trade.* The most obvious effect of a more rapid rise in GNP would be a more rapid rise in imports. Over the years, total U.S. imports have maintained a reasonably stable relationship to total domestic demand. Some imports complement U.S. production, providing both raw materials for expanding industrial production and foreign products to satisfy diversified consumer demand. Other imports compete with domestic products; and as U.S. demand increases, imports can sometimes respond more quickly than domestic output.

However, the net balance of payments impact depends also on the feedback effects. Higher U.S. imports provide additional dollars to foreigners. As already noted, many countries are so hungry for foreign goods that additional foreign exchange earnings are promptly re-channeled into additional expenditures abroad. Additional imports by the United States will increase substantially the foreign exchange earnings of these countries, and the United States will in turn receive a large part of their additional export orders. For example, over one-fifth of U.S. imports come from Latin American countries, and these countries together buy nearly half their imports from the United States. Over two-thirds of Canadian imports normally come from the United States. Whether the United States maintains these shares of Latin American and Canadian markets depends, of course, on the competitiveness of U.S. products and the salesmanship of U.S. firms.

An expanding U.S. economy may also be expected to strengthen some of the primary product markets which have deteriorated in recent years. This too would add to the export earnings of countries relying heavily on sales of primary products, and would maintain their demand for industrial imports while lessening their dependence on U.S. economic assistance. However, even in the best of cases, some primary product markets may remain weak.

Rising domestic demand, by reducing unemployment and excess capacity, may after a time create upward pressure on domestic prices too. Price increases in export industries, or in industries competing with imports, would tend to weaken the U.S. trade position. But . . . raising demand for goods and services will permit more efficient use of existing plant capacity and of underemployed workers still on payrolls—in short, will increase the productivity both of capital and of labor. These factors work counter to the tendency of rising demand to pull costs and prices up. Higher demand will also reduce pressures—by labor, by business, by agriculture—for cost-increasing or protectionist solutions to social and economic strains created by prolonged underutilization of domestic resources.

*Effects of domestic expansion on U.S. investment abroad.* The outflow of private investment funds is influenced by many economic factors, especially the profitability of investment abroad. But it is also influenced by economic activity in the United States. When U.S. capacity is fully utilized, and when capital for domestic investment is in large demand, high profitability will tend to keep capital at home provided that bank credit expansion is not excessive. When capacity is underutilized, unemployment widespread, and the domestic investment outlook discouraging, capital will seek higher profits and interest yields abroad.

Full utilization of capacity will also increase savings in the United States, both corporate and individual. In its impact on the balance of payments, this increase in total savings works counter to the improvement in profitability of domestic investment, since some of the new savings may be sent abroad. But in present circumstances, investment abroad is probably not limited by the supply of savings. Corporations now have a larger cash flow than they are investing both at home and abroad, and both corporations and individuals have had ample opportunity to invest abroad from existing wealth, i.e., from past savings. For these reasons, we can expect the improvement in profitability which full utilization will bring—reinforced by recent and proposed tax measures to improve incentives for domestic investment—to be a major influence in reducing the outflows of U.S. investment funds.

In recent years, Americans have made very large direct and portfolio investments in Europe, especially in the EEC. These investments have reflected in part the weakness of markets and profit prospects in the United States; this can be remedied only by higher utilization of domestic capacity.

They have also responded to important attractions to investment in Europe, but the resulting outflows can be expected to diminish in size.

1. The vigorous growth of European economies has been accompanied by high profit rates, and the steps to create a large internal common market have reinforced expectations of substantial profits.

There are now signs, however, that profitability is declining in Europe; some of the most obvious investment opportunities have already been exploited, and increasing manpower shortages are leading to increases in labor costs which squeeze profit margins. Furthermore, sharp declines in European stock prices—generally much larger than U.S. decline earlier in 1962—have demonstrated to some American investors the thinness of European stock markets.

2. Many American businessmen have built facilities in Europe for fear of being excluded from the EEC by preferential commercial policies. The resulting surge of capital flows to Europe can be expected to taper off. Moreover, successful tariff negotiations under the Trade Expansion Act of 1962 would reduce the tariff discrimination against outside producers inherent in the Common Market.

3. Europe has achieved political, economic, and monetary stability in the past decade, and full currency convertibility only in the last five years. Moreover, in an age of missiles, Europe is no more vulnerable than North America to military attack. These developments have removed certain extra-economic factors which concentrated capital, both American and foreign, in the United States in the 1930's and 1940's. Accordingly, American individuals, business firms, and investing institutions have recently had special reasons to reconsider investment opportunities in Europe, and to diversify their investments to include European assets. This, again, is mainly a once-for-all development, which will spend its force in time.

4. European and U.S. tax laws have, in many instances, favored investment in Europe over comparable opportunities in the United States. Recent legislation should increase the relative attractiveness of investment in the United States. . . .

*The Trade Expansion Act.* The whole free world can benefit from removal of age-old national barriers to the full utilization of Europe's productive strength. But the nations of the free world, both within and outside the EEC, must assure that the EEC uses its new power, not as a lever to secure gains for its members at the expense of nonmembers or for some of its producers at the expense of others, but as an engine to promote economic progress and cooperation throughout the world.

The Trade Expansion Act of 1962, signed by President Kennedy in October, is designed to meet this challenge by enabling the United States to bargain more effectively and comprehensively. The tariff reducing authority provided by the Act . . . greatly increases

U.S. flexibility in tariff negotiations, particularly in negotiations with the EEC. If the United Kingdom becomes a member of the Community, the special authority to negotiate tariff reductions greater than 50 per cent with the expanded EEC on goods for which the United States and the EEC together furnish 80 per cent or more of world exports would apply to a wide variety of products, including coal, organic chemicals, transportation equipment, most kinds of machinery, photographic supplies, paints, cosmetics, and miscellaneous chemical products. In 1960, free world exports of those goods to which the special authority would apply amounted to some $22.5 billion; of this total, exports from the United States were $8.8 billion. Those from EEC countries plus present applicants were $10.4 billion. The United States and the EEC as presently constituted accounted in 1960 for 80 per cent of world exports in only two commodity groups: aircraft, and margarine and shortenings.

It will not be easy for the United States and the EEC to reach a tariff agreement of the comprehensive scope that is essential. But both sides realize the importance of providing a liberal framework for world trade. Since any tariff reductions negotiated by the United States, the EEC, and other participants will be extended to other free world nations on a most-favored-nation basis, these trade negotiations will contribute to a general expansion of free world trade. This extension of tariff reductions to other countries gives them a direct interest in the success of trade negotiations under the Trade Expansion Act. General tariff reductions should benefit all nations, including those exporting products in competition with the exports of former African colonies which now have preferred access to the EEC market. Negotiations under the special authority will also benefit major industrial nations such as Canada and Japan— the two largest trading partners of the United States. To achieve maximum success in tariff reduction, full participation of all major trading nations in the forthcoming negotiations will be essential.

Since trade in many important agricultural products is restricted not only by tariffs but also by quotas and other barriers, negotiations concerning agricultural trade are likely to prove especially complicated and difficult. Both the EEC and the United States may have to make concessions that will be painful to some producers in each area. With the help of the bargaining authority given by the Trade Expansion Act of 1962, the United States hopes to obtain substantial liberalization of trade in agricultural products and to avoid, in the long run, any unfavorable net impact of EEC agricultural policies on U.S. agricultural exports. Some short-run U.S.-EEC understandings along these lines have already been reached. In particular, the EEC has agreed that, if the common policy for grains should result in a reduction in trade in higher quality wheat, corrective action will be taken to restore historical relationships. Also, during the last GATT [General Agreement on Tariffs and Trade] round of tariff reductions, the United States received important concessions on several agricultural commodities, including cotton and soybeans. The EEC has agreed to negotiate further on trade access for ordinary wheat, corn, grain sorghum, rice, and poultry, and to reconsider during the next general round of negotiations the high external tariffs for tobacco and vegetable oils.

These understandings, stemming from the tariff negotiations concluded in early 1962, are limited and do not themselves assure access for U.S. exports that compete with domestic EEC production. However, they point toward rather than away from liberalization. In contrast, the early actions implementing the Common Agricultural Policy indicate a trend toward increased protection. It would be unfortunate if this trend were not reversed. The reversal will be painful to some EEC producers who have envisaged the Community as an assured market for their products, but will be in the general interest of EEC consumers.

In return for assurances that the EEC will set prices at levels which will allow efficient exporters continued access to their markets, the United States may have to limit its own export subsidy program and subject its own domestic price policies to international review. U.S. agricultural policies and programs, like those of other agricultural exporting countries, will be subject to close examination and our waiver in the GATT, permitting us to restrict agricultural imports under certain specific conditions, is likely to come under increasing criticism.

Quantitative restrictions, prohibitive import duties, and subsidies are out of place in the world which both the United States and other industrial nations are trying to build. They do not meet the long-run needs of producers and consumers in these developed countries; they restrict mutually advantageous trade; and they are unfair handicaps to the developing countries in other continents.